MODE

An Introduction

By Jack Harvey

ELEMENTARY ECONOMICS
WORKBOOK FOR ELEMENTARY ECONOMICS
INTERMEDIATE ECONOMICS
MULTIPLE-CHOICE QUESTIONS FOR
INTERMEDIATE ECONOMICS
THE BRITISH CONSTITUTION AND POLITICS (*with L. Bather*)
HOW BRITAIN IS GOVERNED
WORKBOOK FOR HOW BRITAIN IS GOVERNED
PRODUCING AND SPENDING (*with M. Harvey*)
MODERN ECONOMICS: STUDY GUIDE AND WORKBOOK
INTRODUCTION TO MACRO-ECONOMICS
(*with M. K. Johnson*)
INTRODUCTION TO MACRO-ECONOMICS:
A WORKBOOK (*with M. K. Johnson*)
GOVERNMENT AND PEOPLE (*with M. Harvey*)
THE ORGANISATION IN ITS ENVIRONMENT
THE ORGANISATION IN ITS ENVIRONMENT: ASSIGNMENTS
FOR BEC COURSES (*with J. Chilver*)
BASIC ECONOMICS
WORKBOOK FOR BASIC ECONOMICS
URBAN LAND ECONOMICS
MASTERING ECONOMICS
ECONOMICS REVISION GUIDE

By Ernie Jowsey

100 ESSAY PLANS FOR ECONOMICS
URBAN LAND ECONOMICS (*with Jack Harvey*)

MODERN ECONOMICS

An Introduction

Eighth Edition

Jack Harvey and Ernie Jowsey

First edition 1969
Second edition 1974
Third edition 1977
Fourth edition 1983
Fifth edition 1988
Sixth edition 1993
Seventh edition 1998

Eighth edition 2007 Published by
PALGRAVE MACMILLAN
Houndmills, Basingstoke, Hampshire RG21 6XS and
175 Fifth Avenue, New York, N.Y. 10010
Companies and representatives throughout the world.

PALGRAVE MACMILLAN is the global academic imprint of the Palgrave Macmillan division of St. Martin's Press, LLC and of Palgrave Macmillan Ltd. Macmillan® is a registered trademark in the United States, United Kingdom and other countries. Palgrave is a registered trademark in the European Union and other countries.

ISBN-13: 978-0-230-55129-9
ISBN-10: 0-230-55129-7

This book is printed on paper suitable for recycling and made from fully managed and sustained forest sources. Logging, pulping and manufacturing processes are expected to conform to the environmental regulations of the country of origin.

A catalogue record for this book is available from the British Library.

10 9 8 7 6 5 4 3 2 1
16 15 14 13 12 11 10 09 08 07

Printed and bound in China

CONTENTS

Contents

IV THE GOVERNMENT AND THE ALLOCATION OF RESOURCES

Contents

Contents

Contents

LIST OF TABLES AND FIGURES

TABLES

FIGURES

List of tables and figures

List of tables and figures

PREFACE

The primary aim of this textbook is to meet the needs of students taking economics as part of their professional examinations in banking, company-secretaryship, accountancy, insurance, surveying, transport, hospital administration, business studies and commerce. It provides, too, a useful groundwork in economics for GCE 'A' Level and first-degree courses.

This book can claim to deal with 'modern economics' in two senses. First, it presents economics as a method of thought, not a mere body of knowledge. It explains simple economic analysis and shows how it can be applied both to the problems of everyday life and to the particular decisions of the professional man. Instead of being merely a dull grind, economics is shown to be as relevant vocationally as other course subjects. In this way it is hoped to improve the motivation of the student, for only by such an approach will he gain any value from his study.

Second, the book recognises that modern economics is increasingly concerned with the difficulties of maintaining full employment, a stable level of prices, a steady rate of growth, balance-of-payments equilibrium, etc. It is therefore divided almost equally between a study of the determination of prices in individual markets and of the factors which govern the level of activity as a whole.

In deciding what to include, the authors have had two basic considerations – the requirements of the examination syllabus and the level of difficulty with which a student, often studying part-time and without the help of a tutor, can be expected to cope. The first presents few problems, for the syllabuses of the various Examining Boards are fairly similar in their requirements. Thus elementary analysis is supplemented by some description of the economy and its institutions. The second lies far more within the discretion of the authors. Here the basis of selection has been 'when in doubt, leave out'. The dominant aim is that the student should understand, and be able to apply competently, simple basic concepts rather than be confused with half-digested advanced refinements.

Numerous diagrams have been included. Not only do these aid learning by the impact of the visual impression, but they are a neat form of expressing relationships.

Moreover, in order to assist reading and note-taking, the text is, wherever possible, enumerated under headings and sub-headings.

This new edition updates tables and facts and discusses new modern issues such as sustainable development, road traffic and other environmental problems, globalisation, Private Finance Initiatives, changes in the functions of the Bank of England, developments in regional policy and the EU single currency.

2006   JACK HARVEY AND ERNIE JOWSEY

The authors and publishers are grateful to the following for permission to use copyright material: Crown Copyright for Figure 35.1. Every effort has been made to trace all copyright-holders of third-party materials included in this work, but if any have been inadvertently overlooked the publishers will be pleased to make the necessary arrangement at the first opportunity.

GUIDANCE TO THE STUDENT

The saying that 'a little practice is worth a lot of theory' is a dangerous half-truth. There is nothing so practical as sound theory. That is why this book is concerned mainly with simple economic theory. By applying it, the professional person can find the answer to many of the problems with which he or she is continually being confronted. 'Would it be wise to lend so large a sum to Farmer Giles in view of current government policy as regards subsidies to agriculture?' asks the bank manager. 'What effect will the construction of a motorway have on the value of different types of property in the vicinity?' asks the surveyor, valuer and estate agent. 'Is the government likely to increase the rate of income tax or capital gains tax in the next budget?' asks the accountant. 'How best can the liquid assets of the company be invested?' asks the company secretary. And so on.

You are urged to study economics, therefore, not merely to pass an examination, but because it will make you a better professional person. Indeed, if you approach it in this way, the examination will take care of itself.

But you must study systematically and thoroughly. To this end you are advised to proceed as follows:

1. Read through the whole book quickly.
2. Study each chapter carefully in the textbook. Underline important points, and try to find illustrations of these points from your own particular professional experience. Be sure that you *understand* each stage in the argument before proceeding to the next. At times progress may appear slow, but there are no short cuts. Theory cannot be memorised.
3. Write notes covering the chapter material, tabulating points and linking them in diagrams wherever possible. Such notes will give precision to your ideas, consolidate your understanding, and prove invaluable for examination revision.
4. Answer the questions at the end of each chapter. Add to your notes where necessary.
5. Obtain practice in answering the type of question set by the appropriate examining body. Remember that even the simplest-looking question usually requires the statement and application of a fundamental principle.

INTRODUCTION

1

WHAT ECONOMICS IS ABOUT

LEARNING OBJECTIVES

···

After studying this chapter you should be able to:
- explain the meaning of 'allocation of scarce resources';
- define opportunity costs;
- draw a production possibility curve and use it as an analytical tool;
- distinguish between positive economics and normative economics;
- explain the nature, scope and limitations of economics.

1.1 THE ECONOMIC PROBLEM

Wants and limited means

'You must cut your coat according to your cloth.' 'You can't get a quart out of a pint pot.' 'You can't make a silk purse out of a sow's ear.' How many of our every-day sayings draw attention to the fact that, in comparison with all the things we want, our means of satisfying those wants are quite inadequate! Just think of the extra things we could buy if our incomes were larger – new clothes, new furni-ture, a better car, foreign travel, a camcorder. The list has no end, for, even if these wants were satisfied, new wants would arise.

This, then, is the 'economic problem' – unlimited wants, very limited means. And we can never completely overcome the difficulty. But what we can do is to make the most of what we have. In other words, we *economise*.

In order to see more clearly what is meant by 'economising', we can study the spending decisions of a housewife. Indeed, this illustration is more appropriate than it may seem at first sight, for 'economics' is derived from a Greek word meaning 'the management of a household'.

Our housewife's task is to make her fixed housekeeping allowance 'go as far as possible'; in other words, from limited resources she seeks to obtain the maximum satisfaction for the family. Certain goods – those she regards as necessities, such as bread, milk, tea and butter – are purchased in regular quantities almost by habit; but this does not mean that she would not vary her spending on them were there to be any significant change in their prices. Nevertheless, what really lies behind her spending decisions can best be seen if we concentrate on those goods to which she gives frequent consideration. As our housewife walks past the shop windows in the high street, a hundred and one different goods compete for the money in her purse. Should she buy beef or chicken for the Sunday dinner? Peas would be nice – but they are still so dear that cabbage will have to do for one more week. But how everybody would love new potatoes! And they've gone down 4p a pound since last week! Yes, she will buy new potatoes instead of old. And so our capable housewife goes on, comparing the prices of different goods and asking herself whether the pleasure her family will obtain from them will be worth their cost – the inroads they make on her limited housekeeping allowance.

But it is not only the housewife who has to economise. How the school-boy schemes to get the most out of his pocket-money! And the businessman faces the same problems in running his factory. Should he produce this good or that, or some of both? How many of each good? Should he employ extra labourers or would it be better to install a machine to do the work? Would it be more profitable to hire transport or to buy his own lorry? And so on.

Turn to the newspaper any morning, and it soon becomes obvious how often the government, too, is forced to choose as it plans the broad lines upon which the economy shall develop. Better schools, student grants and more hospitals – all are competing for the limited revenue it can safely raise by taxation. Extra houses, new roads and conservation areas – all are claiming a share of the limited land available. In these and many other instances, the government has the task of making the most of the nation's resources.

Opportunity cost

Thus we see that economics is really concerned with the problem of choice – the decisions forced upon us by the smallness of our resources compared with our wants (Figure 1.1). And, as we choose, so we have to sacrifice. If the newspaper boy spends his Christmas tips on a bicycle, then it is likely that he will have to go without the Play Station that he also wanted. In deciding to work overtime on a Saturday afternoon, a worker forgoes leisure time and the football match he would otherwise have watched. When the farmer sows a field with wheat, he accepts that he loses the barley it could have grown. And so with the nation. If extra materials and capital are required to accelerate the building of houses, roads and hospitals, then there will be less left for producing offices, power stations, sport centres, and so on. In all walks of life, having 'this' means going without 'that'. We therefore speak of 'opportunity cost' – the cost of something in terms of alternatives forgone (more accurately, in terms of the *best* alternative sacrificed).

4

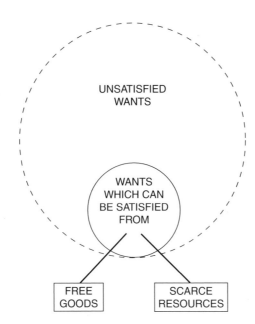

Figure 1.1   The economic problem

In practice, economising is not so much a complete rejection of one good in favour of another, but rather deciding whether to have a little bit more of one and not quite so much of another. It is principally, as we shall see in Chapter 5, an adjustment at the margin.

'Free' and 'scarce' goods

Few goods are so plentiful that nobody will give anything for them. Air, perhaps, is one of the few exceptions. Occasionally, too, there is such an abundant apple harvest that a farmer says 'help yourself'. Such goods are termed 'free' goods. Usually, goods are 'scarce' – they can be obtained only by going without something else. With such goods we have to economise, and so they are often referred to as 'economic goods'. It is worth noting, however, that over time there is no hard-and-fast dividing-line between economic and non-economic goods. Desert wastes can be transformed into rich agricultural land by irrigation; coal-mines are left derelict as new fuels are developed. Scarcity is relative to demand.

In future when we speak of 'goods' we shall be referring to economic goods, including, without further distinction, both commodities and services.

The production possibility curve

We can illustrate the economic problem as follows. Suppose that country X produces only agricultural produce and manufactured goods and that it can, with all its resources fully employed, produce during a year the following alternative combinations (in unspecified units):

Agricultural produce	+	Manufactured goods
100		0
80		25
60		40
40		45
20		48
0		50

By plotting these alternative combinations we obtain a 'production-possibility curve' (Figure 1.2). This shows the various combinations of agricultural produce and manufactured goods attainable by country X with its limited resources and given technology.

The table shows that, with its limited resources, country X can produce either 100 agricultural produce or 50 manufactured goods, or a combination of both. Any larger output is outside the curve and unattainable.

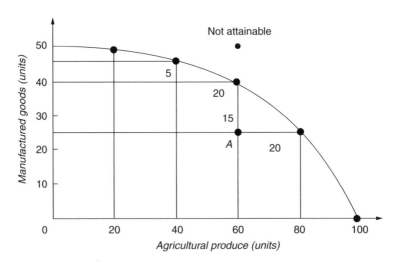

Figure 1.2 A production-possibility curve

Nevertheless, as resources are transferred to manufacturing from agriculture, an ever increasing quantity of manufactured goods has to be given up to obtain an extra 20 units of agricultural produce. For instance, when 40 agricultural units are produced, the opportunity cost of an extra 20 is only 5 manufactured goods, whereas when production is 60 agricultural units the opportunity cost of a further 20 is 15 manufactured goods.

The reason is that resources are not equally suited to producing agricultural produce and manufactured goods. For instance, factory workers would need training in farm work, while land, tractors, etc. would have to be worked more intensively. The result is that the production-possibility curve is concave to the origin.

1.2 THE SCOPE OF ECONOMICS

Definition of economics

Scarcity forces us to economise. We weigh up the various alternatives and select that particular assortment of goods which yields the highest return from our limited resources. Modern economists use this idea to define the scope of their studies. But since there is no one definition which is completely satisfactory, we keep ours as simple as possible. *Economics is the study of how people allocate their limited resources to provide for their wants.*

Amplification

The field which a study of economics covers becomes clearer if we examine certain points of this definition.

1. Economics is a social science

This follows from the fact that economics studies how *people act*. As we shall see, this puts it at a disadvantage compared with the physical sciences which examine various aspects of man's environment.

2. Economics is closely concerned with the findings of other sciences

Because economics studies human behaviour, it must, in reaching conclusions, refer to other branches of study, particularly psychology, sociology and politics. The alternative, advocated by some economists, of restricting economics to pure scientific analysis, curtails its usefulness.

3. *Economics selects a particular aspect of human behaviour*

But, although economics is closely connected with such social sciences, it is distinguished from them by its concentration on one particular aspect of human behaviour – choosing between alternatives in order to obtain the maximum satisfaction from limited resources. This narrower approach is an improvement on Professor Alfred Marshall's definition – 'a study of mankind in the ordinary business of life' – because this, as it stands, would embrace all forms of human activity.

In effect, the economist limits the study by selecting four fundamental characteristics of human existence and investigating what happens when they are all found together, as they usually are. First, the ends of human beings are without limit. Second, those ends are of varying importance. Third, the means available for achieving those ends – human time and energy and material resources – are limited. Fourth, the means can be used in many different ways: that is, they can produce many different goods.

But no one characteristic *by itself* is necessarily of interest to the economist. If, for instance, you have two wants and you cannot choose between them, you are between the devil and the deep blue sea, and you will never get as far as the problem of allocating resources between them. Similarly, 'free' goods are of no interest to the economist since resources do not have to be allocated to obtain them although sometimes a free good such as air can become an economic good because of pollution – in Tokyo, vending machines sell clean oxygen at street corners. Nor is the mere scarcity of means necessarily of significance. Where resources can be used only in one way, e.g. lichen-bearing volcanic land in Iceland for rearing sheep, they do not, although scarce, have to be 'economised'. Using such land for sheep does not mean that the owner has less of other things. Its use therefore gives rise to no problems, and the economist is interested only in the relatively minor point of determining the earnings of such land. Only when all four characteristics are found together does an economic problem arise.

The difficulties

But, in pursuing such studies, economists face two major difficulties:

1. *Economists cannot experiment*

The task of a science is to formulate laws describing what will happen when there is a change in a given set of circumstances. The physicist and chemist can conduct their investigations by experimenting under controlled conditions in a laboratory. But because economists are dealing with human behaviour rather than with physical properties, their laboratory, it has been said, is the real world.

(a) Since facts concerning people are difficult to ascertain, they can never be quite sure of the initial position.

(b) It is impossible to isolate a group of consumers or business people in a test-tube to see how they would react to a given change. The most the economist can usually do as regards consumers' behaviour, for instance, is to take a sample survey which will suggest how groups as a whole will behave.

(c) The economy is subject to continuous change, and so conditions cannot be held constant while the effect of one particular measure is observed.

(d) Because the economy is so complex, no body of economists could follow through all the results of any given change.

(e) Any measurements are usually approximate, and even so take time to collect.

Because of these difficulties, economists can only be approximate in their investigations in real life. Nevertheless, the information available is increasing and becoming more precise, e.g. through market research and government statistical enquiries. Thus economists' predictions are likely to gain in accuracy.

2.   *Economists cannot directly measure welfare*

Since satisfaction, like love or pain, is personal to the individual, there is no absolute scale for measuring welfare. So the economist, using the best approximation, works on the principle that, because two loaves are better than one, an increase in goods represents an increase in welfare.

Even so, he cannot measure all goods. If he gives a value to the vegetables grown in gardens or to do-it-yourself repairs to cars, should he not logically include also something for housewives' cleaning and cooking services? Because it is impossible to know where to draw the line, the economist simplifies matters by confining attention to those goods which are exchanged against money (see p. 344). Since all these have a 'price' it is possible to make use of exact measurement and total dissimilar goods in terms of the common standard.

Nevertheless, the economist must be careful to include any costs or benefits which are not allowed for by an individual in making a decision. Or, if the project is so large that it is likely to have external effects elsewhere, for example a proposed new airport or motorway, a cost-benefit analysis may have to be used to cover these full effects (see Chapter 17). Moreover, since the economist can only quantify in terms of money, some costs and benefits which are not exchanged directly in a market, e.g. environmental costs and benefits, have to be given 'shadow prices'.

Positive and normative economics

Consider how the particulars of different estate agents describe the same room: the first, 'the living room is 4.5 metres by 3.5 metres', the second, 'the living room is deceptively spacious'. One can be verified by measuring; the other is a matter for the eye of the beholder. This leads us to the distinction between positive and normative economics.

Positive economics limits itself to statements that can be verified by reference to the facts. Thus the observation that 'the UK's real national income in 1997 was larger than in 1994, is a positive statement. In other words, positive economics holds that any hypothesis formulated should be testable against empirical evidence.

Normative economics, on the other hand, appreciates that in practice many economic decisions involve subjective judgements; that is, they cannot be made solely by an objective appraisal of the facts but depend to some extent on personal views in interpreting facts. Thus the statement that 'the UK's national income in 1997 should have been larger than it was' is a normative statement. As soon as we introduce the words 'should' or 'ought' we are making subjective valuations, that is normative statements.

Because in practice the distinction between positive economics and normative economics is often blurred, opinion is divided about the exact scope of economics, and so it is instructive to examine their nature in more detail.

1.3 POSITIVE ECONOMICS

Positive economics considers that economics can claim to be a science only if it is strictly scientific in its approach, eschewing normative judgements and adopting scientific methods.

First, it does not attempt to set out criteria for determining what is good or bad, what ought or what ought not to be – any more than physics attempts to say that liquids are 'better' than solids. It is concerned only with positive statements and with the consequences of certain actions. That is why, for instance, the economist must accept ends as given, expressing no opinion as to whether those ends are 'good' or 'bad'. On the other hand, he must point out that individual ends have economic implications for society as a whole. A man, for instance, may decide that he wants to get drunk every day. Here the economist must point out the full cost of this end – the cost to the man of getting drunk, plus the cost to society if he eventually becomes a charge on the National Health Service as an alcoholic.

Nor is the economist concerned directly about the physical aspects of the limited means – the mechanical principles of the plough, the chemical properties of the soil or the biological characteristics of the seed. Both ends and resources are accepted as given. The subject of study is how people mobilise these resources to achieve their ends and how efficient are the methods which they choose.

Second, economics science has a particular object in view – the establishment of principles, propositions, theories or generalisations stating the relationship of one thing to another. In this it goes beyond *descriptive economics*, which concentrates on a mere description of an economy – its institutions (firms, banks, government organisations, etc.), its population, its system of taxation, and so on. But studies ended there could hardly be termed 'scientific'. While descriptive economics is desirable, indeed necessary, it merely describes the mechanism. What we really want to know is how the mechanism operates.

That is the task of *analytical economics*, which sets out to establish general principles about the way in which an economic system works. In discovering these principles, economics makes use of the methods of other sciences. These methods are: (1) induction, (2) deduction.

1.   Induction

In the inductive approach, the economist observes facts, classifies those facts, and then tries to observe any causal relationship between them. For instance, he may discover that the price of eggs falls in the spring. This would be connected with the increase in the supply of eggs at that time of the year, and from this a generalisation can be established that an increase in supply, other things being equal, leads to a fall in price.

The weakness of the inductive approach is that the scientist can never be sure that the principles established are 100 per cent foolproof. Hence, whenever possible, he will try to substantiate by deduction what has been discovered by induction.

2.   Deduction

With deduction, the economist starts from hypothetical assumptions (frequently referred to as postulates). Then, by a process of logical reasoning, he derives propositions from these assumptions. This is often termed 'model-building'. The sequence is as follows:

(a)   The economic phenomenon to be explained is selected. Of course, if the analysis is to be useful, the problem must be of practical significance.

(b)   The initial assumptions are made. These should be as close to reality as possible. But, although he is concerned with human behaviour, realistic assumptions are not impossible. In the main he is interested in market, not individual, reactions. Dealing in large numbers means that patterns of behaviour emerge, and it is possible to think in terms of an 'average economic man'. Thus it is quite reasonable to assume that, in disposing of his income, this average consumer will act rationally, seeking to obtain maximum satisfaction from it.

Of course, the economist has to simplify initially, confining himself to broad assumptions from which he can obtain only broad generalisations. Later, the assumptions can be changed according to particular circumstances, and the conclusions modified accordingly.

11

(c) Logical reasoning establishes what follows from the assumptions. Let us take a simple example. The economist wishes to discover what price will prevail in a market. He makes three assumptions:

    (i) a high degree of competition, on the basis of price, among buyers and among sellers, and between buyers and sellers;

    (ii) more will be demanded the lower the price;

    (iii) more will be supplied the higher the price.

    Demand and supply thus move in opposite directions for a given change in price. The conclusion he comes to is that the price of the good will settle where the amount supplied equals the amount demanded. Any other price will not be a settled price. If it is above, there will be more offered for sale than is demanded. Stocks will pile up, and some suppliers will lower their prices. As the price falls, so more will be demanded, and this will go on until demand equals supply. Similarly, when the price is below that where demand equals supply, shortages lead buyers to offer higher prices. As the price rises, so more will be supplied, and this goes on until demand equals supply (see p. 41). He has thus built up a model showing how price is determined in a market – a very useful piece of economic theory.

    By modifying the assumptions he can make the model closer to real life or show how changes in the economic system work. For instance, suppose that, as a result of an advertising campaign, people's tastes change, so that they want more of the good at the market price than formerly. At the original price, demand now exceeds supply. As before, this will cause the price to rise and supply to expand until a new price is arrived at where once more demand and supply are equal.

(d) As far as possible, propositions derived by deduction are tested by observed data. Often, however, such tests will prove impracticable, if not impossible, to undertake. For instance, the economist may be predicting outcomes which have no past parallels; he has therefore to await events before he can test the validity of his propositions.

    If the principles established are not disproved by such testing, they can be used to predict what will happen in particular instances, for they show how the different parts of a system are related to one another. It should be noted, however, that such forecasts are not unconditional statements of what will occur. The nature of an economic proposition is simply of the form 'if this occurs, then such and such will result'. For example, if demand increases then, other things being equal, price will rise (see p. 43). When we apply general principles to particular cases, we are in the realm of what is often called *applied economics*.

    It is this power to predict which enables firms and governments to plan with some degree of accuracy. The theory of price, for instance, would enable a building firm to make a useful forecast of the effect of an increase in the demand for houses on bricklayers' wages. Or, if there were widespread unemployment in the economy, a knowledge of the principles determining the level of activity could suggest appropriate measures which the government might take to reduce it.

1.4 NORMATIVE ECONOMICS

Normative economics, or 'political economy' as economics was originally called, accepts the analytical methods of positive economics in formulating theories. But it considers that the rigid scientific stance adopted is defective in two main ways.

First, it holds that it is virtually impossible to avoid value judgements. For instance, since facts have to be used to test hypotheses, the *selection* of those facts depends on the judgement of the economist who may unconsciously let his individual bias creep in. Again, in holding that the preferences and ends of individuals in a society are the ones which count, it overlooks that the State may have different ends. Thus the State may ban certain drugs because their abuse can result in ill-health and crime, incurring costs to society. But which drugs are banned involves a value judgement by the State. Finally, in evaluating growth over a period, the economist holds that 'more is better'. However, this view is based only on a consensus opinion, and is thus a value judgement. In any case, even though there may have been an increase in income per head of the population over time, we have no *objective measure* of welfare to assess whether people are obtaining more satisfaction (see p. 9).

Second, and more fundamental, economics is rather sterile if not applied to policy objectives. Positive economics, by restricting itself simply to predicting all the relevant consequences of alternative policies, ends up by 'sitting on the fence'. In contrast, the earlier economists have pursued their studies chiefly because of the social benefits which can result. 'The compelling motive that leads men to economic study is seldom a mere academic or scientific interest in the movements of the great wheel of wealth. It is rather the sense that, in the world of business and of labour, justice stands with biased scales; that the lives of the many are darker than they need be. In these things lies the impulse to economic investigations.' (Professor A. C. Pigou *Unemployment*, 1913).

Thus the normative economist, while still seeking to solve problems as scientifically as possible by following the techniques of the positive economist, applies the results to suggest the course of action which appears to be economically more efficient than the others. In doing so, he enters the region of value judgements.

It means also that, because economics studies human behaviour, the economist's judgement is enhanced by taking into account the findings of other social sciences. For instance, most people would consider that the economist should have something to say on the question, 'Should income tax be made more progressive?' But the reply would have to be along the following lines: 'The tax yield would almost certainly increase; but higher-income groups might not work so hard. While I can suggest theoretical reasons for this, you should also consider what the psychologist has to say. Furthermore, the pattern of consumption may change as the rich have less income to spend. For possible social effects, consult the sociologist. Finally, it will also help in making incomes more equal. That concerns me in that it may increase the proportion of total income spent – but ethics and politics have most weight in deciding whether greater equality of incomes is desirable.'

1.5 CONCLUSIONS

Why economists disagree

The foregoing discussion throws light on the reasons why economists appear to disagree so often. Take the statement, 'Britain must remain in the European Union (EU) because it leads to a faster rate of economic growth.' Why might economists disagree on this?

First, they may not agree on the facts. Can we be certain that Britain's rate of economic growth has accelerated since she joined the EU? Facts are deficient; for example, calculations of Gross National Product (GNP) over time are not unambiguous (see pp. 345–50).

Second, they may disagree on the causal connection. Even if a faster rate of economic growth has been achieved since joining the EU, can we be sure that membership is the cause of this increase? There may be more than one explanation, e.g. the discovery of North Sea oil or increased capital investment in agriculture and industry. It may be difficult to decide which explanation fits the facts best.

Third, the statement really rests on a value judgement – that economic growth is a good thing. Some economists might consider that other objectives – more leisure, less worry, the protection of the environment, and so on – are in a fairly affluent society more desirable.

Fourth, they may unconsciously let individual bias creep into their analysis and interpretation of the facts. While, as scientists, economists try to be as objective as possible, they are often examining subjects upon which they have strong personal feelings. Thus an economist who is an ardent supporter of Anglo-American relationships may unconsciously fail to give full weight to evidence supporting an increase in the growth rate of the EU countries.

The economist as a consultant

Such imperfections do not mean that the economist is without value. If, for instance, he is employed in a business enterprise, the scope of his work is fairly well defined – to promote the success of the business in terms of profits. As regards government policy, however, the advice the economist can give may be less definite. In any case, the final decision will usually rest on the judgement of the politician. A government is seldom faced with a simple choice, since ends are usually a compromise between alternatives. The first task of the economist is to point out any inconsistency between aims. For instance, the aim of economic expansion could conflict with the aim of balance-of-payments equilibrium.

In any case, the economist can indicate the full implications of a particular policy. For example, if a very high level of employment is the aim, then he should point out that this could make it more difficult to maintain a stable price level.

Finally, he may be able to recommend more economic ways of achieving a given end. This is possible because, although ends may be given, there are economic and non-economic means of achieving those ends. Is it better perhaps to obtain food supplies by importing from abroad or by home production?

For his part, the economist tries to be as objective as possible, establishing principles which, given certain conditions, show how the economy works and how it can be made to work better in real life. Furthermore, the principles can be applied to specific problems. Decision-makers may brush these principles to one side, either because facts necessary for a complete answer are not available or because different weight is given to assumptions. But at least economics provides a reminder of where objectivity ends and subjectivity begins.

CHAPTER SUMMARY

....

- Economics is concerned with making choices about the allocation of scarce resources.
- Production possibility curves can be used to illustrate the choices faced by society, and the nature of opportunity cost.
- Positive economics makes statements that can be verified by empirical evidence (reference to facts or data).
- Normative economics recognises that many economic decisions involve subjective judgements.

REVIEW QUESTIONS

....

- Why is economics considered to be a 'social science'.
- Use a production possibilities curve and the concept of opportunity cost to explain the difficulties facing a society in deciding how much of its resources to devote to defence expenditure and how much to consumer goods.

 Visit the companion website for further questions

CHAPTER 2

METHODS OF ALLOCATING RESOURCES

LEARNING OBJECTIVES

After studying this chapter you should be able to:
- describe the functions of the economic system;
- show how market economies allocate resources and explain the deficiencies of such economies;
- show how command economies allocate resources and explain the deficiencies of such economies;
- explain the advantages of mixed economies;
- understand the term 'sustainable development'.

2.1 FUNCTIONS OF AN ECONOMIC SYSTEM

The conditions of economic efficiency

We respond to the economic problem by 'economising'. This means that we have to:

(a) Ascertain what assortment of goods will yield the greatest satisfaction having regard to our limited resources.

(b) Employ those resources as efficiently as possible.

This involves: (i) relating production to the particular assortment chosen; (ii) combining resources in the right proportions; (iii) organising production so that the desired quantity of each type of good is produced with the least cost in scarce resources, e.g. by applying division of labour, considering large-scale production, carefully choosing the location of operations; and (iv) avoiding unemployment of resources.

In terms of Figure 1.2, maximum economic efficiency in the use of scarce resources is achieved when output is at *that point on the production possibility curve* which reflects the demand for agricultural produce relative to the demand for manufactured goods.

If production is technically inefficient or if there is unemployment, production will fall short of the production possibility curve, for example at *A*.

The role of the economic system

In primitive economies, the individual uses his resources directly to provide what he wants. Thus Robinson Crusoe had to decide how much time to spend hunting, fishing, growing corn and relaxing in the sun according to the strength of his preferences for meat, fish, bread and leisure. Similarly, in a subsistence economy the farmer's output is mainly for his own family's needs and he allocates his limited resources accordingly.

Today, however, decisions as to what shall be produced are linked only indirectly with the actual consumer. Man now specialises in production, obtaining the variety of goods he wants by exchange. This involves a multitude of decisions from different people. How much wheat shall the farmer grow? How much shall be milled each day? How many loaves shall the baker bake?

Put briefly, the following questions have to be answered:

(i)   *What* goods and services shall firms produce?
(ii) *How much* of each good and service shall be produced?
(iii) *How* shall the goods and services be produced?
(iv) How shall products be *divided* between households?

Thus if the greatest possible satisfaction is to be obtained from limited resources, there must be a link between producers and consumers. In broad terms this is the function of the 'economic system'.

Basically, any economic system consists of two parts:

(a) *Firms* – the business organisations which decide what goods and services to produce and bring together the different resources required.
(b) *Households* – which consume the goods and services and supply the resources, such as labour, to produce them.

In short, the economic system provides the link between firms and households (Figure 2.1).

Different forms of economic system

Man's first exchanges were quite simple: there was a direct swap of one good for another – a 'market' was established (see p. 30). Eventually a 'go-between' – money – was developed, allowing goods to be 'priced' and sold more easily. The subsistence economy had now evolved into the *market economy*, where answers to the above questions follow from people's decisions in the market.

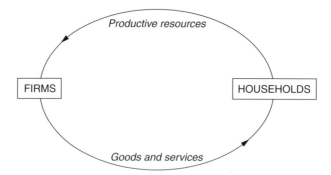

Figure 2.1   The flow of goods and resources in an economic system

In contrast to the market economy, there is the *command* or *centrally directed economy*, where the State decides what to produce and directs the factors of production accordingly. Furthermore, what is produced is distributed according to the decisions of the central body, the emphasis being 'to each according to his need' rather than on financial ability to pay. In the late twentieth century most of the centrally planned economies of the world convented to market economies.

Our task now is to examine in turn the respective strengths of these two systems.

2.2   THE MARKET ECONOMY

Outline of the market mechanism

In the market economy, emphasis is laid on the freedom of the individual, both as a consumer and as the owner of resources.

As a consumer he expresses his choice of goods through the price he is willing to pay for them. As the owner of resources used in production (usually his own labour) he seeks to obtain as large a reward as possible. If consumers want more of the goods than is being supplied at the current price, this is indicated by their 'bidding-up' the price. This increases the profits of firms and the earnings of factors producing that good. As a result, resources are attracted into the industry, and supply expands in accordance with consumers' wishes. On the other hand, if consumers do not want a particular good, its price falls, producers make a loss, and resources leave the industry. In short, the 'consumer is king'.

Prices therefore indicate the wishes of consumers and allocate the community's productive resources accordingly (Figure 2.2). There is no direction of labour; people are free to work wherever they choose.

Efficiency is achieved through the profit motive: owners of factors of production sell them at the highest possible price, while firms keep production costs as low as they can in order to obtain the highest profit margin.

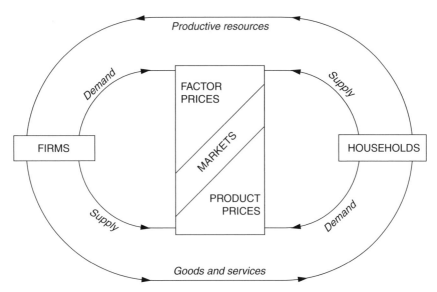

Figure 2.2   The allocation of products and resources through the market economy

Furthermore, factor earnings decide who is to receive the goods produced. If firms produce better goods or improve efficiency, or if workers make a greater effort, they receive a higher reward, giving them more spending power to obtain goods in the market.

In this way the *price system* acts, as it were, like a marvellous computer, registering people's preferences for different goods, transmitting those preferences to firms, moving resources to produce the goods, and deciding who shall obtain the final products. Thus, through the motivation of individual self-interest, the four problems inherent in economising are solved automatically.

Defects of the market economy

In practice the market economy does not work quite so smoothly as this. Nor are its results entirely satisfactory. We speak of 'market failure'.

First, some vital *community goods*, such as defence, police, justice and national parks, cannot be adequately provided through the market. This is mainly because it would be impossible to charge a price since 'free-riders' cannot be excluded (see p. 235).

Second, the *competition* upon which the efficiency of the market economy depends *may break down* (see p. 171).

Third, in practice the price mechanism may through *imperfect knowledge* or *immobility of factors of production*, function sluggishly (see pp. 172, 174). As a result supply is slow to respond to changes in demand.

Fourth, the private-profit motive does not always ensure that *society's* well-being (as distinct from the sum total of *private* wealth) will be maximised. There may be 'spill-over' benefits or costs, e.g. smoke from strawburning usually referred to as *'externalities'* (see Chapter 17).

Fifth, *competition itself may sometimes lead to inefficiency*. Duplication of research and competitive advertising may waste resources (see p. 198). Uncertainty as to rivals' plans may hold back investment.

Sixth, *consumers' choice may be distorted* by persuasive advertising, sometimes of goods injurious to health, e.g. cigarettes.

Seventh, the market economy, where individuals decide what to produce, is subject to instability in the overall level of activity and in the rate of growth, with resources remaining *unemployed* because firms as a whole consider that profit prospects are low (see Chapter 30).

Lastly, the consumers with the most money have the greatest pull in the market. As a result, resources may be devoted to producing luxuries for the rich to the exclusion of necessities for the poor. While this is really brought about by the unequal distribution of wealth and income rather than by the market system, the fact is that the latter tends to produce, and even accentuate, such inequality.

2.3   THE COMMAND ECONOMY

Central decision-making

With the command economy, the decisions regarding what? how much? how? and for whom? are taken by an all-powerful planning authority. It estimates the assortment of goods which it considers people want and directs resources accordingly. It also decides how the goods produced shall be distributed among the community (see Figure 2.3). Thus economic efficiency largely depends upon how accurately wants are estimated and resources allocated.

Merits of the command economy

The merits claimed for the command economy correspond closely to the defects of the market economy. The central planning authority can: (i) ensure that adequate resources are devoted to community and other goods; (ii) use its monopoly powers in the interests of the community, e.g. by securing the advantages of large-scale production, rather than make maximum profits by restricting output;

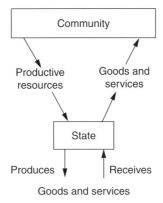

Figure 2.3 The allocation of resources and products through a command economy

(iii) introduce more certainty into production by dovetailing plans and improving mobility by direction of resources, even of labour; (iv) allow for external costs and benefits when deciding what and how much to produce; (v) employ workers in order to keep them occupied although to do so may be unprofitable in the narrow sense; (vi) eliminate the inefficiencies resulting from competition; (vii) use advertising to inform rather than simply to persuade or brainwash; (viii) allow for the uneven distribution of wealth when planning what to produce and in rewarding the producers.

Defects of the command economy

Nevertheless, the command economy has inherent defects, both economic and political:

Estimating the satisfaction derived by individuals from consuming different goods is impossible – although some help can be obtained by introducing a modified pricing system through markets, changes in prices signalling changes in wants. Often, however, prices are controlled, supplies rationed or queues form for limited stocks.

Also, many officials are required to estimate wants and to direct resources. But the use of officials may lead to bureaucracy – excessive form-filling, 'red tape', slowness in coming to decisions and an impersonal approach to consumers. At times, too, officialdom has been accompanied by corruption.

And, even when wants have been decided upon, difficulties of coordination arise. On the one hand, wants have to be dovetailed and awarded priorities. On the other, factors have to be combined in the best proportions. Usually plans are coordinated through numerous committees whose members are primarily politicians with little experience of managing a large organisation.

Furthermore, state ownership of resources, by reducing personal incentives, diminishes effort and initiative. Direction of labour may mean that people are dissatisfied with their jobs; officials may play for safety in their policies.

Perhaps most importantly, there always exists the danger that the State will make it easier to pursue economic objectives by restricting freedom of action, e.g. peasant farms are collectivised, or even by reducing or stifling political expression, e.g. by setting up a one-party system. Individuals would then exist for the State, and not the State for the individual. Thus the ultimate choice between a market economy and a command economy (in their extreme forms) really hinges on whether people prefer to run the risk of dictatorship or to accept the defects of the market economy which allows them greater economic freedom.

2.4   THE MIXED ECONOMY

The 'middle way'

Fortunately, a community does not have to make a complete choice between these two extremes. Instead it can compromise, allowing the State, to act, not as a dictator, but more like a wise parent who gives children much personal freedom but plans ahead to avoid many of the pitfalls into which they may stumble.

Thus, in an attempt to overcome 'market failure', the UK has a 'mixed economy' in which more than half of production is carried out by private enterprise through the market (though subject to varying degrees of government control), while for the rest of the economy the government is directly responsible. Moreover, chiefly by income redistribution and subsidies, the government influences the allocation of the goods and services produced. Our task in this book is to identify how market failure arises and what specific policies the government can adopt to deal with its various forms.

The private and public sectors

In examining how a mixed economy works, it is convenient to distinguish between the 'private sector' and the 'public sector'. The former consists of those firms which are privately owned. Here decisions are taken in response to market signals. The latter includes government departments, local authorities, and public bodies such as the Environment Agency. All are distinguished by the fact that their capital is publicly owned and their policies can be influenced through the ultimate supply of funds by the government. Thus the existence of the public sector enables the government to exercise an important measure of control over the economy. Moreover, decisions on what to produce can be based on need rather than demand (see p. 237).

2.5   MICRO- AND MACROECONOMICS

Microeconomics

A study of the price system is largely concerned with:

(1)   how the supply of a particular good or service is related to the demand for it;
(2)   how the demand for a particular factor of production is related to its supply.

As we shall see, this relationship of demand to supply is based upon prices established in the different product and factor markets (Figure 2.2). Since it is largely a study of the decisions of individual consumers and of individual firms in particular markets – small parts of the economy – it is usually referred to as microeconomics (from the Greek word *mikros* meaning 'small'). Thus if we ask ourselves what forces determine the price of potatoes, the rent of an acre of land in London, or the wage of a Nottingham bus driver, we are dealing with microeconomic questions.

Macroeconomics

However, in addition to studying how resources are allocated to different uses, we have to consider the level at which resources *as a whole* are being employed; that is, the overall level of activity. This gives rise to a series of 'general' questions. How can the total of consumers' demand in the economy change? How do firms in total respond to such a change in demand? What brings about changes in the general level of prices? We are now looking at variables in the aggregate – the aggregate flow of income, aggregate investment, aggregate wages, and so on. Such questions are the concern of macroeconomics (from the Greek word *makros* meaning 'large').

2.6   SUSTAINABLE DEVELOPMENT

Resource allocation decisions may seem very complex in the current time period, but imagine the difficulty of allocating resources efficiently over time. The problem of 'inter temporal' resource allocation has been considered by environmentalists who feel that the present generation should take into account the well-being of future generations in their decision-making. The principle of 'inter generational equity' has become a cornerstone of the principle of 'sustainable development' which can be defined as 'development that meets the needs of the present generation without compromising the ability of future generations to meet their needs'. Questions then arise such as: should we use all North Sea oil reserves now or leave some for people in the future? And if the present generation increases carbon-dioxide emissions by burning fossil fuels in pursuit of economic growth, will this mean catastrophic consequences for future generations through global warming?

There are differing views as to how to allocate resources efficiently and fairly over time. The free-market view argues that self-interest will ensure sustainability because, as resources become scarce, their price will rise encouraging conservation and development of substitutes. The social-efficiency view is that social costs and benefits should be considered in decision-making and not just the private interests of consumers and producers. In this approach, greater importance can be given to future generations and sustainability. The conservationist view suggests that the economic system should not pursue greater consumption and economic growth because it will lead to environmental degradation. The Gaia approach is the strongest advocate of sustainability. This argues that humans should look after the planet's resources and ensure that the land they leave for their descendants (and other species) is in at least as good condition as they found it.

CHAPTER SUMMARY

Economic systems must determine what to produce and the most efficient way to produce it. Market economies rely on the price system to allocate resources, and it usually does this very efficiently, although there are instances of market failure to deal with:

- community goods (or public goods);
- imperfect competition;
- imperfect knowledge;
- externalities;
- instability.

In command or planned economies the state estimates resource requirements and allocates resources accordingly. Estimating wants is very difficult, however, and mistakes are frequent. There are also problems of reduced incentives and authoritarian control in such economies.

REVIEW QUESTIONS

- What are the main aims of any economic system?
- What are the advantages and problems of market economies?
- What are the advantages and problems of command (or planned) economies?
- Why are most of the world's economies mixed economies?
- What is meant by 'sustainable development'?

 Visit the companion website for further questions

PART II

WHAT TO PRODUCE

3

HOW PRICE IS FORMED IN THE FREE MARKET ECONOMY

LEARNING OBJECTIVES

....

After studying this chapter you should be able to:
- explain the meanings of 'value' and 'price';
- define and describe different types of market;
- show how a demand schedule and a demand curve can be formed;
- show how a supply schedule and a supply curve can be formed;
- explain how equilibrium price is determined.

3.1 VALUE AND PRICE

As soon as we wish to know what to produce, there immediately arises the question: 'How can people indicate what they want?' A mere statement of want is meaningless, for, as we showed in Chapter 1, people always *want* something. A want is significant in economics only when a person is prepared to give up something in order to satisfy it. As the strength of the different wants varies, so will the amounts which people are willing to give up. In other words, different goods have a different *value* to them. Value is measured in terms of 'opportunity cost'. For example, if Ms A is willing to work two hours for the money which will buy a DVD, we say that the value of the DVD to her is greater than the value of the two hours' leisure forgone. Value therefore means the rate at which a particular good or service will exchange for other goods. It is important to note, however, that, while to have value a good must be capable of satisfying a want, a good which satisfies a want need not necessarily have value. For example, air satisfies a want; but, in normal circumstances, the supply is so great that nobody will give anything in exchange for it. Because it has no power to command other goods in exchange, it has, in economics, no value.

In modern economic systems we rarely exchange goods directly against other goods. We make use of a 'go-between', or, as it is usually said, a medium of exchange. This medium of exchange is money and the values of goods are expressed in terms of money. In other words, we *price* the goods and services. Price can be defined, therefore, as the value of a commodity or service measured in terms of the standard monetary unit. By comparing prices, we can compare the *rates* at which different goods can be exchanged.

Changes in *relative* prices, if supply conditions have not changed, indicate a relative shift in the importance of those goods. Thus price changes can signal a change in what people want. We must therefore examine the mechanism by which the signals are flashed up. We begin by looking at the 'market' – where values are established by exchange.

3.2 MARKETS

Definition

'I am offered £650 for this heifer. No more offers? For the last time of asking, any advance on £650? Going at £650, going, gone.' Down comes the hammer. 'Sold at £650 to Mr Giles on my right.'

This is the local cattle market. On his stand above the cattle ring is the auctioneer. Inside the ring, a black and white heifer is appraised by local farmers and dealers. Some are buyers, some sellers. The market fixes the price at which those who want something can obtain it from those who have it to sell.

Note that it is only exchange value which is significant here. The farmer selling the heifer may have felt that it ought to have made more than £650. Or, as it was the first calf reared by his son, it may have had great 'sentimental value' to him. Such considerations, however, mean little in the market economy.

Of course, prices are not always fixed by auction. This is the method usually employed where there are many buyers but the seller only comes to the market infrequently, or wishes to dispose of his goods quickly. If there are few buyers and sellers, e.g. in the purchase of a house or a second-hand car, the final price may be arrived at by 'haggling' – the seller meeting the prospective buyer personally and bargaining with him.

But where goods are in constant demand the above methods take too long. Thus most goods, such as foodstuffs, clothing and household utensils are given a definite price by the shopkeeper. But buyers will still influence this price. If it is too high, the market will not be cleared; if it is too low, the shopkeeper's stocks will run out.

A market need not be formal or held in a particular place. Second-hand cars are often bought and sold through newspaper advertisements. Second-hand furniture may be disposed of by a card in a local shop window. Foreign currency, gold, base metals, raw cotton and other goods which can be accurately described are dealt in over the telephone.

However, in studying the market economy it is essential to understand how price is determined. Since this is done in the market, we can define the market simply as *all those buyers and sellers of a good who influence its price*. Within the market there is a tendency for the same price, allowing for costs of transport, to be established for the same commodity.

1. World markets

Today modern transport allows many commodities to have a world market – a price change in one part of the world affects the price in the rest of the world. Examples of such commodities are wheat, coffee, oils, basic raw materials (such as cotton and rubber), gold, silver and base metals. What conditions must a commodity fulfil to obtain a world market?

First, there must be a wide demand. The basic necessities of life (e.g. wheat, vegetable oils, wool, cotton) answer this requirement. In contrast, such goods as national costumes, books translated into little-used languages and postcards of local views have only a local demand.

Second, commodities must be capable of being transported. Land and buildings are almost impossible to transport. Personal services are limited by the distance the consumer can travel. Labour, too, is particularly immobile, especially when it comes to moving to a different country (see Chapter 20). Furthermore, governments, may, by import taxes and quotas, effectively prevent the entry of certain commodities into the country.

Third, the costs of transport must be small in relation to the value of the commodity. Thus the market for diamonds is worldwide, whereas that for bricks is local. Similarly, wheat and oil are cheap to transport compared with coal because they are more easily handled – although, as sea transport is relatively cheap, coal mined near the coast can be sent long distances.

Last, the commodity must be durable. Goods which perish quickly, such as milk, bread, fresh cream and strawberries, cannot be sent long distances. Nevertheless, modern developments, such as refrigeration and air freight transport, are extending the market even for these goods.

2. Perfect and imperfect markets

In any market the price of the commodity in one part affects its price in another part. Hence the same price tends to be established. Where price differences are eliminated quickly, we say the market is a 'perfect' market. (Note that this is not quite the same as 'perfect competition' – see Chapter 11.)

For a market to be perfect certain conditions have to be fulfilled. First, buyers and sellers must have exact knowledge of the prices being paid elsewhere in the market. The development of communications, particularly telecommunications and the internet, has facilitated this. Second, both buyers and sellers must base their actions solely on price, and not favour one particular person out of loyalty or mere inertia. Thus, if one seller puts up the price of his good, his customers immediately go to another who is cheaper. Alternatively, if he lowers his price, customers will so flock to him that he would sell out quickly unless he raises his price to that asked elsewhere.

Examples of perfect markets are the precious stones market of Hatton Garden in London, and above all the organised produce markets and the stock exchange (see below). In these markets the two essential conditions are fulfilled, for prices are watched closely by professional dealers. As a result of their operations, variations in price are quickly eliminated.

But such conditions are rarely satisfied in other markets. Buyers and sellers neither have perfect knowledge nor act solely on the basis of price. The ordinary housewife, for instance, cannot afford the time to go from one shop to another in order to compare the prices of her everyday purchases, though she is usually much more careful when spending on the more expensive goods bought at infrequent intervals. Similarly, shopkeepers do not always know what competing shopkeepers are charging for their goods. Moreover, purchasers may be influenced by considerations other than price. Thus they may continue to deal with one particular trader, even though he is charging a slightly higher price, because he has given them good service in the past. Finally, although two goods may be virtually the same physically, by 'product differentiation' and advertising the merits of his own brand a producer may convince the consumer of its superiority. Such 'persuasive' advertising, makes the market less perfect, and must be contrasted with 'informative' advertising, which increases knowledge and thus helps to make the market more perfect.

Where price differences persist, markets are said to be 'imperfect'. As we have already hinted, such markets are often found in retailing.

3. Organised produce markets

As explained above, the market for certain commodities is worldwide. Moreover, many of these commodities are in constant demand, either as basic raw material or as mainfoods or beverages for a large section of the world's people. They therefore figure prominently in international trade, and are the subject of the following discussion.

England's foreign trade began with the export of raw wool in the thirteenth century, and it was extended by the subsequent development of the chartered companies. These were based in London, and it was there that merchants gathered to buy and sell the produce which the companies' ships brought from abroad.

The big change, however, came about with the expansion of international trade following the industrial revolution. The UK became the greatest importing and exporting nation in the world. London, her chief port and commercial city, not only imported the goods which were required for the people of her own country but built up an important entrepôt business, acting as a go-between in the distribution of such commodities as tea, sugar, hides, skins and wool to many other countries, particularly those of western Europe.

Hence formal 'organised markets' developed. These markets are distinctive in that buying and selling takes place in a recognised building, business is governed by agreed rules and conventions, and often only certain persons are allowed to engage in transactions. They are thus a highly developed form of market. Today, London has exchanges which trade in both spot and forward contracts in such commodities as gold and silver, petroleum, wool, tea, coffee, base metals (tin, copper, lead, aluminium, nickel and zinc), grain, and shipping freights (the Baltic Exchange). It must not be thought, however, that such organised produce markets exist only in London. Liverpool has exchanges for cotton, and most of the other large trading countries have exchanges too. Although today many of the goods go directly to other countries, the earnings of London dealers are part of the UK's income from 'invisible exports' (see p. 489).

Broadly speaking, organised markets fulfil three main functions. First, they enable manufacturers and wholesalers to obtain supplies of commodities easily, quickly and at the competitive market price. Because they are composed of specialist buyers and sellers, prices are sensitive to any change in demand and supply. Thus they are perfect markets.

Second, 'futures' dealings on these markets enable people to protect themselves from heavy losses through price changes. Thus a cotton grower prefers to know what price he will receive before his output is actually delivered to the market. On the other hand, a cotton spinner has to protect himself from a rise in the price of raw cotton between the time he quotes a price for his yarn and the time of its actual manufacture. Where a good is bought today for delivery today, the deal is known as a 'spot' transaction and the price is the 'spot price'. With many goods, however, it is possible to buy today for delivery in the future. The price agreed upon is the 'future' or 'forward' price. For a commodity to be dealt in on a futures market certain conditions must be fulfilled: (i) the commodity must be durable, thereby enabling stocks to be carried; (ii) the commodity must be described in terms of grades which are internationally uniform; (iii) dealings must be frequent enough to occupy professional dealers; and (iv) the commodity must be subject to price fluctuations.

In futures dealings the dealer uses his expert knowledge to make a profit on what he considers will be the future price of the commodity. At any time a dealer will quote a price (according to the view he takes of the future movement of prices) at which he is prepared to buy or sell at some future date. Thus a cotton grower can cover himself against a possible fall in price by selling his produce forward, while a cotton spinner can quote a weaver a price for yarn and guard himself against loss by buying the raw cotton forward.

Such dealing usually performs the third function of organised markets – evening out price fluctuations. At a time when an increase in supply would cause the price to fall considerably, the dealer adds his demand to the normal demand in order to build up his stocks, and thereby keeps the price up. On the other hand, when the good is in short supply he releases stocks and so prevents a violent rise in price. The difficulty is that speculation on the future price may dominate the real forces which influence it, prices fluctuating violently in response to changes in optimism and pessimism.

3.3 FORCES DETERMINING PRICE

Demand and supply

'That animal was cheap,' remarks Phil Archer as the auctioneer's hammer falls. 'And no wonder,' replies Brian Aldridge. 'This has been a long winter. We're now in the middle of April, and the grass is hardly growing. Hay's running short and breeders are being forced to sell sooner than expected. Old Giles is about the only farmer who'll take the risk of buying extra cattle.'

What can we learn from Brian Aldridge's observations? Simply that the £650 at which the heifer was sold was not really determined by the final bid. The real factors producing the relatively low price were the reluctance of farmers to buy and the number of young animals being offered for sale. In short, the price was determined by the interaction of the forces of demand and supply. We shall look at each in turn.

Preliminary assumptions

First, we examine how these forces work in an imaginary market – for eggs. To simplify, we shall assume that:

(i)   All eggs are exactly the same in size and quantity.
(ii) There are no transport costs within the market.
(iii) The market consists of so many small buyers and sellers that there is keen competition.
(iv) It is a perfect market – price differences are quickly eliminated because buyers and sellers (1) have complete knowledge of prices and conditions in other parts of the market, and (2) act solely on the basis of price.
(v)   There is no interference by the government in the operation of market forces, e.g. by price control, regulating supply, etc.

3.4 DEMAND

Demand in economics is the desire for something *plus* the willingness and ability to pay a certain price in order to possess it. More specifically, it is how much of a good people in the market will buy at a given price over a certain period of time.

It is helpful if we separate the factors affecting demand into (i) price, and (ii) the conditions of demand – the determinants of demand other than price.

1. Price (the conditions of demand remaining unchanged)

Normally a person will demand more of a good the lower its price. This is because, once you have some units of a good, you have partly satisfied your want and so will only buy more at a lower price. This conforms to our everyday observations. 'Winter sale, prices slashed' announce the shops when they wish to clear their stocks of clothing.

We can draw up a table showing how many eggs a person would be willing to buy at different prices. If they are very expensive, other foodstuffs will, as far as possible, be substituted; if they are cheap, people may even buy them to pickle. By adding up the demand from all buyers of eggs in the market at different prices over a given period of time, it is possible to obtain a *market demand schedule* (Table 3.1).

Note that this schedule does not tell us anything about the actual market price or how much is in fact sold. It is an 'if' schedule. All it says is: '*If* the price is so much, then this quantity will be demanded.' Plotting this schedule on a graph, and assuming that demand can be obtained for intermediary prices, gives the demand curve *D* in Figure 3.1.

Table 3.1 Demand schedule for no-such market for the week ending 31 January 2006

Price (pence per egg)	Eggs demanded* (thousands)
12	3
10	9
8	15
6	20
4	25
2	35

* What buyers would take at each price.

What to produce

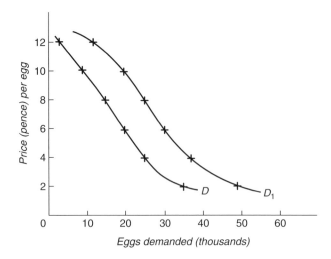

Figure 3.1 Quantity demanded and price

Table 3.2 An increase in demand

Price (pence per egg)	Eggs demanded (thousands)
12	12
10	20
8	25
6	30
4	37
2	49

2. The conditions of demand

Something may occur to cause housewives to demand more eggs at a given price. In other words, the demand schedule alters. Suppose, for instance, farmers unite in an advertising campaign describing tasty egg dishes. As a result more eggs are demanded at all prices (Table 3.2).

Plotting this revised demand schedule gives curve D_1 to the right of D. Had conditions so changed that demand decreased, the new demand curve would have been to the left.

The influence of both (1) price, and (2) the conditions of demand, on the quantity demanded is thus shown on the graph. The former determines the shape of the

36

demand curve – its slope downwards from left to right. The latter determines the position between the axes – an increase in demand shifting the curve to the right, a decrease to the left. For clarity's sake, a change in demand resulting from a change in price will in future be referred to as an *extension* or *contraction* of demand; a change in demand due to new conditions of demand will be described as an *increase* or *decrease* in demand.

Conditions of demand may change in a *short* period of time through:

(1) A change in the price of other goods. Goods compete for our limited income and are thus, to some extent, substitutes for each other. When the prices of other goods fall, the particular good under discussion becomes relatively dearer and therefore less of it is demanded. When the prices of other goods rise, it becomes relatively cheaper, and so more of it is demanded.

But the effect on the demand for a particular good is more pronounced when the price of a close *substitute* changes. Suppose that fried tomatoes are an alternative to eggs for breakfast. If the price of tomatoes falls, housewives will tend to buy them rather than eggs. Thus, although there has been no initial increase in the price of eggs, demand for them has decreased. Similarly, where goods are *complements*, a change in the price of one good has a pronounced effect on the demand for the other. For example, a fall in the price of cars results in more cars being purchased, leading eventually to an increase in the demand for petrol and tyres (see also p. 50).

(2) A change in tastes and fashion. A campaign advertising eggs would increase demand; a scare that eggs were the source of infection would decrease it.

(3) Expectations of future price changes or shortages. The fear that the price of eggs may rise considerably next week may induce people to increase their demand now in order to have eggs in stock.

(4) Government policy. A selective tax on eggs paid by the consumer would raise the price and lead to a decrease in demand; a rebate paid to the consumer would have the opposite effect.

Over a *longer* period the conditions of demand may change through:

(5) A change in real income. If there were an all-around increase in real income (that is, money income adjusted for any change in the price level) people could afford more eggs, and demand would probably increase. Or it might now be possible to afford mushrooms for breakfast, and these would take the place of eggs, now an 'inferior good' (see p. 59).

(6) Greater equality in the distribution of wealth. The wealth of a country may be so distributed that there are a few exceptionally rich people whereas the remainder are exceedingly poor. If many poor people felt they could not afford eggs, greater equality of wealth would be likely to increase the demand for eggs.

(7) A change in the size and composition of the population. Additional people coming into the market will, with their extra income, increase demand, especially if eggs figure prominently in their diets.

Supply in the economics refers to how much of a good will be offered for sale at a given price over a given period of time. As with demand, this quantity depends on (i) the price of the good, and (ii) the conditions of supply.

1. Price (the conditions of supply remaining unchanged)

Normally, more of a good will be supplied the higher its price. The real reason for this is explained in Chapter 5. But even a brief consideration of how the individual farmer reacts to a change in price will show that it is likely to be true. If the price of eggs is high, he will probably consume fewer himself in order to send as many as possible to market. Moreover, the higher price allows him to give his chickens more food so that they can lay a few extra eggs. When we extend our analysis to the market supply it is obvious that a higher price for eggs enables other farmers – the less efficient – to produce.

Hence we are able to draw up a *market supply schedule* – the total number of eggs supplied at different prices by all the sellers in the market over a given period of time (Table 3.3).

Once again it must be noted that this is an 'if' schedule, for all it says is: '*If* the price is so much, then this quantity will be offered for sale.'

Table 3.3   Supply schedule for no-such market for the week ending 31 January 2006

Price (pence per egg)	Eggs supplied* (thousands)
12	40
10	32
8	25
6	20
4	13
2	7

* What sellers would offer at each price.

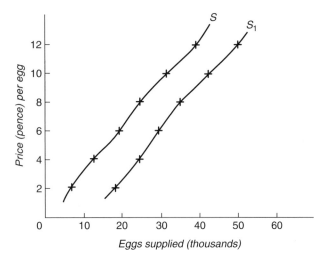

Figure 3.2 Quantity supplied and price

We can plot this schedule (Figure 3.2); assuming supply for all intermediate prices, a supply curve *S* is obtained.

However there is a fundamental difference between demand and supply. Whereas demand can respond almost immediately to a change in price, a period of time must usually elapse before supply can be fully adjusted. For the first day or two the only way in which the farmer can send more eggs to market is by eating fewer himself. By the end of the week he may have increased output by giving the hens more food or by leaving the light on in the hen-house all night; the higher price covers the extra cost. But to obtain any sizeable increase the farmer must add to his hens; if all farmers are following the same policy, this will take about five months, the period required to rear laying hens from chicks.

These different periods of time are dealt with more fully in Chapter 12.

2. The conditions of supply

The number of eggs supplied may change even though there has been no alteration in the price. In the spring, for instance, chickens lay more eggs than in winter. Thus more eggs will be supplied at all prices in the spring, and fewer in winter as shown in Table 3.4.

Table 3.4 shows that compared with winter when only 25,000 eggs were supplied at 8p each (Table 3.2), during the spring 36,000 were supplied. Or, looked at in another way, 25,000 eggs can be supplied in the spring at 4p each compared with

39

Table 3.4 An increase in supply in the spring

Price (pence per egg)	Eggs supplied (thousands)
12	50
10	43
8	36
6	30
4	25
2	19

8p in the winter. When plotted, the revised supply schedule gives a curve S_1 to the right of the old one (Figure 3.2). Had supply decreased, the new supply curve would have been to the left.

Like demand, therefore supply is influenced by both (i) price, and (ii) the conditions of supply. The former determines the shape of the curve – its upward slope from left to right. The latter determines its position between the axes – an increase in supply shifts the curve to the right, a decrease to the left. To distinguish between the two we shall refer to a change in supply resulting from a change in the price of a commodity as an *extension* or *contraction* of supply; a change in supply due to new conditions of supply will be described as an *increase* or *decrease* in supply.

In general, conditions of supply may change through:

(1) *Price expectations.* Where a commodity is durable and the relative cost of storage low, e.g. gold, wheat, antiques, price expectations can, as with consumers' demand, affect supply. Thus if the price is expected to rise, stocks will be held or even augmented. If the price is expected to fall, stocks will be depleted. Supplies of perishable goods such as eggs are at a disadvantage here.

(2) *A change in the prices of other goods, especially when it is easy to shift resources into producing those goods.* Suppose, for instance, that there is a considerable increase in the price of chicken meat, including boiling fowls. It may pay the farmer to cull more of his older hens. Thus fewer eggs are supplied at the old price.

(3) *A change in the prices of factors of production.* A fall in the cost of pullets or of their food would reduce the cost of producing eggs. As a result more eggs could be supplied at the old price, or – looked at in another way – the original quantity could be produced at a lower price per egg. A rise in the wages of workers on chicken farms would have the opposite effect.

(4) *Changes resulting from nature.* (E.g. the weather, floods, drought, pest) and from *abnormal circumstances* (e.g. war, fire, political events).

(5) *Government policy.* A tax on the output of eggs or an increase in employers' national insurance contributions for farm workers would result in fewer eggs being offered for sale at the old price. That is, the supply curve moves

to the left. On the other hand, a subsidy, by decreasing costs, would move the supply curve to the right.

Other changes in supply take longer, occurring through:

(6) *Improved techniques*. Technical improvements reduce costs of production, shifting the supply curve to the right. Thus improved automatic feeding devices might be developed, or selective breeding producing hens which lay more eggs.
(7) *The discovery of new or the exhaustion of old supplies of raw materials.*
(8) *The entry of new firms into the industry.* If new farms begin to produce eggs, then supply would be increased and the supply curve would move to the right.

3.6 THE DETERMINATION OF PRICE: MARKET CLEARING

The demand and supply curves can be combined in a single diagram (Figure 3.3).
    Let us see how this analysis helps as a first approach to understanding how the market is cleared. The assumptions we have made so far are:

(i) Many buyers and sellers.
(ii) Keen competition between buyers, between sellers, and between buyers and sellers.
(iii) More will be demanded at a lower price than at a higher price.
(iv) Less will be supplied at a lower price than at a higher.

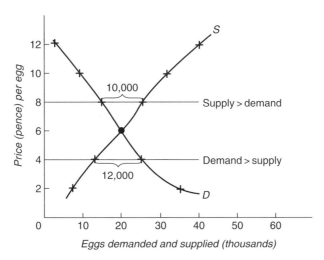

Figure 3.3 The determination of the equilibrium price

Given assumptions (iii) and (iv), the two curves slope in opposite directions. Thus they cut at a single point – in our example, where the price is 6p. It can be predicted that in No-Such Market, where these conditions of demand and supply exist, the price of eggs will move towards and eventually settle at 6p. This is the *market* or *equilibrium* price, the price where the plans of both buyers and sellers are consistent.

This proposition can be proved as follows. Suppose that initially the price of eggs is fixed at 8p. Here 15,000 will be demanded but 25,000 supplied. There is thus an excess supply of 10,000. But some sellers will want to get rid of their surplus, and therefore reduce the price being asked. As this happens some supplies are withdrawn from the market, and there is an extension of demand. This continues until a price of 6p is reached, when 20,000 eggs are both demanded and offered for sale. Thus 6p is the only price at which, given existing demand and supply, the market is 'cleared'.

Similarly, if the initial price is 4p, 25,000 will be demanded, but only 13,000 offered for sale. Because of this shortage, housewives queue to buy eggs, and sellers see that their supplies will quickly run out. Competition among buyers will force up the price. As this happens, more eggs are supplied to the market, and there is a contraction of demand. This continues until a price of 6p is reached, when demand equals supply at 20,000 eggs.

3.7 CHANGES IN THE CONDITIONS OF DEMAND AND SUPPLY

The equilibrium price will persist until there is a change in the conditions of either demand or supply.

Let us begin with our market price of 6p. Suppose tastes alter, and people eat more eggs. The conditions of demand have now changed, and the demand curve shifts to the right from D to D_1 (Figure 3.4).

At the original price of 6p we now have an excess of demand over supply – 30,000 eggs are demanded, but only 20,000 are supplied. As explained in the previous section, competition between buyers will now force up the price to 8p, a new equilibrium where 25,000 eggs are both demanded and supplied.

Similarly, a decrease in demand – resulting, for instance, from a significant fall in the price of tomatoes – would cause the curve to shift to the left and the price of eggs to fall.

Alternatively a change may occur in the conditions of supply. At any given price more eggs can be produced during the spring, when the supply curve shifts to the right from S to S_1 (Figure 3.5).

At the original price of 6p we now have an excess of supply over demand – 30,000 eggs are supplied, but only 20,000 are demanded. Here competition amongst sellers will mean that the price falls to 4p, where 25,000 eggs are both demanded and supplied.

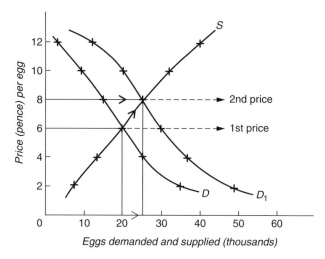

Figure 3.4 The effect on price of a change in the conditions of demand

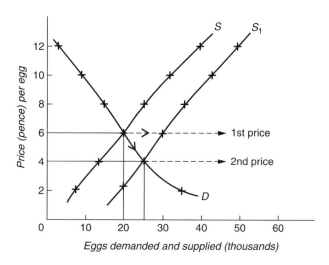

Figure 3.5 The effect on price of a change in the conditions of supply

Similarly, a decrease in supply, resulting, for instance, from higher costs of feedingstuffs for hens, would cause the supply curve to shift to the left and the price of eggs to rise.

Later we have to allow for the time element when looking at the response of supply to a change in the conditions of demand.

3.8 LATEST THEORIES

A great deal of academic study in economics over the past century has been devoted to 'General Equilibrium Theory'. This was developed first by Léon Walras (1834–1910) as the study of simultaneous equilibria in a group of related markets. Walras showed that, if all consumers were utility maximisers and firms were perfectly competitive, then a unique stable equilibria can exist.

The modern concept of general equilibrium was put forward by Kenneth Arrow and Gerard Debreu in 1954. The key issues concern the conditions under which the equilibrium will be efficient and whether the equilibrium will be unique and stable. The Arrow–Debreu model analysed the economics of the whole economic system and proved the existence of a multimarket equilibrium in which no excess demand or supply exists. The theory is based on two assumptions – that a competitive equilibrium will be achieved if each person in the economy possesses some quantity of every good available for sale in the market; that exploitable labour resources exist which are capable of producing goods and services.

There has been a great deal of subsequent attention in economic literature to the aesthetically pleasing idea of simultaneous equilibrium in all markets, but much of it is highly theoretical, using advanced mathematics, and it has been criticised for being far removed from reality. (Arrow, K. J. and Debreu, G. (1954) 'The Existence of an Equilibrium for a Competitive Economy', *Econometrica*, xxii, 265–90.)

CHAPTER SUMMARY

- A market can be defined as 'all buyers and sellers of a good or service who influence its price'.
- There are many different types of market, including world markets in commodities, organised markets where futures dealings are possible, and perfect and imperfect markets.
- In perfect markets, price differences are eliminated quickly.
- In imperfect markets, price differences can persist.
- The price of a good or service is determined by the interaction of the forces of demand and supply. Since demand and supply curves slope in opposite directions, they intersect at a single point. This is the market or equilibrium price where demand equals supply – the 'market clearing price'.

REVIEW QUESTIONS

....

- Why would a market be described as 'imperfect'?
- Explain briefly why demand curves slope downwards from left to right.
- Explain briefly why supply curves slope upwards from left to right.
- What is meant by the term 'equilibrium price'?

 Visit the companion website for further questions

APPLICATIONS OF DEMAND AND SUPPLY ANALYSIS

LEARNING OBJECTIVES

....

After studying this chapter you should be able to:
* explain the functions of price in a free market;
* show the effects of excess demand;
* illustrate the effects on price of changes in demand;
* illustrate the effects on price of changes in supply.

We have shown how price is determined in the free market, illustrating the explanation with demand and supply curves. Our task now is to show how this analysis can be applied to practical problems. First, we consider questions concerned with the role of price in the free market economy; second, we look at other problems, especially those relating to government policy, and examine how demand and supply analysis can help.

4.1   THE FUNCTIONS OF PRICE IN THE FREE MARKET

In a free market, price both *indicates* and *motivates* by conveying information to buyers and sellers and evoking a response.

How price 'rations out' scarce goods

At any one time the supply of a good is relatively fixed. It therefore has to be apportioned among the many people wanting it. This is done by adjusting price. As price rises, demand contracts; as it falls, demand expands. At the equilibrium price, demand just equals the supply. Should supply increase, the total quantity can still be disposed of by lowering the price; should supply decrease, price would have to be raised.

We can illustrate how price works by considering two current problems:

(a) *Who shall be allowed to park in a congested area?* There is traffic congestion in the centre of Barthem City because of the many cars parked at the kerbside. The city council decides that this is because parking is a free good – it costs motorists nothing to park their cars. It is decided to limit car-parking to one side of the road and to 240 places, each with a parking meter. The demand schedule for one-hour parking is estimated to be as follows:

Price (pence)	Demand
90	135
60	240
30	360
0	540

The council therefore fixes a charge of 60p.

This introduction of parking meters: (1) makes parkers pay for the space they occupy; (2) bars the all-day parker by limiting meter time to one hour; (3) forces the all-day parker and those 300 short-stay parkers who will not pay 60p to travel by public transport or to park off the street or out of the city centre; (4) causes the demand for off-street parking to increase, thereby encouraging firms to expand supply; (5) helps to relieve congestion by limiting parking to one side of the street or prohibiting it in busy roads.

(b) *Why do 'touts' obtain such high prices for Cup Final tickets?* To ensure that the regular football supporter can afford a Cup Final ticket, prices are fixed by the Football Association. Let us simplify by assuming that the Football Association has one price, £10, for 100,000 tickets, but that a free market price would be £30. In Figure 4.1, when the price is £30 demand equals the available supply, but at the controlled price of £10 demand exceeds supply by 150,000.

But some tickets are obtained by touts, who resell at a profit in a free market where demand and supply determine price. Keen club supporters, not lucky enough to have been allocated a ticket, are willing to pay more than £10. As the price rises, some people possessing tickets may be induced to sell them to the touts. Thus the demand and supply curves are roughly as shown in Figure 4.2, giving a 'spiv-market' price of £100.

An important conclusion can be drawn from this example: where price is controlled below the market price, only some form of rationing can ensure that everybody gets a share of the limited supply. Normally this is achieved by the Football Association, which, after allocating so many tickets to each finalist, limits each affiliated club to approximately two. The alternative would simply be a 'first come, first served' method of distribution, penalising those who could not queue and increasing the scope for tout activity.

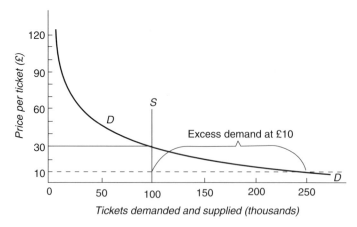

Figure 4.1   Excess demand for Cup Final tickets

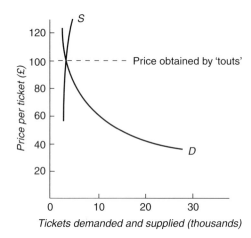

Figure 4.2   The 'tout' price of Cup Final tickets

How price indicates changes in wants

Prices are the signals by which the community indicates the extent to which different goods are wanted and any changes in those wants.

Consider how the demand for housing accommodation in London has increased over the last thirty years, largely through increased demand resulting from the rise in real income. As a result, rents have risen from *OP* to *OP*₁ (Figure 4.3).

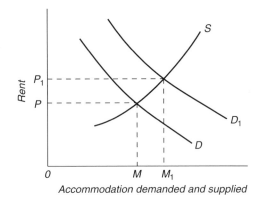

Figure 4.3 The effect on rents of an increase in the demand for accommodation

How price induces supply to respond to changes in demand

When demand increases, price rises and supply expands; when demand decreases, price falls and supply contracts. Thus in Figure 4.3, the increase in price has made it profitable for extra housing accommodation, MM_1, to be supplied by converting existing houses into flats and by new building.

In Chapters 11 and 12 we explain in more detail how supply responds to changes in demand.

How price indicates changes in the conditions upon which goods can be supplied

If the cost of producing a given commodity rises, this should be signalled to consumers who can then decide to what extent they are prepared to pay these higher costs by going without other goods. Again this is achieved through price. Assume in Figure 4.4 that the cost of producing good X has increased because raw materials have risen in price. Where demand is depicted by D, most consumers meet the higher costs (price rises by PP_1) rather than do without the good. Where demand is depicted by D_1, consumers tend to go without the good as its price rises (demand falls by MM_1), substituting other goods for it.

How price rewards the factors of production

Payments for factors of production (for example, wages for labour) give their owners spending power. The relative size of this spending power determines the

49

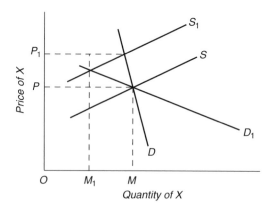

Figure 4.4 The effect of a change in the conditions of supply on price and quantity traded

division (usually termed 'distribution') of the total output produced. If the price of a good rises, producers can afford to offer higher rewards in order to attract factors from other uses.

4.2 FURTHER APPLICATIONS

Why do the prices of agricultural products fluctuate more than the prices of manufactured goods?

Price changes occur through changes in the conditions of demand and supply. Generally speaking, the conditions of demand for both agricultural products and manufactured goods are, over not too long a period, fairly stable. But the supply of agricultural products, unlike that of manufactured goods, varies from season to season, and, because of weather, plant disease and farmers' decisions, from year to year. Nor is storage easy, particularly in the case of foodstuffs. Thus the amount of agricultural products coming on the market fluctuates considerably, and so prices also fluctuate. The difference between the two can be seen by comparing tomatoes and carpets (Figure 4.5). Whereas the price of tomatoes varies between OP_1 and OP_2, that of carpets remains steady at OR.

How would an increase in the demand for cars affect the price of tyres?

Cars and tyres are 'jointly demanded'. In Figure 4.6 the increased demand for cars leads to an increased demand for tyres, and the prices of both rise. Later it will be

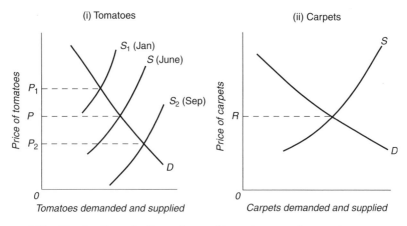

Figure 4.5 Fluctuations in the prices of tomatoes and carpets

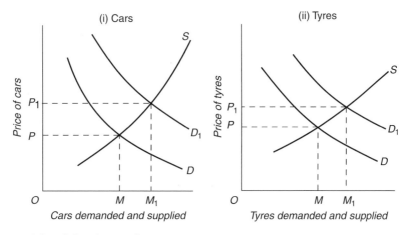

Figure 4.6 Joint demand

shown how slight modifications could be made to the supply curve for tyres to allow for differences in the length of time under consideration (see pp. 146–7).

How would an increase in the price of petrol affect the price of paraffin?

Petrol and paraffin are 'jointly supplied'; an increased production of one automatically increases the production of the other. Suppose that demand for petrol

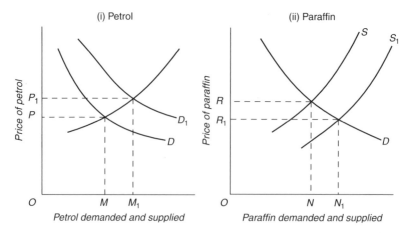

(i) Petrol   (ii) Paraffin

Price of petrol

Price of paraffin

Petrol demanded and supplied

Paraffin demanded and supplied

Figure 4.7   Joint supply

increases, but that there has been no change in the demand for paraffin. The price of petrol rises from OP to OP_1 and supply expands from OM to OM_1 (Figure 4.7). But this means that the supply of paraffin is automatically increased, though there is no change in price. Thus the supply curve for paraffin moves from S to S_1, and the price of paraffin falls from OR to OR_1. In practice, it is probable that the oil companies would try to increase the demand for paraffin, e.g. by advertising oil-fired central heating. If this proved successful, the price of paraffin would recover.

How could the government secure greater use of unleaded petrol?

Here the government must operate to alter the relative prices of leaded and unleaded petrol by increasing the tax on the former and reducing it on the latter. The effect is shown in Figure 4.8. Because of the increased tax on leaded petrol, demand decreases at all prices, the demand curve now being D_1 instead of D. Price, including the higher tax rises from OP to OP_1, and the amount sold contracts by MM_1 (Figure 4.8 (i)).

In contrast, the reduced tax on unleaded petrol allows the same amount to be obtained at a lower price, as shown by the higher demand curve, D_1. Price falls to OP_1 and the amount sold expands by MM_1 (Figure 4.8 (ii)).

Note that it is also possible to show the effects of a tax per unit by shifting the supply curve upwards (to the left) by the amount of the tax. The effects are the same.

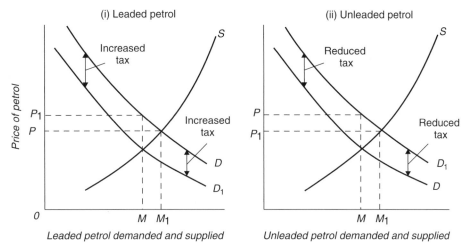

Figure 4.8 The effect on quantity bought of a change in the tax on a good

CHAPTER SUMMARY

Price performs a number of important functions in a free market, including:

- 'rationing out' scarce goods;
- indicating changes in wants;
- inducing supply to respond to changes in demand;
- indicating changes in conditions of supply;
- rewarding the factors of production.

Demand and supply diagrams can be used to show price changes in response to changes in the conditions of demand and supply.

REVIEW QUESTIONS

- How does price 'ration out' available supply?
- Explain, using a diagram, why tickets for Wimbledon can command very high prices when sold by ticket touts.
- Show how an increase in demand for cars will affect their price.
- Show how a decrease in supply of tomatoes will affect their price.
- Explain how a unit tax on cigarettes could change the quantities consumed.

 Visit the companion website for further questions

CHAPTER

5

A FURTHER LOOK AT DEMAND

LEARNING OBJECTIVES

....

After studying this chapter you should be able to:

- use marginal utility theory to explain why demand curves normally slope downwards from left to right;
- explain the circumstances necessary for exceptional demand curves;
- calculate price elasticity of demand;
- explain the significance and applications of price elasticity of demand;
- understand and give examples of cross-elasticity of demand;
- understand and give examples of income elasticity of demand.

5.1 WHY THE DEMAND CURVE NORMALLY SLOPES DOWNWARDS

Our conclusion in Chapter 3 – that more of a good will be demanded the lower its price – was based solely on our everyday observations. Can we put this conclusion on firmer ground?

The answer is 'yes'; and we shall use what is known as the 'marginal utility theory'. Other theories, such as the indifference curve analysis or revealed preference, may from the point of view of method be more satisfying, but the marginal utility theory is shorter to explain and often more useful in simple analysis.

Our method of approach will be as follows. Our main interest is in the market demand curve. But the market demand is made up of the demand of all the individuals who comprise the market. If, therefore, we study the individual buyer as he spends his income, and it can be said that other buyers act similarly, we can conclude that the market and individual patterns of behaviour are similar.

54

Maximising satisfaction

We assume that every individual has limited resources – represented by a limited money income – and that each acts 'rationally'. 'Rational' must not be interpreted in a value sense as being 'sensible'. It might not be sensible for someone to spend a large part of his income on cigarettes, but that is up to him. All the economist means by 'rational' is that the individual is consistent in his behaviour in the sense that he tries to get the most out of his limited resources. This is a reasonable assumption. There may be the odd consumer who acts frivolously, but since we are dealing with many consumers in the market we can think of a typical consumer who does act 'rationally'.

Because resources are limited, buying one good involves going without something else. In disposing of incomes, therefore, people weigh up the various 'opportunity costs', and try to obtain the maximum satisfaction from their expenditure. Normally their choice does not necessitate making an absolute decision between one good and another, but rather having a little more of this by sacrificing a little bit of that.

It might be questioned whether the consumer really does follow this careful procedure. How many people when purchasing a good weigh up its pros and cons and compare it, according to its price, with other goods? Surely, most expenditure is purely automatic? Admittedly, much expenditure is habitual – but this does not mean that people give no thought to it. Our immediate reaction to an increase in the selective tax on petrol or cigarettes, for instance, is to ask whether we cannot make do with less. In any case, following a routine for minor matters (including everyday purchases) allows more time for thinking about those things which are outside the usual run of events. Thus while we may not consciously consider the satisfactions to be obtained from other goods every time we buy a packet of washing powder, we are careful when furnishing a home to weigh up the merits and price of a video recorder as opposed to a dish-washer.

Questions to be answered

There are three basic questions we have to answer:

1. What conditions will hold when the consumer has obtained the maximum satisfaction from limited resources? In other words, what are the equilibrium conditions?
2. How does the consumer achieve this equilibrium?
3. What happens when the equilibrium is disturbed by a price change?

Let us deal with each in turn.

Preliminary assumptions

(a) Our consumer runs a home.
(b) He/she has a limited housekeeping allowance per week.
(c) He/she acts rationally to maximise satisfaction from this limited income.
(d) During the period of time under consideration, income and tastes do not change.
(e) He/she knows how much satisfaction each unit of a good will give.
(f) He/she is one of a large number of buyers; as a result his/her demand does not directly affect the price of the good.

1. The equilibrium condition

Our consumer will be in equilibrium when he/she would not switch a single penny of expenditure on one good to spending on another.

We can be more explicit by introducing the term 'utility'. In economics, this simply means that a good has the power to satisfy a want, irrespective of whether it is useful or commendable. Utility merely implies that the good is wanted by somebody. Note, too, that we cannot measure utility objectively; like love, pain or fear, it is purely subjective to the individual.

Our consumer knows in his/her own mind how much satisfaction each good affords him/her. The objective is to obtain the greatest possible utility from his/her income; that is, to *maximise total utility* (Figure 5.1).

The consumer achieves this by careful allocation of spending – say between cheese and margarine. All the time he/she is asking: 'If I spend a penny more on

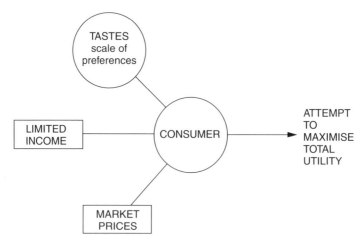

Figure 5.1 Factors affecting the equilibrium of the consumer

cheese, will I obtain more or less utility than if I spent the penny on margarine?' Only when the satisfaction he/she obtains from the last penny spent on cheese is equal to that from the last penny spent on margarine will he/she be in equilibrium. That is, spending adjustments take place at the margin.

Note that we did *not* say that the consumer obtained the same utility from the last pound of cheese as he/she obtained from the last pound of margarine. If for instance, a pound of cheese were four times as expensive as a pound of margarine, that would obviously be unreasonable; we would expect four times the amount of utility.

Sometimes, however, we cannot buy goods in 'pennyworths' – the good is 'lumpy' and we have to take a whole 'lump' of it or nothing at all. Can we restate our equilibrium condition to allow for this? Yes, but first we must define more carefully the concept of the margin and what we mean by 'marginal utility'.

Each small addition to a given supply of a good is called the *marginal increment,* and the utility derived from this increment is known as the *marginal utility*. Our original condition of equilibrium can therefore be stated in general terms:

$$\frac{\text{The marginal utility of}}{\text{1p spent on good } A} = \frac{\text{The marginal utility of}}{\text{1p spent on good } B}$$

But the marginal utility of 1p spent on good *A* depends on how much of a unit of good *A* you get for 1p. Thus:

$$\frac{\text{The marginal utility of 1p}}{\text{spent on good } A} = \frac{\text{The marginal utility of one unit of good } A}{\text{The number of pence it costs to buy a unit of good } A}$$

Similarly with good *B*. Thus our original equilibrium condition can be rewritten as:

$$\frac{\text{The marginal utility of one unit of good } A}{\text{Price of a unit of } A \text{ in pence}} = \frac{\text{The marginal utility of one unit of good } B}{\text{Price of a unit of } B \text{ in pence}}$$

That is:

$$\frac{\text{Marginal utility of good } A}{\text{Price of } A} = \frac{\text{Marginal utility of good } B}{\text{Price of } B}$$

The argument can be extended to cover more than two goods.

2. How does the consumer achieve this equilibrium?

The question must now be asked: how can our consumer arrange that the utility of the last penny spent on different goods is the same? The answer is to be found in the so-called *law of diminishing marginal utility*. Although wants vary considerably in their nature, they all possess the underlying characteristic that in a given period they can be satisfied fairly quickly. Thus, if a boy drinks lemonade to quench his thirst, the first glass will yield him a great amount of satisfaction. Indeed, the second glass may be equally satisfying. But it is doubtful whether he will relish the third glass to the same extent, since his thirst has now been partially quenched. If he continues to drink the lemonade, there will come a time when a glass gives him no additional satisfaction whatsoever and, in fact, it might be that he would be better off without it – there is a *disutility*. We can therefore state a general rule that the utility derived from any given addition to a consumer's stock of a good will eventually decline as the supply increases.

This means that our consumer can arrange that equal utility is derived from the last penny spent on each good by varying the quantity he/she buys. If more of a good is bought, the stock of other goods remaining fixed, its marginal utility relative to other goods falls. Similarly, if less of a good is bought, the marginal utility of the good relative to other goods rises. The consumer makes such marginal adjustments until he/she is in equilibrium.

3. What happens when the equilibrium is disturbed by a price change?

Suppose the price of cheese falls from 230p to 210p per pound while the prices of other goods remain unchanged. How will this affect the consumer's demand for cheese? We can proceed in either of two ways:

(1) The fall in the price of cheese will enable the consumer to obtain more cheese than before for every penny, including the last, spent on it. More cheese usually implies greater satisfaction. The last penny spent on cheese, therefore, now yields greater satisfaction than the last penny being spent on other goods. Hence the consumer reduces the utility obtained from the last penny spent on cheese by buying more cheese.

(2) The alternative form of the equilibrium condition is:

$$\frac{\text{The marginal utility of the last lb of cheese}}{\text{Price of lb of cheese}} = \frac{\text{The marginal utility of one unit of good } B}{\text{Price of one unit of good } B}$$

A fall in the price of cheese destroys this relationship; the marginal utility of cheese to its price is now higher than with goods B, C, etc. To restore the equilibrium relationship, the marginal utility of cheese must be decreased. To do this our consumer buys more cheese.

The reasons for this expansion in the demand for cheese can be analysed more closely. A reduction in the price of cheese means that our consumer is now able to purchase all the cheese he/she had before and still have money left over. This is an *income* effect of a price fall – he/she can now buy more of all goods, not only of cheese. But, in addition to this 'income effect', more cheese will tend to be bought because of a *substitution* effect. At the margin this means that a penny spent on cheese will now yield more satisfaction than a penny spent on other foods. Thus cheese is substituted for other foods. If cheese is a good substitute, marginal utility will diminish comparatively slowly as the consumption of it increases. A given price fall, therefore, will lead to a considerable increase in the quantity of cheese demanded.

Although we have explained the behaviour of only one consumer, it is reasonable to expect other buyers in the market to act similarly. Since the *market-demand curve* is made up of the demand schedules of all the individual purchasers, we can conclude that more of a good will be demanded the lower its price.

5.2 EXCEPTIONAL DEMAND CURVES

Normally the demand curve slopes downwards from left to right, showing that demand extends as price falls. It is possible, however, to envisage circumstances in which the reverse occurs – a fall in price bringing about a contraction of demand, and a rise in price an extension.

1. Inferior goods

Certain goods can be termed 'inferior' in that less is spent on them as income increases, people preferring other goods as incomes rise. Bread, cheap cuts of meat and low-quality floor-coverings are examples.

Now with most goods, e.g. strawberries, demand is likely to increase with a rise in income. The income effect on demand of a price fall will therefore be positive, reinforcing the substitution effect which is always in a positive direction. But with inferior goods the income effect on demand is negative, working in the opposite direction to the substitution effect. Take the case of cheap meat. A fall in its price would result in a tendency to substitute it for better cuts, such as steak, but the income effect would work in the opposite direction, people tending to replace cheaper meat with steak. If the income effect were greater than the substitution effect, the net result would be that less cheaper meat would be demanded at the lower price.

The income effect of a price fall will be more significant the greater the proportion of one's income which is spent on the good. And, if a large part of one's income is spent on an 'inferior' good (as may happen when income is low), the income effect may be so considerable as to outweigh the positive substitution effect. Suppose, for instance, that a person is so poor that 40 per cent of income has to be spent on bread in order to obtain the necessary calories to live. Now suppose that a loaf of bread falls in price from 40p to 20p per lb. The same amount of bread can now be obtained for only 20 per cent of money income, the other 20 per cent being available for spending on different goods. In other words, there has been a substantial increase in real income. As the person is now better off, it is quite likely that more varied foods will be bought but, since these will yield calories formerly provided by bread, they will tend to replace bread, the demand for which will thus contract even though its price has fallen.

The above is really an extreme case. What is an 'inferior' good depends largely upon one's level of income. Take a cheap joint of meat, for instance. To a particular person this may be an 'inferior' good, the negative income effect of a price fall outweighing the substitution effect. But there would also be poor people who could not have afforded even this joint at the old price. For them both the income effect and the substitution effect of a price fall would be positive. Thus, when we look at the *market* demand curve (as opposed to an individual's demand curve), we could find that it follows the normal shape, with more demanded as price falls.

2. Price movements are linked with expectations

With certain goods, expectations are an integral part of demand. The best example is securities bought and sold on the Stock Markets, where a person's current demand is largely determined by what he thinks will be the price of the security in the future. In this case, a rise or fall in the price of a security may well be associated with a larger or smaller quantity respectively being demanded if people think that the rise or fall will continue. A similar situation can arise in the residential housing market when prices begin to rise. Buyers want to purchase before the price rises further still and so there are more sales of houses after a price rise.

3. Goods having 'snob appeal'

Certain goods, e.g. diamonds, designer dresses and mink coats, may be wanted chiefly for ostentation – the desire to impress others. Should the price of such a good fall so much that it comes within the reach of many more people, original purchasers may no longer want it. Hence total demand could be less. Here again, however, we must distinguish between the individual and market demand curves. Although 'snob' buyers may leave the market when the price of the good falls, it is likely that large numbers of new buyers would enter, thereby adding to demand at these lower prices.

In each of the above types of situation, we have analysed the abnormality of the demand curve as a direct link between price and demand. With all three, however, we cannot ignore the fact that there is a close connection with changes in the conditions of demand. The first has a change in income, the second a change in expectations, and the third a change in tastes. Our theory explaining consumers' behaviour should be able to cope at one and the same time with a change in conditions of demand which are implicit in a change of price. It is a weakness of the marginal-utility approach that it fails to do so.

5.3 PRICE ELASTICITY OF DEMAND

Consider Figure 5.2. At price OP, demand for both commodities A and B is OM. But when the price of both falls by PP_1, demand for A expands by only MM_1, whereas that for B expands by MM_2. It is possible, therefore, to refer to differences in the 'price elasticity' of demand. This always refers to the elasticity at a particular price, and in what follows when we talk about 'elasticity' it will be assumed that there is some price in mind.

Measurement of elasticity of demand

Elasticity of demand (strictly, own-price elasticity) is defined by comparing the *rate* at which demand expands with the *rate* at which price falls. Using this definition, elasticity of demand can be measured in two ways. One is direct, showing the degree of elasticity; the other is indirect, merely indicating whether the demand for the good is elastic or inelastic.

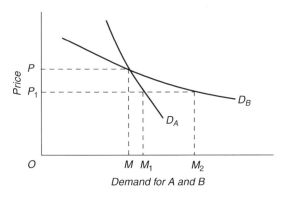

Figure 5.2 Elasticity of demand

1. A direct comparison of the rate at which demand changes with the rate at which price changes

When we wish to compare *rates* of change, we have to work in terms of proportionate (or percentage) changes. We can therefore define elasticity of demand as *the proportionate change in the amount demanded in response to a small change in price divided by the proportionate change in price*. That is,

$$\text{Elasticity of demand} = \frac{\text{Proportionate change in demand}}{\text{Proportionate change in price}}$$

$$= \frac{\dfrac{\text{Change in quantity demanded}}{\text{Original quantity demanded}}}{\dfrac{\text{Change in price}}{\text{Original price}}}$$

$$= \frac{\dfrac{\text{New Quantity} - \text{Old quantity}}{\text{Old quantity}}}{\dfrac{\text{New price} - \text{Old price}}{\text{Old price}}}$$

We can illustrate by an example from the demand schedule on page p. 35. When price falls from 10p to 8p, demand for eggs expands from 9,000 to 15,000. Elasticity of demand is thus equal to:

$$\frac{6000/9000}{2/10} = \frac{0.66}{0.2} = 3.33$$

Similarly, for a fall in price from 4p to 2p, elasticity of demand equals 0.8.

It will be noted that there is a difference in elasticity when we measure for a price rise or a price fall. Thus when price fell from 10p to 8p, elasticity was 3.33; but when it rises from 8p to 10p, elasticity is 1.6. This occurs because we were measuring from different prices and for a relatively large change. Were the price change only 1p instead of 2p, the two results would be more nearly equal. Where the price change is infinitely small, measurement of elasticity of demand is at the same point, and there is only one elasticity.

2. A comparison of total outlay as price changes

For the purpose of economic analysis, it is usually sufficient to refer to elasticity of demand in broad terms. Where elasticity is greater than 1 (the change in the quantity demanded is more than proportionate to the change in price), we say demand is elastic. Where it is less than 1 (the change in the quantity demanded is less than proportionate to the change in price), we say demand is inelastic. If it is 1 (the change in the quantity demanded being proportionate to the change in price), elasticity is described as being equal to unity.

This broad approach can be used to measure elasticity in a slightly different way. If the proportionate expansion in demand is greater than the proportionate change in price, the total amount spent on the good will increase. In other words, demand is elastic when, in response to a fall in price, total outlay (expenditure) increases; or, in response to a rise in price, total outlay decreases. Similarly, demand is inelastic when, in response to a fall in price, total outlay decreases; or, in response to a rise in price, total outlay increases. Elasticity of demand is equal to unity when as price changes, total outlay remains the same. This is the form of measurement which is most used in practice.

The rule can be remembered as follows:

price change, then total outlay changes in *opposite* direction – demand elastic;
price change, then total outlay changes in *same* direction – demand inelastic.

Thus, with the demand schedule on p. 35, we have:

Price of eggs (pence)	Demand (thousands)	Total outlay (thousand pence)	
10	9	90 }	Elastic demand
8	15	120	
6	20	120 }	Inelastic demand
4	25	100	

Between 8p and 6p, elasticity of demand equals unity.

Important points regarding elasticity of demand

1. *Demand curves are unlikely to have the same elasticity throughout their length.* Thus for the demand schedule on page p. 35, we have seen that demand is elastic at prices above 8p and inelastic at prices below 6p.
2. *The important exceptions to the above*, when elasticity of demand is the same throughout the whole length of the curve, are:

(a) *Demand absolutely inelastic*, people buying exactly the same amount of a commodity whatever its price (Figure 5.3a).
(b) *Demand perfectly elastic*, people ceasing to buy the commodity at all if its price rises slightly (Figure 5.3b). This is the demand curve for his good which faces an individual seller under conditions of perfect competition (see p. 129).

(c) *Elasticity of demand equal to unity*, where total outlay is constant at all prices. The curve here is known as a 'rectangular hyperbola', and all rectangles representing outlay (price x quantity demanded) are equal. For example, rectangle $OABC$ equals rectangle $OPQR$ (Figure 5.3c).

3. *Any other straight-line demand curve has a different elasticity of demand for each different price.* Take the demand curve D_A (Figure 5.4), for example. For a price fall of a penny: (a) at 5p, elasticity of demand is 5; (b) at 2p, elasticity of demand is 0.5.

The reason for this is that although a constant slope means that demand changes by the same amount for a given price change, the *rate* of change depends on the price and quantity from which we start.

4. *Usually we cannot compare the elasticities of demand of different goods by comparing the slopes of the respective demand curves.* The slope of the demand curve depends not only upon elasticity of demand, but also on the vertical and horizontal scales chosen. Furthermore, even if the same scales are chosen for different commodities, we cannot safely say that, where the demand curve for one commodity slopes more steeply than another, the demand for the first commodity is less elastic. Compare, for example, the parallel demand curves D_A and D_B in Figure 5.4. For a price fall from 4p to 3p, elasticity of demand for commodity A is equal to 2, while for commodity B it is equal to 1.

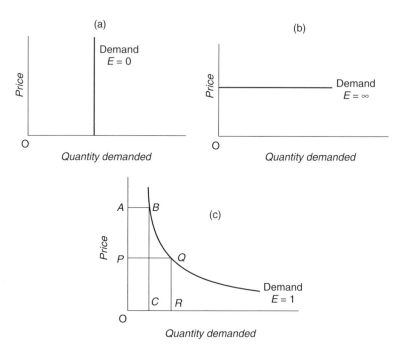

Figure 5.3 Constant elasticities of demand

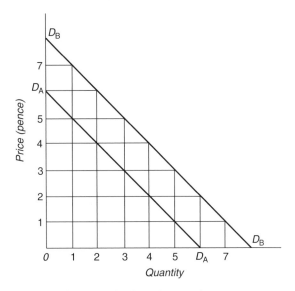

Figure 5.4   Elasticity of a straight-line demand curve

The reason is that, although we have taken the same price, we have started measuring proportionate changes in quantity demanded from different quantities. Only at the position where two demand curves with different slopes cut can we be *certain* that the difference in their slopes will reflect a difference in the elasticity of demand at that particular price (Figure 5.2).

Factors determining elasticity of demand

1.   *The availability of substitutes at the ruling market price*

As a good falls in price, it becomes cheaper relative to other goods. People are induced to buy more of it to replace goods which are now relatively dearer. How far they can carry out this replacement will depend upon the extent to which the good in question is, in their own minds, a substitute for the other goods. Goods within a particular class are easily substituted for one another. Beef is a substitute for lamb. Thus if the price of beef falls, people will buy more beef and less lamb. Between one class and another, however, substitution is more difficult. If the price of meat in general falls, there will be a slight tendency to buy more meat and less fish, but this tendency will be very limited, because meat is not nearly so perfect a substitute for fish as beef is for lamb.

We must be careful, however, over labelling the demand for the accepted necessities of life as 'inelastic' and the demand for luxuries as 'elastic'. With both, the substitution factor may be more important. Thus, although bread is a necessity, at a high enough price demand for it might be elastic because it has to compete with potatoes or cake. Similarly, a Rolls-Royce is a luxury, but demand for it will be inelastic if no substitute gives a similar prestige. In any case it is difficult to state categorically which goods are necessities and which luxuries. But we can use the concept to help, saying that where the demand for a good is very inelastic over a wide price range, that good can be regarded as a necessity, and where demand is very elastic over a wide price range, that good can be regarded as a luxury.

2. The number of possible substitute uses

Where a good can be substituted for another good, its demand tends to be elastic. And the more goods it can be substituted for, so the more will demand for it extend as its price falls. Thus reductions in the price of plastics have led to large extensions of demand as they have been substituted for materials used in such articles as enamel bowls, galvanised buckets, paper wrappings, glass garden cloches, wooden toys and tin containers.

3. The proportion of income spent on the good

When only a very small proportion of a person's income is spent on a good, as (for example) with pepper, salt, shoe polish, newspapers, matches and toothpaste, no great effort is made to look for substitutes when its price rises. Demand for such goods is therefore relatively inelastic. On the other hand, when the expenditure on a good is fairly large, as (for example) with most groceries, a rise in price would provide considerable incentive to find substitutes. Thus supermarkets have succeeded because, when they cut prices, large numbers of customers are attracted from other retailers who are selling the same good at a higher price.

4. The period of time

Since it takes time to find substitutes or to change spending habits, elasticity may be greater the longer the period of time under review. In practice, many firms try to overcome the ignorance or conservatism of consumers by advertising, giving free samples, or making special offers.

5. The possibility of new purchasers

In discussing the possibility of substitution above, we have looked at elasticity of demand from the point of view of the individual consumer. But when we are considering the market demand curve, we must allow for the fact that, as price falls, new consumers will be induced to buy the good. In fact with many goods, such as cars, video-recorders, washing machines, etc., of which people require only one, it is the fall in price bringing the good within the range of the demand of new consumers which leads to the increase in demand. Hence a fall in price which induces people in a numerous income-group to buy will result in a considerable elasticity of demand.

Uses of the concept of elasticity of demand

The concept of elasticity of demand figures prominently in both the theoretical analysis of the economist and the practical decisions of the businessman and government. The following are a few examples.

1. Theoretical economics

(a) *To define 'perfect competition' in selling a good.* The economist, in order to explain the working of the economy, usually begins by constructing a model of how it works under theoretical conditions known as 'perfect competition' (see pp. 128–38). On the selling side, one essential criterion of perfect competition is that everybody in the market produces so small a quantity of the total supply that no one seller can influence the price of the good by the amount he puts on the market. He has to accept market price as given for any output he might produce. That is, he sees the demand for his good as perfectly elastic (see p. 63). (Similarly, on the buying side, no one purchaser must be able to influence the price by the size of his demand – see pp. 135–6.)

(b) *As a helpful tool in analysing problems connected with changes in the conditions of supply.* Many problems analysed by the economist can be tackled adequately only by making use of the concept of elasticity of demand. Consider, for example, the question 'What effect will a rise in wages have on the numbers employed in the car industry?' The answer hinges largely on the elasticity of demand for the product made by that labour. An increase in wages will move the supply curve of the product to the left, from S to S_1 (Figure 5.5). Output will contract – but how much it contracts depends upon the elasticity of demand. If demand is elastic, it will contract to OM_1; if inelastic, to OM_2.

The general rule is that where demand is elastic, a change in supply will cause the quantity sold to change rather than price; where demand is inelastic, price changes rather than the quantity sold. Thus a trade union will find it more difficult to obtain a wage increase for its members without creating unemployment where the elasticity of demand for the product made is high.

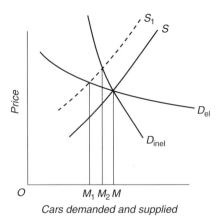

Figure 5.5 Elasticity of demand and a change in the conditions of supply

2. Business decisions

(a) *The supermarket.* The policy of the supermarket rests largely on the high elasticity of demand for its products. When it cuts the price of a good, the supermarket expects a considerable expansion in demand by winning customers from retailers selling at a higher price. Thus it is most successful in selling standardised goods, such as branded groceries, but less successful where customers form a personal attachment to the shopkeeper, as with butchers, tailors, etc.

(b) *The monopolist.* A monopolist is not faced with a perfectly elastic demand curve when selling his product, for the price of the good is affected by the quantity he puts on the market (see Chapter 15). Therefore, he looks at the demand schedule for his good and fixes the amount, and thus the price, at which he makes the highest profit.

Let us imagine a football club which is staging a European Cup match. Let us further imagine that there is no comparable attraction within fifty miles and that the price of admission is fixed by the club, which pursues the policy of making as big a profit as possible. Expenses of the club will be roughly the same whether few or many watch the game. The relevant portion of the demand schedule is as follows:

Price of admission (£)	Number of spectators willing to pay that price	Total outlay by spectators (£)
10	60,000	600,000
20	56,000	1,120,000
30	50,000	1,500,000
40	32,000	1,280,000

The club therefore fixes the price of admission at £30, and the total number of spectators at the game is 50,000.

A rail operator, too, has to consider elasticity of demand when fixing fares. Should it, for example, raise fares in order to reduce losses? If, at existing fares, the demand is relatively elastic, then a fare increase would mean that total revenue would fall. Losses would be reduced only if operating costs (through carrying fewer passengers) fell more than revenue. On the other hand, if demand were inelastic, raising fares would increase total revenue without adding to operating costs.

3. Government policy

Throughout this book we shall find that, in discussing government economic policy, elasticity of demand looms large. For instance, the Chancellor of the Exchequer must take it into account when considering the effect of a selective tax on a particular good: the demand may be so elastic that the increase in price might cause such a falling-off in demand that the total tax received was less than formerly. Suppose, for instance, the demand schedule for a commodity is as follows:

Price (£)	Quantity demanded (000s)
4	200
3	600
2	1,000

Assume also that supply is at constant cost per unit and that the market price is £2 at which 1 million units are being sold. The Chancellor of the Exchequer now decides to tax the good, imposing a tax of £1 on each unit. The result is that sales drop to 600,000 and his total tax receipts amount to £600,000. Later he goes further, increasing the tax to £2 per unit. This raises the total price of the good from £3 to £4. Between these two prices, demand is very elastic. Only 200,000 are now sold, and the Chancellor's tax receipts are reduced to £400,000. Thus if the Chancellor wishes to raise revenue without increasing VAT generally, he selects a good which has an inelastic demand. This is one reason why tobacco and alcohol bear selective rates of tax. Since they are regarded as luxuries, the higher price which results is not considered to be too serious a burden on the consumer.

Other examples of the application of elasticity of demand to government policy are: (a) How will a selective tax or subsidy on its products affect the size of an industry? (See pp. 464–5.) (b) How is the burden of a selective indirect tax shared between the consumer and the producer? (See p. 461.) (c) Would devaluation or depreciation of the country's currency improve the balance of payments? (See p. 509.) (d) Will an improvement in the terms of trade improve the balance of payments? (See p. 478.)

5.4   OTHER ELASTICITIES OF DEMAND

When we refer to 'elasticity of demand' without qualification, we are speaking, as above, of what is more precisely *'own-price* elasticity of demand'. But the concept has other applications.

Income elasticity of demand

An increase in real income usually increases the demand for goods, but to a varying degree. Thus it is possible to speak of *income elasticity of demand* – the proportionate change in demand divided by the proportionate change in real income which has brought it about. If demand increases 20 per cent, for instance as a result of a 10 per cent increase in real income, income elasticity of demand equals 2. Which goods have a high income elasticity of demand depends upon current living standards. In Western Europe today, it is the demand for such goods as cars, washing-machines, dish-washers, central-heating, video-recorders, new houses and personal services which expands the most as income increases. In contrast, necessities, such as potatoes, salt, eggs and soap, have a low income elasticity of demand and may even come into the category of 'inferior goods' where the quantity demanded actually falls as income increases.

Cross-elasticity of demand

Where two goods are related, e.g. as substitutes or complements, a change in the price of one will lead to a change in demand for the other. Thus a rise in the price of oil leads to an increase in the demand for coal, while a fall in the price of DVD players leads to an increased demand for DVDs.

The extent to which the demand for a good changes in response to a price change of another good is known as *cross-elasticity of demand*:

$$\text{Cross-elasticity of demand} = \frac{\text{Percentage change in the quantity demanded of good } X}{\text{Percentage change in the price of good } Y}$$

With substitutes, cross-elasticity is positive. For example, an increase in the price of Y would lead to an increase in the demand for X (as with oil and coal in the example above). With complements, cross-elasticity is negative, since a fall in the price of Y leads to a rise in the demand for X (as with DVD players and DVDs in the example above). The closer the substitutes or complements, the larger will be the figure for cross-elasticity. A cross-elasticity near zero signifies that there is little relationship between the two goods (Figure 5.6).

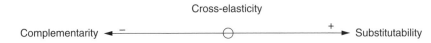

Figure 5.6   Cross-elasticity of demand

CHAPTER SUMMARY

··

- The demand curve of an individual for a commodity slopes downwards from left to right showing that demand extends as price falls. A fall in the price of a commodity means that the marginal utility of that commodity in relation to its price is now higher than that of other goods. To restore the equilibrium relationship – that the marginal utility of any commodity in relation to its price must be equal to the marginal utility of any other commodity in relation to its price – the marginal utility of the commodity whose price has fallen must be decreased. To do this, more of it must be bought. Although there are circumstances where more of a commodity is bought after a price rise, these are exceptional circumstances.
- Price elasticity of demand measures the responsiveness of quantity demanded to a change in price. Goods with inelastic demand do not suffer a large reduction in quantity demanded when price rises. Goods with elastic demand do suffer a large reduction in quantity demanded when price rises.
- Income elasticity of demand measures the responsiveness of quantity demanded to a change in income; and cross-elasticity of demand measures the responsiveness of quantity demanded of one good to a change in the price of another good.

REVIEW QUESTIONS

··

- Why does buying more of a commodity reduce its marginal utility?
- If the elasticity of a demand curve is zero, what is its shape?
- What factors determine elasticity of demand?
- Explain why elasticity of demand is a useful concept for:
  (a)   retailers;
  (b)   government.

 Visit the companion website for further questions

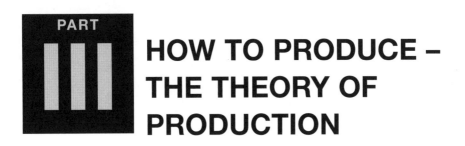

PART III

HOW TO PRODUCE – THE THEORY OF PRODUCTION

6

THE FIRM

So far we have given only a very approximate explanation of how supply responds to a change in price. For the next nine chapters our task will be to examine the supply curve a little more closely. As with demand, we have to study the actions of individuals (in this case the firms producing goods). By considering the decisions a firm has to make, we try to establish general principles governing its behaviour.

6.1 THE ROLE OF THE FIRM

Definition of the firm

In Chapter 2 we showed that an economic system consists of two main parts: (1) *households*, the units which provide productive resources and consume the goods produced; (2) *firms*, the units which hire productive resources in order to produce goods and services. As we shall see, this definition of a firm is very wide, including all forms of organisation from the sole trader to government department. In the chapters which follow, however, we shall be concentrating on firms which produce goods for sale in the market. Chapters 6 to 10 will be concerned mainly with the decisions on hiring and combining the factors of production.

Chapters 11 and 12 will look at problems connected with output. First, however, we must consider what economists are really referring to when they talk about the different 'factors of production' and 'production'.

The factors of production

The classical economists divided the factors of production into four groups – land, labour, capital and organisation, with their rewards being respectively rent, wages, interest and profit.

But such a classification, based on physical characteristics, has serious weaknesses, e.g. the training of a worker represents an input of capital. Thus present-day economists conduct much of their analysis by talking about factors of production generally – resources which cooperate in the production of goods and services wanted by the community. But they also recognise that certain factors do have some common, broad and important characteristics which permit a general classification useful for purposes of analysis and so the old classical economists' terminology has been retained.

Land now refers solely to the resources provided by nature, e.g. fresh water, sunshine, rain and space to employ other factors of production and to dispose of waste. In practice, it is treated as a separate factor in order to examine the nature of the earnings of any factor which is fixed in supply.

Labour refers to the actual effort, both physical and mental, made by human beings in production. It is this 'human' element which distinguishes it from other factors, for it gives rise to special problems regarding mobility, unemployment and psychological attitudes.

Capital, as opposed to land, is man-made. Goods can be classified as:

(a) *Consumer goods*: those goods which directly satisfy consumers' wants and are in the hands of the consumer, e.g. a loaf, a bicycle, a table.
(b) *Producer goods*: those goods which are not wanted directly for their own sake, but for the contribution they make to the production of consumer goods, e.g. buildings, machines, tools, raw materials. Sometimes the same good may be either a consumer good or a producer good, depending on its use. A car, for instance, may be used simply for pleasure, or by a sales representative for business.

Capital, as a factor of production, consists of producer goods and stocks of consumer goods not yet in the hands of the consumer. It is treated as a separate factor of production in order to emphasise (a) the sacrifice of present enjoyment which is necessary to obtain it, and (b) the fluctuations in economic activity which occur because its use extends over a period of time (see Chapters 21 and 30).

Enterprise refers to the acceptance of the risks of production which arise through uncertainty. This is a somewhat narrower meaning than that given by the classical economists to the *entrepreneur* – the person or persons who decided what goods to produce and brought the factors of production together to produce them.

Today the role of organising the factors of production is regarded as a managerial function which can be performed by a paid manager, i.e. by a highly skilled form of labour. What really distinguishes enterprise from other factors is that it has to carry all the *risks of production*. How these risks arise will be examined in more detail later. Briefly, they occur because production takes time. The entrepreneur engages labour and buys raw materials and machinery now in order to produce a good which will not be sold until some time in the future. Whether costs are recovered will depend upon the demand for the good when it comes to be sold. There may be a change in tastes in the meantime; or a rival may, through a better process, be putting the good on the market at a lower price. In such ways, an expected profit may turn out to be a loss.

Profit or loss is the reward of uncertainty-bearing. Whoever accepts this ultimate risk is the true entrepreneur – the farmer working on his own account, the doctor who starts his own practice, the persons who buy shares (the 'risk' capital) in a company, or the citizens of a state (who gain should a nationalised industry achieve a profit, but ultimately bear any losses made).

Production

Early economists, such as the French Physiocrats of the eighteenth century, considered that only work in the extractive industries (agriculture, mining and fishing) was productive. In his *Wealth of Nations* in 1776, Adam Smith added manufacturing, but he was specific in excluding workers who merely rendered services. 'The labour of the menial servant does not fix or realise itself in any particular subject or vendible commodity … Like the declamation of the actor, the harangue of the orator, or the tune of the musician, the work of all of them perishes in the very instant of its production.' The weakness of this definition can be easily appreciated: the persons who make the dresses for the actresses and the scenery for the stage would be productive, while the actresses themselves are not, and the farmer who grows the food is productive while the cook is not!

To arrive at a more satisfactory definition we have to ask: 'Why do people work? What is the reason for production?' The answer is simple – to satisfy wants. Consequently people who render services must be regarded as being productive. The soldier, nurse, footballer and hairdresser are all satisfying wants. Similarly in a factory, the clerk who calculates the wages and the boy who sweeps the floor are as productive as the machine-tool operator making the nuts and bolts. All are helping to produce the final product – a good that satisfies wants.

Wants can take different forms. Most people like a newspaper to read at the breakfast table; thus the boy who takes it from the shop to the customer's letterbox is productive. Most people, too, prefer to buy their potatoes weekly; thus the farmer or merchant who stores them through the winter is satisfying the wants of consumers, and is similarly productive. Utility is created by changing not only the *form* of our scarce resources, but also their *place* and *time*.

For certain purposes it may still be useful to classify industries broadly. *Primary industries* cover the first steps in the productive process – agriculture, fishing, mining and oil prospecting. *Secondary industries* use the raw materials of the extractive industries to manufacture their own products – flour, clothing, tinned salmon, steel girders, petrol and so on. *Tertiary industries* are concerned with the provision of services – transport, communications, distribution, commerce, government, and professional and other services.

6.2 THE OBJECTIVES OF THE FIRM

In a market economy a firm has to cover its costs if it is to stay in business. Thus regard must be paid to 'profitability'.

But in practice are firms always single-minded in seeking to *maximise money profits*? The answer is no; there is a range of possible objectives.

Personal motives may be important, especially where the manager is also the owner of the firm. Thus emphasis may be placed on good labour relations, the welfare of the workers, the desire for power, political influence, public esteem or simply 'a quiet life'. To cover such objectives profit would have to be interpreted in a wider sense than 'money profit'.

With major companies there is in practice a gap between the ownership and administration. The business is run by professional managers, and is too complex for shareholders to be able to exert effective control. This applies even to the institutional shareholders, who avoid being directly involved in the running of the business. Thus the motives of the full-time executive managers tend to override the shareholders' desire for maximum return on capital invested. Managers may be anxious for the security of their own jobs and, instead of taking the calculated risks necessary to earn maximum profits, tend to play for safety. More likely, they will be motivated by personal desires for status. Provided they achieve a level of profit which keeps shareholders content, their positions and salaries can be enhanced by expanding the firm to where it *maximises sales* rather than profits. Alternatively, the rate of growth may be maximised. Either objective becomes a possibility when competition is imperfect.

Even when there is an emphasis on money profit, a firm may stress its long-term position rather than immediate maximum profit. Security of future profits may be the dominating motive for mergers and takeovers as an alternative to developing new products and techniques. Moreover, where there is an element of monopoly, a firm can follow its own pricing policy rather than have it determined by competitive market conditions (see Chapter 15). In such circumstances it may not adjust prices to short-term changes in demand and supply conditions. For one thing, there are the administrative costs of printing and distributing new price lists. For another, frequent changes in price tend to offend retailers and customers.

Again a firm enjoying a degree of monopoly has always to assess what effect the pursuit of maximum profit may have on its overall position in the long term. Will a high price attract new entrants or encourage the development of a rival product? Will it lead to adverse publicity and eventually to government intervention by a reference to the Office of Fair Trading?

Finally, a firm has often to modify its objectives in deference to government policy. Thus it may be expected to follow government guidelines regarding wage increases, to have regard to the environment in the disposal of its waste products and even to retain surplus workers for a time rather than add to an already high level of unemployment.

Yet, while we must take account of these other objectives, our analysis cannot proceed far if any are seen as the main motive force of the firm. In any case, they merely supplement the profit objective, for profits have to be made if the firm is to survive. Thus the best general assumption is that firms seek to maximise profits. We can then establish principles concerning how resources should be combined and what output should be produced.

6.3 THE DECISIONS OF THE FIRM

To achieve its objective of maximising profit, a firm has to assess the demand of potential customers for its product and produce that output which secures the greatest difference between total revenue and total cost. Moreover, the cost of producing this given output must be the lowest possible.

This means that the firm has to answer the following questions:

(1) What goods shall it produce?
(2) How shall it raise the necessary capital and what shall be its legal form?
(3) What techniques shall be adopted, and what shall be the scale of operations?
(4) Where shall production be located?
(5) How shall its product be distributed?
(6) How shall resources be combined?
(7) What shall be the size of output?
(8) How shall it deal with its employees?

We consider the first two problems in the remainder of this chapter; the rest are examined in Chapters 11, 15 and 20.

6.4 WHAT TO PRODUCE

The first approach

Other things being equal, a firm will produce those goods which enable it to make the greatest return on capital (profit). However, in practice, this usually means that it has to choose a line of production within the limited range of its specialist knowledge. Let us assume that the firm is manufacturing light farm machines and that it is contemplating producing lawnmowers.

Since it is likely that some firms are already producing lawnmowers, the market economy throws up two guidelines. First, there is the current price of mowers. The firm would have to estimate its own costs for producing similar mowers, the number it could expect to sell at this price, and its likely profits, and thus calculate the return on capital employed. Second, the accounts of companies have to be filed with the Registrar of Companies, and the profit earned by public companies is publicised in the financial pages of leading newspapers and specialist journals. If existing producers of lawnmowers were shown to be earning a high rate of profit, the prospects for a new competitor would look favourable.

Market research

Where the proposed market is new or different from that for existing products, the above indicators are not so useful. Here the firm must fall back on some form of market research.

Initially, it may be producing similar goods, e.g. light agricultural machinery, and some indications of potential demand may come from wholesalers, retailers or even customers in conversation with the firm's representatives. Such suggestions can be cross-checked with those of other distributors.

Where the reaction is generally favourable, more thorough market research can be carried out, probably through a specialist market research organisation. Market research can cover desk research, field studies and test marketing.

Desk research examines the broad determinants of the potential demand by using (i) published material, e.g. government statistics, and (ii) the firm's own sales records. As we saw in Chapter 4, these determinants are price and the various conditions of demand. More specialist facts could be obtained from relevant periodicals and trade journals, e.g. *Gardeners' World* (where circulation figures indicate the number of keen gardeners). Membership figures for the Royal Horticultural Society could also be used.

More precise information on potential sales necessitates a planned, consumer-oriented *market research programme* in potential markets. This would cover many aspects of market behaviour, particularly consumer reaction to the product – especially with regard to its quality, packaging, delivery dates and after-sales service, and to price cuts.

Before a national or major sales campaign is undertaken, some form of *test marketing* would probably be carried out so that modifications could be made to correct any deficiencies. For instance, such a test might reveal that certain features of the product were unnecessary, thus permitting greater standardisation. Moreover, not all potential customers have identical preferences. The firm would therefore consider (i) a 'marketing mix' – producing different models at different prices – and (ii) varying sales methods and channels of distribution.

6.5 THE LEGAL FORM OF THE FIRM AND RAISING THE NECESSARY CAPITAL

After deciding what to produce, the firm must consider what legal form its business shall take and how to raise finance in order to employ the desired factors of production. It may be that the two decisions are closely linked from the beginning. But it must be remembered that a business has to be fairly successful before it can induce outsiders to subscribe finance on a large scale for its development. Hence initially it is likely that the legal form of the business will rest primarily on the degree of control which the entrepreneur wishes to exercise personally and the various legal and tax advantages which different types afford. The position is summarised in Figure 6.1.

The finance required by a firm is usually classified as (a) working capital, and (b) fixed capital.

(a) *Working capital* is for purchasing 'single-use' factors – labour, raw materials, petrol, stationery, fertilisers, etc – more or less the factors we refer to in Chapter 11 as 'variable factors'. Finance for working capital can be obtained from a variety of sources: banks, trade credit, finance companies, factor houses (which discount outstanding invoices), tax reserves, intercompany finance, advance deposits from customers and the government (e.g. through the Business Start-up Scheme which on conditions provides a £1,500 equipment grant and an allowance of £50 per week for 30 weeks when starting a new business).

(b) *Fixed capital* covers factors which are used many times – factories, machines, land, lorries, etc. Some finance for fixed capital is therefore required initially for advance payments on factory buildings, machinery and so on before the firm is earning revenue, though it is possible to convert fixed capital into working capital by renting buildings, hiring plant and vehicles or by leasing or buying on deferred payments through a finance company. Normally, fixed-capital requirements are larger than those for working capital. Moreover, lenders recognise that they part with their money for a longer period and accept a greater risk. Thus finance for fixed capital tends to be more difficult to raise than for working capital, unless the business starts as an offshoot of a parent company.

The sole proprietor

The sole proprietor is the oldest form of entrepreneurial organisation. Even today, from the point of view of numbers, small firms predominate, but in their total

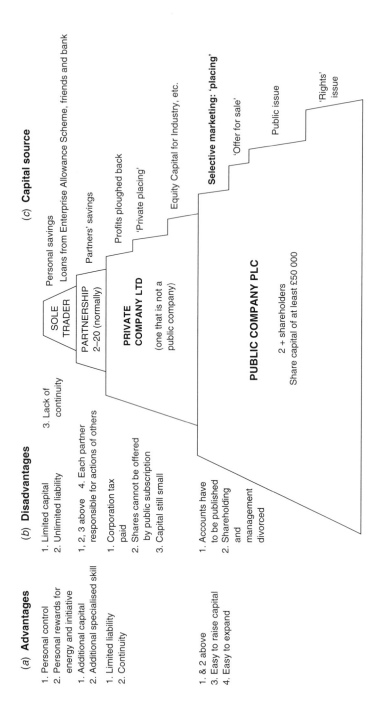

Figure 6.1 The forms of enterprise and the raising of capital

productive capacity, they are far less important than joint-stock companies. Such one-person firms range from the jobbing gardener and window-cleaner working on his or her own account to the farmer, shop-keeper and small factory-owner who employ other workers and may even own many separate units. Nevertheless, these businesses all have the same characteristic of being owned and controlled by a single person. It is this person's task to make all decisions regarding the policy of the firm, and it is he or she alone who takes the profits and bears the brunt of any losses which are made. This makes for energy, efficiency and a careful attention to detail.

However, the sole proprietor suffers from three main disadvantages. First, the development of such a firm must proceed slowly because the sources of capital are limited. The success of the venture, especially in its early stages, depends very largely on the person in charge, and nobody is likely to provide capital for the business unless there is that confidence in the proprietor which comes from personal contact. Hence the main source of capital is the personal savings of the owner himself together with such additional sums as can be borrowed from relatives, close friends, a bank or perhaps the Rural Development Commission. In time, development and expansion may take place by 'ploughing back' profits, but this will probably be an extremely slow process, and such firms generally remain comparatively small.

Second, in the event of failure, not only the assets of the business but also the private assets and property of the proprietor can be claimed against by creditors. In short, there is no limited liability.

Third, there is lack of continuity; on the retirement or death of the owner, a one-person firm may cease to function.

Because of these disadvantages, the sole-proprietor form of organisation is, in the main, confined to those businesses which are just starting up, or to certain industries, such as agriculture and retailing, where requirements of management make the small technical unit desirable.

The partnership

A larger amount of capital is available when persons combine together in a 'partnership'. Except for certain professional partnerships, e.g. accountants or solicitors, where membership is unlimited, not more than twenty may so join. Each partner provides a part of the capital required and shares the profits on an agreed basis. Yet the amount of capital which can be raised in this way is still inadequate for large-scale organisations. The result is that partnerships remain relatively small, being particularly suitable to that type of business, such as retailing and the professions (doctors, dentists, consulting engineers and lawyers), where the capital provided is not so much in the form of money as in professional skill and experience, each partner probably specialising in a particular branch.

But partnerships have disadvantages. The risk inherent in unlimited liability is increased because all partners are liable for the firm's debts irrespective of the amount of capital which each has invested, and private fortunes may be called upon to meet the demands of creditors. Only if a partner takes no share in the management of the firm, and there is at least one ordinary partner, can the privilege of limited liability be enjoyed. Second, any action taken by one partner is legally binding on all other partners. From this it follows that not only must each partner have complete confidence in the others but that, as the number of partners increases, so does the risk inherent in unlimited liability. Finally, by giving notice to the others, one partner may terminate the partnership at any time, while it is automatically dissolved upon the death or bankruptcy of any one partner. This means that surviving partners have either to buy his share or find a purchaser who is acceptable to everyone. In such circumstances, therefore, the continuation of the business often involves great trouble and expense.

The joint-stock company

The joint-stock company first developed in Tudor times when England's foreign trade began to expand. Instead of a trading ship being owned by one person, it was financed by a number of people who bought 'shares' in a company formed for the purpose. Yet, until the middle of the nineteenth century, people were reluctant to take shares in such companies since they enjoyed no limited liability. By purchasing only one share a person risked not merely the money invested but, should the company be forced into liquidation, the whole of his or her private fortune. Moreover, this unlimited liability made it virtually impossible to adopt the technique of spreading risks by investing in different companies.

The Industrial Revolution made it essential that more capital should be available to industry. Hence, in order to induce small savers to invest, the privilege of limited liability was bestowed by Parliament in 1855.

Today the joint-stock company is the most important form of business organisation. The advantages it enjoys over the partnership are limited liability, continuity, the availability of capital (since investors can spread their risks and sell their shares easily), and, should the need arise, ease of expansion. Indeed, some kinds of business could not be conducted on a small scale, and these have to start as joint-stock companies, either being sponsored by important interests, or else developed as subsidiaries of existing large firms.

Against these advantages, however, certain disadvantages, which could add to costs, have to be considered. Even small companies have to file with the Registrar of Companies a balance sheet and an Annual Return giving the names of the directors and secretary, while companies with a turnover above £1 million have to submit audited accounts. Furthermore, any assets of the company which have been built up over the years will increase the value of the original shares (usually owned by the family). When the time comes to wind up the company, e.g. owing to retirement, any increase in the value of the shares may be subject to capital gains tax.

The *long-term finance* of a company is obtained in four main ways: (a) selling 'shares' in the company; (b) borrowing; (c) obtaining a government grant or loan; (d) retaining profits.

(a) Shares

A 'share' is exactly what the name implies – a participation in the provision of the capital of a company. Shares may be issued in various units, usually from 5p upwards, and people can vary the degree to which they participate by the number of units purchased. The investment of money in a company does involve certain risks, of which two are paramount. The first is that the return on the capital invested may be less than expected because profits are disappointing. The second is that share prices in general may have fallen at the moment when the owner wishes to sell. To minimise these risks, investors usually spread their holdings over different companies and vary the magnitude of the risks undertaken by having a portfolio of shares, debentures and government bonds.

(i) *Ordinary shares*. The dividend paid to the ordinary shareholder depends mainly on the prosperity of the company. If profits are high, the dividend is usually correspondingly high; if there are no profits, then there may be no dividend. Moreover, the payment of a dividend to an ordinary shareholder ranks last in the order of priority, while if the company should be forced into liquidation the ordinary shareholder is repaid only after other creditors have been paid in full. Thus the 'ordinary share' is termed 'risk capital' (and often referred to as an 'equity'). In return for bearing the risks of the business venture each ordinary shareholder has a say in the running of the company, voting according to the number of shares held. At the general meeting, directors are appointed or removed, changes made in the company's method of raising capital and conducting business, and auditors appointed. Thus the ordinary shareholders, because they take the major risks and decisions regarding the policy of the company, are the real 'entrepreneurs'. In practice, however, their rights are rarely exercised. Providing the company appears to be doing reasonably well, few share-holders trouble to attend meetings. Moreover, unless the company is very large, the directors are often in a strong position in that they may hold or control a large proportion of the ordinary shares. Indeed, at times voting rights are specifically excluded (usually signified by 'A' shares).

(ii) *Preference shares*. If investors wish to undertake a slightly reduced risk, they can buy preference shares. Such a shareholder is entitled to a dividend payment before the ordinary shareholder, but only at a fixed per cent no matter how high the company's profits. In addition, only in exceptional circumstances, such as when it is proposed to alter their rights or to wind up the company, or when their dividends are in arrears, can these shareholders vote at ordinary meetings. Should, however, the company be forced into liquidation, the preference shareholder ranks above the ordinary shareholder in the redemption of capital.

Preference shares may also be 'cumulative'. If the company cannot pay a dividend one year, arrears may be made up in succeeding years before the ordinary shareholders receive any dividend. Since 1965 preference shares have lost popularity through their unfavourable tax treatment (see below).

(b) Borrowing

Long-term loans are usually obtained by issuing 'debentures'. These bear a fixed rate of interest irrespective of the profit made by the company. Since this interest payment is a first charge on the income of the company, the risk to the investor's income is not so high. Moreover, should the company fail, debenture-holders are paid out first. In fact, 'mortgage debentures' are secured on definite assets of the company. One other advantage of debentures is that they are redeemable after a specified period. Should the company be unable to meet its interest charges or to redeem the loan when due, the debenture-holders can force it into liquidation.

Unlike the ordinary shareholder whose investment is bound up with the fortunes of the company, the purchaser of a debenture eliminates risk as far as possible. In essence, such a person is merely lending the company money. Hence he or she enjoys no ownership rights of voting on management and policy. But a company whose profits are subject to frequent and violent fluctuations is not in a position to raise much of its capital by debentures. Such a method is really suitable only to a company making a fairly stable profit (sufficiently adequate to cover the interest payments), and possessing assets (such as land and buildings), the value of which would not depreciate a great deal were the company to go into liquidation.

A company having a large proportion of fixed-interest loans to ordinary shares is said to be 'highly geared'. Such a company will be able to pay high dividends when profits are good, but unable to make a distribution when profits are low. Where profits are expected to rise in the future, therefore, a company may prefer to raise capital for expansion by issuing debentures.

But it is the present-day corporation tax which is the main impulse in this direction. Debenture interest (but not preference-share interest) is included in the costs of a company for the purposes of calculating tax. Thus it reduces taxable profits. On the other hand, if finance is raised by shares, there is no prior interest charge and profits (which are subject to tax) are that amount higher. This tax situation has, since the introduction of corporation tax in 1965, led companies to finance capital expansion as far as possible by fixed-interest loans rather than by the sale of shares. Preference shares are now rarely issued.

(c) Government grants and loans

Grants and loans are available for venture capital (see p. 88), to firms setting up in Assisted Areas (see p. 442), and also to farmers on a percentage basis for expenditure on certain improvements, e.g. woodland and hedge-planting, slurry disposal.

(d) Retained profits

Not all profits are distributed to shareholders. In addition to providing for depreciation and for a contingency fund, profits will be regarded by a successful company as its major source of capital for future expansion.

Private and public companies

Joint-stock companies are of two main kinds, private and public. Each has to submit to the Registrar of Companies its;

(a) *Memorandom of Association*, giving its name, the address of its registered office, the amount of the authorised capital it can raise and the objects of its activities, (usually affording it as wide a scope as possible); and
(b) *Articles of Association*, containing the rules and regulations which govern how it will be run as regards the issue of shares, the company's borrowing powers, the election of officers, the powers of directors and the frequency of meetings.

The private company

A private company is simply a company that is not a public company and the formalities involved in its formation are few and inexpensive.

The private company, while conferring limited liability, allows the business to be privately owned and managed. It is thus particularly suitable for either a medium-sized commercial or industrial organisation not requiring finance from the public, or for a speculative venture where a small group of people wishes to try out an idea and is prepared to back it financially to a definite limit before floating a public company. While private companies are considerably more numerous than public companies, their average capital is much smaller.

Nevertheless, because the shares of a *private company* are illiquid in that they cannot be offered for sale by public issue, a difficult stage in its growth may be reached when its capital is in the region of £250,000. The gap can be bridged in four main ways. First, as part of the government's desire to encourage growth of the economy through the development of small businesses, banks and other institutions have been more willing to provide medium-term loans especially as, under the Small Firms Loan Guarantee Scheme (SFLGS), the Department of Industry guarantees 75 per cent of loans up to £250,000 for up to ten years. Second, a stockbroker may effect a 'private placing' of shares or debentures with a life insurance company or an investment trust, who are usually in a position to ignore the disadvantages of holding securities of private companies. Third, help might be obtained from the new issue market, where both issuing houses and merchant bankers assist firms to raise capital, even providing some themselves.

Fourth, new 'venture' capital companies (including specialist arms of the clearing banks) now provide medium and long-term equity financing for new and developing businesses. And, to encourage the provision of such funds for small unlisted firms, it has been possible since 1996 to form venture capital trusts.

The public company

When a large amount of capital is required, the first step is usually to form a public company. This must have at least two shareholders, an authorised minimum capital of £50,000 (a quarter of which is paid up) and carry the designation 'public limited company' – abbreviated to Plc – after its name. But it is the second step which is really important – getting its shares 'quoted' on the Stock Exchange or the Alternative Investment Market (AIM) (see pp. 318–19). This entails an exhaustive examination of the company's affairs which have to be advertised very fully in at least two leading London newspapers.

The capital required can be raised by a 'placing', an 'offer for sale' or a 'public issue by prospectus'. The first is the usual method when under £15 million is required, for the costs of underwriting and administration are less. An issuing house, licensed dealer or investment company agrees to sell blocks of the shares directly to institutions and persons who it knows are likely to be interested in them.

For larger amounts an offer for sale is a likely method. The shares are sold *en bloc* to an issuing house, which then offers them for sale by advertisement similar to a public issue.

For more than £50 million, a public issue by prospectus can be employed. Here the company's object is to obtain in a single day the capital it requires. Hence it must advertise well and price its shares a little on the cheap side. The advertisement is in the form of a prospectus which sets out the business, history and prospects of the company together with its financial standing and the security offered.

In practice, the sale is usually conducted through an *issuing house*, which advises on the terms of the issue. It will also arrange to have the issue underwritten: that is, it will find a number of institutions, such as merchant bankers, which, in return for a small commission, will take whatever part of the issue is left unsold. However, such underwriters do not have to rely entirely on permanent investors to buy the securities on the day of issue, for speculators, known as *stags*, are usually operating, and they buy the shares hoping to resell them quickly at a small profit. Furthermore, where a company is raising additional capital, existing shareholders are now usually given the right to purchase new shares through a *rights issue* in proportion to shares already held and usually at a favourable price.

Some of the advantages and disadvantages of different enterprises are summarised in Figure 6.1.

Co-operative societies

Although there were many co-operative societies in operation before the Rochdale Pioneers in 1844, it was these twenty-eight artisans, mostly cotton weavers, who started the modern co-operative movement. By subscribing a few pence per week, they accumulated an initial capital of £28, with which they rented a small store and started trading with small stocks of flour, oatmeal, sugar, butter and candles. Profits were distributed to members in proportion to their purchases. In 2006 there were 46 retail co-operative societies in the UK with an aggregate membership of over 8 million and 69,000 employees. Turnover was £7.5 bn per annum, accounting for 5 per cent of Britain's retail trade, and making them Britain's largest retailer. In addition, they largely provide the capital and control the operation of the Co-operative Wholesale Society.

The minimum shareholding in a retail co-operative society is usually £1. Only if a full share is held does a member enjoy voting rights, but not more than one vote per member is allowed irrespective of the number of shares held. Some societies still distribute profits as a dividend in proportion to the value of a member's purchases as recorded at checkout through a numbered plastic card. Others use the National Dividend stamp scheme operated by the Co-operative Wholesale Society. Stamps are given to customers in proportion to their purchases, and a book of stamps can be redeemed for cash, goods or a deposit in a share account, in which case a bonus is usually added. In the main, however, price cuts have allowed co-operative shops to compete with supermarkets and stores.

Co-operative societies described above are organised directly by consumers and are therefore called 'consumer co-operative societies'. Producers have also formed 'producer co-operative societies' to market their members' produce. They are chiefly important in the marketing of agricultural produce where production is carried on by small farmers, as in Denmark, New Zealand and Spain.

Nevertheless, apart from some formed to purchase inputs, there has been little development in the UK. But they could become more prominent, e.g. in the selling of milk, as the government has now wound up the Marketing Boards (except for the British Wool Marketing Board, which collects and sells the British wool clip).

The public sector

The organisation of production in the public sector takes different forms: government department, public corporation, an executive agency quasi-government body, local authority. These are dealt with in Chapter 19.

CHAPTER SUMMARY

The objectives of firms may be wider than simply 'maximising profits'. They may have a desire for rapid growth or sales maximisation or long-term goals. Nevertheless, the main motivation for firms is profit, and in order to make the most profit, firms make decisions about what to produce, how to raise capital and the legal form to adopt.

REVIEW QUESTIONS

- Why might a firm be pursuing an objective other than profit maximisation?
- What are the advantages of 'joint-stock' companies?
- What are the advantages and disadvantages of partnerships?
- Distinguish between working capital and fixed capital.

 Visit the companion website for further questions

CHAPTER 7

THE ORGANISATION AND SCALE OF PRODUCTION

LEARNING OBJECTIVES

After studying this chapter you should be able to:
- explain the advantages and disadvantages of division of labour;
- identify and explain different advantages of large-scale production;
- suggest reasons why small firms continue to thrive in certain industries.

When assembling its plant, organising its factors of production and deciding how to get the finished product to the customer, the firm will consider the advantages of specialisation and of producing on a large scale.

Because specialisation is the fundamental principle upon which modern production is organised, we begin this chapter by examining it. We do so under the traditional heading of 'the division of labour' but, as we shall see, it is equally applicable to machines, the distribution of goods, localities and even countries.

7.1 THE DIVISION OF LABOUR

Advantages of the division of labour

Increased production results when the labour force is so organised that each person specialises on a particular job. Thus in the simple task of making a table, one worker will be sawing the wood, another planing it, a third cutting the joints, a fourth gluing together the various parts, and the last polishing the finished article.

This increased production is achieved because:

1. Each worker is employed in the job in which his or her superiority is most marked

Suppose that, in one day, Smith can plane the parts for 20 tables *or* cut the joints for 10, whereas Brown can either plane 10 tables *or* cut the joints for 20. If each do both jobs, their combined production in a day will be 15 tables planed *and* 15 table joints cut. But Smith is better at planing, while Brown is better at cutting joints. If they specialise on what they can do best, their combined production will be 20 tables planed *and* 20 table-joints cut – an increase in output of a third. Later, when we consider international trade, we shall develop this argument to show that specialisation can still be advantageous even if one person or country is superior in both lines of production.

Even if, initially, workers were equally proficient at the different jobs, it might still pay to specialise, for the following reasons.

2. Learning is facilitated

Not only is less time taken in learning a particular job, but 'practice makes perfect' so that skills are developed by repetition of the same task.

3. Economy in tools allows specialised machinery to be used

This is illustrated in Figure 7.1 where in (b) division of labour has been introduced. Not only are specialised tools in constant use but their output is much

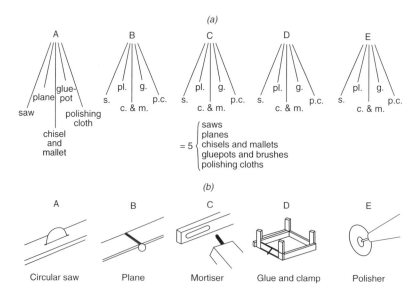

Figure 7.1   Economy in tools through specialisation

greater. Thus division of labour sets free talented men for research – and allows their inventions to be used profitably.

4. ***Time is saved through not having to switch from one operation to another, e.g. in obtaining and replacing different tools.***

5. ***The employer can estimate costs of production and output more accurately***

Disadvantages of the division of labour

While the division of labour leads to lower costs of production, it may have disadvantages both for the workers and for society. The worker may find the job monotonous, and this could affect the quality of work. With some occupations such as paint spraying there is a risk of occupational disease. Moreover, the skilled specialist may face redundancy if demand falls, while a strike by a few key workers can lead to widespread unemployment. Finally, standardised products tend to replace individual craft work.

Nevertheless, it must be emphasised that these drawbacks are but a small price to pay when compared with the great benefits resulting from the division of labour.

Limitations on the division of labour

Naturally, the scope for the division of labour varies from one industry to another. Countries like Switzerland which have too few workers to permit much specialisation concentrate on manufacturing a narrow range of products. Again, in industries such as agriculture and building where the same operations are not taking place each day, many 'Jacks of all trades' are required. Moreover, an exchange system using money is essential: we must first unite in exchange before we can divide in production. Finally, the division of labour has to be related to current demand for the product. It is no use specialising in making something which nobody wants; conversely, minute division of labour is only possible when there is a large demand. The complex organisation of car production, for instance, rests on a mass demand for a standardised product made up from a multitude of small parts.

7.2 THE ADVANTAGES OF LARGE-SCALE PRODUCTION

As a firm's output increases, costs per unit may fall as a result of the advantages of large-scale production. These are often referred to as 'internal economies' to distinguish them from 'external economies', which arise indirectly from the growth of the *industry* (see p. 96).

Internal economies

Internal economies are of five main kinds:

1.   Technical economies

In making a good, as distinct from distributing it, increased output permits more division of labour, greater specialisation of machines, the economy of large machines (e.g. a double-decker bus can carry twice as many passengers as a single-decker, though neither the initial cost nor running costs are doubled) and the linking of processes (e.g. in steel-making, where re-heating is avoided).

Generally, technical economies fix the size of the unit actually producing, e.g. supermarket, rather than the size of the firm, which may consist of many units, e.g. Tesco. Where technical economies are great, the size of the typical unit tends to be large – as, for example, in the production of cars, sheet steel, gas and electricity. Where, however, increased output merely means duplicating and reduplicating machines, the tendency will be for the unit to remain small. For instance, in farming at least one combine harvester is necessary for about 600 acres. Thus UK farms tend to remain small, for as yet there are no great technical economies to be derived from large machines. Where few technical economies can be gained and yet the firm is large, consisting – as with chain stores – of many operating units, it is usually because other types of economy are possible, as follows.

2.   Managerial economies

When output increases, division of labour can be applied to management. For example, in a shop owned and run by one man, the owner, although having the ability to order supplies, keep accounts and sell the goods, has yet to do such trivial jobs as sweeping the floor, weighing articles and packing parcels – tasks within the capability of a trainee. His sales, however, may not warrant employing an assistant. The large business overcomes this difficulty: a brilliant organiser can devote all his time to organising, the routine jobs being left to lower-paid workers.

The function of management can itself be divided, e.g. into production, sales, transport and personnel. These departments may be further subdivided – sales, for instance, being split into sections for advertising, exports and customers' welfare.

3. Commercial economies

If a bulk order can be placed for materials and components, the supplier will usually quote a lower price per unit, since this enables him also to gain the advantages of large-scale production.

Economies can also be achieved in selling the product. If the sales staff are not being worked to capacity, the additional output can be sold at little extra cost. Similarly, advertising costs are spread. Indeed, the large firm often manufactures many products, so that one acts as an advertisement for the others. Thus Hoover vacuum cleaners advertise their washing machines, dishwashers and steam irons. In addition, a large firm may be able to sell its by-products, something which might be unprofitable for a small firm.

Finally, when the business is sufficiently large, the division of labour can be introduced on the commercial side, with expert buyers and sellers being employed.

Such commercial economies represent real gains to the community, reducing prices through better use of resources. On the other hand, where a large firm uses its muscle to *force* suppliers into granting it favourable prices, it will simply result in higher prices to other buyers.

4. Financial economies

In raising finance for expansion the large firm is in a favourable position. It can, for instance, offer better security to bankers – and, because it is well known, raise money at lower cost, since investors prefer shares which can be readily sold on the Stock Exchange.

5. Risk-bearing economies

Here we can distinguish three sorts of risk. First, there are those which can be insured against, enabling large and small firms alike to spread risks.

Second, certain businesses usually bear some risk themselves, saving some of the profits made by the insurance company. Here the large firm has a definite advantage. London Transport, for instance, can cover its own risks, while a large bank can call in funds from other branches when there is a run on the reserves in a particular locality.

The third kind of risk is one that cannot be reduced to a mathematical probability and thus cannot be insured against – risk arising from changes in demand for the product or in the supply of raw materials: this is usually referred to as risk arising from 'uncertainty'. To meet fluctuations in demand the large firm can diversify output (like British American Tobacco) or develop export markets. On the supply side, materials may be obtained from different sources to guard against crop failures, strikes, etc.

External economies

While the firm can plan its internal economies, it can only *hope* to benefit from external economies which arise as the *industry* grows.

First, the concentration of similar firms in an area may produce mutual benefits: a skilled labour force; cooperating in providing common services, such as marketing and research; better roads and social amenities; technical schools catering for the local industry; product reputation; ancillary firms supplying specialised machinery, collecting by-products, etc. The firm must take into account such economies when deciding where production shall take place, for the lower costs may outweigh any diseconomies which arise through traffic congestion, smoke, etc.

Second, external economies can take the form of common information services provided either by associations of firms or even by the government.

Finally, as an industry grows in size, specialist firms may be established to provide components and services for all producers thereby extending economies of scale.

7.3 THE SIZE OF FIRMS

Horizontal, vertical and lateral combination

The advantages of large-scale production provide firms with a strong impetus to combine.

Horizontal integration occurs where firms producing the same type of product combine. Thus Nestlé took over Rowntree, and Ford acquired Jaguar (Figure 7.2).

Vertical integration is the amalgamation of firms engaged in the different stages of production of a good. Thus Britoil, an oil exploration company was taken over by BP. Vertical integration may be 'backward' towards the raw material; or 'forward' towards the finished product.

Both of the above can improve efficiency, thereby lowering costs per unit and increasing profits. Thus horizontal integration can allow greater specialisation, commercial economies and a saving on administrative overheads. Vertical integration facilitates linked processes and reduces risk by increasing direct control over the supply and quality of raw materials and components. Moreover, all parts can be manufactured to an integrated design, and there is direct control over the distribution of the final product (see below).

Lateral integration occurs where a firm increases the range of its products. Concentration on one product may make a firm vulnerable to a change in fashion, a switch in government policy or a recession. Thus the firm diversifies, often by taking over other firms producing completely different products. For instance, P & O is engaged in shipping, cross-Channel ferries, road transport and construction through its subsidiary companies.

Apart from increased efficiency and security of profits, integration may enhance a firm's prestige. One other aim, however, must not be overlooked – monopoly power. This is discussed in Chapter 15.

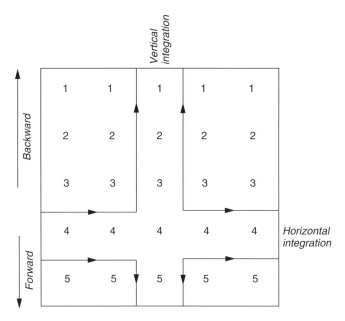

Figure 7.2 Horizontal and vertical integration

Integration may result from internal development or combining with exist-ing firms either by merger or a takeover – when a company buys all the shares of a smaller firm and absorbs it completely – or by the formation of a holding company in which the parent company obtains enough shares to give it effec-tive control, though the smaller company preserves its identity and enjoys considerable independence of action. Many large companies, e.g. Unilever, GEC and Great Universal Stores, hold such controlling interests in subsidiary companies.

7.4   THE PREDOMINANCE OF THE SMALL FIRM

In spite of the advantages enjoyed by the large firm, we must not conclude that every firm has to be large to be competitive. Indeed the small firm still predomi-nates in all forms of production. In agriculture two-thirds of all holdings are less than fifty hectares in size, while in retailing nearly nine-tenths of all firms consist of only one shop although independent retailers are under severe threat from supermarkets, with more than 2,000 closing down in 2005. Even more remarkably, small firms are important in manufacturing where one would have thought that technical economies of scale would be all-important. Table 7.1, which covers the size of the establishment – the factory or workshop – in manufacturing, shows

Table 7.1 Size of manufacturing establishments in the UK, 2006

Employees	Number of firms	Percentage of total firms
1–9	109,630	70.8
10–99	39,015	25.2
100–999	5,920	3.9
Over 1000	160	0.1
TOTAL	154,725	100

the small establishment is also typical of manufacturing in the UK, with 96 per cent employing less than 100 people.

Any explanation of this predominance of the small firm has to deal with two salient facts: (i) small firms are especially important in certain industries, such as agriculture, retailing, building, and personal and professional services; (ii) variations in the size of firms exist even within the same industry. Both result from the nature of the conditions of demand and supply.

Demand

Large-scale production may be only *technically* efficient; it is not *economically* efficient unless a large and regular demand justifies it.

The market may be small because demand is local (e.g. for personal services and the goods sold by the village store), or limited to a few articles of one pattern (e.g. for prestige luxury goods and highly specialised and individually designed machine tools) or because transport costs are high (e.g. for bricks and perishable market garden produce), or because product differentiation divides it artificially (see p. 194).

Where demand fluctuates (e.g. in construction), the overhead cost of idle specialised equipment is heavy – but the smaller the firm, the less the burden.

Supply

Even if demand is large, factors on the supply side may make for small firms. While in certain industries, e.g. retailing and building, it is possible to start with little capital or be supported by franchising (e.g. McDonald's) or by joining a wholesale chain (e.g. Spar), the difficulty of obtaining further funds and the taxation of profits are obstacles to expansion. Furthermore, government policy may give specific support to small companies, e.g. by levying a reduced rate of corporation tax. Alternatively, where vertical dis-integration is possible, firms need not expand internally but simply employ specialist firms for advertising, research, supplying components and selling by-products. Important, too, is the fact that many small owners do not have the drive to expand or the ability to manage a large concern. Or, as in farming and retailing, they will work long hours (that is, accept a lower rate of profit) simply to be their own bosses.

Above all, as the size of the firm increases (Figure 7.3), management difficulties occur. If management is vested in heads of department, problems of coordination arise and rivalries develop. This means that one person must be in overall command – yet people with such capabilities are in very limited supply. In certain industries these difficulties may soon occur. Rapid decisions are

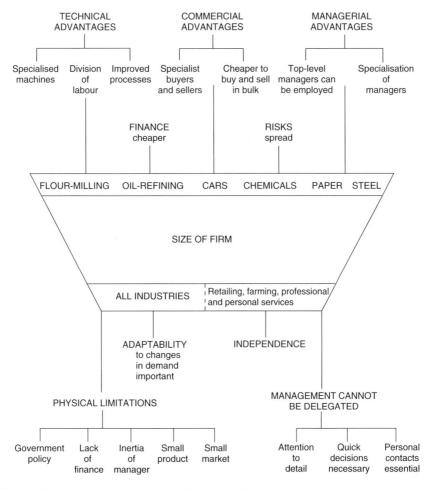

Figure 7.3 Factors influencing the size of a firm

required where demand changes quickly e.g. in the fashion trades, or supply conditions alter, e.g. through the weather in agriculture. Or care may have to be given to the personal requirements of customers, e.g. in retailing and services. This may necessitate the close supervision of management, and thus the firm has to be small.

CHAPTER SUMMARY

- Increased production results from labour specialisation.
- As a firm's output increases, costs per unit may fall due to internal and external economies of scale.
- Small firms can continue to thrive in sectors where demand is small or local or specialised, and where supply conditions require close managerial control.

REVIEW QUESTIONS

- What are the benefits of division of labour?
- Explain why technical economies in an industry may not be sufficient to justify large-scale production.
- Give three examples of industries where small firms continue to predominate and suggest reasons why this is so.

 Visit the companion website for further questions

CHAPTER 8

THE DISTRIBUTION OF GOODS
TO THE CONSUMER

LEARNING OBJECTIVES

After studying this chapter you should be able to:
- explain the functions of wholesalers and retailers;
- describe, and suggest reasons for, recent trends in retailing.

8.1 THE SCOPE OF PRODUCTION

A manufacturer will have to decide on how to get his finished goods to the consumer. If he undertakes the task himself, he must be willing to employ sales representatives, run delivery transport, carry stocks, organise exports, advertise his product, advise customers, give credit and establish servicing centres. Many of these are highly specialised functions and the employment of full-time experts requires a large output. Furthermore, the manufacturer's main ability lies in organising the production of the good rather than its distribution.

Hence division of labour is applied to getting the good to the consumer. Just as the manufacturer buys raw materials and components from other producers, so specialists perform the task of distributing to the consumer – the final stage of the productive process. This represents a form of forward vertical disintegration.

These specialists may perform many different tasks, or each separate task may itself be further hived off to a specialist. To simplify, we group them together under the headings of 'wholesalers' and 'retailers'. Figure 8.1 shows their place in the various stages of the production of chocolate.

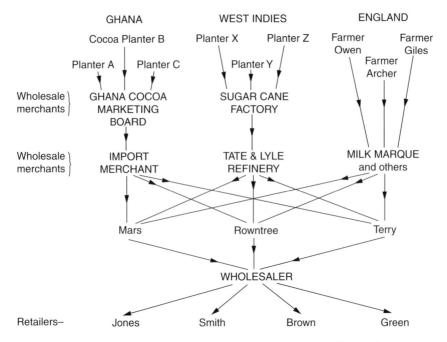

Figure 8.1 The parts played by the wholesaler and retailer in the 'production' of chocolate

8.2 THE WHOLESALER

The wholesaler buys goods in bulk from producers and sells them in small quantities to retailers according to their requirements. In doing so, he helps the process of production in a number of ways.

1. Economising in distribution

Since many shops, especially those stocking a large variety of goods, order their supplies only in small quantities, it is not economical for each producer to sell directly to them.

Figure 8.2 shows that, when the four chocolate firms deliver in bulk to a wholesaler, the number of contacts and journeys is reduced from sixteen (a) to eight (b).

Particularly in agriculture, where the goods are perishable, the farmer finds it easier if, instead of trying to contact retailers himself, he delivers his produce to a

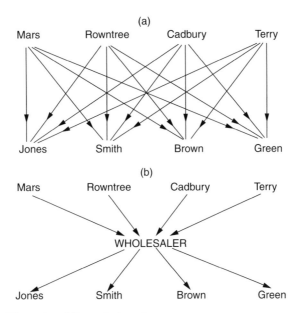

Figure 8.2 The role of the wholesaler

wholesaler or commission salesman, for example at New Covent Garden, and leaves the actual selling to him.

Similarly, in the construction industry, where there are numerous small builders, it is easier for manufacturers to deliver through builders' merchants.

2. Keeping stocks

Consumers like the convenience of being able to obtain a good at a shop just when they require it. This means that stocks have to be held. Often, however, neither the producer nor the retailer has the necessary storage facilities or the extra capital required, and so it is left to the wholesaler.

In other ways, too, the costs of storage are removed from the producer or retailer. While loss through fire, flood or rats can be insured against, no insurance can be taken out to cover a fall in demand. Thus a wholesaler or dealer, who holds stocks of a good which is liable to go out of fashion, relieves manufacturers and retailers of that risk.

The holding of stocks is, in itself, a valuable economic function in that they help to even out fluctuations in price resulting from temporary fluctuations in demand or supply. Thus merchants replenish brick stocks during the winter, and run them down during the rest of the year.

3. Arranging imports from abroad

Manufacturers could rarely be bothered to ship small parcels to individual retailers abroad or to undertake the currency and documentary arrangements. These tasks are left to a wholesaler, the import merchant, who is known and trusted. Often the import merchant goes abroad to establish and develop trade.

4. Carrying out certain specialised functions

Not only does the wholesaler advertise goods but, in order to make selling easier, he may process goods. Thus milk is pasteurised, hams are cooked, tea is blended and sugar is refined, while certain commodities, such as cotton, wheat and wool tops, are graded.

5. Channelling information and advice

Suggestions which customers make to the retailer are passed on to the wholesaler, and the latter, especially when such suggestions are widely representative, conveys them to the manufacturer. Thus the manufacturer discovers how his product could be improved or how fashion changes can be anticipated.

6. Assisting in the day-to-day maintenance of the good

With many products, particularly vehicles and machinery, an efficient maintenance service is essential. The manufacturer can be relieved of this task by the wholesaler, who can provide a local and quick maintenance, repair and spare-part service.

8.3 THE RETAILER

Functions of the retailer

The retailer performs the last stage of the productive process, for it is he who puts the goods in the hands of the actual consumer. His work has been summarised as having 'the right goods in the right place at the right time'. The functions set out below are really an enlargement on this. In practice, however, there is not always a clear distinction between the wholesaler and the retailer so that in some cases their functions overlap.

1. Stocking small quantities of a variety of goods

What is the 'right good' depends on the customer, for different people have different tastes, and what suits one may be undesirable to another. Thus having the 'right good' depends largely on stocking many varieties of the good so that each customer can make his or her individual choice, pay for it, and take delivery there and then. In part, a shop is a showroom where the customers can examine and compare the different goods one with the other and make their own selection. This is particularly helpful when customers are choosing goods which are only bought infrequently.

The size of the stocks the retailer carries depends on many factors. Some manufacturers even stipulate that a certain minimum stock shall be carried before allowing a retailer to sell their goods. Usually, however, it is left to the retailer. He will consider the popularity of the product, the possibility of obtaining further supplies quickly, the perishability of the good or the likelihood of it going out of fashion, the season (especially if it is approaching Christmas or if there is a seasonal demand for the good) and the possibility of a future change in its price. Above all, he must allow for the cost, the interest on a bank overdraft.

2. Taking the goods to where it is most convenient for the customer

Taking the goods to where it is most convenient for the customer may merely mean that the retailer sets up his shop within easy reach. It is for this reason that we find retailers congregated together in town centres, though, with goods in everyday use, such as groceries, small shops are often dotted around residential districts. Where customers are very dispersed (as in country districts) the retailer may have a 'travelling shop'. The introduction of Internet shopping and delivery by the larger supermarkets is a development of this.

While, with the majority of goods, customers take their purchases with them, the retailer may arrange delivery. This occurs with goods such as coal and furniture where transport is essential, but it also applies where the customer requires the extra convenience of having goods delivered, as (for example) with milk, the early-morning newspaper, laundry, and groceries supplied by high-class stores.

3. Performing special services for customers

In the course of running the main business, the retailer performs many services for the convenience of customers, all of which help to build up goodwill. Where the good is not in stock, it will be ordered, and, in other matters where contact with the manufacturer is necessary the retailer often acts for the customer. Thus goods are returned to the manufacturer for repair, though, in order to effect such repairs more quickly, a repair service may be maintained, e.g. cycle, radio and television retailers.

With many goods, too, such as fishing tackle, photographic equipment, musical instruments, machinery and sports gear, special advice can be provided. Indeed, some manufacturers insist on their retailers having technical competence.

Finally, for the greater convenience of customers, goods may be sent on approval or finance arranged through hire purchase, credit accounts, etc.

4. Advising the wholesaler and manufacturer

A retailer maintains close contact with customers. From them he discovers, either through a chance remark in the course of conversation or by direct suggestion, how a good could be improved or the type of good people would like. Eventually this information finds its way to the manufacturer who will probably act upon it.

Types of retail outlet

Retailing might be widely defined to include all shops, mail-order firms, garages, bus companies, launderettes, betting shops or indeed any organisation which sells products or services to the consumer. It is usual, however, to take a narrower view and to confine retailing to shops and mail-order outlets, as follows.

1. Independents

These are mainly small shops with no other branches, and they account for nearly two-fifths of retail trade turnover. Yet, in spite of their advantages of individual attention to customers, 'handy' locations for quick shopping trips, and the willingness of owners to accept a lower return for the benefits of being their own boss, these independents have steadily lost ground to the larger stores.

A major bid to avert the decline has come through the voluntary chains, such as Spar, Londis, of which about a third of the independents are members. While retaining their independence, members buy in bulk from the wholesaler and use common advertising and display techniques.

A more recent development enabling an individual trader to set up in business is 'franchising', that is, buying a concession from a major firm, e.g. Kentucky Fried Chicken, McDonald's, 'K' shoes, United Dairies, to sell the brand-name product. The concessionaire advertises and advises on presentation.

2. Multiples

These can be defined arbitrarily as organisations of ten or more shops. Some, such as Mothercare and Dorothy Perkins, sell a particular type of good. Others, such as Marks & Spencer, Boots, F. W. Woolworth and British Home Stores, have a fairly extensive range of products. Together with the supermarkets they comprise some 48 per cent of the market.

Their chief advantages are that they can obtain the economies of bulk buying and centralised control, eliminate the wholesaler, invite instant recognition through their standardised shop fronts, and establish a reputation through brand names.

3. Supermarkets

These may be defined as self-service shops with a minimum selling area of 200 sq. metres, but the trend in recent years, especially among the multiple grocery companies, has been towards superstores (of at least 2,000 sq. metres) and hypermarkets (see below). While organisationally they would count as multiples, their share of the food trade warrants separate attention. In 1996 they accounted for half the grocery trade and two-fifths of retail food sales.

The field is led by the five major retail grocery chains: Tesco, Sainsbury's, Morrison's, ASDA and Somerfield. Their strength lies in economies of scale, low labour costs, a clear and attractive display of merchandise, bulk buying and selling under their own label (e.g. Sainsbury cornflakes, Tesco coffee). Marketing via the Internet with home deliveries has enabled the major supermarkets to increase sales. As a result they have highly competitive prices and have gained ground rapidly.

Indeed, many of these self-service organisations have extended their activities beyond groceries to self-service of goods showing higher profit margins, e.g. clothing, hardware, cosmetics, pharmaceuticals, do-it-yourself and garden supplies. The opening of offshoot branches of the major supermarkets (e.g. Tesco Express) in residential areas poses a considerable threat to independent small shops.

4. Hypermarkets

Urban congestion, inadequate parking space and rising rents have made high street sites increasingly expensive. The answer to these problems has been the very large 'out-of-town' shopping centre or 'hypermarket', catering mainly for the car-borne weekly shopper, and these outlets are now expanding rapidly.

5. Department stores

Competition from multiples has forced department stores to alter somewhat their traditional pattern of having separate departments under the control of a responsible buyer, often described as 'many stores under one roof', in favour of bulk-buying by central office, more self-service, and extended credit facilities. As a result they have retained some 4 per cent of the retail market.

The main groups are House of Fraser, Debenham's, the John Lewis Partnership and Great Universal Stores.

107

6. *Co-operatives* (see p. 89)

7. *Mail order*

Mail-order business, which accounts for nearly 3 per cent of the retail market, is particularly susceptible to higher postal charges.

The major companies, Great Universal Stores, Littlewoods Mail Order, Freemans and Empire Stores, sell by agency and illustrated catalogues, purchases usually being arranged through weekly interest-free payments. Over one-half of all sales are accounted for by women's clothing and household goods.

Factors affecting the type of retail outlet

Over the last thirty years, the pattern of retailing has moved away from the small, independent shop towards the larger organisation, notably the multiples, super-market chains and mail-order firms. This trend reflects a greater emphasis on competition through lower price rather than by better service.

The larger firms are in a strong position to cut prices. Not only do they obtain the advantages of large-scale production (particularly those of selling a whole range of goods and of buying in bulk), but they can use their bargaining strength to secure further price discounts from manufacturers. Indeed, the largest may force the manufacturer to supply goods under the retailer's 'own-brand' label at a price below that at which other retailers can buy the manufacturer's national brand. Moreover, since large retailers cater for a whole range of shopping, e.g. food, they can attract customers into stores by 'loss-leaders'.

Economic factors influencing this trend have been:

1. *Increased income*, which has led to a swing towards the more expensive processed foods and consumer durable goods and facilitated less frequent shopping trips.
2. *An increase in car ownership*, which has enabled people to move from the city centre to the outer suburbs. Shops have followed, not only to be near their customers, but also to obtain larger sites with parking facilities, lower rents and less congestion. The car has also made customers more mobile, enabling them to travel to good shopping centres where they can purchase all their requirements at a single stop.
3. *An increase in the number of married women going to work*, which has promoted the demand for convenience foods and labour-saving devices. It has also led to the reduction of the number of shopping expeditions, a trend helped by the wider ownership of refrigerators and freezers.

These factors are likely to remain important in the future. It seems probable, therefore, that new supermarkets will take the form of discount stores or hypermarkets selling a wider range of products having a higher profit margin than groceries. Moreover, the more favourable response to recent planning applications is enabling new stores to be developed outside towns, while cash-and-carry warehouses are now available to consumers who can buy in quantity.

Such changes are likely to be at the expense of the medium-sized business, and some smaller local retailers despite their 'convenience' services.

8.4 THE FUTURE OF THE MIDDLEMAN

Criticisms of middlemen

Wholesalers and dealers who come between the manufacturer and the retailer or the consumer are often referred to as 'middlemen'. They are frequently criticised on the ground that they take too large a share of the selling price. It is argued that, if the manufacturer sold direct to consumers, prices could be reduced.

But, as we have seen, wholesalers relieve producers of essential functions, allowing them to obtain the advantages of specialisation in marketing products. Such forward vertical disintegration is usually the cheapest way of getting the good to the consumer.

However, this does not mean that all criticism of middlemen is unjustified. Sometimes their profit margins are too high. This may occur through continuing with antiquated methods or by a single middleman playing off one small producer, such as a farmer, against another (hence the formation of producers' co-operatives).

The elimination of the wholesaler

In recent years a tendency for the wholesaler to be eliminated has been due to: (i) the growth of large stores, which can order in bulk; (ii) the development of road transport, which reduces the necessity of holding large stocks; (iii) the desire of manufacturers to retain some control over retailing outlets in order to ensure that their products are pushed or that a high standard of service, freshness, etc., is maintained; (iv) the practice of branding many products, which eliminates many specialised functions. In other cases, however, the elimination of the wholesaler has been confined to sales of high value goods such as furniture and television sets; to circumstances where the producer and retailer are close together, as with the market gardener who supplies the local shop; and to cases where the manufacturer does his own retailing.

To some extent the wholesaler has responded to this challenge by developing in two main directions: (a) by establishing the cash-and-carry warehouse, sometimes called the 'the retailers' supermarkets'; (b) by becoming the organiser of a voluntary chain of retailers, who are supplied, and to some extent controlled, by him, e.g. Spar.

Direct selling by manufacturers

Selling direct to consumers by the manufacturer occurs chiefly where: (a) the manufacturer wishes to push the product (e.g. beer and footwear) or to ensure a standard of advice and service (e.g. sewing-machines); (b) the personal service element is important (e.g. made-to-measure clothing); (c) the manufacturer is a small-scale producer-retailer, often selling a perishable good (e.g. cakes and pastries), or serving a local area (e.g. printing); (d) so wide a range of goods is produced that a whole chain of shops can be fully stocked (e.g. Thornton confectionery); or (e) the good is highly technical or made to individual specifications (e.g. machinery).

CHAPTER SUMMARY

- Wholesalers perform a range of functions, including holding stocks, importing, limited processing, communication and some maintenance.
- Retailers stock small quantities of a variety of goods in locations which are convenient for customers.
- Increased incomes of consumers, increased car ownership and social changes have led to an increase in numbers of larger retail outlets, such as supermarkets and hypermarkets, selling a wide range of goods. Many of these are successfully offering Internet shopping services.

REVIEW QUESTIONS

- How do wholesalers help the process of production?
- Give reasons for the trend towards larger retail outlets over the last 30 years.

 Visit the companion website for further questions

CHAPTER 9

THE LOCATION OF PRODUCTION

LEARNING OBJECTIVES
....

After studying this chapter you should be able to:
- analyse the determinants of firms' location decisions;
- distinguish between natural and acquired advantages of industrial location.

A firm has to decide where to produce. It will reach its decision by considering: (a) the advantages of producing in different areas; (b) the level of rents in these different areas. Thus, although the rent of sites in an area may be high, it can pay a firm to go there if other factors cost less.

9.1 THE ADVANTAGES OF DIFFERENT LOCALITIES

These can be classified as: (1) natural, (2) acquired, (3) government-sponsored.

1. Natural advantages

Costs are incurred both in assembling the raw materials and in distributing the finished product. In manufacturing some products, the weight of the initial raw materials is far greater than that of the final product. This is particularly true where coal is used for heat and power, e.g. in iron and steel production (Figure 9.1). Here transport costs are saved by producing where raw materials are found (e.g. on coal and iron-ore fields), or are easily accessible (e.g. near a port).

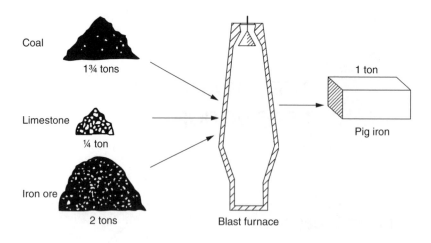

Figure 9.1   The production of pig-iron

On the other hand, with some industries the costs of transporting the finished product are greater than those of assembling the raw materials, e.g. ice-cream, furniture, beer, mineral waters, metal cans, and glass containers. With these, it is cheaper for a firm to produce near the market for its goods. Thus, Walls has ice-cream factories close by most large concentrations of population.

What is really important as regards transport costs is their ratio to the value of the product. Thus sand and gravel are excavated locally, whereas special types of brick are transported long distances.

Generally speaking, transport improvements and new developments (e.g. electrical power, lighter materials) have helped firms to move away from their sources of raw materials. The tendency now is, therefore, for firms to concentrate, not on the coalfields, but on the outskirts of areas of high population which provide both a supply of labour and a market for the finished good.

A river, estuary or coastal location may be essential when huge quantities of water are required by an industry (e.g. chemicals, atomic power), and this may also be important for waste disposal.

Besides accessibility to raw materials and nearness of markets, suitability of climate is a further natural advantage which may have to be considered when locating production. Indeed, in agriculture, it is usually decisive, provided soil conditions are not adverse.

Under 'natural advantages' we can also include an adequate supply of the type of labour required. Thus high technology industries have been attracted to the south-east of England by the skilled labour available, while the abundance of cheap labour has been important for the development of mass-production in Taiwan and Hong Kong.

2. Acquired advantages

Improved methods of production, the development of transport, inventions and new sources of power may alter the relative importance of natural advantages and so change an industry's location. Thus, as high-grade iron-ore fields became exhausted and improved techniques reduced coal consumption, it became cheaper to transport the coal than the iron ore to produce pig iron, and production shifted to near the ports importing iron ore and the low-grade iron-ore fields of the east Midlands. Similarly, improved transport may attract industry nearer to motorways or airports. Finally, new inventions, such as 'humidifiers' and water-softeners (cotton and wool), can make an industry less dependent upon a particular locality.

Yet we must not overstress the importance of the above changes. Even when natural factors have disappeared, an industry often remains in the same region because of the 'man-made' advantages it acquires as it expands. Indeed, it has been said that the ability of a locality to hold an industry greatly exceeds its original ability to attract it (e.g. steel, cotton). A skilled labour force, communications, marketing and commercial organisations, nearby ancillary industries (to achieve economies of scale or to market by-products), training schools and a widespread reputation for the products of the region, all help to lower costs of production, thereby making the locality attractive to new firms (see also p. 96).

3. Government-sponsored advantages

Unemployment in such highly localised industries as coal, cotton and ship-building, and environmental problems (traffic congestion, pollution, housing stress) in regions attracting new and expanding industries, have led the government to offer firms financial inducements to set up plants in Assisted Areas (see Chapter 35).

Such financial advantages have to be considered by a firm when deciding where to site its factory. But while government grants were a major inducement for Nissan to establish its car factory in Sunderland, the area's history of engineering skill, the availability of a large flat site and proximity to major port facilities for exporting all influenced the decision.

9.2 THE LEVEL OF RENTS IN DIFFERENT AREAS

In addition to the advantages of being in a particular locality, a firm will also have to consider the cost of land there relative to that elsewhere.

The cost of the land will be decided by the price system. Other firms, possibly from other industries, may be looking for the same site advantages. Thus the cost (that is, the price) of the land will be fixed by competition among the various firms wanting to go there, and it will settle at the highest price which the keenest firm has to pay – its opportunity cost.

Now the firm that can pay the most will be the one which values its advantages the highest compared with the advantages of land elsewhere. Thus, early in its history, it seemed that the cotton industry might settle on the Clyde, for the locality had all the natural advantages of south-east Lancashire. But the Clyde had advantages for producing iron and steel and for building ships, and in these her superiority was most marked. Thus shipbuilding firms were prepared to pay extra for this advantage. For cotton manufacturers this extra cost of a site on the Clyde exceeded any disadvantage of being in Lancashire. Hence ship-building firms settled along the Clyde, and cotton firms in Lancashire.

In the final analysis, therefore, it is not the absolute advantages of a district which decide where a firm locates but the advantages relative to those of every other district. Thus an industry whose outlay on unskilled labour forms a high proportion of its production costs would, other things being equal, be able to bid more for land in an area of cheap labour than one whose spending on such labour was minimal. And, in any town centre, we see the same principle at work – shops oust other businesses, and houses are converted into offices.

Other influences on location

A firm will normally choose the site where the advantages are greatest compared with its cost. But even for a comparatively new industry, where natural advantages are important, we cannot assume that they will be decisive. Thus it is largely historical accident which accounts for the development of the Rover plant at Cowley on the outskirts of Oxford, for the old school of William Morris came up for sale just as the production of cars at his original cycle works was being expanded.

Moreover, electricity has now practically eliminated dependence on a coalfield site. Yet firms may still go to the original areas because of the advantages acquired over time. Others may choose to be nearer their markets. Some 'footloose' firms have even located in certain districts, particularly south-east England, largely because the managing directors (or their wives) have preferred living there!

The various factors influencing location are summarised in Figure 9.2.

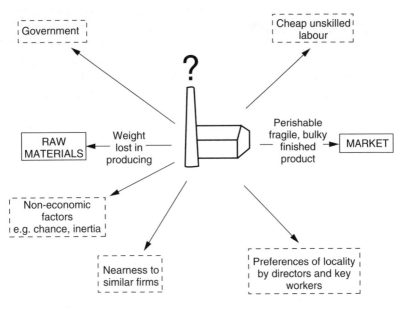

Figure 9.2 Factors influencing the siting of a business

Globalisation

Globalisation is the process by which most economies in the world have become more interdependent. Reductions in transport costs over the last 20 years have led to transnational corporations locating the production of each component part of a product in the country that can produce it in satisfactory quality at least cost. National and regional boundaries have become less important and components of products, such as cars, are now made in a number of countries. Many workers in the USA, Germany, the UK, France and Japan now work for foreign-owned firms. Many worldwide companies, such as McDonald's, Coca-Cola and Guinness, have a decentralised management structure. Markets are also globalised through worldwide media, such as satellite television channels, so that tastes in such things as designer clothes and methods of playing music are the same in cities everywhere. The reduction of regulatory barriers to international finance flows has led to integration of worldwide financial markets. Investment flows now take place in and out of most countries with the help of the revolution in information technology. The result of these major changes in the last 25 years is that an increasing share of jobs and incomes are created in the global economy.

CHAPTER SUMMARY

- Firms reach decisions on where to locate based on the advantages of producing in different areas and on the level of rents in different areas.
- A particular location can have natural, acquired and/or government-sponsored advantages.
- Increasing globalisation of production and deregulation of financial markets has led to greater wealth being created in the global economy and a reduction in the importance of national economic boundaries.

REVIEW QUESTIONS

- Analyse the location decision of a firm manufacturing glass.
- Describe the influences on location of the older 'staple' industries of the UK (coal, steel, textiles, shipbuilding).
- Explain what is meant by 'globalisation'.

 Visit the companion website for further questions

CHAPTER 10

COMBINING THE FACTORS OF PRODUCTION

Even the simplest form of production requires at least two factors of production. Thus the manna which fell from Heaven, although a free gift of Nature, needed labour to collect it before it could satisfy wants (Exodus 16). But since factors can usually be combined in different proportions, a firm has to decide how much of each it will hire. In other words, how will it allocate its spending in order to obtain the greatest possible output from a given outlay? For example, the same amount of concrete can be mixed by having many men with just a shovel each or by having only one man using a concrete-mixer. Can we discover any general principle governing the firm's decision? We can begin by seeing what happens to output when one factor is held fixed while the amount of another factor is increased. From this we derive the law of diminishing returns.

10.1 THE LAW OF DIMINISHING (OR NON-PROPORTIONAL) RETURNS

The present-day formulation of the law is as follows: provided that all units of the variable factor are perfect substitutes for each other and that techniques or organisation do not change, if one factor is held fixed, but additional units of the varying factor are added to it, eventually the extra output resulting from an additional unit of the varying factor will become successively smaller. Since the additional output resulting from an extra unit of the varying factor is known as the 'marginal product', the law refers to eventual diminishing marginal productivity.

The law can be illustrated as follows. Assume: (i) production is by two factors only, land and labour; (ii) all units of the variable factor, labour, are equally efficient; (iii) there is no change in techniques or organisation.

Table 10.1 shows how the output of potatoes varies as more labourers work on a fixed amount of land. Until three men are employed, the marginal product of

Table 10.1 Variations in output of potatoes resulting from a change in labour employed

Number of men employed on the fixed unit of land	Total output	Output (50-kilo bags) Average product	Marginal product
1	2	2.0	2
2	16	8.0	14
3	54	18.0	38
4	80	20.0	26
5	95	19.0	15
6	108	18.0	13
7	120	17.1	12
8	130	16.2	10
9	138	15.3	8
10	142	14.2	4
11	142	12.9	0
12	132	11.0	−10

Notes:
(a) *Total output* is the total output (bags) from all factors employed.
(b) *Average product* refers to the average output per man. It therefore equals

$$\frac{\text{total output}}{\text{number of men employed}}$$

(c) *Marginal product* refers to the marginal output (bags) to labour, and equals the addition to total output which is obtained by increasing the labour force by one man. That is, marginal output equals total output ($n + 1$) men minus total output of n men.
(d) There is a fundamental relationship between average product and marginal product. Marginal product equals average product when the latter is at a maximum (Figure 10.1). This relationship is bound to occur. So long as the marginal product is greater than average product, the return to an additional labourer will raise the average product of all labourers employed. On the other hand, as soon as the marginal product falls below average product, the additional labourer will lower the average product. Hence when average product is neither rising nor falling, that is, at its maximum, it is because marginal product equals average product.

This relationship can be made clearer by a simple example. Suppose Flintoff has played 20 innings and that his batting average is 60 runs. Now if in his next innings he scores more than 60, say 102, his average will increase – to 62. If, on the other hand, he scores less than 60, say 18, his average will fall – to 58. If he scores exactly 60 in his twenty-first innings, his average will remain unchanged at 60.

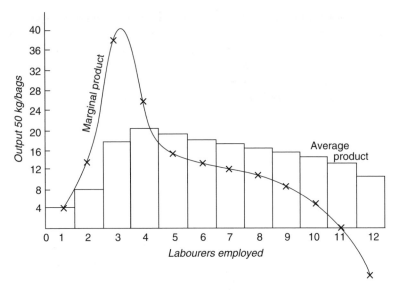

Figure 10.1 The relationship between the number of labourers employed, average output and marginal output

labour is increasing – the third labourer, for instance, adding thirty-eight bags. Here there are really too few labourers for the given amount of land. Thereafter the marginal product falls, the fourth labourer adding only twenty-six bags, and so on; total output is still increasing, but at a diminishing rate. The maximum return per labourer occurs when there are four labourers to the plot. If we increase the number of labourers to eight, the maximum return per labourer can only be maintained by doubling the amount of land. When eleven labourers are employed they start to get in one another's way, and from then on total output is declining absolutely.

In order to avoid any misconceptions, it is helpful to call attention to certain fundamental points.

1. The units of the variable factor are homogeneous. The marginal product of labour does not fall because less efficient labourers are being employed. Diminishing returns occur because more labourers are being employed on a fixed amount of land – and, through physical considerations, labour is an imperfect substitute for land. (If it were otherwise, all the world's food supplies could be grown on a garden plot: extra land would not be necessary, since output could be increased merely by adding labourers.)
2. The law applies only if one factor is held fixed. (If both factors can be varied, we have a change of '*scale*', see p. 135.)

3. The law is not applicable if the factors can only be combined in fixed proportions. If, for instance, you must have one labourer to one shovel to obtain any output, then merely increasing the number of labourers by one will add nothing to output; the marginal product is nil. For the law to hold, the proportions in which the factors can be combined must be variable.
4. The law does not formulate any *economic* hypothesis or theory; it merely states physical relationships. While the physical productivity of an extra labourer is important to a farmer in deciding how many men to employ, it will not *determine* his decision. He must also know the relative costs of factors; that is, he requires economic data as well as technical facts.
5. There are no changes in techniques.

The practical applications of the law of diminishing returns

The law is significant both in our everyday life and in the theoretical analysis of the economist.

First, it helps to explain the low standard of living in many parts of the world, particularly Africa. Increasing population is cultivating a fixed amount of land. As marginal product falls, average product is dragged down – and with it, therefore, the average standard of living.

Second, it shows how a firm can adjust the marginal physical products of factors by altering the proportion in which they are combined. Thus few labourers to the plot gave a high return per labourer; after four labourers, the average product began to fall. So the law is often referred to as 'the law of varying proportions'. The firm will choose that combination of factors which yields the maximum output from a given outlay, as follows.

10.2 THE OPTIMUM COMBINATION OF VARIABLE FACTORS

So far we have assumed that there are just two factors, land and labour, and that land is fixed. But suppose that there is another variable factor, say capital. Now the farmer will have to decide how he will combine labour with capital. The problem is similar to that of the consumer seeking to obtain the maximum satisfaction from the expenditure of limited income.

How much of each he employs will depend upon its productivity relative to its price, since he will alter the combination until, for the last pound spent on both labour and capital, he obtains the same amount of product. Suppose, for instance, the last pound's worth of labour is yielding more potatoes than the last pound spent on capital. It will obviously pay the farmer to transfer this pound from capital to buying more labour, for this will increase his total physical yield.

But labour and capital are obtained in different units, their units being different in price. Thus we cannot directly compare the productivity of one man with that of one unit of capital, say a mechanical hoe; we must allow for their respective prices. If the cost of one man is only one-third of the cost of a mechanical hoe, then the marginal product of a man need only be one-third of the hoe's to give the same yield for a given expenditure. Thus the farmer will be in equilibrium in combining factors when:

$$\frac{\text{Marginal product of labour}}{\text{Price of labour}} = \frac{\text{Marginal product of capital}}{\text{Price of capital}}$$

A corollary of this is that, like the housewife in purchasing her goods, the firm will tend to buy more of a factor as its price falls, and less as it rises. Suppose the wage-rate rises but the marginal product of labour remains unchanged. The fundamental relationship stated above has now been destroyed. To restore the position it is necessary to raise the marginal product of labour and to lower that of capital by combining less labour with more capital: in short, a rise in wages without a corresponding increase in the productivity of labour will, other things being equal, tend to bring about the replacement of labour by machines (see p. 264).

The above argument helps to explain why in Britain more capital is combined with a given amount of labour in agriculture compared with Ireland; relative prices are different. Similarly, if land is variable as well as labour, agriculture will be extensive where land is relatively cheap (as in Canada) and intensive where it is relatively dear (as in Britain).

A third application of the law of diminishing returns is to show how costs vary with changes in output when one or more factors are fixed. It is to this problem that we now turn.

CHAPTER SUMMARY

- Production of goods and services involves the use of factors of production.
- These factors of production can be either variable (the amount used can be varied) or fixed (the amount used cannot be varied).
- If one factor of production, such as land, is fixed, the law of diminishing returns means that if increasing quantities of a variable factor, such as labour, are used, output at first increases but must eventually reach a peak and even decline.
- The optimum combination of variable factors of production will be achieved when the marginal product of each factor relative to its price is equal to the marginal product of the other factor(s) relative to its (their) price(s).

REVIEW QUESTIONS

••

- Identify the factors of production involved in the opencast mining of coal.
- Are any of the factors you have identified (in question 1) fixed?
- Does the law of diminishing returns apply to opencast coal production (explain your answer)?

 Visit the companion website for further questions

11

DECIDING ON THE MOST PROFITABLE OUTPUT

LEARNING OBJECTIVES

After studying this chapter you should be able to:

- distinguish between normal and supernormal profit;
- explain the nature of fixed costs;
- describe the market conditions of perfect competition;
- analyse the behaviour of firms in perfect competition.

11.1 THE COSTS OF PRODUCTION

Costs as alternatives forgone

Suppose a man sets himself up as a shopkeeper. He invests £6,000 of his savings in the business, and in the first year his receipts are £80,000 and his outgoings £44,000. The accountant would say that his profits over the year were £36,000. The economist, however, would disagree.

The reason for this is that the economist is not so much concerned with money costs as with 'opportunity cost' – what a factor could earn in its best alternative line of production. This concept of cost has a bearing on (i) the economist's concept of 'profit', and (ii) how long production should continue when total costs are not covered.

'Implicit costs'

The £44,000 money outgoings of the shopkeeper above can be regarded as 'explicit costs'. But when we look at costs as alternatives forgone we see immediately that the shopkeeper has certain 'implicit costs' – the rewards his own capital and labour could earn elsewhere. If, for instance, his capital could be invested at 8 per cent, there is an implicit cost of £480 a year. Similarly with his own labour. His next most profitable line, we will assume, is to be a shop manager earning £23,520 a year. Thus a total of £24,000 in implicit costs in addition to the explicit costs should be deducted from his receipts.

Normal and supernormal profit

But we have not finished yet. The shopkeeper knows that, in running a sweet shop, some risk arises through uncertainty – a risk which he avoids if he merely works for somebody else. The shopkeeper must therefore anticipate at least a certain minimum profit, say £4,000 a year, before he will start his own business. If he does not make this minimum profit, he feels he might as well go into some other line of business or become a paid shop manager. Thus another type of cost (which we call 'normal profit') has to be allowed for – the minimum return which keeps a firm in a particular industry after all other factors have been paid their opportunity cost. Normal profit is a cost because, if it is not met, the supply of entrepreneurship to that particular line of business dries up.

We have, therefore, the following costs: explicit costs, implicit costs and normal profit. Anything left over after all these costs have been met is 'supernormal' profit. In terms of our example, we have:

	£	£
Total revenue		80,000
Total costs: explicit	44,000	
implicit	24,000	
normal profit	4,000	72,000
Supernormal profit		8,000

Fixed costs and variable costs

For the purpose of our analysis, we shall classify costs as either *fixed* or *variable*.

Fixed costs are those costs which do not vary in direct proportion to the firm's output. They are the costs of *indivisible* factors, e.g. buildings, machinery and vehicles. Even if there is no output fixed costs must be incurred, but for a time, as output expands, they remain the same.

The entrepreneur has to pay for fixed costs (for fixed factors) in advance, and if what he makes turns out to be a 'white elephant', there is little he can do about it short of selling up for what he can get.

Variable costs, on the other hand, are those costs which vary directly with output. They are the costs of the variable factors, e.g. operative labour, raw materials, fuel for running the machines, wear and tear on equipment. Where there is no output, variable costs are nil; as output increases so variable costs increase.

In practice it is difficult to draw an absolute line between fixed and variable costs; the difference really depends on the length of time involved. When current output is not profitable, the firm will have to contract production. At first overtime will cease; later, workers will be paid off. In time, more factors, e.g. salesmen, become variable, and if receipts still do not justify expenditure on them they too can be dismissed. A factor becomes variable when a decision has to be taken on whether it shall be replaced, for then its alternative uses have to be considered. Eventually machines need renewing; even they have become a variable cost. A decision may now be necessary on whether the business should continue.

The distinction between fixed and variable factors and costs is useful in two ways. First, in economic analysis it provides a means of distinguishing between differences in the conditions of supply which result from changes in the time period. The *short period* is defined as a period when there is at least one fixed factor. While, therefore, supply can be adjusted by labour working overtime and more raw materials being used, the time is too short for altering fixed plant and organisation. Thus the firm cannot achieve its best possible combination for a given output. In the *long period* all factors are variable; they can therefore be combined in the best possible way. Now supply can respond fully to a change in demand.

Second, as we shall see later, the distinction is fundamental when the firm is considering whether or not to continue producing. In the long period all costs of production, fixed and variable, must be covered if production is to continue. But in the short period fixed costs cannot be avoided by ceasing to produce; they have already been paid for, simply because it was necessary to have some 'lumpy' factors even before production could start. Only variable costs can be saved; and so, provided these are covered by receipts, the firm will continue to produce. Anything that it makes above such costs will help to recoup its fixed costs (see pp. 134–5).

11.2 HOW DO COSTS BEHAVE AS OUTPUT EXPANDS?

Changes in costs as output expands

In discussing the law of diminishing returns we referred to quantities of factors and yields in physical terms. But in deciding how to maximise profit, the firm will be concerned with those quantities translated into money terms. It can then see directly the relationship between costs and receipts at different outputs and is thus able to decide what output will give the maximum profit (see Table 11.1). Our first task, therefore, is to consider how costs are likely to change as output increases. We shall assume perfect competition in buying factors of production – the demand of each firm is so small in relation to total supply that any change in demand will not directly affect the price of those factors.

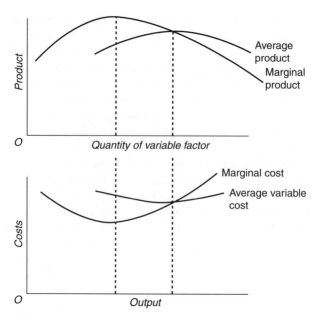

Figure 11.1   The relationship between returns and costs

In the short period there are, by definition, bound to be fixed factors. And when considering the law of diminishing returns we found that when a variable factor was added to a fixed factor the marginal product might increase for a time but would eventually diminish. How will this affect costs as output expands?

Let us assume that two factors are being used, one of them fixed. If each unit of the variable factor costs the same, but the output from additional units is increasing, the firm is obtaining an increasing output for any given addition to expenditure. In other words, the cost of each additional unit of output is falling as output expands. On the other hand, if the marginal product of the variable factor is diminishing, the cost of an additional unit of output is rising. This cost of an additional unit of output is known as *marginal cost* (MC).

The above conclusions are represented diagrammatically in Figure 11.1, where average product = total product of n units of the variable factor/n, and average variable cost = total variable costs of n units of output/n.

Cost schedules

Table 11.1 illustrates this relationship between output and costs. The figures, which have been kept as simple as possible, are for an imaginary firm,

Rollermowers, manufacturer of lawnmowers. Fixed costs (FC) amount to £10,000, and, as variable factors are added, output expands. At first, there is an increasing marginal product; as a result MC is falling. This has its effect on average total cost (ATC) until approximately 75 units are being produced. From then onwards, as the fixed factors are being worked more intensively, diminishing returns cause the ATC curve to rise. These figures can be plotted on a graph (Figure 11.2).

Table 11.1   Costs, revenue and profits of Rollermowers (in £)

Output per week (units)	Fixed cost (FC)	Total Variable cost (TVC)	Total cost (TC)	Marginal cost (MC)	Average fixed cost (AFC)	Average variable cost (AVC)	Average total cost (ATC)	Total revenue (TR)	Profit, super-normal (TR − TC)
0	10,000								
				200					
10	10,000	2,000	12,000		1,000	200	1,200	4,500	−7,500
				140					
20	10,000	3,400	13,400		500	170	670	9,000	−4,400
				100					
30	10,000	4,400	14,400		333	146.7	480	13,500	−900
				100					
40	10,000	5,400	15,400		250	135	385	18,000	2,600
				135					
50	10,000	6,750	16,750		200	135	335	22,500	5,750
				185					
60	10,000	8,600	18,600		167	143.3	310	27,000	8,400
				240					
70	10,000	11,000	21,000		142.9	157.1	300	31,500	10,500
				300					
80	10,000	14,000	24,000		125	175	300	36,000	12,000
				390					
90	10,000	17,900	27,900		111.1	198.9	310	40,500	12,600
				510					
100	10,000	23,000	33,000		100	230	330	45,000	12,000
				660					
110	10,000	29,600	39,600		91.1	269.1	360	49,500	9,900
				840					
120	10,000	38,000	48,000		85	316.7	400	54,000	6,000

Notes:
(a)   TC of n units = FC + VC of n units.
(b)   MC is the extra cost involved in producing an additional unit of output. That is, MC of the n th unit = TC of n units −TC of n − 1 units. Here output is shown in units of 10, so that this difference in total costs has to be divided by 10.
(c)   AFC of n units = $\frac{FC}{n}$
(d)   AVC of n units = $\frac{TVC \text{ of } n \text{ units}}{n}$
(e)   ATC = $\frac{TC \text{ of } n \text{ units}}{n}$

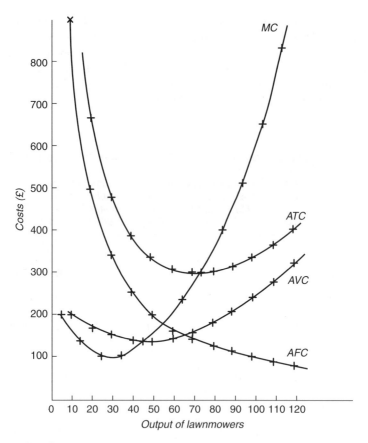

Figure 11.2 Cost curves

The following relationships between the curves should be noted:

(i) AFC and AVC added vertically give ATC.
(ii) The MC curve cuts both the AVC and ATC curves when they are at a
     minimum, the same reason applying as in Table 10.1, note (d).

11.3 PERFECT COMPETITION

In order to ascertain whether a firm is maximising profits, we have to know (i) the
price at which it can sell different outputs and the price at which it can buy different quantities of factors, and (ii) whether it is free to enter another industry
where it can make higher profits. Both questions involve us in a study of the
extent to which competition prevails.

First, we build up a model assuming that the conditions of 'perfect competition' –
the highest form of competition – apply. In chapters 15 and 16 we show how

relaxing these conditions leads to imperfect competition, forms of which prevail in real life.

The conditions necessary for perfect competition

For perfect competition to exist the following conditions must hold:

1. A large number of relatively small sellers and buyers

If there are a large number of sellers relative to demand in the market, any one seller will know that, because he supplies so small a quantity of the total output, he can increase or decrease his output without having any significant effect on the market price of the product. In short he takes the market price as given, and can sell any quantity at this price. He is a *price-taker*.

This is illustrated in Figure 11.3, where (a) shows market price *OP* determined by the demand for and supply of the goods of the industry as a whole. But the industry supply, we will assume, comes from a thousand producers, each of about the same size. Each producer therefore sells such a small proportion of the total market supply that he can double his output from *ON* to *OM* or halve it from *OM* to *ON* without affecting the price – Figure 11.3b.

In other words, in perfect competition a seller is faced with an infinitely elastic demand curve for his product (Figure 11.4a). If, in our example, he charges a higher price than *OP*, nobody will buy from him; if he charges less than *OP*, he will not be maximising his revenue, for he could have sold all his output at the higher price, *OP*.

In contrast, the producer in Figure 11.4b sells such a large proportion of the market supply that a change in his output affects the price he receives for his product.

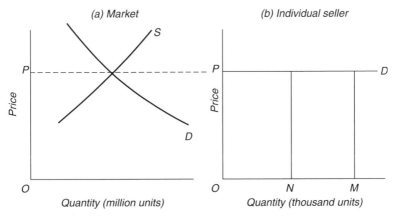

Figure 11.3   The firm's demand curve under perfect competition

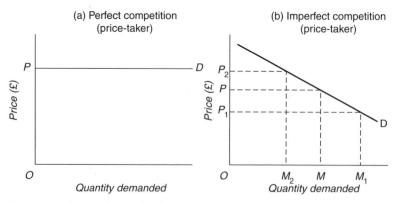

Figure 11.4 The firm's demand curve under perfect and imperfect competition

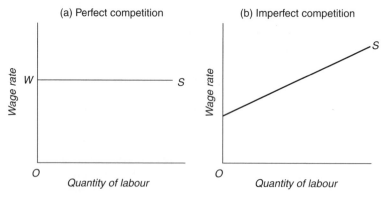

Figure 11.5 The supply of a factor under perfect and imperfect competition

When he supplies OM, the price is OP. If he increases his supply to OM_1, the price falls to OP_1. Similarly, if he decreases his supply to OM_2, the price rises to OP_2. Alternatively, such a producer can decide on the price he charges, leaving it to the market to determine how much is sold at that price. But he cannot fix both price and quantity at the same time. We can call such a producer a *price-maker*. Any change in market conditions is reflected in the quantity the firm can sell at the price it has fixed. Here the firm can respond by changing the price it charges.

Similarly, on the buying side, purchasers of goods and of factors of production where there is perfect competition are faced with an infinitely elastic supply curve. For example, one producer can increase his demand for a factor of production but the price of the factor does not rise as a result (Figure 11.5a). Here the producer's demand is so small relative to the market supply that he can buy all the labour he requires at the prevailing market wage rate OW. On the other hand,

130

in Figure 11.5b the producer employs such a large proportion of the market supply of labour that when he takes on more workers the wage rate rises.

2. Homogeneous product

Buyers must regard the product of one producer as being a perfect substitute for that of another, and purchase solely on the basis of price, switching to a competitor if one producer raises his price. Where goods are graded, e.g. wheat and cotton, there is identity of product in the same grade.

Such identity of product does not exist where there is a real or imaginary difference (e.g. a special wrapping or brand name) or where reasons other than price (e.g. goodwill) influence buyers. Here an individual producer can raise his price without necessarily losing all his customers. In short, *product differentiation* leads to some downward slope in the demand curve.

3. A perfect market, especially perfect knowledge of market conditions

There are two aspects of perfect knowledge:

(a) sellers and buyers must know the prices being asked in other parts of the market, both product and factor, so that they can act accordingly;
(b) in order to make free entry effective, a would-be producer must also know what profits are being made by existing producers.

The above conditions give a perfectly competitive market. For a situation of perfect competition to exist we must also have:

4. Free entry

(a) If the number of sellers is to remain large, there must be free entry to the industry, otherwise existing firms could combine to influence price or they could grow in size as existing firms leave the industry.
(b) Free entry allows the profit motive to function. If demand increases, causing the price of a product to rise, the possibility of profits will attract other firms into that industry. Likewise, if the demand falls, losses sustained by some firms will cause them to leave the industry.

5. Perfect mobility of the factors of production in the long period

A change in the demand for a product must, in the long period, result in factors of production being transferred from one line of production to another. Moreover, all factors, including entrepreneurship, must be equally available to all firms. In real life, however, this does not occur (see p. 144).

6.   No transport costs

This is not an essential condition, but it will simplify our analysis.

In practice these conditions never apply simultaneously, and perfect competition must be regarded primarily as an analytical device which enables us to arrive at some fundamental conclusions.

11.4   THE SHORT-PERIOD EQUILIBRIUM OUTPUT OF THE FIRM UNDER PERFECT COMPETITION

Since the firm is seeking to maximise its profits, its equilibrium output will be that amount where the difference between total revenue and total costs is greatest. At this output, the firm will have no incentive to increase or decrease production.

The firm will therefore be concerned with two broad questions:

1.   How much will it obtain by selling various quantities of its product?
2.   How much will it cost to produce these different quantities?

At first sight it may seem that maximum profit will occur at the minimum average cost output. But this is unlikely to be so. The real question which the entrepreneur will be continually asking is: 'If I produce another unit, will it cost me less or more than the extra revenue I shall receive from the sale of it?' That is, he concentrates his attention at the margin: if an extra unit of output is to be profitable, *marginal revenue* (the addition to total revenue received from the last unit of output) must at least equal its *marginal cost*.

Under perfect competition the firm will obtain the market price for its goods, whatever its output. In other words, marginal revenue (MR) equals price, with the price line horizontal (Figure 11.6). On the other hand, although under perfect competition the firm can buy increasing quantities of its factors at a given price, marginal cost (MC) eventually rises because of diminishing returns.

The equilibrium output of Rollermowers

Let us return to our imaginary firm, Rollermowers, and its cost curves (Table 11.1). These curves are plotted in Figure 11.6. Assume that the market price of mowers is £450. We can impose this MR curve on the cost curve diagram.

Now at any output where MR (price) is above MC, Rollermowers can increase profits by expanding output. Where MC is above MR (price), it can increase profits

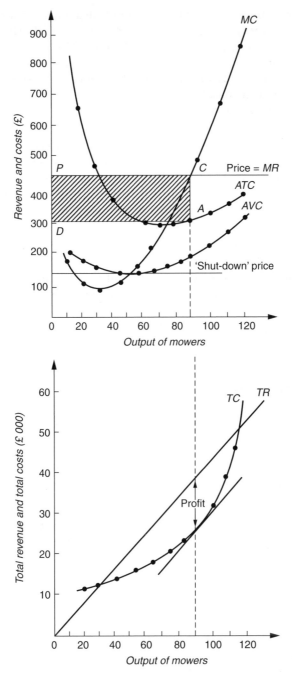

Figure 11.6   The equilibrium output of the firm under perfect competition

by contracting output. Its equilibrium output, therefore, is where MR (price) equals MC: that is, at an output of 90 units. Here ATC is £310. Thus supernormal profit equals total receipts (£40,500) – total costs (£27,900) = £12,600 = shaded area *PDAC* (Figure 11.6). (The reader can check this by seeing whether, from the total costs given in Table 11.1 the difference between total revenue and total costs would be greater at any other output).

Two provisos should be noted:

(1)   The MC curve must cut the MR curve from below. (It is possible for the MC curve to cut the MR curve at a smaller output while it is falling, but in this case the firm would increase profit by expanding output.)
(2)   Current revenue must cover current costs overall. Now 'current revenue' is simply the number of goods currently produced times their price. But as we have seen, 'current costs' depend upon whether we are dealing with the short or the long period.

Alternatively, we can plot TR and TC at different outputs (Figure 11.6, lower part). Profit is maximised at 90 mowers where the slopes of the two curves are equal. Here the *rate* of change of TR, that is MR, equals the *rate* of change of TC, that is MC and the gap between TR and TC is greatest.

The short-period 'shut-down' price

A firm will only *start* to produce if it expects that total revenue will be sufficient to cover:

(a)   the cost of replacing fixed factors;
(b)   the cost of variable factors, e.g. labour, raw materials;
(c)   normal profit.

We will imagine that the firm does think it can make a go of it. It buys highly specific machinery (fixed costs) which, we will assume for the sake of simplicity, has no value to any other firm, together with labour and raw materials (variable costs), and starts producing.

But as time goes by it finds that its original expectations are not being fulfilled. The price at which it can sell its good is lower than estimated. Although the cost of variable factors is being covered, the firm sees that, unless price rises the margin between the two is too small to provide sufficient cash to replace machines when they wear out. In other words the business as a whole will prove unprofitable.

But what will our firm save by stopping production forthwith? Obviously its variable costs, for these vary directly with output. But what of its machines, which, since they have no alternative use, have no resale price? These are fixed factors which have already been paid for, and ceasing to use them now cannot recoup past expenditure. Their opportunity cost is zero.

Consequently our firm takes a philosophic view of the situation. It has some perfectly good machines which, if used, will add nothing to costs. So, provided the cost of the variable factors is being covered, it goes on producing. Anything earned above such cost will help to recoup the cost of the fixed factors.

How can we tell if variable costs are being covered? Simply by looking at the AVC curve. If we take Rollermowers as an example, a price of £135 for a mower would just enable it to produce in the short period. Here MC would equal MR and, with an output of 45 units, TVC would just be covered. Any price lower than this, however, would mean that, for any output where MC = MR, total receipts (price times output) would be less than TVC (AVC times output). Rollermowers could not make a 'go' of it even in the short period; and so we can call £135 the 'shut-down' price.

11.5 THE LONG-PERIOD EQUILIBRIUM OF THE FIRM AND INDUSTRY

In the long period, all factors are variable. This has two effects:

1. The *firm* can vary the size of its plant in order to obtain a given output at the lowest possible cost through economies of *scale*.
2. New firms can obtain plant in order to enter the industry; or alternatively firms need not renew plant and can leave the industry.

We shall develop each of these effects in turn.

Returns to scale

The firm must have started off with some plant, and, in deciding on its size, have taken into account the advantages of producing on a large scale. But it may have misjudged its future sales. They may be larger than originally expected; as a result, plant capacity is too small. On the other hand, sales may have been overestimated; as a result, plant capacity is too large.

Let us assume that Rollermowers has underestimated what it can sell. As a result of starting with too small a plant for its output, it has had to work it more intensively by increasing its variable factors – labour, etc. That is, it is working under conditions of diminishing returns.

But in the long period it can remedy this situation. It decides to enlarge its *capacity* to combine more capital with labour. This gives it the chance to acquire more specialised machines, for those are justified by the larger output. Probably,

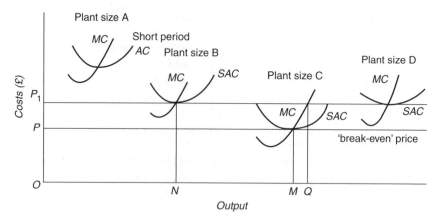

Figure 11.7 Increasing and decreasing returns to scale

too, it will be able to introduce more division of labour and even secure commercial and other economies.

Thus, as we saw in Chapter 7, as the *scale* of output increases, costs per unit fall. In other words, up to a certain point (an output of *OM* in Figure 11.7), additions to plant produce new short-run cost curves for any given capacity, each lower than the other. Here there are increasing returns to *scale*.

Beyond output *OM*, decreasing returns to scale set in. The fixed nature of entrepreneurship may result in increased difficulties of coordinating decisions and administration or more remote contact with workers and customers. And, from *OM* onwards, these diseconomies outweigh any economies still being achieved of a technical, commercial, financial or risk-bearing nature.

The optimum size of the firm

In the above example, the firm's long-period costs of production per unit are at a minimum when output is *OM*. This is known as the optimum size of the firm; it is its *most efficient* size.

As we have seen, this 'most efficient' size varies from one industry to another. When technical economies of scale are important, as (for instance) in the production of steel and cars, decreasing costs occur over a large output. On the other hand, in some industries, such as farming and retailing, reductions in average cost which may be obtained by working with large machines are exhausted at a relatively small output. From then onwards, only economies of a commercial, financial, risk-bearing, or managerial nature can be secured. But as output increases, management problems are more likely to arise. Personal attention to detail is impossible, quick decisions are more difficult, and flexibility is lost. As a result, diseconomies occur, and eventually these diseconomies outweigh the economies of increased size, thereby producing increasing costs. The optimum size is thus a compromise of forces pulling in opposite directions.

In practice, the optimum size of a firm is not a fixed one. Not only do the relative prices of different factors of production change (resulting in changes in the shape of the cost curves), but techniques are improved (again changing the position of the curves). Hence the concept of an optimum size of firm is theoretical; it is, as we shall see, the size to which firms *tend* to conform in the long period as, in their efforts to survive, they compete with other firms.

The industry

We now consider the effects of competition between firms. In the long period not only can existing firms alter the size of their plant to secure greater efficiency, but new firms, observing the supernormal profits being earned by firms already producing, will be able to obtain plant to enter the industry. Output will increase.

But this increased supply by the industry will cause the market price to fall. That is, the horizontal price line facing the individual firm will fall in the long period, e.g. from OP_1 to OP (Figure 11.7). Furthermore, this adjustment will continue until no supernormal profits are being made, for only then will there be no incentive for firms to enter the industry.

If one firm is more efficient than the others, it will be making supernormal profits. This could occur, for instance, because it was producing OQ with plant size C, when other firms were each only producing ON with plant size B. In the long period, some of these firms would increase their size of plant towards plant size C. As a result of the increased supply, price would fall. Firms failing to adjust towards the more efficient size would be forced out of business.

Thus competition forces existing or new firms towards plant size C, and increased output forces price down to OP. If there were a higher price, some firms could be making supernormal profits, and new firms entering would increase supply and force down the price. On the other hand, if price were less than OP, no firm could break even in the long period when all factors had to be paid their current price. OP is therefore referred to as the 'break-even price'.

We can illustrate the above from Rollermowers' cost curves (Figure 11.2). Let us assume that it chose the optimum size of plant in the first place – all firms have to conform to its cost curves in the long period or go out of business.

In the long period, all costs must be covered – but with no supernormal profits if the industry is to be in equilibrium. This will occur when Rollermowers' output is 75 units and the market price of mowers is £300. Here total revenue (£300 × 75) equals total cost (average cost × output, £300 × 75). £300 is thus the 'break-even' price.

To summarise: in the long period and assuming conditions of perfect competition, each firm will be producing at the 'optimum' size *OM* and the price of the product will be *OP*. Each firm, too, will be in equilibrium at output *OM* because price equals marginal cost. The industry is in equilibrium because: (a) each firm is in equilibrium; (b) there is no incentive for firms to enter or leave the industry, because no supernormal profits or losses are being made.

CHAPTER SUMMARY

- Normal profit is the minimum return necessary to keep the firm in the industry. Any greater profit is known as 'supernormal profit'.
- Fixed costs do not vary with output – they are fixed in the short-run.
- Variable costs do vary with output – they can be avoided by stopping production.
- If the conditions necessary for perfect competition (sometimes called 'assumptions') are fulfilled, each firm will be a price-taker, will be producing at the optimum size, and, as only normal profits are being made by all firms the industry, is in equilibrium.

REVIEW QUESTIONS

- For a firm producing motor cars, give examples of fixed and variable costs.
- Why are profits maximised when marginal costs equal marginal revenue (and marginal costs are rising)?
- Why is the demand curve for individual firms in perfect competition perfectly elastic (horizontal)?
- Identify the firm's 'shut down price' in the short-run and the long-run.

 Visit the companion website for further questions

12

THE SUPPLY CURVE OF
THE INDUSTRY UNDER
PERFECT COMPETITION

LEARNING OBJECTIVES

After studying this chapter you should be able to:
- distinguish between short-period and long-period supply;
- show how the supply curve of an industry can be constructed;
- explain the concept of elasticity of supply;
- identify practical uses of the concept of elasticity of supply.

12.1 INTRODUCTION

So far we have concentrated our attention on the behaviour of the firm. But the individual firm is only one of a large number comprising the industry. To obtain the supply curve of the industry, therefore, we have to add together the supply curves of these firms. This will give us the market supply curve, the one which interacts with the demand curve to fix price.

In practice, the term 'industry' presents difficulties. In everyday speech 'industry' includes firms producing goods which differ slightly, e.g. cars, washing-machines, furniture, etc. But the reader is reminded that, when we defined perfect competition, we assumed a homogeneous product. Our definition of an industry must therefore be the group of firms producing the total amount of an identical good supplied to the market. Variations in this definition can be allowed for later (see Chapter 16).

We total the output of the individual firms at different prices to obtain the market supply schedule. Generally speaking, more is supplied the higher the price. But why this is so differs in principle according to whether we are considering the short or the long periods. Each must therefore be examined separately.

12.2 THE SHORT PERIOD

Consider, for example, Rollermowers' cost schedules, Table 11.1. Any price below £135 per mower will stop production, because TVC are not covered. At higher prices, however, it will produce an output where price = MC. That part of the MC curve above the AVC curve (see Figure 11.6), therefore, is its short-period supply curve as follows:

Price (£)	Outputs (units)
135	45
185	55
240	65
300	75
390	85

In the short period, no new firms can enter the industry because, by definition, they cannot obtain fixed factors. The supply curve of the industry, therefore, is obtained simply by adding the output of all existing firms at each given price.

Suppose, for the sake of simplicity, that the industry consists of four firms, the other three being less efficient than Rollermowers. Their outputs (*starting from minimum AVC*) are given under A, B and C in Table 12.1.

This is shown graphically in Figure 12.1. The MC curves of the four firms are summed horizontally to obtain the short-period supply curve of the industry. Since all firms under perfect competition must produce where MC is rising, their output will be greater the higher the price. Thus the short-period market supply curve rises from left to right, showing that more is supplied the higher the price. It will be influenced by any change which affects the firms' MC curves, e.g. the prices of factors, productivity, taxes.

It will be observed that the supply curve derived above is not smooth, but stepped. This is because we have taken only four firms. If there had been very many firms each differing only slightly in efficiency, we should have had a much smoother curve.

Table 12.1 Short-period supply schedule

Price (£)	Output (units)			Rollermowers	Total
	Firm A	Firm B	Firm C		
135				45	45
185			45	55	100
240		45	55	65	165
300	50	55	65	75	245
390	55	65	75	85	280

The supply curve of the industry under perfect competition

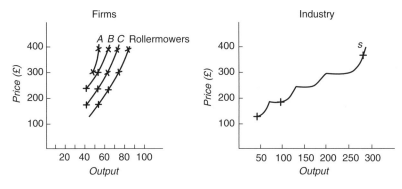

Figure 12.1   The short-period supply curve of the industry

12.3   THE LONG PERIOD

The long-period equilibrium of the firm and industry

The long-period supply curve of the industry must be derived from conditions where the industry itself is in equilibrium, for it represents the supply offered, given no change in demand or techniques, when all factor adjustments have been made.

This requires two conditions:

(a)   Each and every firm must be in equilibrium. That is, there must be no incentive for a firm to change its output. In both the short and the long periods, this occurs when marginal revenue equals marginal cost (with provisos as to a minimum price of the product).

(b)   There must be no incentive for firms to enter or leave the industry (which they can do in the long period if they so wish). This means that, for the industry to be in equilibrium, no supernormal profits or losses are being made by any firm. Given our assumptions regarding perfect competition, the forces of competition will bring this about in the long period.

Our discussion of the firm showed that, in the long period, each existing firm (including any attracted into the industry) will be producing at its optimum size *OM* and at a price *OP* where total costs are just covered (Figure 11.7). Since new firms can now come into the industry on identical terms, there would be a long-period supply curve for the industry which will be perfectly elastic at price *OP*. In other words, the supply curve would be horizontal.

But such a conclusion can be arrived at only on the very theoretical assumptions of perfect competition. In particular, this assumed that:

(a)   each firm is so small that its demand for a factor does not affect the price of that factor;

(b)   there is perfectly free entry into the industry.

141

A rigid acceptance of these conditions, however, is impossible. First, it creates a theoretical difficulty – if all firms are at the peak of efficiency since they are operating at a minimum average cost, which goes out of business if the price of the goods falls slightly? Second, it leads to a conclusion – that supply can be increased indefinitely at constant cost – which is most unlikely. We can overcome both objections by making either of the above assumptions more realistic.

The price of factors of production and the size of the industry

While an individual firm may be so small that its demand will not affect the price it has to pay for factors of production, the collective action of all firms in the industry will have repercussions. In the past, we have referred to these 'industry results' as *external* economies and diseconomies of scale.

Now it could happen that, as the industry expands, there are external economies of scale – growing reputation, skilled labour availability, transport improvements, etc. These will tend to lower the cost curves for individual firms as the output of the industry expands. On the other hand, there may be diseconomies which will raise costs. One such likely result of the expansion of the industry will be an increasing price of the factors of production. Given full employment, as the size of the industry's output expands, higher rewards will have to be paid to attract factors from other industries.

In practice, therefore, at the same time as the increased supply resulting from the entry of new firms tends to lower the price of the product, the cost curves of the firm are tending to be pushed down by external economies and pushed up by external diseconomies of scale. In other words, external economies will make for increased supply at a lower cost – there are decreasing costs to the industry; external diseconomies will make for increased supply at a higher cost. The actual slope of the long-period supply curve – downwards or upwards – will depend upon the balance between the two.

Suppose, for instance, that the entry of a fourth firm, D, to the industry in Figure 12.2 drives up the prices of the factors of production without gaining any external economies. As a result the cost curves of all firms move from (a) to (b), each firm in (b) having a higher minimum average total cost. This gives a new supply for the industry, M_4, at a higher price OP_1, as compared with the previous supply, M_3 at a price OP (Figure 12.2c). That is, there is an upward-sloping industry supply curve.

Perfectly free entry

Even if there were no institutional barriers to entry into an industry (e.g. through cartel or other agreements or through conditions imposed by the government),

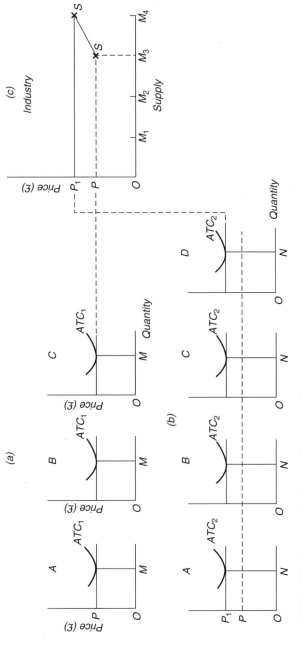

Figure 12.2   The long-period supply curve of the industry

143

the condition of free entry is effective only if:

(a) there is perfect knowledge
(b) factors of production are perfectly mobile and equally available to all firms.

As soon as either of these conditions is relaxed, firms of differing degrees of efficiency will result.

Is it likely that these conditions will apply as regards entrepreneurship? The answer is 'no'. Our assumption of 'perfect knowledge' means that entrepreneurs outside the industry are aware of any supernormal profits being earned by existing firms, of the prices of all factors of production, and of all the different ways in which the good can be produced.

Obviously, the extent of such knowledge is so vast that entrepreneurs must differ in the degree to which they possess this knowledge. And this disparity becomes even more marked when we introduce dynamic considerations. Fluctuations in demand, improvements in techniques and changes in the relative prices of factors of production are continually giving rise to changes in the conditions of demand and supply. Entrepreneurs therefore have to plan ahead according to their estimates. Some entrepreneurs will make more accurate estimates than others.

What this means is that equally efficient entrepreneurs are not available to all firms. At any one time, therefore, some firms are making supernormal profits of varying degrees, while others are marginal in that they are just making normal profits. The situation is shown diagrammatically in Figure 12.3.

Firm D, the highest-cost firm, is also a marginal firm – it is only just induced to stay in the industry by the present price, *OP*, and it will be the first to leave the industry if the price falls, e.g. to OP_1. If the price falls below OP_1 firm C will leave the industry, and so on. Once again, therefore, we can plot the supply of the industry at different prices. This will give a supply curve sloping upwards from left to right.

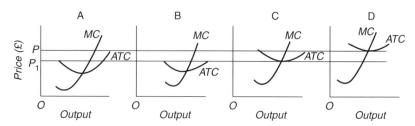

Figure 12.3 Differences in efficiency of entrepreneurs

12.4 ELASTICITY OF SUPPLY

Definition of elasticity of supply

Consider Figure 12.4. For a rise in price from OP to OP_1, supply extends from OM to OM_1 with S_1 and to OM_2 with S_2. At price OP, therefore, S_2 is said to be more elastic than S_1.

More precisely, the elasticity of supply of a good at any price or at any output is the proportional change in the amount supplied in response to a small change in price divided by the proportional change in price. In the supply schedule on p. 38, for instance, when the price of eggs rises from 10p to 12p supply expands from 32,000 to 40,000. Elasticity of supply is therefore equal to:

$$\frac{\frac{8}{32}}{\frac{2}{10}} = 1.25$$

As with elasticity of demand, we say that supply at a given price is elastic if elasticity is greater than 1, and that it is inelastic if elasticity is less than 1.

Limiting cases

There are two limiting cases of elasticity of supply which are of economic significance:

1. Elasticity of supply equal to infinity

The main uses of this concept are: (a) where a single firm demands so small a proportion of a factor of production that it can obtain an infinite amount at a given price – that is, there is perfect competition in buying factors of production;

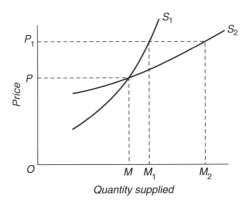

Figure 12.4   Elasticity of supply

(b) where production takes place at constant cost. In both cases, the supply curve is horizontal (Figure 12.5a).

2. Supply absolutely inelastic

Here a good is fixed in supply whatever the price offered (Figure 12.5b). It applies to rare first editions and Old Masters, and, by definition, to fixed factors in the short period.

Whereas elasticity of demand equal to 1 was significant because it described the case where total expenditure on the good remained constant at all prices, unitary elasticity of supply has no such significance. (Any straight line passing through the origin will give a supply curve with a constant elasticity of 1, for such a line describes a situation where supply always changes in the same proportion to a given price change.)

Factors determining elasticity of supply

Elasticity of supply is determined by: (i) the period of time under consideration; (ii) the relationship between the individual firms' minimum-supply points; and (iii) the cost of attracting factors from alternative uses. We shall consider each in turn.

1. Time

We distinguish three main periods:

(1) Momentary equilibrium

Here the supply is fixed and elasticity of supply = 0. An example is Christmas trees on Christmas Eve. With many goods, some increase in supply can take place by drawing on stocks, switching factors of production from one product to

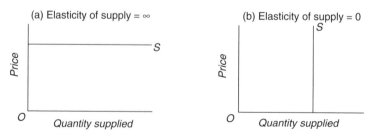

Figure 12.5 Extremes of elasticity of supply

another (where a firm makes two or more different products) or utilising any spare capacity.

(2) Short-period equilibrium

Usually varying supply requires a change in the factors of production employed. Unless there is surplus capacity this takes time – and the period differs for each factor. In the short period, as we have seen, it is possible to adjust supply only by altering the variable factors (raw materials, labour, etc.).

(3) Long-period equilibrium

Other factors – the fixed factors, e.g. land already sown and capital equipment – can be altered in the long period, allowing supply to adjust fully to a change in price. Thus elasticity is greater in the long period.

This is because the difference between the short and the long periods has an important effect on costs. Since, in the short period, supply can be expanded only by adding to the variable factors, it means that, unless there is surplus capacity, the best possible combination of the factors of production cannot be achieved. Too many of the variable factors are being applied to the fixed factors, and the law of diminishing returns operates. Increased production, in other words, is obtained only by decreased efficiency, and we have increasing marginal cost.

In the long period, because all factors can be varied, the optimum combination can be achieved. Increased efficiency produces a smaller rise in costs per unit as output expands. But it may take a long time before this position is reached. Expanding rubber production, for instance, takes seven years while new trees mature.

It follows that, because the supply curve of an industry consists of the MC curves of the firms in it, a given rise in price will produce a smaller expansion of supply in the short period than in the long period. The longer the period of time under consideration, the greater elasticity of supply will tend to be. If we refer to Figure 12.4, S_1 could well represent the short-period supply curve, and S_2 the long.

2. The relationship between the firms' minimum-supply points

The supply curve is obtained by aggregating the supply of individual firms. If these firms each offer a supply to the market at more or less the same minimum price, supply will tend to be elastic at that price. Similarly, as price rises, the greater the number of firms coming in, the greater is the elasticity of supply.

3.   *The cost of attracting factors of production*

In order to expand production additional factors have to be attracted from other industries. For an industry as a whole, this means that higher rewards will have to be paid. What we have to ask, therefore, is how much of a factor will be forthcoming in response to a given price rise. In other words, what is the elasticity of supply of factors of production? And, of greater significance, what influences determine this elasticity?

In answering this question we can first consider what happens when one particular industry, e.g. office-building, wishes to expand. Let us concentrate on one factor: labour. With increased demand for building labourers, wages rise. But they rise not only for the office-building industry but for all other industries employing such labourers – house-building, road construction, public works, etc. How will it affect these industries?

First, they will try to substitute other factors, e.g. cement mixers, bulldozers, etc., for the labour, which now costs more. Is such substitution physically possible? If so, is the supply of these alternative factors elastic or will their prices rise sharply as demand increases? If physical substitution is fairly easy and the supply of alternative factors is elastic, it will mean that a small rise in wages will release much labour for the office-building industry.

Second, higher wages will lead to increased costs in building houses, constructing roads, etc. The supply curve of these products, therefore, moves to the left; and, the higher the proportion of wages to total costs, the further will it move. The extent to which this leads to a reduced production of these alternative goods will depend upon the elasticity of demand for them. If elasticity is high, the small rise in the price of the good will cause a considerable contraction of demand, and labour will be released for office-building. If, on the other hand, demand is inelastic, even a considerable rise in wages will have little effect on the output of houses, etc., and the increase in the supply of labour to office-building will be correspondingly small.

We see, therefore, that the two main influences affecting the elasticity of supply of a factor to a particular industry are (1) the extent to which other factors can be substituted, and (2) the elasticity of demand for the alternative goods it produces.

Practical uses of the concept of elasticity of supply

1.   *The elasticity of supply of a good is a major factor in determining how much its price will alter when there is a change in the conditions of demand*

This is apparent in the following examples:

(a)   *Why does a crisis in the Middle East lead to a sharp increase in the price of gold?*
The threat of war in the Middle East leads holders of assets, particularly the local oil-rich rulers, to seek a store of wealth which will hold its value. Because of its

The supply curve of the industry under perfect competition

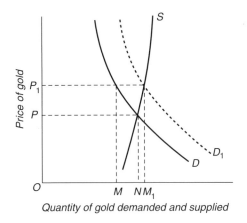

Figure 12.6 The effect of a Middle East crisis on the price of gold

general acceptability, such an asset is gold. There is thus an increased demand for gold, D_1, and, since supply is almost inelastic, the price rises from OP to OP_1 (Figure 12.6).

(b) *Given free markets how would the price of cane sugar be affected in the short period and the long period if the demand for sugar increased?* Once again we can assume a fairly inelastic demand curve for sugar. The original price is OP (Figure 12.7). Demand then increases from D to D_1. The supply of cane sugar in the short run is inelastic, for supply can be expanded only by adding labour, fertilisers, etc. Price therefore increases to OP_1. But in the long period more land can be planted with sugar cane.

Supply is therefore more elastic, and is represented by the curve S_1. The long-run price falls to OP_2.

(c) *Given free markets, why is the price of butter likely to fluctuate more than the price of margarine?* Generally speaking, the prices of primary products tend to fluctuate between wider limits than the prices of manufactured goods. This is because (i) demand is often more inelastic for primary products, and (ii) supply is usually more inelastic, particularly in the short period. We shall concentrate on supply.

Margarine is processed chiefly from vegetable oils. If the price of margarine falls, these oils can be transferred to other uses, e.g. soap manufacture. The supply of butter, on the other hand, depends chiefly on the number of cows. If the price of butter falls, roughly the same amount of milk still has to be processed into butter, for other outlets are very limited. No real change can take place in the number of cows for some time. This would still apply should the price of butter rise. In short, the supply of butter is more inelastic than the supply of margarine, and the price varies more for a given change in demand (Figure 12.8). The price of margarine rises from OP to OP_1, whereas that of butter moves from OP to OP_2.

The general rule is: a change in the conditions of demand or supply will tend to produce wide fluctuations in price but small fluctuations in the quantity bought where supply or demand respectively are inelastic; and small fluctuations

149

The theory of production

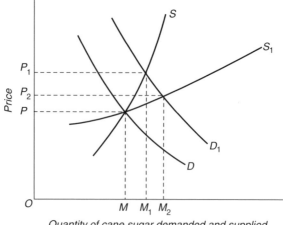

Figure 12.7 Changes in the price of sugar cane over time in response to a change in demand

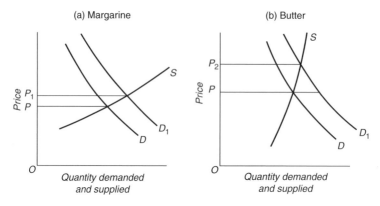

Figure 12.8 Changes in the prices of margarine and butter in response to a change in demand

in price but wide fluctuations in the quantity bought where supply or demand respectively are elastic.

2. *The elasticity of supply is significant with regard to taxation*

(a) Where the supply of a good is inelastic, the Chancellor of the Exchequer can impose a tax on the producer without it having a great effect on the amount of the good offered for sale. Suppose, for instance, that a person owns a field which is suitable only for sheep-grazing, and that the most any farmer will pay for the use of this field is £10 a year, which the owner accepts. Now suppose that the government puts a tax of £5 a year on this type of land. This means that the owner will have to pay the tax, for the farmer will pay no more, and the land cannot be put to any other use. In fact, the government could tax almost all the rent away before it would make any difference to the number of sheep being grazed on it; but, if all the rent went on tax, the owner might leave the land standing idle (see p. 279).

(b)   The relative elasticities of demand and supply determine the proportion of a selective indirect tax borne by the producer as compared with the consumer (see pp. 461–2).

CHAPTER SUMMARY

- The supply curve of the industry (or market supply curve) can be obtained by the addition of the outputs of the individual firms at different prices.
- Differences in efficiency of entrepreneurs mean that at any one time some firms are making supernormal profits, while others are making only normal profits.
- Less efficient firms can only supply at higher prices and so the supply curve of the industry will slope upwards from left to right.
- Elasticity of supply is the proportional change in amount supplied in response to a small change in price divided by the proportional change in price. It is a major factor in determining how much the price of a good will alter when there is a change in demand.
- Elasticity of supply is also significant when deciding which goods to tax heavily.

REVIEW QUESTIONS

- How can the long-period supply curve of the industry be determined?
- Why will differences in the efficiency of entrepreneurs lead to a supply curve that slopes upwards from left to right?
- Give examples of goods and/or services with a) elasticity of supply equal to infinity; b) absolutely inelastic supply; c) inelastic supply; d) elastic supply.
- Why is the concept of elasticity of supply of practical significance?

 Visit the companion website for further questions

13

REWARDING THE FACTORS OF PRODUCTION: THE MARGINAL PRODUCTIVITY THEORY OF DISTRIBUTION

LEARNING OBJECTIVES

After studying this chapter you should be able to:
- explain why the earnings of factors of production vary;
- derive the marginal physical product of labour;
- derive the marginal revenue product of labour;
- show how the prices of factors of production are determined.

13.1 INTRODUCTION

Sharing the national 'cake': factor rewards

Factors of production co-operate together to produce the national product. Each of these factors is owned by somebody. How much of the cake each individual obtains depends upon (i) how much of the factors is owned, and (ii) the reward each factor receives.

Differences in individual incomes therefore depend upon both inequalities of ownership and inequalities in earnings. It is the latter, concerned with the theory of distribution, which is the subject of this chapter.

Before proceeding, however, two important points must be made:

(1) Some factors are consumed in one use (e.g. raw materials), while others are durable, rendering services over a period. In what follows we are examining the price of the *service* rendered by a factor, not the factor itself, though of course the two are directly related. This proviso must be borne in mind when, in what follows, we abbreviate by talking about the 'price of a factor of production'.

(2) Here we are concerned only with the reward to factors in a given industry, occupation or district. In other words, we examine how the price of a factor

is fixed in a particular market. Analysis by ordinary demand and supply curves is therefore possible. When, as in Chapter 30, it becomes necessary to examine the economy as a whole, we have to abandon this partial-equilibrium analysis for a more general one, and we then speak of labour, capital, investment, wages and the rate of interest in broad terms.

Our approach will be as follows. The price of a factor service is determined, like that of a good, by demand and supply. First, therefore, we look at the demand for and supply of factor services in general.

But, as we have seen, factors can be classified according to certain broad and important characteristics. In the chapters that follow, therefore, we shall examine how these special characteristics influence the return to these different factors.

13.2 THE MARGINAL PRODUCTIVITY THEORY: PERFECT COMPETITION

The marginal productivity theory is primarily concerned with what determines the *demand* for factors of production. It shows that, *under perfect competition*, an employer will always pay a reward to a factor equal to the value of its contribution to the product. Its most serious weaknesses are that in the real world perfect competition seldom prevails and that it tends to ignore the supply side. Nevertheless, it does give precision to what determines the demand for a factor, and thus some examination of the theory is a necessary preliminary to a more detailed discussion of the rewards of individual factors in the real world. It is a general theory applying to all factors of production. Illustration, however, is usually in terms of labour and wages, and we shall adopt this practice.

Demand of the individual firm

The demand for a factor is made up of the individual demands of all the firms using it. It is a *derived* demand – the factor is not wanted for its own sake, but simply because it can contribute to the production of particular goods. Hence the actual price which a firm is willing to pay for a factor depends upon the addition to its receipts which results from the employment of a particular unit of that factor. By examining this in more detail precision can be given to what constitutes the demand for a factor.

Let us begin by making the following assumptions:

1. There is perfect competition in the market where the product is sold.
2. There is perfect competition in buying the factor – with labour, each firm is so small relative to the size of the market that it cannot, by varying its own demand, alter the wage rate.

3. All workers offering the particular type of labour are homogeneous.
4. In changing output, only the quantity of labour employed is varied; all other factors remain fixed in supply.

The law of diminishing returns (Chapter 10) showed that, as additional quantities of a variable factor (labour) are added to a fixed factor (land), the marginal return (physical product) of that variable factor would eventually decline. The analysis was conducted in terms of the physical returns to factors (Table 10.1, p. 118), and columns (1) and (2) of Table 13.1 are extracted from that earlier table.

But when demanding labour (or any other factor) the firm is not so much interested in the marginal physical product as in the amount of money it will receive from the sale of that product. It pays for a factor because it contributes to ultimate receipts. What it has to ask, therefore, is: 'How much will total revenue increase if an additional worker is employed?' The value of this contribution to total revenue of an additional factor is known as its *marginal-revenue product* (MRP).

The MRP depends not only on the marginal physical product, but also on the price at which the product sells. Under perfect competition, the producer can sell any quantity at a given price. Hence the MRP is equal to the marginal physical product x the price of the product. Thus, in Table 13.1, by assuming that potatoes sell at £10 per 50 kg bag, we can arrive at the MRP in column (3). For example, when 2 labourers are employed, the total physical product is 16 bags, which at £10 a bag yields a total revenue of £160. When 3 are employed, the total physical product is 54 bags, giving a total revenue of £540. The MRP of the third worker is thus £380. Table 13.1 gives the MRP for each additional labourer, and the figures are plotted in Figure 13.1. The MRP curve shows the increase in total revenue as each extra worker is added to the labour force.

Table 13.1 Schedules of marginal physical productivity and marginal-revenue productivity of labour – product sold under conditions of perfect competition

Number of labourers employed (1)	Marginal physical product (50 kg bags potatoes) (2)	Marginal-revenue product (£) (3)
1	2	20
2	14	140
3	38	380
4	26	260
5	15	150
6	13	130
7	12	120
8	10	100
9	8	80
10	4	40
11	0	—

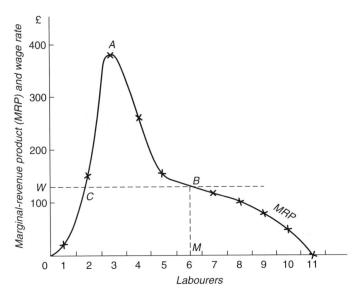

Figure 13.1 Changes in the marginal-revenue product as the number of labourers is increased

How the farmer decides on the number of labourers to employ can be seen from this example. An extra labourer will be employed so long as the resulting addition to total revenue is greater than the cost of employing the additional worker. In our example, because labour is the only variable factor, the farmer is equating MR and MC.

MR is shown by the MRP curve. But what of MC, the cost of engaging each additional labourer? Here it must be remembered that we have postulated perfect competition in buying factors of production. This means that the farmer's demand for labour is so small relative to the market that he cannot directly influence the price of labour. He has to accept the market wage rate as given, and, at this ruling wage rate, the supply of labour is perfectly elastic. MC and AC are one and the same thing, and are represented by a horizontal straight line equal to the wage rate (Figure 13.1).

The firm therefore equates MRP and the wage rate. Thus, in Figure 13.1, if the wage rate were £130 per week, the farmer would engage 6 workers. If fewer, say 5, were employed, the farmer could add more to receipts than to costs by taking on another worker, for the MRP (£150) would exceed MC (£130). On the other hand, if 7 were employed, the farmer would be paying the seventh worker £10 more than he was contributing to receipts.

Some difficulties examined

It might be asked whether the firm can always estimate the marginal-revenue productivity of each factor of production. The following two cases are particularly difficult.

First, with certain factors, such as secretaries, teachers, etc., there is no definite and immediate physical product resulting from their work. How, then, can the marginal physical product, and thus their marginal-revenue productivity, be measured? The answer is simply that they cannot be – but that does not alter the fact that, in practice, a firm proceeds to engage factors as though it can so estimate.

Second, how do we separate the contribution of factors when, for technical reasons, they have to be combined in fixed proportions? In our example this difficulty does not arise. Because labour is the only variable factor, the physical product of an additional worker is measured simply by seeing the difference made to total product. Even when there is more than one variable factor, the marginal product of one factor can be estimated if it is possible to hold the other factors fixed while the one is varied. But where a driver and a lorry, or a carpenter and a plane, have to be combined together in a fixed ratio, how much of the additional total product should be attributed to the extra labourer and how much to the extra machine or tool employed?

In practice, this problem arises only in the case of labour, for it is usually possible to vary the proportion of capital employed by such means as giving the driver a larger lorry or providing the carpenter with a mechanical plane. But where an addition to labour necessitates an automatic addition to capital equipment, the marginal productivity theory comes up against a real obstacle. All we can do is measure the MRP to each factor in turn by deducting from the MRP of the whole unit the cost of all the other factors. This will give us what we can call the 'marginal net revenue product' of the particular factor.

13.3 THE DETERMINATION OF THE PRICE OF A FACTOR SERVICE

Like all other prices, the price of a factor service is determined by demand and supply.

Demand

The concept of marginal-revenue productivity gives precision to what determines the demand of an individual firm for a factor.

The *position* of the demand curve of the individual firm will depend upon the following.

1. The physical productivity of the factor

Productivity could be increased through: (a) additional capital being combined with labour, though in the short period some labour might be displaced; (b) technical progress and improved organisation, e.g. increased division of labour, though here again there may be some initial unemployment; (c) higher wages increasing the efficiency of undernourished or discontented workers ('the economy of high wages').

2. The price of the product that the factor is producing

A rise in the price of the product resulting from an increase in demand would raise the marginal-revenue productivity of labour (see p. 262).

3. The prices of other variable-factor services employed by the firm

In our example above we assumed that there was only one variable factor. But most firms employ, even in the short run, many variable factors – workers, fuel, raw materials, etc. In order to obtain the maximum return from a given outlay, the firm has to combine its variable factors so that:

$$\frac{\text{MRP}_A}{\text{Price}_A} = \frac{\text{MRP}_B}{\text{Price}_B} = \dots = \frac{\text{MRP}_Z}{\text{Price}_Z}$$

(See p. 121). It is obvious, therefore, that if the prices of other services, e.g. *B*, rise, the demand curve for *A* (when *A* can be substituted for *B*) will move to the right. Similarly, if the price of *B* falls, the demand curve for *A* will shift to the left.

However, we have so far avoided two complications – the *shape* of the demand curve and imperfect competition in the demand for a factor. Both will be postponed until we consider trade-union activity in the next chapter.

The *industry's demand curve* for a factor service is the sum of the demands of the individual firms. This would be a simple horizontal addition at each given price if we assumed that the price of the product remained unchanged as the quantity of the factor demanded by firms increased. But it is much more realistic to assume that, as firms obtain more of the factor service, the supply of the product will increase and its price fall. The result will be that the industry's demand curve for a factor will fall more steeply than the curve obtained by a straightforward addition of firms' marginal-revenue product curves.

Supply

By the supply of a factor we mean the amount which is offered as the reward is varied. Usually we should expect a higher price to extend supply, for factors

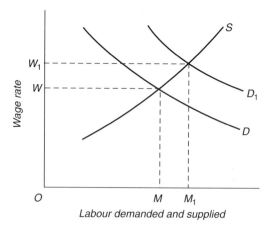

Figure 13.2   The determination of the price of a factor

would be attracted from other industries and occupations. Thus the supply curve normally slopes upwards from left to right (Figure 13.2).

Nevertheless, the actual shape of the supply curve, i.e. the elasticity of supply, will vary according to (a) the nature of the factor, (b) the institutional background and (c) the period of time involved. It is considered in the chapters which follow, where each class of factor is dealt with separately.

Demand, supply, and the price of the factor

The reward of a factor, in this case the wage rate, is determined by the interaction of demand and supply. Thus in Figure 13.2, with demand curve D and supply curve S, the wage rate is OW.

A change in the price of the product will affect the marginal-revenue productivity of the factor. This will be reflected by a change in the position of the demand curve. Suppose, for instance, that the price of the product rises. This will mean that the demand curve for labour will shift to the right, say from D to D_1. As a result, the wage rate is higher, OW_1, and the number employed increases from OM to OM_1.

13.4   WEAKNESSES OF THE MARGINAL PRODUCTIVITY THEORY

The marginal productivity theory shows that, given perfect competition, each factor receives a reward the size of which depends upon the total supply of the factor and the value of its contribution to the finished product. The latter depends upon the price placed by the market on the particular product made. The wage rate, for instance, will increase if the supply of labourers decreases or if the price of the product rises; similarly, it will decrease if the supply of labourers increases or the price of the product falls.

However, although the marginal productivity theory gives precision as to how the demand for a factor arises, it has to be modified for the conditions of the real world, largely because many of its assumptions do not hold strictly.

First, it assumes that a producer knows the value of marginal products whereas at best he may only know the *expected* value.

Second, prices, particularly wages, are not flexible. Rather than accept a wage that lowers the accepted 'status' of an occupation or the traditional wage differential, workers may prefer to remain unemployed.

Third, time-lags in adjusting supply through the immobility of factors mean that, in the short period, factor earnings may contain an element of 'economic rent' (see p. 282).

Fourth, and most important, the theory ignores imperfections in the market, both for goods and services. If, for instance, the firm is selling its product under imperfect competition, the price received will fall as output increases. This means that the marginal-revenue product of an extra labourer will be less than the marginal physical product multiplied by its price, since the lower price applies to all previous units produced.

Similarly, a firm may be the only employer of a factor in a locality, so that, as this firm demands more, the factor price rises not only for the additional factor but for all previous factors. Thus the marginal cost of employing such factors is higher than the market price. In both instances the demand for the factor will be less than it would have been had competition prevailed.

Finally trade unions may exert a monopoly power in the sale of labour, a subject discussed in Chapter 20.

CHAPTER SUMMARY

- The price of a factor service is determined by demand and supply. The demand for a factor is a derived demand – it arises from demand for the product of the factor.
- The value of the contribution to the revenue of the firm provided by a factor is its marginal revenue product (MRP), and this is the marginal physical product multiplied by the product price. A change in the product price will change the value of the MRP of the factor and thus the position of the demand curve.
- The supply curve of a factor normally slopes upwards from left to right, meaning that more of it will be supplied at higher prices.
- Although there are problems associated with measurement of the value of marginal products, time lags in supply, market imperfections and inflexible wages, marginal productivity theory provides an explanation of how prices of factors of production are determined.

REVIEW QUESTIONS

- What is meant by 'derived demand'?
- Why might it be difficult to determine the marginal revenue product of a teacher?
- Explain how the demand curve for a factor of production can be determined.
- Use a diagram to explain how the prices of factors of production are determined.

 Visit the companion website for further questions

PART IV

THE GOVERNMENT AND THE ALLOCATION OF RESOURCES

CHAPTER 14

MARKET FAILURE AND THE ROLE OF GOVERNMENT

LEARNING OBJECTIVES

After studying this chapter you should be able to:

- explain the three types of efficiency in allocation of resources;
- show how market failure can arise;
- explain why it is necessary for governments to intervene in the market economy;
- show why the model of perfect competition is useful.

14.1 EFFICIENCY IN THE ALLOCATION OF RESOURCES

Efficiency in the allocation of resources is achieved when society has so allocated its limited resources that the maximum possible satisfaction is obtained. To ensure that no reshuffling of resources will increase satisfaction, there must be exchange efficiency, technical efficiency and economic efficiency. Let us examine what each involves and how the market economy can bring about all three simultaneously.

(a) *Exchange efficiency* means that no overall gain in satisfaction can be obtained by an exchange of goods between persons. To avoid the difficulty of measuring satisfaction, we can state the condition more precisely: it is not possible for one person to achieve a gain in satisfaction by an exchange of goods without another person losing.

In the market economy this requirement is achieved by consumers relating their preferences to market prices in order to maximise satisfaction from their limited resources. There is equilibrium within and between markets when all

163

consumers have arranged their purchases so that:

$$\frac{\text{Marginal utility of good } A}{\text{Price of } A} = \frac{MU \text{ of good } B}{P_B} = \frac{MU \text{ of good } Z}{P_z}$$

which can be rewritten $\dfrac{MU_A}{MU_B} = \dfrac{P_A}{P_B}$ \hfill (1)

But since in competitive markets there is a *single price* for each good and all consumers seek to maximise satisfaction, it follows that each consumer will buy that quantity of the good which will make the marginal utility he obtains from it equal to that obtained by other consumers. Should, for instance, one consumer have a higher marginal utility for good A, he will demand more of A and less of other goods, i.e. he offers 'other goods' to other consumers in exchange for good A. As a result, an adjustment in the set of relative prices takes place until all consumers are in equilibrium.

(b) *Technical efficiency in production* means that no increase in output can be obtained by producers substituting one factor for another or reorganising the scale of production.

In the market economy individual producers combine resources, e.g. land and capital, to obtain maximum output of a given good from a limited budget. Demand and supply in the factor market will establish prices at which resources are exchanged, the demand for each factor being dependent upon its productivity and the price of the finished product. Each producer employs that quantity of a factor where:

$$\frac{\text{marginal physical product of factor } M}{\text{Price of factor } M} = \frac{MPP_N}{P_N} = \ldots \frac{MPP_Y}{P_Y}$$

which can be rewritten $\dfrac{MPP_M}{MPP_N} = \dfrac{P_M}{P_N}$ \hfill (2)

Since there is only one price at which one factor exchanges for another, and since each producer adopts for his limited resources the same profit-maximising criterion, it follows that in equilibrium the marginal physical product of a factor is the same in all lines of production. If the marginal product is higher in one particular line, producers there will demand more of that factor, substituting it for other factors. As a result the relative factor prices change until the equilibrium condition is fulfilled.

(c) *Economic efficiency* means that, out of the various total combinations of goods which can be obtained from society's limited resources, that particular assortment is produced which affords the greatest possible satisfaction. In short, supply must be related to demand.

In the market economy a network of relative prices is established which link individual preferences with the conditions of supply, as follows.

Given perfect competition and no external costs or benefits, the opportunity cost of producing an additional unit of a good is reflected in money terms by marginal cost. Thus the production of good A will be where (i) $P_A = MC_A$; and of good B, where (ii) $P_B = MC_B$. By dividing (i) by (ii) we have:

$$\frac{P_A}{P_B} = \frac{MC_A}{MC_B}$$

That is, the relative prices of A and B are equal to their relative marginal costs, the opportunity cost of supplying an addition unit.

We can now marry equations (1) and (3):

$$\frac{MU_A}{MU_B} = \frac{P_A}{P_B} = \frac{MC_A}{MC_B}$$

Therefore, $$\frac{MU_A}{MU_B} = \frac{MC_A}{MC_B}$$

That is, the extent to which people prefer one good to another is equal to the relative cost of supplying those goods. Thus economic efficiency in the allocation of resources is achieved through the system of relative prices established in the market economy.

14.2   HOW DOES 'MARKET FAILURE' ARISE?

For the market economy to achieve the efficiency outlined above, certain conditions must apply. These are dealt with more fully in later chapters, but they can be summarised as follows:

1.   *The basic assumptions of perfect competition must hold*

If market prices are to reflect both consumers' preferences and producers' costs, there must exist:

(a)   *A perfect market*, where price differences are quickly eliminated and participants choose on the basis of price (see also p. 122).
(b)   *Perfect knowledge*, so that consumers and producers have adequate market and technical information upon which to make their decisions (see p. 122).
  Only if conditions (a) and (b) apply will there be common prices throughout the market for each product or factor of production.
(c) $P = MR$, and firms produce that output where $MR = MC$.

However, this will only represent economic efficiency if $MR = P$, since production must proceed to the point where the satisfaction which the consumer derives from an additional unit of the good equals the cost to society of producing that unit, that is $P = MC$.

But price will only equal marginal revenue under conditions of perfect competition (see p. 176), where many producers each supply so small a quantity that no single producer can influence the market price. Furthermore, there must be freedom of entry into the industry. Similar conditions must apply in selling factors of production.

In contrast, where there is imperfect competition, marginal revenue is less than price (see Chapter 16).

(d) *Increasing costs*, so that the MC curve is rising to cut the horizontal demand curve from below (see Figure 8.5). However, certain industries which have to produce with large fixed costs often have decreasing costs (a falling MC curve). This means that, to obtain an equilibrium output, the MR curve would have to be downward-sloping in order to cut the MC curve (Figure 14.1). Consequently at the profit-maximising output (OM), price (OP) is greater than marginal cost (OC) and so the conditions of economic efficiency are not fulfilled.

(e) *Perfect mobility of factors of production* in response to changes in relative prices.

(f) All the necessary conditions for perfect competition should exist everywhere in the economy simultaneously.

2. No external benefits or costs

In the market, private consumers and producers seek to maximise their own benefits and profits. However, this assumes that their decisions impose no indirect benefits or costs on others. In practice, this is often not so. For example, the design of a new house may destroy the architectural harmony of a whole street.

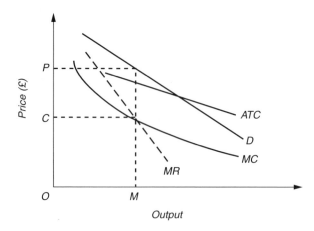

Figure 14.1 Equilibrium output under conditions of decreasing cost

In the decision-making process allowances should be made for such spillover benefits and costs, referred to later as 'externalities' (see Chapter 17).

3. All economic goods can be priced in the market

The pure price system implicitly assumes that all economic goods are capable of being priced in the market, but this is possible only if the enjoyment of a good or service can be confined to those people willing to pay for it. With some goods and services, such as defence, street-lighting, common land and National Trust open spaces, it is impossible or impractical to exclude non-payers since anybody can be a 'free-rider'. Such goods, therefore, have to be provided collectively and financed, not by charging individuals a price as they use them, but by subscription (e.g. the Royal Society for the Protection of Birds), by advertising and sponsorship (e.g. commercial television) or, more usually, by taxation (e.g. defence, street-lighting, common land).

The necessity of government intervention in the market economy

Only if the above conditions are fulfilled will there be an *efficient allocation of resources*. This is an important conclusion and, as we shall see, has implications for government policy.

But it does not go far enough in that it fails to deal with the fact that the market economy is itself dynamic, producing in the short-term the instability of booms and recessions, and yet in the long-term being capable of generating a growing output capacity.

Thus the overall performance of the economy has to be monitored with the objects of achieving: (a) *full employment* of current resources, and (b) adequate *long-term growth*.

Nor does the working of the market economy ensure that it results in an *equitable distribution of wealth*.

Thus to achieve the advantages of the market economy – the decentralisation of decision-making by households and firms, and the incentive of the profit motive for efficiency and innovation – some government intervention is necessary. This must go further than simply providing a framework of rules covering, for example, the protection of private property, the enforcement of contracts. The government has to take an active part in improving the efficient working of the market economy and, making normative judgements, ensuring more equity in the distribution of income.

14.3 THE ECONOMIC FUNCTIONS OF GOVERNMENT: A SUMMARY

The economic functions of the government, therefore, fall under three broad headings: the allocation of resources, stability of the economy, the distribution of income.

The allocation of resources

Our discussion of the possible reasons why defects in the allocation of resources can occur, suggest that the government must be concerned with:

(a) imperfect competition, particularly with regard to monopoly and the immobility of resources;
(b) external costs and benefits;
(c) imperfect knowledge, both in the present and as regards the future;
(d) community goods, where a pricing system cannot be operated.

Stability

Stability of the economy involves the government taking measures to achieve:

(a) full employment;
(b) a stable price level;
(c) a balanced regional development;
(d) a healthy balance of payments;
(e) a steady and acceptable rate of growth.

As we shall see, the government faces difficulties in achieving all these objectives simultaneously.

The distribution of income

Since satisfaction is personal to the individual (see p. 9), welfare resulting from a redistribution of income cannot be dealt with scientifically by objective measurement (see p. 9). However, many people do feel that poverty in the midst of plenty is unacceptable, and their satisfaction is increased by giving to voluntary agencies, e.g. the Salvation Army, the Child Poverty Action Group. Yet while voluntary bodies play a part in the redistribution of income, their efforts are limited and concentrated mostly on sectional interests. Only the government can achieve the degree and fairness of redistribution which is acceptable.

The government may carry out redistribution by deliberate policy measures (as with public spending and taxation). But redistribution may take place only as an offshoot of measures designed to achieve other objectives e.g. parking-meter charges. The economist's task is to reveal where such redistribution occurs and suggest the likely economic effects; the ultimate decision has to be left to the politician.

14.4 A NOTE ON THE VALUE OF THE ASSUMPTION OF PERFECT COMPETITION

Since conditions of perfect competition are so stringent that they are rarely met with in real life, it might be asked why economists should assume it for purposes of analysis.

The first reason is that model-building has to start at a simple level. From this first step modifications can be made to the original assumptions to make the model conform more closely to real life. The analysis of a private enterprise economy operating under conditions of perfect competition provides a simple jumping-off board from which more complex situations can be analysed as the conditions of perfect competition – such as rational decision-making profit-maximisation, perfect knowledge, perfect mobility, etc. – are relaxed.

The second reason for assuming perfect competition follows from the first. Since certain assumptions have to be made when beginning to build a model, it is desirable to be as realistic as possible, even though they will be modified later. Now, an alternative model could start from monopoly – one seller. Yet, as we shall see later, there can be no absolute monopolist, since all goods are to some extent competitive with one another. In real life, too, a deviation from perfect competition is probably a much nearer approximation than a deviation from monopoly.

Third, perfect competition does provide some indication of economic efficiency. Production, for instance, takes place where price (what consumers are prepared to give up at the margin) equals marginal cost (what it costs in factors of production to produce this marginal increment). Moreover, in the long period, production also takes place at minimum average total cost; no supernormal profits are being made. The conditions necessary for perfect competition, e.g. mobility of the factors of production and perfect knowledge, can often be promoted by a government seeking to improve the efficiency of an economic system.

On the other hand, we must not go so far as to say that complete perfect competition would provide maximum economic efficiency. For one thing, it considers only private costs and benefits. But there are likely to be external costs and benefits. Thus it may be efficient for society to produce where marginal costs exceed price if, as (for instance) with an underground railway line which reduces congestion on the roads, there is also a social benefit. Furthermore, to achieve maximum efficiency, perfect competition would have to rule throughout the economy: promoting it in just one part might result in a worse allocation of resources.

Above all, our analysis of perfect competition has been conducted for purely static conditions. It may be that some other market form is more adaptable to future change or more conducive to innovation and therefore to growth (see p. 182).

CHAPTER SUMMARY

- Efficiency in the allocation of resources involves: exchange efficiency; technical efficiency; and economic efficiency.
- Economic efficiency in the allocation of resources is achieved through the system of relative prices established in the market economy.
- Market failure arises when all of the conditions of perfect competition are not met and where there are external benefits or costs, and where some goods cannot be priced in the market.
- Governments intervene in market economies in order to improve the allocation of resources, to try to improve economic stability and to redistribute income.

REVIEW QUESTIONS

- What is the condition for exchange efficiency?
- Give three examples of 'market failure'.
- What objectives might the government have when trying to stabilise the economy?
- Why is the theoretical model of perfect competition useful?

 Visit the companion website for further questions

MONOPOLY

15.1 IMPERFECT COMPETITION

What do we mean by imperfect competition?

In Chapter 11 we stated the assumptions of perfect competition and examined their implications. What happens if *any* of these assumptions is broken?

1. Many small sellers and buyers

Suppose that, instead of many sellers, there are only a few, or even one. Each seller now provides a substantial part of the market supply. As a result, the market price will be affected whenever he varies the amount he supplies of the commodity. In other words, he is faced with a downward-sloping demand curve (see p. 130).

Similarly, on the buying side, when any buyer takes a significant proportion of the total market supply, he will be faced by a rising supply curve.

In both cases we have some element of 'imperfect competition'. As we shall see, a downward-sloping demand curve has particular significance as regards marginal revenue.

2. Homogeneous product

Products may not be homogeneous. The seller may split up the market to some extent by (*a*) product differentiation, or (b) goodwill. The result will be that even though he raises his price a little, he still retains some of his customers. Again he faces a downward-sloping demand curve. Nevertheless, there may still be freedom of entry to the 'industry' (see Chapter 16).

3. Perfect knowledge, free entry and perfect mobility of the factors of production

A breach of any of these conditions can give rise to demand or supply curves which are not perfectly elastic. Consumers, for instance, may not have complete knowledge of prices ruling elsewhere, e.g. in retail markets. Thus sellers can raise their price without losing all their custom. Similarly, there may not be free movement into the industry. This may arise when again outside firms do not have complete knowledge of the profits being made by existing firms. Or entry may be legally prohibited or made impossible by the inability to obtain essential factors of production. In such cases, existing firms can combine to exert some control over the market supply.

Thus, whenever any of our conditions for perfect competition is broken, some form of 'imperfect competition', indicated by a downward-sloping demand curve or an upward-sloping supply curve facing the individual seller or buyer, results.

Forms of imperfect competition

There are many 'shades' of imperfect competition. At one extreme, we have a single producer of a certain product; at the other, the only difference from perfect competition is that firms in the industry are each producing a slightly different brand. The first we call 'monopoly', the second 'monopolistic competition'. In between, we can have just a few sellers of the same or of a slightly different product – 'oligopoly'. The broad market forms are shown in Figure 15.1.

15.2 WHAT DO WE MEAN BY 'MONOPOLY'?

Comparison with perfect competition

Under perfect competition, there are many sellers each producing a very small amount of the total supply of a homogeneous product. The result is that each producer is faced with an infinitely elastic demand curve. It would be nice, therefore, if, at the other extreme, we could define a monopolist, which literally means 'one seller', as a producer who is faced with an absolutely inelastic demand curve.

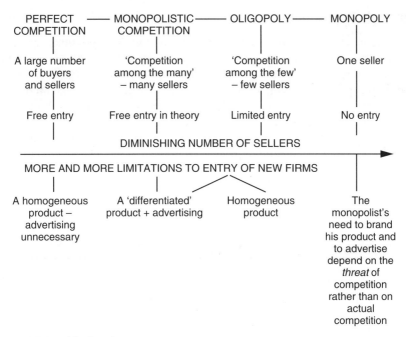

Figure 15.1   Market forms

Unfortunately this is impossible. Because income is limited, goods compete with one another for this income. To a greater or lesser degree, therefore, all goods are substitutes for each other.

Has the monopolist's demand curve a constant elasticity of 1?

It has been suggested, therefore, that the only true monopolist is one who sold all goods and therefore obtained all consumers' spending. The demand curve facing him would then be of unit elasticity at all prices. Any rise in the price of goods would simply mean that, although less were bought, total expenditure was unchanged.

But if we follow this argument through we can see that this definition is untenable for two reasons:

1. Any reduction in output will result in the same receipts, but lower costs. Where, then, does the reduction stop?
2. What the monopolist pays to the factors of production (his costs) is also the income of households (Figure 2.2) which they spend on the goods he produces (see Chapter 30). If he goes on reducing output (in order to lower costs), where do receipts come from?

Monopoly in practice

Since, therefore, a theoretical definition of monopoly is impossible, we have to consider the situation from a practical point of view. While to some extent all goods are substitutes for one another, there may be essential characteristics in a good or group of goods which give rise to gaps, as it were, in the chain of substitution. If one producer can so exclude competitors that he controls the supply of such a good, he can be said to be a 'monopolist' – a single seller.

In practice, 'pure' monopoly is seldom found in real life. But one producer may dominate the supply of a good or group of goods. Monopoly legislation in the UK now considers that, where a dominant seller controls one-quarter of market sales, it can be considered to be a 'monopoly'.

15.3 FOUNDATIONS OF MONOPOLY POWER

A monopolist is the sole supplier of a good for which there are no very close substitutes, and can exclude competitors. His control over the supply of a good may be either in its production or sale. The sources of this power can be classified under four main headings:

1.   Immobility of the factors of production

Immobility of the factors of production means that new competitors cannot compete with existing suppliers. Such immobility may arise through:

(a) *Legal prohibition of new entrants.* In the seventeenth century James I granted monopolies as a means of raising revenue, but today prohibition of entry of new firms is chiefly confined to certain 'public utility' undertakings, e.g. water supply, natural gas pipelines, and some public corporations, e.g. letter delivery (Post Office) and the Civil Aviation Authority where many firms would create technical difficulties.

(b) *Patents, copyrights and trademarks,* with the object of promoting invention and the development of new ideas.

(c) *Government policy of establishing a single providing agency,* e.g. the post office letter service.

(d) *Control of the source of supply by one firm,* e.g. diamonds (De Beer), white salt (ICI and British Salt), mineral springs, a secret recipe (Kentucky Fried Chicken), specialist workers (e.g. dress-designers), trade unions and professional associations.

(e) *Restrictions on imports,* by tariffs, quotas, health controls, etc.

2. Ignorance

A monopoly may persist largely through the ignorance of possible competitors. They may not know about the supernormal profits being made by the existing firm, or they may be unable to acquire the necessary know-how, e.g. for involved technical processes.

3. Indivisibilities

Whereas the original firm may have been able to build up its size gradually, new firms may find it difficult to raise the large capital required to produce on a scale which is cost-competitive, e.g. with cars, drugs, computers.

In some cases, too, the efficient scale of plant may be so large relative to the market that there is only room for one firm. These 'natural' monopolies cover many of the public utilities, e.g. gas supply, water, electricity generation, but given certain conditions, there are possibilities of making such markets 'contestable' (see p. 188).

4. A deliberate policy of excluding competitors

Restriction of competition falls into two main groups. On the one hand, we have the sources of monopoly power described so far. These have, as it were, resulted indirectly rather than from any deliberate action by producers. Such 'spontaneous' monopolies must be contrasted with 'deliberate' monopolies – those which are created specifically to restrict supply (e.g. OPEC).

Deliberate action to exclude competitors takes various forms. Firms producing or selling the same good may combine, or a competitor may be subject to a takeover bid. Monopolies are often formed in the sale of services. Trade unions are primarily combinations of workers formed with the object of obtaining higher wages (see Chapter 20). Certain professions, such as medicine and the law, have their own associations which regulate qualifications for entry, professional conduct, and often the fees to be charged.

Some practices designed to exclude competitors are highly questionable – vicious temporary price-cutting, collusion in submitting tenders, collective boycotts, intimidation of rivals' customers by threats to cut off the supply of another vital product, etc.

As we see later (p. 181), it is essential to distinguish between the two types when formulating policy.

15.4   THE EQUILIBRIUM OUTPUT OF THE MONOPOLIST

The effect of the downward-sloping demand curve on marginal revenue

Consider Figure 15.2. In (a) the producer is selling under conditions of perfect competition. His marginal revenue is equal to the full price, since all units sell at this. Thus, for the fourth unit, MR is the shaded area *A*.

In (b), however, the producer is selling under conditions of imperfect competition. If he wishes to sell a fourth unit, he must lower his price from £5 to £4. But this lower price applies not only to the fourth unit but also the first three units. Thus his net addition to receipts is equal to what he gets for the fourth unit, *A*, less what he loses on the three previous units, *B*. Under imperfect competition, therefore, MR is always less than price at any given output.

The relationship between the costs, revenue and output of a monopolist

Let us consider another imaginary manufacturer of lawnmowers, Airborne Mowers. To simplify, we shall assume that it has identical cost curves to those of Rollermowers, but differs in that it has a patent for its particular mower, thereby excluding competitors. In short, Airborne Mowers is a monopolist. Since its output is also the market supply, the number of the mowers which it puts on the market affects the price. Thus if it produces only twenty mowers a week, each will sell at £790; if total output is increased to ninety, the price drops to £440.

Airborne Mowers has the same problem as Rollermowers – to decide which output yields maximum profit. But it has an extra complication on the revenue

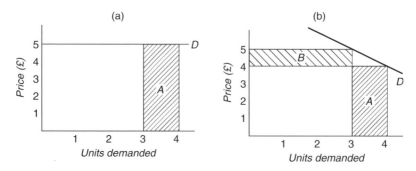

Figure 15.2   Marginal revenue under perfect and imperfect conditions

Table 15.1 Costs, revenue and profits of Airborne Mowers (in £)

Output per week (units)	Costs Total	Costs Average total	Costs Marginal	Price per unit	Revenue Total	Revenue Marginal (per unit)	Profits
0	10,000						−10,000
			200			840	
10	12,000	1,200		840	8,400		−3,600
			140			740	
20	13,400	670		790	15,800		2,400
			100			640	
30	14,400	480		740	2,200		7,800
			100			540	
40	15,400	385		690	27,600		12,200
			135			440	
50	16,750	335		640	32,000		15,250
			185			340	
60	18,600	310		590	35,400		16,800
65	19,825	305	240	595	36,725	240	16,900
70	21,000	300		540	37,800		16,800
			300			140	
80	24,000	300		490	39,200		15,200
			390			40	
90	27,900	310		440	39,600		11,700
			510			−60	
100	33,000	330		390	39,000		6,000
			660			−160	
110	39,600	360		340	37,400		−2,200
			840			−260	
120	48,000	400		290	34,800		−13,200

side – as output increases, price falls for the *whole* of the output. The result can be seen in the marginal receipts (Table 15.1). These figures are plotted in Figure 15.3.

By inspection we can see that the maximum profit is made when sixty-five Airborne mowers are produced each week. At this output MR = MC (both £240), as in perfect competition. But MR is no longer equal to, but is less than price (£565). Total weekly receipts are £36,725 and total costs £19,825 (by interpolation), giving a maximum profit of £16,900.

Alternatively, we can use the price and ATC at an output of 65 units to calculate profit. In Figure 15.3, total receipts equal the rectangle *OMCP* (output times price) = 65 × £565; total cost equals the rectangle *OMAD* (output times average cost) = 65 × £305. Thus profit is the difference between the two: the rectangle *DACP* equals 65 × £260, i.e. £16,900.

177

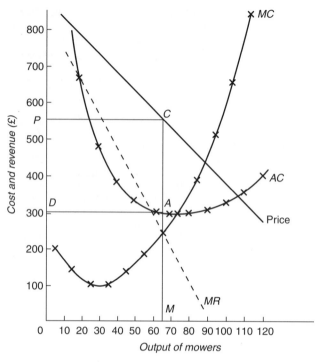

Figure 15.3   The equilibrium output of a monopolist

Some important analytical points concerning the monopolist

1.   MR is related to elasticity of demand

As we have seen, demand is elastic when, as a result of a fall in price, total expenditure increases. In terms of MR, demand is elastic when MR is positive. Similarly, demand is inelastic when MR is negative. This is shown in Figure 15.4, where we have assumed a straight-line demand curve for simplicity.

From Figure 15.4 we can draw the following conclusions:

(a)   A monopolist will never produce at a price where demand is inelastic, i.e. below *OP* (Fig. 15.4). (Here MR is negative; so the monopolist can increase total revenue by reducing output.)

(b)   Where a monopolist has no marginal costs (e.g. the owner of a mineral spring gushing from the earth), the MC curve will be horizontal along the *x*-axis. Production will therefore take place where elasticity of demand equals unity for here MR = 0.

(c)   Where a monopolist firm has marginal costs, it will always produce at a price where demand is elastic. (If MR = MC, MR must be positive, too.)

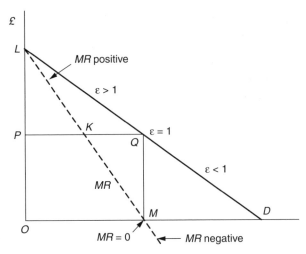

Figure 15.4   Elasticity of demand and the monopolist's output

2. With a straight-line demand curve, the MR curve bisects the horizontal distance between the price axis and quantity demanded

This can be proved as follows:

Total revenue = Sum of revenue for each unit of output = *LOM* at output *OM*
Total revenue =   Price × Output   = *POMQ* at output *OM*

Therefore *LOM* = *POMQ*

But area *POMK* is common. Therefore *LPK* is equal in area to *KMQ*. But identical angles are equal. Therefore, Δ *LPK* is congruent with Δ *KMQ*. Therefore, *PK* = *KQ*, and thus *OM* = *MD*. This also means that *LQ* = *QD*. Thus the mid-point of a straight-line demand curve is where elasticity of demand equals 1, with MR = 0.

3. The greater the absence of substitutes, the greater the power of the monopolist to make profits

While the monopolist will never produce at an output where demand is inelastic, the greater the inelasticity of demand, the greater will be monopoly power – a higher price will drive fewer purchasers elsewhere. This can be seen from Figure 15.5.

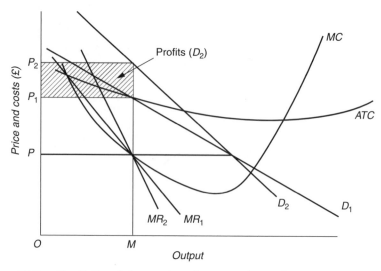

Figure 15.5   Elasticity of demand and monopoly profits

At any given price above *OP*, D_1 is more elastic than D_2. Since these demand curves cut each other at price *OP*, the MR of each must be the same at output *OM* (from proposition (2) above). Suppose the monopolist's MC curve cuts these MR curves at output *OM*. This will give the same equilibrium output for both D_1 and D_2. But the price charged will be OP_1 for D_1, and OP_2 for D_2. Profits are therefore greater for D_2 (shaded) than for D_1 (nil).

4.   The monopolist can produce at an output where MC is falling even in the long period

At an output where MC is falling, AVC must be greater than MC (see Figure 11.1). Under perfect competition, therefore, an output where price = MC (falling) must mean that TVC are greater than TR. There will thus be no production.

With monopoly, however, MR is below price. Thus a profit is still possible provided ATC at the equilibrium output, e.g. *OM* (Figure 15.5), is less than the price at which the monopolist sells.

5.   It is impossible to derive a supply curve for the monopolist

Under perfect competition, MC is equated with MR to obtain equilibrium output. Since the producer is faced with a demand curve of infinite elasticity, MR also equals price. There is thus a direct relationship between the amount supplied and price.

A monopolist, too, equates MC and MR, but now MR is less than price. But the MR corresponding to a given price depends upon the elasticity of demand at that price. It is possible, therefore, to have many different outputs at the same price, or many different prices for the same output. Thus we cannot show a *unique* supply at any given price as we can under perfect competition.

This can be illustrated from Figure 15.5, for at the output *OM* different elasticities of demand give different prices. The reader can construct a similar diagram showing different quantities supplied by the monopolist for the same price according to differences in elasticity of demand.

6. Even in the long period, the monopolist can retain supernormal profits

Under perfect competition, the existence of profits in the short period attracts new entrants, and supernormal profits are competed away. Under monopoly, the producer is the industry, and, by definition, no new firms can enter. Thus, even in the long period, the monopolist's profits remain. Indeed, his profits are likely to increase because he can now combine his factors to produce his profit-maximising output at the lowest possible average cost.

15.5 PUBLIC POLICY AND MONOPOLY

Policy considerations

Monopoly is an emotive word, and often the immediate reaction is that it should be replaced by competition. But two considerations suggest a more cautious approach may be preferable.

First, we must refer to our earlier distinction between 'spontaneous' and 'deliberate' monopolies. While the 'spontaneous' monopolies may still abuse their fortunate position in order to make high profits, to a large extent they are inevitable, and usually policy should seek to control rather than destroy them. On the other hand, 'deliberate' monopolies, those designed solely to follow restrictive practices detrimental to the consumer should, where possible, be broken up. In practice, however, it is often difficult to draw a distinct line between the two.

Second, we have to examine more carefully the view that the monopolist will always follow policies harmful to the consumer. The argument runs as follows.

Where there is perfect competition, output for all firms in the industry will take place where price equals MC, i.e. at *OM* (Figure 15.6). In other words, production is carried to the point, *OM*, where the cost of producing an extra unit, MP, just equals the value which consumers place on that extra unit in the market. Moreover, in the long period, this will be the output where, for all firms, ATC is at a minimum. There are no supernormal profits.

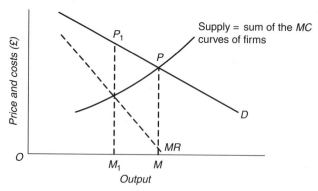

Figure 15.6 Output under perfect competition and monopoly

Now suppose a cartel formed from all the individual firms becomes responsible for selling the product. In order to maximise profits the cartel will sell an output where MC = MR, i.e. OM_1 at price M_1P_1. Thus consumers get less of the product and at a higher price than under perfect competition. It means, too, that demand for factors of production in this particular activity is lower than it would be in the absence of monopoly, and so there is a distortion of factor prices – which has its repercussions on more competitive sectors of the economy.

But the above analysis is not infallible. For one thing, it makes certain implicit assumptions; for another, it ignores dynamic considerations.

First, it rests on the assumption that the competitive industry's supply curve will be the same as the MC curve of the monopolist. But this is unlikely to be so. A single firm may be able to achieve economies of scale which are not open to the comparatively small firms which comprise the competitive industry. In addition its investment may be higher since there is now no fear of over-capitalisation of the industry through rival firms carrying out similar investment.

It is probable, therefore, that the monopolist will, at the relevant market output, have lower costs than the firms producing under conditions of perfect competition. Indeed, we can envisage a situation where, even though the monopolist is producing at the maximum profit output, the consumer nevertheless obtains more of the product and at a lower price than under perfect competition. Thus, in Figure 15.7, perfect competition between firms would give an output of OM at price OP. But, since the monopolist has lower cost curves, OM_1 would be produced at a price OP_1. Even so this does not achieve maximum economic efficiency for price is above MC, and supernormal profits are still being made.

Second, our competitive model was purely static in its approach. Profits were maximised on the basis of *given* prices of products and factors. No consideration was given to other influences on the growth of firms over time.

But the *development* of firms depends upon innovation and investment in research. Thus we have to ask the question: 'Are firms more likely to innovate and

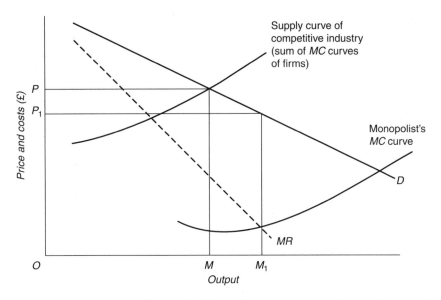

Figure 15.7 A monopolist producing a larger output and at a lower price than a perfectly competitive industry

spend on research if, by being granted monopoly powers, they can be assured of the rewards?' In short, are monopolies more conducive to growth than perfect competition? We cannot develop the argument here, but the mere existence of the Patents Acts suggests that there is some truth in it. On the other hand, there have been instances where monopolies have bought up patents in order that they would *not* be developed in competition with them.

Third, price and output may be more stable under monopoly. Where there are many competing producers, as in agriculture, the reactions of each can bring about sharp swings in the total supply and price of the commodity. In contrast, the monopolist can view the market as a whole in assessing likely future demand, probably finding that only marginal adjustments to supply are necessary. Partly for this reason Marketing Boards (now ended) were set up as selling monopolies in certain branches of agriculture, e.g. potatoes, milk.

Finally, in criticising monopoly, we must remember that restriction of output may permit a discriminating monopolist to charge prices which will allow certain markets to be supplied (see pp. 189–93).

The control of monopoly

While monopolies may be 'spontaneous' or 'deliberate', the division does not make the first group 'white' or the second 'black'. In the first place, our analysis has shown that, no matter how the monopoly has arisen, it will restrict output if its aim is to maximise profits. Second, while a monopoly may be 'deliberate', there may still be benefits for reasons given above. All we can say is that some control of monopoly is desirable, but that it must usually be done on an empirical basis. The degree of monopoly power has to be established and the benefits weighed against the possible economic and social disadvantages – restriction of output, a waste of resources in maintaining the monopoly position (e.g. by advertising), a lack of enterprise through the absence of competition, the exertion of political pressure to secure narrow ends (e.g. by trade unions), and a redistribution of wealth from consumers to the monopolist.

As a result, monopolies in the UK are regulated rather than prohibited. Yet any policy is fraught with difficulties. An exact assessment of the public benefits and disadvantages resulting from a monopoly is impossible. Very often, too, the decision as to whether a monopoly is useful or anti-social in character depends on circumstances and therefore varies from one period to another (note the fostering of monopolies in the 1930s). Moreover, if legislation is proposed, the term 'unfair competition' has to be closely defined by lawyers, though, for the purposes of control, it really requires an elastic interpretation based on economic issues. Last, government policy in another field may influence the problem of monopoly. Thus tariff protection, by restricting competition from abroad, enhances the possibility of establishing monopolies in the home market.

Broadly speaking, policy can take five main forms:

1. State ownership

When it is important not to destroy the advantages of monopoly, the State may take it over completely; the public then appears to be effectively protected. Freed from the objective of maximising profit, there should be no tendency for the state-owned industries to use their monopoly position to make high profits. Should, however, such profits be made they would eventually be passed on to the public in lower prices, or in reduced taxation.

In practice, however, lower profits may mask inefficiency in operation or the payment of wages to employees above those in comparable occupations elsewhere. Consequently, provision must be made for the prices charged to be examined by an independent body and for efficiency checks to be carried out by independent experts.

2. Legislation and administrative machinery to regulate monopolies

This method is usually employed when it is desired to retain monopolies because of their benefits but to leave them under private ownership.

The Monopolies and Restrictive Practices Act 1948 (since amended) set up a Monopolies Commission to investigate monopoly situations. Upon the Commission's report, a ministerial order can declare certain arrangements or practices illegal. Subjects investigated have included: supply of household detergents, breakfast cereals, cross-channel sea-ferries, video games, travellers cheques; and proposed mergers, e.g. GEC and Plessey, Lonrho and the House of Fraser, Capital Radio and Virgin Radio. Alternatively the commission can suggest conditions which would make a monopoly's proposals or practices more acceptable.

3. Breaking up or prohibition of the monopoly

Where the monopoly is, on balance, 'against the public interest', policy can take the form of breaking it up or prohibiting it by legislation. Thus the State could reduce the period for which patents are granted or make their renewal more difficult. When the owner of a particular site uses his monopoly power to frustrate a comprehensive city centre development, the site can be compulsorily purchased by the local planning authority.

Alternatively, it could outlaw attempts to eliminate competition, whether by unfair practices, the formation of cartels or restrictive agreements. Total prohibition was the policy at one time followed in the USA.

In the UK, an investigation by the Monopolies Commission led to the Restrictive Trade Practices Act 1956. This (1) allowed manufacturers and traders to enforce *individual* resale price maintenance through the ordinary civil courts; (2) banned the *collective* enforcement of resale price maintenance through such practices as private courts, stop lists and boycotts; (3) required other restrictive pacts, such as common-price and level tendering, to be registered with a new Registrar of Restrictive Trading Agreements, appointed by the Crown; and (4) set up a new Restrictive Practices Court. The court sits as three-member tribunals, each consisting of at least one judge and two lay members. For a practice to be allowed it must be justified as being 'in the public interest' according to one of seven closely defined 'gateways'. The tribunal's decision is made on a majority basis.

But the 1956 Act still permitted individual suppliers to enforce resale price maintenance for their own products. This was amended by the Resale Prices Act 1964, which made minimum resale price maintenance illegal, except for goods approved by the court. So far only minimum prices for proprietary medicines and books have been authorised, and in practice the Net Book Agreement has been undermined because publishers found it difficult to enforce.

The Monopolies and Mergers Act 1965 strengthened and extended the legislation on monopolies. A merger or proposed merger can be referred to the Monopolies Commission where it would lead to a monopoly or would increase the power of an existing monopoly. The Act also increased the government's powers to enforce the findings of the Commission (for example, by allowing it to prohibit mergers or dissolve an undesirable monopoly).

The Fair Trading Act 1973 introduced a new concept with regard to monopoly and consumer protection. Unlike the earlier Monopolies Acts, whose primary concern was whether monopolies might be harmful to economic efficiency and thus not in the public interest, the object of this new Act was stated to be to 'strengthen the machinery of *promoting competition*'. The Act:

(a) created an Office of Fair Trading under a Director-General. Not only did the Director-General take over the functions of the Registrar of Restrictive Trading Agreements, but he now also has the responsibility for discovering probable monopoly situations or uncompetitive practices. Thus the Office of Fair Trading provides ministers with information and advice on consumer protection, monopoly, mergers and restrictive practices.

(b) empowered the renamed Monopolies and Mergers Commission (MMC) to investigate local as well as national monopolies and extended its powers of enquiry to the nationalised industries and even to restrictive labour practices (though with limited follow-up powers).

(c) reduced the criterion for a monopoly situation to a one-quarter (minimum) market share, thereby defining a monopoly according to the degree of market concentration.

These powers were strengthened by the Competition Act 1980, the government seeking to place greater emphasis on the promotion of competition. The Director-General can investigate any business practice which may restrict, distort or prevent competition. If found to be uncompetitive, he may accept an undertaking from the business responsible, or in default refer the practice to the Monopolies and Mergers Commission to establish whether it operates against the public interest. In 2003, the Competitions Commission recommended that bids for Safeway by Asda, Tesco and Sainsbury's should be prohibited but that by Morrisons should be permitted, subject to some disposals. Nevertheless the Secretary of State at the Department of Trade and Industry (DTI) can reject the MMC's recommendations, as happened in 1997 when the Bass take-over of fellow brewers Carlsberg–Tetley was blocked since it would have given Bass 35 per cent of the British brewing market.

Agreements and concerted practices with anti-competitive effects or purposes are prohibited outright unless the MMC accepts special circumstances. Thus in 1993 it allowed leading perfume houses to refuse supplies of 'luxury' perfumes to downmarket retailers who were cutting prices.

Single market regulations require British law on monopolies and restrictive trade practices to be compatible with EU law so that UK firms operating in Europe do not have to deal with two fundamentally different forms of legislation. At present the Commission has responsibility for all mergers having a 'Community dimension' where the firms involved have an aggregate worldwide turnover of 5bn euros or community wide turnover of 250m euros.

4. Price control

The object here is to remove the monopolist's power of influencing price. Thus if the government controls the maximum price at OP_C (Figure 15.8) the demand (MR) curve facing the monopolist is perfectly elastic up to that price, and the equilibrium output is OM_C instead of OM_M. Here $P = MC$, but it is only a second-best solution because, although price is lower and output greater, supernormal profit could still be made. This solution should be compared with that where production takes place where costs are decreasing (see below).

5. Market solutions

The Conservative government of the 1980s, with its preference for market solutions rather than regulation, has introduced three new methods for dealing with monopolies, chiefly those monopolies given more independence as a result of privatisation.

1. Franchising

With respect to independent television programmes, for example, companies have to tender for the right to broadcast programmes, the idea being to foster competition and divert at least a part of the profits to the State. However, some device seems to be required to ensure that quality programmes, for example the existing Channel 4, are not completely ousted by the more profitable low-brow shows.

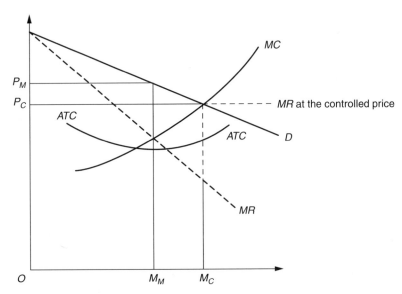

Figure 15.8 Monopoly and price control

2. Contestable markets

The supernormal profits earned by a monopolist firm should attract competitors into the market. But, as we have seen, this may be impossible when fixed costs are so heavy that the penalty of failure is unacceptable. On the other hand if 'sunk costs' (those of specific assets which are of little or no value in other uses) are slight, the risk of having to withdraw should profits disappear is small. The existence or mere possibility of a 'hit and run' competitor therefore produces a contestable market.

This concept can be used to introduce competition into the natural monopolies. With these decreasing-cost monopolies the initial fixed capital required is so high that would-be entrants could not accept the risk, for in the event of failure they would be left with irrecoverable fixed costs. But suppose those high initial costs can be circumvented. Firms would then be willing to compete because withdrawal would be easier should the venture prove unprofitable.

We can illustrate the method and its results from British Gas (BG). The Oil and Gas (Enterprise) Act 1982 permits independent gas producers to negotiate a contract direct with large consumers and deliver supplies through the BG pipelines system. This the independent supplier would do if BG was making a monopoly profit $P_M LRS$ (Figure 15.9). An independent supplier could now use the pipeline to negotiate a price OP_C which would enable it to break even. In fact when a large American oil company proposed to do this, BG cut its own contract price. Thus the *threat* may be sufficient to avert monopoly pricing, though it should be noted

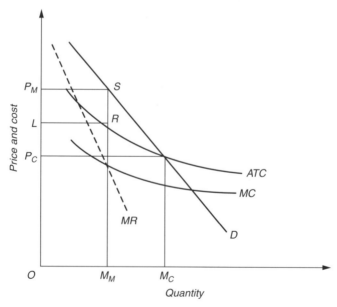

Figure 15.9 Price and output under a contestable market

that $P = AC$ (rather than $P = MC$) and so is again only a second-best solution. However it does succeed in a lower price (P_C rather than P_M) and increases output by $M_M M_C$.

This is the best that can be achieved, without government subsidy, in a decreasing MC situation. Of course, a watchdog body would have to ensure that BG's *pipeline* (TransCo) charges to the independent supplier were not excessive, covering only a reasonable rate of return on its investment. Competition by contestable markets can be seen in Talk Talk's competition with BT and the periodic tendering for regional franchises by TV companies.

3. Price regulation by formula to control profits

To prevent newly privatised monopolies charging a profit-maximising price and yet give them an incentive to be efficient, price increases have been regulated according to a formula which is varied periodically. Usually this incorporates a specific figure, say 2 per cent, by which any price rise must fall behind the rate of inflation as measured by the Retail Price Index. This means that 2 per cent is the productivity increase target, but provides the supplier with an incentive to do better since any surplus revenue can be retained (see also p. 244).

15.6   DISCRIMINATING MONOPOLY

A discriminating monopolist is one who can, and does, sell the *same* product at different prices to different consumers.

Examples of discriminating monopoly are: (a) a doctor who varies fees for the same treatment according to estimates of the wealth of the patients; (b) a car manufacturer who sells cars in export markets at a lower price than on the home market (even allowing for differences in taxation); (c) electricity taken during the night and charged at a lower tariff than that consumed during the day; (d) a small builders' merchant who charges the professional builder less than the 'do-it-yourself amateur for paint and wallpaper; (e) rail fares.

The necessary conditions for discriminating monopoly

For discriminating monopoly to be practicable, certain conditions must be fulfilled.

(1)   *There must be some imperfection in the market.* Under conditions of perfect competition, discrimination is impossible. But where there are different markets, or where parts of the market are separated by transport costs or time (e.g. off-peak electricity, rail travel), type of customer (e.g. senior citizens), consumers' ignorance or national barriers, sellers can exercise some control over the supply in each market, or in each part of the market, separately.

(2) *Elasticities of demand in the markets must be different.* This means that the demand curves must slope differently. As a result, different prices can be charged by the monopolist in order to maximise profits.

(3) *No 'seepage' is possible between markets or different parts of the market.* If an exporter in one country, for instance, sells the good much more cheaply in another country, then either transport costs or physical controls must prevent re-importation to the country of origin.

The equilibrium position of the discriminating monopolist

Suppose that a discriminating monopolist is faced with two markets, A and B. The demand curves for each of these markets are shown in Figure 15.10. In order to maximise his profits he will have to decide: (a) the total output he will produce; (b) how to divide this output between the two separate markets; (c) what price to charge in each market. We shall examine each problem in turn.

(a) *What shall be his total output?* Since we assume that the product is homogeneous, the monopolist must consider the MC for the *whole* output irrespective of which market it is sold in. This MC he will equate with the combined MR curve of the two markets (CMR). This curve is found by adding the two MR curves horizontally – the output of market A for any given MR is added to the output of market B for that MR. This is repeated for all values of MR. Thus in Figure 15.10 the monopolist will produce OQ. At that output the addition to his cost of producing the last unit just equals the addition to his revenue from selling that unit in either market.

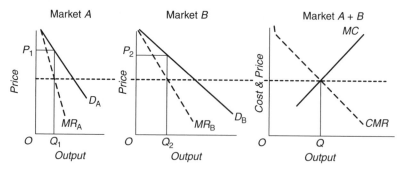

1 For simplicity, straight-line revenue and cost curves have been assumed.
2 Demand is more elastic in market B at all prices.

Figure 15.10 The equilibrium output of a monopolist who sells in different markets

(b)   *How shall he divide this output between the two markets?* The monopolist will maximise profits by equating the MC of the *whole* output with the MR in market A (MR_A) and the MC of the *whole* output with the MR in market B (MR_B). This means that he will sell OQ_1 in market A and OQ_2 in market B, for the combined output OQ (where CMR equals marginal cost) is obtained by summing the output in A and in B. MR must be the same in both markets, for it has to be equated with MC for the total output. If it were not the same, the monopolist could increase profits by transferring output from where marginal revenue was lower to where it was higher.

(c)   *What will be the price in each market?* This, too, can be seen from the diagram. An output of OQ_1 in market A will sell at OP_1; an output of OQ_2 in market B will sell at OP_2. Since demand is less elastic in market A than in market B, a smaller quantity is sold and at a higher price in A than in B.

Can price discrimination be in the interest of consumers?

The term 'discrimination' suggests that consumers are exploited in order to increase the profits of the monopolist. Now price discrimination will enable the monopolist to obtain a higher total revenue (and thus higher profits) than if he merely charged a single price for the whole of the market. But this means he must produce a larger output than with a single price. He is able to do this because, by being able to separate the markets, he does not force down the price in one market by selling extra goods in another market. Indeed, if there were different markets for all units of his product (that is, 'perfect discrimination'), the marginal revenue for each unit of a good would be the price at which it sold. The monopolist's output would then be identical with the perfectly competitive output (Figure 15.11).

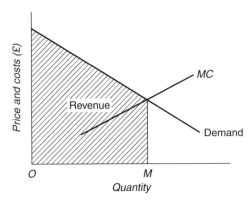

Figure 15.11   Receipts under 'perfect discrimination'

Two points of significance to the consumer follow from this.

1. Price discrimination may make it possible to supply a particular market

Two examples come to mind. British Rail charges all passengers at so much per mile. Main line services are profitable at the standard rate; many local services are not. Local lines are therefore closed down. It is possible, however, that local passengers would be willing to pay higher fares to maintain the service.

Or we can consider a doctor whose services are demanded by both wealthy and poor patients (Figure 15.12). Their demand curves, D_1 and D_2 respectively, will, with price differentiation, allow the monopolist doctor to supply OM_1 at price OP_1 to the wealthy patients and OM_2 at price OP_2 to the poorer patients. But if he has to charge a single price (and wishes to maximise his profits), he will supply OM at a price OP – and this only to his wealthy patients. This is because his total demand curve is still D_{1+2} but, without price discrimination in separate markets, a negative MR_1 outweighs increased revenue from D_2 at the price and output where that becomes effective, K.

2. Price discrimination may make it possible to supply a good when no single price would cover total costs

Suppose the demand for the product and the costs of producing are as shown in Figure 15.13. Where a single price is charged, no firm could cover its total costs. But it may be possible for a firm (e.g. a public utility) to charge discriminating prices and thus cover its costs. If the monopolist could discriminate perfectly between every purchaser, he could produce an output up to the point where $\Delta SRC = \Delta PLS$, for $LOMC$ are his total costs and $POMR$ would be his total revenue.

The firm might be able to cover its costs by imposing a fixed standing charge on consumers irrespective of the quantity bought. But, if this is impossible, without price discrimination the firm would either have to close down or have its revenue shortfall covered by a subsidy.

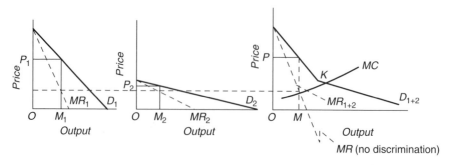

Figure 15.12 How price discrimination allows an extra market to be supplied

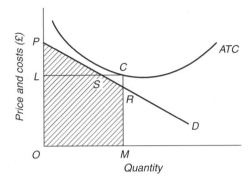

Figure 15.13   The possibility of supply with price discrimination

---

CHAPTER SUMMARY
....

- There are many sorts of imperfect competition, from a single seller of a certain product to many sellers of different brands of a product. A firm in imperfect competition is faced with a downward-sloping demand curve which means that MR is always less than price.
- Restrictions on the entry of new firms into a monopolised industry mean that supernormal profits can be made in the long-run.
- Monopolies in the UK are regulated rather than prohibited because there may be benefits such as lower costs to offset against the possible economic and social disadvantages.
- The Monopolies and Mergers Commission can investigate local and national monopolies and recommend appropriate action to the DTI.
- Price discrimination in monopoly is the practice of charging different prices for the same product to different consumers.

REVIEW QUESTIONS
....

- What is meant by 'imperfect competition'?
- How can monopoly power arise?
- Why can supernormal profits persist in the long-run in monopoly?
- Are there any possible benefits of monopoly?
- Use a diagram to show how a monopolist can use price discrimination to increase profits.

 Visit the companion website for further questions

16

IMPERFECT COMPETITION: OTHER FORMS

LEARNING OBJECTIVES
....

After studying this chapter you should be able to:
- explain the nature of monopolistic competition;
- illustrate the short- and long-run equilibrium of monopolistic competition;
- describe the market form of oligopoly;
- explain how pricing decisions are made in practice.

Perfect competition and monopoly represent two extreme market forms. The first, we have seen, occurs where identical goods are made by a large number of producers and there is completely free entry to the industry. The opposite market condition, monopoly, is possible where a good which has no close substitutes is made by a single producer who can prevent competitors entering the industry.

In the real world, however, there is more likely to be a situation somewhere between the two where many firms or perhaps just a few compete *imperfectly* in the market.

16.1 MONOPOLISTIC COMPETITION: IMPERFECT COMPETITION WITH MANY FIRMS

The nature of monopolistic competition

An industry may consist of many firms each making a product which differs only in detail from that of its rivals. Each firm, since its product is not homogeneous with that of other firms, enjoys some monopoly power. On the other hand, because there is no real gap in the chain of substitution, there is competition from other firms. What we really have is a number of small 'monopolists' competing with one another – 'monopolistic competition'. How does this come about?

Conditions giving rise to monopolistic competition

On the demand side, we have a situation which is closely akin to monopoly. Few goods are completely homogeneous. Indeed, nearly every firm tries deliberately to give its product some distinction from those with which it competes. This 'product differentiation', as it is called, takes various forms. Special characteristics of the good are extensively advertised, competitions are run periodically, free gifts are offered, distinctive wrappings are used. Or, quite simply, the brand name is splashed across television screens and street hoardings in the hope that constant repetition will lead consumers to prefer the good. Apart from product differentiation, a seller may depend upon 'goodwill' (arising through habit or social contacts), rather than the actual price charged, to retain customers.

Whichever method is used, product differentiation or goodwill, the result is the same. The producer is not faced with a market demand which is beyond control. If the firm raises its price, some customers will buy competitors' brands. But not all customers will do this. Some will consider other brands inferior, and only a large price rise will induce them to change. Similarly, if the firm lowers its price, it will attract only a limited number of customers from rival producers. In short, the producer of a brand good or a seller possessing goodwill is, like a monopolist, faced with a demand curve which slopes downwards from left to right. Nevertheless, demand tends to be elastic. Although there are not perfect substitutes available, there are fairly good ones – the different brands of rival producers.

On the supply side, because entry to the industry is possible, the situation is similar to perfect competition. Where one producer is seen to be making supernormal profits, existing producers tend to copy the product and new competitors start producing a somewhat similar brand.

The equilibrium of the industry under monopolistic competition

We simplify the analysis by making two important assumptions: (a) individual producers can obtain all their supply of any factor at a given price; (b) external economies do not affect costs as the number of firms in the group increases. While the latter can be allowed for by subsequent modification, the former is to some degree unrealistic. The industry consists of many but not an infinite number of firms. The demand of one firm for a factor of production may therefore be sufficient to affect its price. Nevertheless, our assumption enables us to analyse a situation where all firms can, in the longer period, achieve identical cost curves, and where cost curves will not rise as new producers enter.

1. The short period

In the short period existing firms cannot increase production by employing additional fixed factors, nor can new firms enter. Each firm, therefore, is a little 'monopolist', having a downward-sloping demand curve for its product and producing where MC equals MR. Because there are many firms, each firm can set its price without having to consider the reactions of competitors. This price will be greater than MR, and supernormal profits are made (Figure 16.1a).

2. The long period

In monopolistic competition the full long-period equilibrium position is possible only when both firms and the industry are in equilibrium. Whereas for each firm the condition of equilibrium (MR = MC) will apply whatever the output, for the industry we must allow, as with perfect competition, for the entry of new firms and for increased production by existing firms. This is where monopolistic competition differs essentially from monopoly; with the latter, *one* firm is *the* industry.

The increase in supply in the long period will lead to a fall in the price of the good, and the demand curve facing each producer shifts its position downwards to the left, for more producers are now dividing up the total market. At the same time, it is likely that the demand curve will become more elastic, for all products of the group will tend to become more similar to that of the most successful. In other words, each brand becomes a better substitute for other brands.

This will continue until supernormal profits have disappeared. Each firm will be earning only normal profits. (In practice the full equilibrium position is unlikely to be reached. Differences between firms will persist, and most will be earning small supernormal profits.)

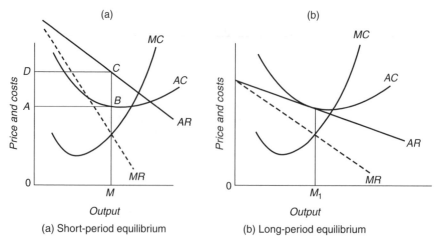

(a) Short-period equilibrium   (b) Long-period equilibrium

Figure 16.1 Monopolistic competition: equilibrium of firms in the short and long periods

A comparison of the equilibrium position of the firm in the short period and the long period under monopolistic competition is shown in Figure 16.1. In the short period, output is *OM*, where MR = MC. But the inability of other firms to add to fixed factors means that supernormal profits exist, equal to *ABCD*. In the long period, the entry of close substitutes causes the AR curve to fall. Supernormal profits disappear, and the equilibrium output is OM_1, where MC = MR, and AC = AR (Figure 16.1b).

Certain points regarding this long-period equilibrium output should be noted:

(a) No supernormal profits are made; as in perfect competition, there is free entry to the industry.

(b) The same conditions of full equilibrium hold as in perfect competition – MC = MR (equilibrium of the firm), and AC = AR (equilibrium of the industry). That both conditions hold at the same output is due simply to a mathematic relationship. At an output less than OM_1, AC is falling more rapidly than AR. This means that MC must be pulling down AC more than MR is pulling down AR. In other words, MC must be less than MR. At any output greater than OM_1, AC is rising more rapidly than AR. MC must therefore be greater than MR. The only point where AC and AR are falling at the same rate is at output OM_1 where they are tangential, and here MC is neither less nor greater than MR – it is equal to it.

(c) Price is greater than MC and MR – a result of the falling AR curve.

(d) The equilibrium output is less than that under perfect competition. This again is the result of the downward-sloping AR curve, which can be tangential to a U-shaped average-cost curve only at an output less than the minimum average cost.

The economic and social effects of monopolistic competition – the 'wastes of competition'

1. Even in the long period firms operate at less than the optimum size

Under perfect competition, not only are supernormal profits eliminated, but in the long period each firm is producing where AC is a minimum – the optimum output. At this output factors of production are combined in the correct proportions and the full advantages of large-scale economies are achieved. What happens under monopolistic competition is that firms operate at less than their optimum size and thus there is inefficiency in the allocation of factors of production.

But we should not assume from the above argument that monopolistic competition is necessarily a 'bad' thing. Not every consumer will want to buy goods which are identical with those bought by other consumers. Different individuals have slightly different tastes. Thus waste in the use of the scarce resources can be regarded as the part of the price that has to be paid for variety of choice.

2. Costs are incurred in competitive advertising

Perfect competition assumes perfect knowledge and homogeneous goods. Advertising is therefore unnecessary. If any one firm incurred costs in this way, it would benefit no more than its rivals.

In practice, however, knowledge is not perfect, and most firms marketing a new product have to spend money in bringing its merits to the notice of the public. Such costs are as justifiable as those incurred in the actual production of the good. Indeed, they may even be beneficial in that, by expanding demand, they allow the advantages of large-scale production to be achieved.

But 'informative' advertising forms only a small proportion of modern advertising. The main object is to *persuade*. Firms, having made their product somewhat different, then incur large costs in advertising this difference and in persuading the customer that their brand of good is superior to other brands. Put in economic terms, they aim at decreasing the elasticity of demand for their particular product as well as shifting the demand curve to the right. In reality, there may be little basic difference between brands – but labour and other scarce resources are wasted in trying to convince the public that it is otherwise. The *AC* curve includes this cost of advertising, so raising the final equilibrium price (Figure 16.1b).

In practice it is not always easy to draw the line between informative and persuasive advertising. If you adhere to the principle of allowing people to exercise freedom of choice, then you must accept what follows – that they are open to be persuaded. What consumers lack is knowledge of the good, and they are thus easy victims to the pressures of advertising. Today there is only a private body, the Consumers' Association (publishers of *Which?*), to report on goods to subscribers.

16.2 OLIGOPOLY: IMPERFECT COMPETITION WITH FEW FIRMS

Pricing where there are few firms

In real life many goods and services are produced by just a few firms, e.g. cigarettes, cars, petrol, tyres, screws, detergents, electric cable, newspapers and lawnmowers. Here we have 'oligopoly', where pricing and output policy conforms to no given principles. Sometimes one large firm is a 'price leader', setting the price which will maximise its profit and taking its share of the market. Smaller firms have to take this price as given and consider themselves as operating in a competitive market.

In other cases, firms may be of fairly equal strength but, since their number is small, no one firm can set a price *without considering the likely reaction of its competitors*. If, for instance, it reduces its price, it cannot guarantee that it will win a greater share of the market since other firms may retaliate and cut their prices.

It is impossible, therefore, to predict the exact behaviour of the oligopolist. Whereas with monopoly and monopolistic competition the relationship of marginal revenue and marginal cost determines price and output, the oligopolistic firm has the added dimension of having to make a guess about the reaction of its competitors to a change in price. There are many different assumptions it can make, and each will give a different solution.

Thus, there is no single theoretical model to cover the oligopolist's pricing policy. A likely assumption by firms is that price cuts will be matched by competitors, but not price increases. From this has developed the theory of the kinked demand curve.

The kinked demand curve

The oligopolist firm reasons that if it cuts prices, its competitors will follow suit in order to avoid losing customers. On the other hand, if it raises its price, its rivals will do nothing, being content to pick up the extra customers driven away by the price increase. This means that its demand curve is relatively inelastic for price cuts, but relatively elastic for price increases. Thus in Figure 16.2, if the original price is P, the firm would expect to move down along the curve towards D and upwards towards D_1.

For two reasons, the kinked demand curve makes for price stability. First, the oligopolist firm is likely to be conservative in its pricing policy, not changing its price from P. Second, even though its costs change, the firm would not change its price or output. This is the result of the broken marginal revenue curve, MR, which follows from the kinked demand curve. Thus marginal cost can change between MC to MC_1 without exerting any pressure on the firm's policy. Only if costs change more would the firm consider risking the loss of customers by raising its price or risk a price war by lowering its price.

The model, however, does have weaknesses in that: (a) it cannot explain how price P was originally determined; and (b) there is little empirical evidence to support the assumption that a price cut, but not a price rise, will be matched by competitors – though provided the oligopolist *acts* on this assumption it makes no difference to the outcome.

Oligopoly policy in practice

Since in an oligopolistic market situation firms are reluctant to engage in price-cutting, other policies are often pursued in practice.

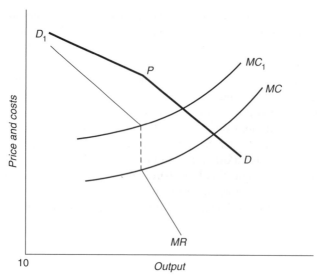

Figure 16.2 The kinked demand curve

First, the few firms concerned are able and usually willing to come to a tacit agreement on price in order to achieve joint profit maximisation. Often this takes the form of following the price set by the largest firm. Thus Brooke Bond Oxo appears to give the lead in tea prices. The extent to which such collusion is possible depends on the ability to exclude new firms, for example because production has to be on a large scale from the outset.

Second, non-price competition is prevalent, e.g. through extensive advertising (detergents), discounts, free gift stamps, competitions, temporary special offers (newspapers), low interest rates (cars), better after-sales service, etc.

16.3   PRICING POLICY IN THE REAL WORLD

Difficulties of the MC = MR principle

Following the above brief discussion of oligopoly, we have to admit that in many other cases the strict principle of fixing a price where MC equals MR may not be rigidly adhered to. For one thing the optimum output may be unobtainable because of cash-flow difficulties, the result of the capital market not being perfect. For another, few markets are so perfectly competitive that individual producers have no control over their price and have such an exact knowledge of the shape of their demand curve that MR can be equated with MC at all outputs.

Pricing policy therefore usually follows more pragmatic methods. Sometimes, for example with government contracts, the firm may follow a 'cost-plus' approach, being allowed what is considered to be a fair percentage addition to basic costs to cover overheads and normal profit; or the firm will, by a process of trial and error, seek to charge 'what the traffic will bear', e.g. the 'black-market' ticket seller.

Mark-up pricing

More usually where a producer has some control in fixing a price, pricing is on a 'mark-up' basis. Only the cost of manufacturing is calculated accurately, and to this is added a rather arbitrary percentage for overheads in order to arrive at the final selling price. Thus, in selling a book, the publisher calculates the cost of printing and binding, adds a percentage (say 40 per cent) to cover overheads and normal profit, and fixes a final bookshop price which covers these costs plus the author's royalty and the bookseller's margin based on the retail price.

Indeed, this may be the only practicable method when, as is usual, firms are producing more than one product. A publisher, for instance, could not exist on the sales of one book and, in any case, would want the extra security of publishing different types of books. Furthermore, in order to survive, producers have to pay regard to what is known as 'the product life-cycle', which consists of innovation, growth, maturity, saturation and decline (Figure 16.3). In the growth period the product shows increasing profitability, for the firm enjoys almost a monopoly position. With time, competitors enter: sales increase, but only at the expense of rising advertising costs. Thereafter the market becomes oversupplied or competitors produce improved models, and sales decline. Thus the go-ahead firm will

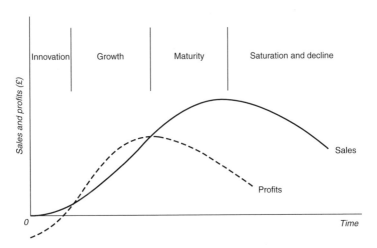

Figure 16.3 The product life-cycle

always be planning new products so that one replaces another as each passes through its life-cyle.

With a many-product firm the exact share of overheads attributable to any one product would be difficult, if not impossible, to ascertain. The mark-up method sidetracks this difficulty. Furthermore, it allows control by the cost accountant, especially as regards maintaining cash flow and ensuring profitable production. Where pricing is on the MC = MR principle, there is no certainty that total costs are covered.

CHAPTER SUMMARY

- A firm in monopolistic competition produces a differentiated product and so faces a downward-sloping demand curve.
- In the short-run supernormal profits can be made, but because there is freedom of entry to the industry, these are competed away by new firms and in the long-run only normal profits are possible.
- In oligopoly, the firm must consider the reactions of its competitors to any change in its price. And because there are only a few firms in the industry, it is easier for anti-competitive agreements to be made.
- Most firms in the real world exist in monopolistic competition or oligopoly.

REVIEW QUESTIONS

- What is meant by 'product differentiation'?
- Is competitive advertising 'wasteful'?
- Explain why prices in oligopoly may be quite stable.
- Explain why 'mark-up pricing' may be common in the real world.

 Visit the companion website for further questions

LEARNING OBJECTIVES
....

After studying this chapter you should be able to:
- define and give examples of externalities;
- illustrate how externalities increase marginal social costs;
- suggest ways that externalities can be allowed for;
- explain the nature of cost-benefit analysis.

17.1 EXTERNALITIES

Definition

So far we have referred to 'externalities' only in passing (p. 19). But with the growing complexity of economic activity and decision-making, the concept has increased in importance, and before we can analyse problems of the environment it is necessary to examine it in more depth.

In the pure market economy, resource allocation is the result of the decisions of consumers (households) and producers (firms) who seek to maximise the difference between benefits and incurred costs. We refer to these as *private benefits and private costs*.

But one weakness of the market economy is that it may fail to take account of any additional benefits or costs which 'spill over' from the original decisions. A firm may decide to build a new factory on a derelict site in a depressed district. In doing so it confers external benefits – tidying up the site and reducing the cost of government unemployment benefit payments. External benefits are often referred to as 'positive externalities'. On the other hand, should the factory be built in a predominantly residential district, it would incur spill-over costs of heavy vehicle movement, noise, loss of visual beauty, etc. External costs are often referred to as 'negative externalities'. If we add these spill-over benefits (and costs) to the private benefits (and costs) of a transaction we have the full *social benefits* (and costs) involved. It is usual to refer to these 'spill-overs' as 'externalities' – the costs or benefits additional to those which are the immediate concern of the parties to a transaction and which are not provided for directly in the market price.

Diagrammatic representation

We can present the problem of allowing for externalities diagrammatically. Suppose, for instance, that a farmer applies nitrates to his field up to the point where the marginal revenue product (in terms of the value of the extra grass which will result) equals the marginal cost. Thus in Figure 17.1, given no government control over the use of nitrates, OC kilos per hectare will be applied.

However, some of the nitrate may not be taken up by the grass, but finds its way into the water supply. There is now an external cost to be taken into account which increases as the application of nitrate per hectare increases. This external cost has had to be added to the private cost (MC) to obtain the true marginal social cost, shown by the curve MSC, and the socially efficient application of nitrates is reduced to OD per hectare.

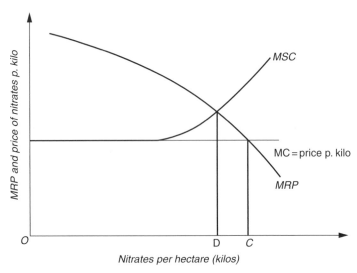

Figure 17.1 The external cost of nitrates applied to land

17.2   METHODS OF DEALING WITH EXTERNALITIES

Externalities and the price system

If an economically efficient allocation of resources is to be achieved, externalities, provided they are not too trivial, must be allowed for.

It should not be assumed, however, that the *price system* completely fails to respond to externalities. Thus one property developer has responded to environmental pressures by providing a barn owl tower in a new office building to rehouse the birds which were previously on the site. Often externalities may be reflected in the market price. Thus shops where traffic congestion is a serious problem will, other things being equal, command lower rents than shops having nearby parking facilities.

Private action may also provide for externalities, e.g. by a store itself providing parking for customers. Or such 'internalisation of externalities' may be achieved by negotiation. Thus within a local community rules may be drawn up governing car parking, standards of house maintenance, children's play areas, etc. Alternatively, such matters may be covered more rigidly by covenants in the leases. Similarly, owners of the fishing rights on the Hampshire chalk-streams mutually agree to confine weed-cutting to three specified weeks during the fishing season.

Taking this a stage further, persons adversely affected by a new road proposal, e.g. routeing the M3 through Twyford Down, Winchester, may subscribe to a *pressure group* to oppose the scheme. More pervasively, some form of private trust, such as the Royal Society for the Protection of Birds or the Woodland Trust may be established to deal with a general environmental externality.

Possible government action to allow for externalities

Nevertheless private arrangements often prove inadequate. Not only may the costs be exorbitant relative to the benefits to be shared, but where 'free-riders' cannot be excluded, it may be impossible to organise sufficient collective bargaining strength to negotiate effectively. In any case, costs (or benefits) are often so far-ranging e.g. the detrimental effects of exhaust fumes, that not all the losers (or beneficiaries) can be identified. Finally, uncertainty and selfishness may prevent a satisfactory solution by private action. Usually, therefore, some form of government action is necessary.

Because there are a variety of methods by which externalities can be allowed for the government can choose according to the particular case.

First, it may introduce a pricing system to bring externalities into the reckoning. For example, to deal with traffic congestion, parking-meters may be installed, with even local residents charged for reserved parking permits.

Second, taxation and subsidies may take the idea of 'charging' a stage further. Thus the rating of empty houses can be regarded as a tax imposed to offset the external costs resulting from homelessness and the overall shortage of accommodation. On the other hand, external benefits may be allowed for by subsidies, e.g. towards the costs of repairing ancient monuments and listed buildings where, because private costs of upkeep exceed private benefits, rapid deterioration and eventual demolition would otherwise result.

Third, externalities may be covered by physical controls. Most evident are the building consents required under the Town and Country Planning Acts (see below).

Fourth, externalities may be internalised by widening the area of control. The National Trust, for instance, harmonises the interests of both farmers and walkers in order to secure maximum benefits from its Lake District properties.

Fifth, the government may itself assume responsibility for providing certain goods and services. This is usual when externalities are: (a) so extensive that only government authority can adequately allow for them, e.g. providing a major airport; (b) cumulative, e.g. a slum area, vaccination against smallpox.

Externalities and the environment

The concept of externalities is central to many of the problems confronting governments today, especially those concerning the environment. Indeed, we now have to recognise that externalities are not now confined to national boundaries, e.g. acid rain, nuclear fallout from Chernobyl. It is in the context of the environment (Chapter 18) that the implementation of the methods listed above will be examined.

However, we must first consider the extent to which externalities can be incorporated into economic decision-making by quantifying them in money terms. We do this in the wider context of cost-benefit analysis (CBA).

17.3 COST–BENEFIT ANALYSIS (CBA): REASONS FOR

The allocation of resources in the public sector

In the market economy, resources are allocated through the interaction of demand and supply in the market. Prices are the signals which coordinate the wishes of consumers with the cost of supplying goods.

But market signals may be either non-existent or defective. This applies particularly to many of the goods supplied by the government, such as roads, bridges, airports, parks, amenity land, education, health services, new urban areas and housing. Not only are such goods provided free or at less than cost, but they are on such a large scale that externalities loom large.

Without firm market signals, decisions on the desirability of a project may rest mainly on subjective political considerations. For example, redistribution of income is a factor in providing free education, while egalitarian and social reasons are prominent in requiring schools to be organised on comprehensive lines.

But allocating resources largely through the ballot box has serious defects in deciding investment in many public projects. First, the one-man, one-vote principle does not weight votes according to the intensity of satisfaction gained or lost. Thus, the simple majority decision could allow two voters marginally in favour of, say, a by-pass to outvote one who would suffer considerably from it. Second, political decisions are essentially subjective. Economic efficiency in resource allocation requires that objective criteria should be used as far as possible. Third, government involvement in the economy has so increased the burden and complexity of public-sector decisions that decentralisation of decision-making is desirable.

The nature of CBA

CBA is a technique which seeks to bring greater objectivity into decision-making. It does this by identifying all the relevant benefits and costs of a particular scheme and quantifying them in money terms. This allows all the benefits and costs to be aggregated, as it were, in the form of a balance sheet upon which the ultimate decision can be made.

For example, the benefits of a new motorway would obviously include the time saved in travel, fuel economies, reduced congestion in towns through which motor traffic formerly passed, fewer road accidents and the pleasure derived by the extra motorists who could now make day trips. Against this, however, would have to be set the cost of constructing the motorway, the additional noise suffered by nearby residents, the congestion on the feeder roads, the toll of animal life and so on.

17.4 DIFFICULTIES OF CBA

However, in giving a monetary value to such benefits and costs, we run up against both theoretical and practical difficulties.

First, there is likely to be some form of income redistribution. Thus those who suffer from the noise of the traffic on the by-pass, lose; the motorists and lorry drivers who save travelling time, gain. Only if the losers can be fully compensated by the gainers can we be satisfied that there has been no loss of satisfaction. But can we identify all those who are adversely affected by noise, and the extent of the noise on them? This difficulty of identification occurs frequently e.g. the countrylovers who lose pleasure through electricity pylons intruding on the landscape. This means that compensation is not actually paid.

Second, even if market prices are available, they may not, through indirect taxes, subsidies, imperfect competition or government price control reflect true opportunity costs. It is impossible, therefore, to achieve consistency in making adjustments.

Third, if no charges are made for the use of the by-pass, how do we know the possible value of the benefits received? The number of motorists likely to use the road can be estimated, but how do we value the journey each makes, since some are travelling on business and others on leisure pursuits? Similarly with the reduction in accidents; we can estimate the saving to the hospital service, in police time, etc., but how do we value the physical suffering avoided? And the by-pass may result in fewer deaths: what price do we put on the saving of human life? Similar problems arise in valuing such intangibles as noise, traffic congestion and the toll of animal life. It may be possible to obtain a price by analogy, e.g. the fall in the value of houses resulting from the noise, and the life-span earning-power of people dying in accidents, but no such calculation can be completely satisfactory.

Fourth, when estimating spillover costs and benefits which are not priced in the market, e.g. noise and human life, should we attach the same importance to them as for actual market prices when drawing up the balance sheet? Errors in such estimates, especially when 'shadow prices' form a large proportion of the balance sheet, could affect the viability of a project.

Fifth, there is the problem of deciding the cut-off point for externalities and the 'time horizon' for the benefits and costs to be included. The viability of a project could rest on these, and there is always the temptation for interested parties to extend the cut-off point or the time horizon in order to justify particular preferences.

Finally, in order to compare competing projects, we have to reduce them to present values by discounting future costs and benefits. But there are many different rates of interest to choose from, e.g. the rate at which the government can borrow, the rate for firms, the current rate determined largely by short-term monetary considerations. If there is less risk in a public project than in a private one, the lower government borrowing rate could be used. This lower rate is also supported by the fact that the government must consider the needs of future generations. Thus the social time preference rate is lower than the market rate since the latter is influenced by the limited time preferences of individuals.

17.5   AN ASSESSMENT OF THE ROLE OF CBA

Limitations of CBA

The theoretical and practical difficulties outlined above weaken CBA's effectiveness as a tool for decision-making. But its use is further limited by other considerations.

In particular, CBA cannot be used where political decisions dominate. For instance, local authority housing may be provided in areas of high land values, e.g. Hampstead, in order to achieve a 'social mix'. While social factors can be identified, it is almost impossible to measure them satisfactorily.

Moreover, it may be difficult to apply CBA to certain decisions. Consider, for instance, a local authority which is spending £9 million on swimming facilities. The decision rests between: (i) one swimming-bath of Olympic standards which, while it could be used for local people, would also bring prestige to the town; (ii) three smaller swimming-baths, each capable of providing training facilities and holding galas; and (iii) six very small baths specifically designed to teach children to swim. The advantages of each are largely immeasurable by CBA since they embrace so many intangibles. As a result councillors decide subjectively (perhaps on political lines) at a council meeting.

Nor can a firm CBA decision be taken for a project which involves irreversible decisions, such as the survival of a species of animal or plant, since it is impossible to estimate the current cost of a decision which would deny future generations the opportunity to choose.

Conclusion

CBA provides a rational technique for appraising projects where market information is either non-existent or deficient. But it must not make false claims for objectivity by dealing in precise sums. While it is an aid to decision-making, it is not a substitute for it. Its role is to present systematically all the information relevant to a decision, indicating the weight which can be placed on the accuracy of the calculations submitted. Drawing up such an agenda ensures that the claims of rival pressure groups are assessed and that all the relevant issues are fully debated before the ultimate political decision is taken.

CHAPTER SUMMARY

- Externalities are 'spill-over' effects (both costs and benefits) which are not taken account of by the market.
- The price system can respond to externalities but where they are wide-ranging some form of government action (such as taxation or subsidies) will be required to account for them.
- Cost-benefit analysis tries to identify and value all of the relevant private and social costs and benefits of an investment proposal. There are many practical difficulties in doing this, however, including assigning values or 'shadow prices' to non-market goods and services.

REVIEW QUESTIONS

- Identify possible externalities (both positive and negative) from a proposal to quarry limestone from a site within the Peak District National Park.
- Give five examples of ways in which the government can allow for externalities.
- Describe the process of cost-benefit analysis.
- What are the main limitations of cost-benefit analysis?

 Visit the companion website for further questions

CHAPTER 18

THE ENVIRONMENT: CONSERVATION, POLLUTION AND ROAD TRAFFIC

LEARNING OBJECTIVES

After studying this chapter you should be able to:
- explain why the natural environment is an economic good;
- illustrate the problems associated with over-exploitation of a renewable resource;
- describe methods that can be used to preserve historic buildings;
- explain the economics of pollution and the policies that can be applied to deal with it;
- describe the nature of urban traffic problems and analyse possible solutions.

18.1 INTRODUCTION

The environment as an economic good

The term 'environment' extends our earlier concept of land (p. 76) to include the sea and the atmosphere. As such it provides:

(a) materials (such as soil, minerals and timber) and energy (from fossil fuels, tides and wind);
(b) space, on which to produce food (including fish), erect buildings, develop communications and facilitate sporting activities;
(c) the 'natural world', a consumer good in that it affords utility directly for walking, holidays, safaris, nature study or just contentment from peaceful surroundings;
(d) a 'sink' for waste products.

In essence, the natural environment is 'nature's capital' or 'natural infrastructure' providing a flow of goods and services. As such it is an economic good. First, because natural resources are finite, it is 'scarce'. K. Boulding, an American Professor, likens the earth to a spaceship which, apart from receiving continuous

211

energy from the sun, is a closed system where those on board have initially a stock of food and water resources which, because they cannot be added to, must not be wasted, but recycled. Second, the natural environment can be put to *competing* alternative uses. We cannot, for instance, enjoy clean holiday beaches if there is no restriction on ships emptying their oil bilges into the sea. Third, such resources as tropical rain forests, ancient woodland, fossil fuels, historical buildings and species of flora and fauna can be lost for ever as man seeks to produce more food, manufactured goods, buildings, roads and airports. Indeed, the dumping of waste products, such as nuclear waste, cadmium and sulphurous gases can even threaten man's very existence.

18.2 CONSERVATION

The nature of conservation

With the exception of the special case of protecting an irreplaceable resource conservation is not simply preservation. Instead it seeks *creative continuity* by promoting vitality of use of the environment while ensuring that change is sympathetic to the quality of life for both present and future generations. Thus, in the UK, conservation embraces a wide field – green belts around towns, national parks, public bridle-ways and footpaths, animal, fish, butterfly protection, Sites of Special Scientific Interest, National Trust property, mineral and oil reserves, museums, buildings of special architectural and historical interest, and so on.

Certain aspects of conservation need emphasising. First, as mentioned above, there is an *opportunity cost* of a better environment. A 'green belt', for instance, keeps land in agriculture at a lower current market value than, say, housing, and also extends the journey to work of those city workers who live beyond it.

Second, externalities loom large. A farmer who rips out a hedge does so because a larger field will cost less to work. The owner of an old Georgian building may wish to demolish and rebuild with a block of flats in order to maximise his gain over cost. Both, however, are considering only their private costs and benefits. Yet there may be other costs in *lost* external benefits, e.g. for nature lovers and walkers who prefer the patchwork landscape of small fields, or for passers-by for whom a Georgian building has an aesthetic appeal.

Third, conservation is concerned with changes over time in both demand and supply. Individuals may have a restricted time horizon resulting in inadequate conservation of existing resources. In essence conservation is synonymous with the optimum use of resources over time and therefore reflects many of the problems concerned with investment in general. But, largely on account of the distant time horizon involved and its far-reaching effects on the community at large, there are special aspects of conservation which make it unsuitable to be left entirely to market forces – estimating future demand, allowing for externalities, preserving stocks of renewable resources, the impossibility of reversing wrong decisions.

The role of economics

Since economics is concerned with the allocation of scarce resources between alternative uses, we have to ask what contribution it can make towards solving problems of the environment, such as those of conservation, pollution and traffic congestion especially in city centres.

First, it can identify the major economic aspects. With conservation, for instance, it highlights the link between a rising standard of living and the increasing demand of future generations for open spaces and buildings of historical interest. For both conservation and pollution it can define sustainable growth. Second, it can indicate how externalities can be measured by CBA, thereby giving substance to the claims of rival pressure groups and producers' interests. Third, it can suggest appropriate measures, especially those that can operate through the market.

Fourth, it should draw attention to the limitations of economic policy, especially as regards the cultural and moral aspects. For instance, should it be left to the market to decide where a plant for processing poisonous substances is located? Local people may be so poor that they require the employment opportunities it can provide. Thus their economic weakness may force them to accept the accompanying health hazard.

The indivisibility of the environment

Although in what follows the environment is discussed under the headings of 'conservation', 'pollution' and 'traffic', it must be emphasised that the problems are interlocking. Woodlands and forests may be conserved because of their richness in trees and flowers or because of their historical uniqueness. Yet their very existence fulfils the further function of absorbing the emissions of CO_2 from cars and power stations and releasing oxygen. In other words, they are recycling waste and helping to prevent global warming.

Conservation of stocks

Using a resource in excess of its capacity to reproduce itself eventually reduces supply to the point where its price rises. This increasing opportunity cost produces a contraction of demand and a search for substitutes. Such market responses help to conserve non-renewable stocks, such as fossil fuels and minerals.

Some environmental resources, e.g. fish, whales, grouse, are renewable, but only if the contraction in demand occurs soon enough to leave a stock which does not fall below the minimum necessary for recovery. Conservation here has to be concerned with limiting what is harvested in order to maintain a stable stock.

However, some resources are not only non-renewable but, if lost, irreplaceable, e.g. an historic building, ancient woodland, species of animals, birds, insects and flowers on the verge of extinction. Once they disappear, they are lost for ever. This is a special case of conservation for here the over-riding objective is preservation.

In order to illustrate how economic analysis may assist in both forms of conservation, we take two examples – maintaining fish stocks and preserving an historic building.

18.3   MAINTAINING STOCKS OF FISH

The function of private property rights

Overfishing means that over a period catches are so large that they exceed the rate of growth of the stock, which therefore declines in size. This could be a cumulative process resulting in the progressive shrinking of safe catches.

The basic reason for the failure to conserve the stock is the absence of private property rights over the fishing grounds. As a result, no one fisherman will voluntarily limit his catch, because that simply means that others can catch more.

Overfishing

We assume:

(a)   the price of fish is constant;
(b)   as the size of the catch increases beyond a certain level, the stock of fish declines because the catch exceeds the rate of fish renewal;
(c)   the marginal productivity of effort falls as the stock of fish falls (shown by the declining slope of the total revenue curve);
(d)   the marginal cost of effort is constant.

If there were individual property rights over the fishing grounds – only with shellfish would this be possible – the owner would fix an annual catch which maximised profit. In Figure 18.1 this would be OS where TR – TC is at a maximum. For the sake of simplicity we will assume that this catch equals the renewal rate of the present stock; it is the sustainable catch. But up to OP supernormal profit can still be made. Competition between boats would eliminate this by pushing the catch to OP. This represents gross overfishing for the sustainable stock is only OS.

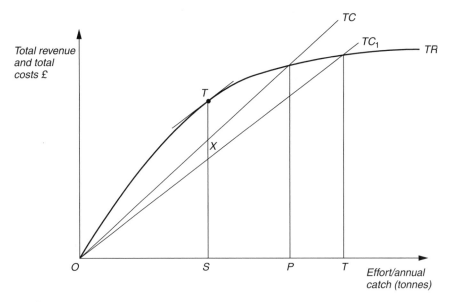

Figure 18.1   Overfishing

It should be noted that larger ships and new techniques will lower costs, e.g. TC to TC_1. This will have the effect of increasing the catch size to OT, thereby aggravating the problem of maintaining the stock.

Methods of controlling overfishing

On our simplifying assumptions, overfishing occurs between S and P. To maintain the stock the annual catch has to be restricted to OS. Possible ways in which this can be achieved are:

(1)   *Vesting fishing rights in a single body* which owns the fishing boats. Thus Iceland took the first step in this direction by confining fishing within 200 miles of its coast to Icelandic vessels. But this only goes a part of the way. Unless the Icelandic government also owns the fishing fleet, there must be some further control over the catch.

(2)   *Imposing such physical controls* as: restricting the number of vessels by licence; enlarging the net mesh to ensure only mature fish of a certain size are taken; requiring each boat to stay in harbour for so many days a year.

The difficulty with most physical controls is enforcement. They are also resented by the fishermen since some suffer a loss of livelihood as marginal boats are forced out of the industry.

(3)   *Taxing catches at so much a tonne* is administratively easier. In Figure 18.1 the tax would have to yield TX. Such a tax is also flexible in that different rates

of tax can be applied to different types of fish according to their relative scarcity.

(4) *Introducing quotas* for each ship, which in total will allow an aggregate catch of OS. Since abnormal profit can be made by those fishing, these quotas could be sold to cover the administrative costs. Once in existence, quotas can be traded on a 'quota market' (see p. 223).

(5) *Establishing no-fishing areas.* Fish can thrive in such areas to the point where stocks are replenished and then move out in search of food to areas where they can be caught. With the use of satellite technology and global positioning systems, fishing boats can be monitored to ensure that they do not stray into the no-fishing zones.

18.4 PRESERVING AN HISTORIC BUILDING

Where a building of historical importance, e.g. an Elizabethan manor house, has outlived its usefulness as a residence, conservation has to take into account the irreversibility of a decision to demolish it. Moreover, while demolition may be the current market solution, it could be based on defective criteria, e.g. in estimating future demand and in choosing the appropriate discount rate for arriving at present values. Consider the following example.

The market solution

The historic building (which we will assume is a house in the centre of town) will be demolished when the site can be put to a more 'profitable' use. This necessitates calculating its present capital value, obtained by totalling the discounted flow of net benefits expected in the future. It is likely that, ignoring inflation, the value of the house will fall over time as it becomes increasingly unsuitable for modern living requirements. This is shown by the curve *PP* (Figure 18.2).

In contrast, the capital value of a new office block (*RR*) will eventually be such that, even allowing for the cost of rebuilding, the cleared site is worth more than the historic house. If left to market forces, therefore, demolition of the historic house occurs in year D.

Possible weaknesses of the market solution

On what grounds may *economics* justify interference with this market solution?

First, it is unlikely that the curve *PP* reflects the true opportunity cost of the historic house at any one time. For one thing, certain benefits are likely to have been ignored.

Apart from *external benefits* (such as the pleasure which the view of a historic house gives to passers-by), we should recognise the existence of an 'option

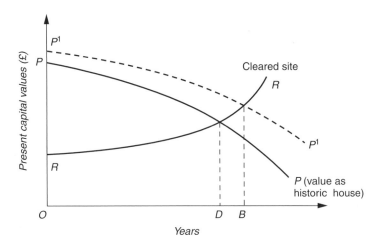

Figure 18.2 Adjustments to the present value of a historic building for different uses

demand'. Where decisions are irreversible (as with the destruction of a historic building), many people would pay something just to postpone such a decision. The difficulty lies in quantifying such 'option demand', but its existence is evident in the fact that many people subscribe voluntarily to the National Trust and the Worldwide Fund for Nature, for example. The rest enjoy the option as 'free riders', but their demand should also be included.

Furthermore, because the rate of social time preference is lower than that of private time preference (see p. 208), a present capital value derived from the lower rate of discount appropriate to the social time preference would be higher than one based on a rate of discount which merely reflected *private* time preference.

These additional benefits and the lower discount rate would give the historic house a higher capital value curve, $P^1 P^1$, with demolition being postponed until year B.

Second, and even more important, we have to recognise that, when dealing with the future, knowledge is not perfect. Thus a decision to demolish a building may be based on a defective assessment of the future conditions of demand and supply. This is not serious when we are dealing with *flows*, such as the services provided by offices, since new offices can always be built if demand increases in the future. But demolishing a historic building diminishes a stock which cannot be replaced.

Government policy for preserving historic buildings

The above analysis suggests that the government must intervene in the free operation of the price system in order to preserve historic buildings. Its action can take a variety of forms.

First, the building could be brought under public ownership. Such a policy would usually be followed where the cost of excluding free-riders would be prohibitive, e.g. Hadrian's Wall. Equally important, it would allow welfare to be maximised (see p. 235). Finally, public ownership would automatically allow external benefits to be internalised.

Second, the historic building could be left in private ownership but a subsidy given through repair grants or tax concessions on the grounds of the external benefits conferred. Such a subsidy would increase net benefits to the owner and so raise the present value. However, there are difficulties. Many external benefits cannot be quantified while shortage of funds could mean that the subsidy was insufficient to raise the present-use value curve permanently above the cleared-site curve so that demolition is only postponed to year B, unless other action is taken.

Third, any building of special architectural or historic interest may be 'listed'. This means that it cannot be altered or demolished without the consent of the local planning authority. While this gives protection against positive acts of demolition, it may not cover destruction by the neglect of the owner. Such neglect occurs because high maintenance costs result in negative net benefits. Even though in such circumstances the local authority can appropriate the building, there is reluctance to do so since the cost of maintenance now falls on public funds. Thus, in practice, 'listing' in year D may be only a 'stop-gap' measure, bridging the years between D and B (Figure 18.2) until increasing demand raises the value of the historic building above that of the cleared site. More frequently, 'listing' simply imposes a prohibition on demolition until an alternative policy can be formulated.

Fourth, giving permission for the building to be adapted to a more profitable use provides such a policy. Thus stables may be converted into a dwelling, and houses into offices. This has the effect of increasing net benefits and thus raising the present value curve so that it is above the cleared-site curve.

In consenting to a change of use of a historic building, the objective of the authorities must be to retain as many of the original features as possible. Thus some flexibility of building regulations is necessary, for example, as regards height of rooms, window space and even fire precautions. The distinctive character of the converted building may produce increasing rentals over time, e.g. for prestige reasons, so that not only is it preserved but there is no charge on public funds.

18.5 POLLUTION

Aspects of pollution

Pollution occurs when man introduces waste matter into the environment directly or indirectly causing damage to persons (or wildlife) other than himself.

While residual waste is created in consumption (e.g. household waste, scrapped consumer durables, litter), it is pollution resulting from production which is more serious (e.g. acid rain, smoke, gases, toxic chemicals, pesticide contaminants, liquid effluents, noise, oil spillages) for it affects the whole of the environment – land, sea and the atmosphere. It is harmful to human health, e.g. through carbon monoxide fumes; to agriculture, e.g. resulting in lower yields or poorer quality; to buildings, e.g. in corrosion of stonework; to amenity, e.g. causing damage to fish, fauna and flora; and to the life of the whole planet through the 'greenhouse' effect produced by carbon dioxide discharged into the atmosphere.

It is the rapid increase over the last century in population and economic growth, with its accompanying industrialisation, that has given rise to pollution. What is new, however, is the recognition of the *problem* of pollution. Paradoxically, while economic growth may cause pollution, growth may be an essential prerequisite of environmental improvement. Economic poverty compels people to accept visual squalor, poor buildings and polluted watercourses. Prosperity enables us to buy a better environment. For example, the EU's excess production of foodstuffs has made it easier to switch to preserving the landscape.

Degradation of the environment: definition of pollution

Everybody can recognise evidence of pollution. The economist, however, must have a precise definition. Present-day concern is with the increasing environmental pollution resulting from both population and economic growth. Production involves unwanted residuals – smoke, poisonous chemicals and gases, noise, household waste etc. Some, such as carbon dioxide gas, can be transformed by the environment into harmless or even beneficial materials (e.g. oxygen). But this takes time, and *pollution occurs when the flow of residual emissions exceeds the natural environment's capacity to absorb them*. Indeed pollution may even reduce the environment's ability to assimilate waste.

Technology and the control of pollution

While technological developments stimulate growth, it could be that new technology will allow growth, while containing pollution. Such developments could take the form of: (a) substitute products which are more environmentally friendly, e.g. degradable containers; (b) greater efficiency in production to reduce waste; (c) on-site treatment of controlled disposal of waste, e.g. desulphurisation of gases by power stations, catalytic converters on cars; (d) the replacement of coal and oil with 'greener' sources of energy, e.g. natural gas, wind power and tidal power.

But while such technical developments are likely to occur eventually, what is 'sustainable pollution' must be assessed in the context of the current technology employed. It is here that economic analysis can contribute to a solution of the problem by suggesting and examining a range of broad options.

The economist's approach

As we have seen in previous chapters, the economist emphasises *marginal* decisions. While everybody likes clear air, pure water, a peaceful environment, clean pavements, roads free from congestion, etc., pollution abatement incurs costs. Thus the choice is not the simple one between clean air and polluted air, but between various levels of dirty air. In short, we have to apply the marginal principle and accept that level of pollution where the cost of further abatement exceeds the extra benefit which results.

Why does the market economy fail to control pollution?

In most cases pollution represents external costs. The right to peace and quiet, the right to enjoy a landscape unspoiled by electricity pylons, the right to swim from an oil-free beach are not private legal rights which can be easily enforced. Often, therefore, no *private* cost is incurred for infringing those rights. Thus in Figure 18.3 if there is no cost to a chemical manufacturer of discharging effluent into the river, he will produce chemicals up to the point *OC*. But when we take into account the poisoning of fish, the destruction of vegetation which provides a habitat for insects and birds and the overall loss of visual beauty for ramblers, such spill-over costs have to be added to private costs to obtain the aggregate social cost. This means that while *OC* is the efficient level of production for the chemical manufacturer, the *socially* efficient level of production is *OD*, because here marginal social cost equals marginal social benefit (assuming marginal private benefit equals marginal social benefit). In other words, if more than *OD* is produced there is a misallocation of resources.

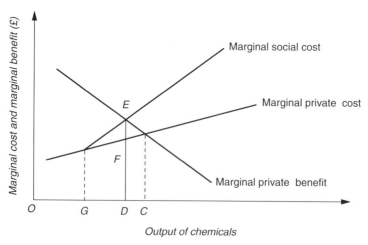

Figure 18.3   Efficient output with external costs

Policy difficulties

While this analysis of the nature of the problem is fairly straightforward, difficulties occur in devising and applying an appropriate policy.

First, although the costs of pollution control can be measured in money terms, the benefits are 'intangibles', having no price-tag since they are not traded in the market. Take as an example the chemical factory which discharges effluent into a river. While the value of the fishing rights lost can be measured by market information, the value of the loss suffered by bird-watchers and ramblers has no direct market price. This means that the technique of shadow pricing, with all its weaknesses, has to be employed (see p. 208).

Second, most economic assessments of damage are made after the pollution has occurred. But adjustments in response to such pollution may already have been made. For example, the cabbage yield in a market garden may be 20 per cent below that which could have been expected in a clean-air environment. Yet this loss would understate the damage if, in an environment originally free from smoke, more profitable tomatoes would have been grown. In practice, it is extremely difficult to ascertain and measure this 'adjustment factor'.

Third, since pollution occurs in different forms, circumstances and scale, it is necessary to apply different policies to deal with the problem.

Possible policies

1. 'Greening' public opinion

Publicity drawing people's attention to the nature of the pollution problem by the government and pressure groups, such as the Green Party and Friends of the Earth, has had a remarkable success in recent years. Households have become waste-recycling conscious and climate change has become part of everyday conversation whenever there is a prolonged spell of hot weather.

Firms have responded. Pilkington Glass, for instance, encourage managers to integrate environmental responsibility in all business decision-making, covering such matters as waste and emission reduction, recycling waste and energy saving. Similarly, B&Q, Homebase and MFI have pledged to supply only goods made with timber from sustainable forests, with the sources being monitored.

2. Setting up an environmental protection agency

Externalities arise because of non-existent, ill-defined or unenforceable private property rights. To overcome this, it may be possible to create an agency in which these property rights are vested, in effect internalising externalities in order to maximise benefits and minimise costs. For example, the Environment Agency coordinates drainage, water supply, waste disposal and angling interests.

3. Market negotiation

If a 'market' in the pollution can be established, the optimum amount of pollution can be arrived at. Suppose a garden owner wishes to burn all his rubbish at the weekend when his neighbours just want to enjoy sitting in their gardens. They could negotiate with the burner to burn at some other time, either by arrangement or at a price. In the latter case, the externality is being 'priced'.

The same principle could apply on the international scale. Brazil could be paid not to clear her equatorial rain forests, and Sweden already assists Poland in reducing acid rain, because the acid rain from Poland damages Sweden.

Usually, however, if the market is to be used to control pollution there must be incentives to avoid pollution by conserving energy or to reduce pollution by the controlled disposal of waste products.

4. Direct regulation imposing a maximum level of pollution

Here the government decides what each polluter must do to reduce pollution, and enforces it under penalty of law, e.g. environmental conditions of planning, no discharge of oil waste by ships within so many miles of the coast. Such a policy, however, provides little incentive to instal antipollution devices so that the specified standard becomes the target, involves constant inspection, and tends to impose national (sometimes international) standards instead of allowing for different local circumstances. On the other hand, the policy does allow the polluter to find the cheapest means of achieving the specified maximum.

It should be noted that rigid control is essential where: (a) pollution is a threat to existence, e.g. blue asbestos dust in workshops; and (b) pollution is cumulative and becomes dangerous at a certain level, e.g. cadmium absorption by the soil.

5. Subsidising the reduction of pollution

Where it is impossible or too costly to identify the polluters (e.g. litter louts) the government itself takes responsibility for pollution control, the cost being covered from the proceeds of taxation. Alternatively, the government may decide that specific compensation is adequate to deal with the particular pollution, especially where this is localised. Thus in clean-air zones, people are given subsidies to instal smokeless fuel appliances. On the other hand, losers may be compensated, e.g. grants to provide double glazing to reduce noise from aircraft. The difficulty is that such public schemes simply mean that polluters are passing on the cost to the taxpayer. Often, therefore, where polluters can be identified, control has to be enforced through individual penalties imposed by the courts, e.g. for dropping litter, polluting watercourses.

Alternatively, the government could seek to reduce pollution by directly subsidising: (a) the development of new techniques to reduce pollution or save energy; (b) the production of cleaner substitutes e.g. a reduced tax on unleaded petrol; or (c) the recycling of waste, e.g. bottles.

6. Taxing pollution

A charge or tax according to the level of pollution seeks to ensure that the 'polluter pays'. In terms of Figure 18.3 a tax of *EF* would induce the factory-owner to limit his production to *OD*.

Such a policy has the merit of flexibility, and is thus particularly desirable where the benefits can only be ascertained by trial and error or where the aim is to achieve a progressive reduction in pollution since charges can be adjusted accordingly. Moreover, charges have the effect of 'internalising externalities': once the tax is set, the polluter can respond to it as he chooses. Thus a profit-maximising polluter would instal his own pollution control to the point where the marginal cost of doing so was less than the tax saved. Furthermore, the proceeds of a tax can be used to compensate those losing by the residual pollution. Finally, in as much as the charge raises the price of the product, the actual consumer now pays the full opportunity cost of production – a fairer solution than passing on the external costs to society at large.

Even so, a charges policy has its limitations. First, a tax can only be imposed if the individual polluter can be identified. Second, there is the problem of *how* to tax. If it is on units of output, e.g. tonnes of nitrate fertiliser, the larger producer pays more as his pollution is likely to be greater. But this does nothing to encourage a reduction in the pollution *per unit*. If, however, the degree of pollution can be measured, e.g. the quantity of toxic waste being discharged into the river, and taxed accordingly, there would be an incentive to instal an anti-pollution device.

Second, there are distributional implications if the product whose price rises is one which is bought mainly by poor persons, though the proceeds of the tax can be used to compensate.

Third, if a country imposes a tax unilaterally, e.g. on the burning of fossil fuels, it may give an unfair advantage to its foreign competitors.

7. Tradeable permits

Suppose in Figure 18.3 that output represents the aggregate of all chemical firms on a given river. The government decides to limit pollution to *GD*. Each firm is given a licence to emit a share of *GD*. If the government wishes to raise revenue (equal, say to *EF*), it can sell or auction the licence. The essence of these pollution permits is that they can be traded on the 'permit' market. Those firms having a high cost of reducing emission will want to buy permits from the efficient firms who sell them for more than it costs them to abate.

This method provides an incentive to those who sell permits to instal equipment which reduces pollution. At the same time, it uses the market to cover much of the regulation required. One difficulty is that as firms become more abatement-efficient, the supply of permits coming on to the market will increase, and their fall in price will allow firms inefficient in pollution control to buy them. Here the government could itself buy on the market and, by confiscating permits, keep up the cost of pollution. Since the 1970s the United States Environmental Protection Agency has used an emissions trading programme with considerable success in combating air pollution. The European Union has a carbon emissions trading scheme as the cornerstone of its climate change policy.

18.6   ROAD TRAFFIC

The benefits and costs of motor transport

In the twentieth century motor transport has increased accessibility for both resources and people through the mobility, flexibility and convenience it affords. It has thus contributed to the improvement of living standards.

Unfortunately as the use of road vehicles has increased, the benefits they afford have been progressively diminished by external costs. In providing a motorway network and by passing cities and towns, inroads are made into the countryside, even on occasions intruding on areas of natural beauty or of special scientific interest.

But it is the concentration of motor traffic in urban areas which presents the major environmental problems. The greater mobility afforded by the car has enabled workers to live some distance from their place of employment and has thus been a major cause of urban sprawl. Moreover, people still have to travel from the suburbs to the city centre for work, shopping and leisure activities. Whereas traffic increases as we approach the centre, road capacity decreases. The resulting concentration of traffic imposes social costs on non-car users by exhaust-fume pollution, noise, the danger of accident, visual blight, inconvenience to pedestrians and loss of time to bus travellers. More than that, the expansion of motor transport has led to the demand for road space exceeding supply so that one road-user imposes on other road-users the extra costs of congestion – higher fuel consumption, reduced speed and time spent in traffic jams. Indeed, the problem is likely to become more acute as income and population increase and the use of cars and commercial vehicles expands.

The urban traffic problem

The major external cost is congestion, for this undermines the chief advantage – accessibility – which motor transport affords. It is necessary, therefore, to analyse the problem and to consider possible ways of dealing with it.

Two salient points should be noted. First, it is basically a peak-hour problem, confined to approximately five hours a day on fewer than 250 working days of the year. Second, it is largely the result of the increased use of the private car for journeys to work. The former tends to restrict the amount of investment which can be profitably undertaken in the transport system. The latter indicates that some effort should be directed towards making the road-user pay the full costs (including external costs) of taking his vehicle on the road.

Bearing these principles in mind, actual policy can follow six main lines:

(1) do nothing;
(2) invest in the construction of more roads;
(3) impose physical controls to improve traffic flows;
(4) restrict parking;
(5) use the price system to allocate existing road space;
(6) use the existing road system more efficiently through a better distribution of the means of travel as between the car and public transport.

(1) Do nothing

Some people argue that trying to improve movement on the roads is self-defeating: the easier it is to travel, the more people use their cars. As congestion increases, there comes a point where the cost in terms of wasted time and frustration is such that motorists switch to public transport.

But such a policy has snags. First, it provides no *incentive* for motorists to switch to public transport. There should be such an incentive, since those who do switch make travelling easier for those who do not. Second, the high level of congestion envisaged would become a permanent feature, penalising equally the essential car-users and the optional users, those for whom using public transport would impose no severe hardship. Third, the congestion would affect non-car users, such as pedestrians.

(2) Invest in more roads

The long-term solution is increased investment to improve the urban environment and the circulation of traffic. This could take the form of comprehensive redevelopment of existing city centres and improved town planning, such as siting industry away from city centres.

The main thrust, however, would be to build more roads linking the suburbs and city centre. But by-passes also play a part, in that through traffic is siphoned off.

It is doubtful, however, whether this would be a complete solution.

(a) As it is difficult to impose tolls on short-run roads, they have to be financed from taxation and made freely available to all wishing to use them. But as the amount which can be devoted to public investment in general is limited, roads have to compete with defence, health care, social welfare, the modernisation of public transport, and so on. Yet, without direct pricing of road use, there is no precise indication of what people are prepared to pay for more roads and therefore no firm basis for comparing the rate of return with that of alternative capital projects (though CBA may help). Thus there is no answer to the basic question of whether vast investment in new urban road systems is economically viable, bearing in mind that it is largely to provide only for peak-hour travel between the suburbs and the city centre.

(b)   Investment in roads, as opposed to extending public transport, involves an income redistribution, since public transport is used mainly by poorer persons. The result is that the decision on whether to invest in more roads is eventually a political one and pressure groups in favour may be successful in spite of the very high cost of urban road construction.

(c)   It would take many years for a complete road network to be built. In the meantime, movements in industry and population and transport developments could change needs considerably.This factor largely accounts for the wide discrepancies between forecasts and actual flows, as in the case of the M25 or the M6.

(d)   The demand for road space seems to respond to supply, with better roads generating more motor transport. Demand and supply, therefore, are never in equilibrium. This was recognised in 1994 when the government announced a major curtailment of its road-building programme.

This means that we are always faced with a short-term situation of making the best possible use of existing road-space, as follows.

(3) Manage traffic flows

Some immediate improvement in traffic flows can be achieved by clearways, reversible lanes, linked traffic signals, bus lanes, miniroundabouts, etc. Such adaptation can often be combined with schemes which improve the environment e.g. designating pedestrian-only areas, constructing culs-de-sac in residential districts or simply restricting the movement of heavy vehicles in residential zones.

In the longer term attempts can be made to spread the flow of rush-hour traffic over a longer period (e.g. by staggering working hours) or to reverse the flow (e.g. by encouraging offices to locate in the suburbs and the building of out-of-town shopping centres). Nevertheless care must be taken to ensure that the commercial heart of the city is not destroyed as a result. This latter consideration has led to government discouragement of further out-of-town shopping developments.

It must be noted, however, that traffic management can only increase the capacity of the road network when the initial *pattern* of movement is sub-optimal. Even then it only provides a short-term relief from congestion since, unless entry is restrained, improving the traffic flow eventually generates additional traffic.

(4) Restrict parking

Perhaps the greatest advantage of the motor vehicle is the convenience of door-to-door travel. This needs parking facilities. These contribute to accessibility and – by increasing catchment areas – to the prosperity of shopping and business centres. Yet, paradoxically, too many facilities lead to congestion, and so an appropriate balance between parking and movement has to be sought. Indeed the old Greater London Council proposed taxing each private office parking space provided, in order to divert commuters to public transport.

Parkers are of two sorts: the 'long-term' parker (the commuter) and the 'short-term' parker (the shopper and the business visitor). The problem is largely one of removing the 'long-term' parker from the streets, so that there will be sufficient accommodation for 'short-term' parkers to pursue their shopping or business activities. Two approaches are possible: physical control and road pricing. Both involve costs of adequate administration.

Physical controls take various forms, from the restriction of parking to certain days, time, side of street or type of vehicle (such as taxis only) to the complete prohibition of all kinds of waiting, including the loading and unloading of commercial vehicles. Permits may also be issued to give priority to essential users and residents. Furthermore, planning consents for new buildings usually stipulate the minimum number of parking spaces to be provided.

While physical controls are unrelated to ability to pay, they lack the subtlety of the price mechanism's rationing function. Where parking is possible, charges can be imposed to bring demand into line with the limited number of spaces available. In order that street parking should be confined to short-term parkers, it is usually linked with the physical control of limiting the time which can be spent at any one bay.

Kerbside parking has to be supplemented by off-street parking, especially for the long-term commuter. Since the cost of this is high, it is more likely to be provided where meter charges are also high. Local-authority car parks are mostly hardstands and tend to be for short-term parkers only. Multistorey and underground garages are expensive to build. Since demand drops off at night, they are largely dependent financially on there being sufficient day-time parkers to pay the relatively high charges. If these, however, induce commuters to travel by public transport, there is a net benefit to the community through reduced congestion and less cost of road construction. This would justify any shortfall in revenue being underwritten by the local authority.

The provision of cheaper parking for shoppers and other short-term parkers has also to be considered, especially in the light of current government policy of protecting the vitality of city centres by restricting new out-of-town shopping developments. But without massive local authority subsidy, such parking cannot be provided in the city centre. This suggests that 'park and ride' arrangements will have to be the preferred solution.

(5) Use the price system to allocate scarce road space

The principle of allocating limited parking space by charges can also be applied to moving vehicles by imposing a tax to reduce the use of vehicles and so relieve congestion.

In addition to his running costs, the private motorist allows for the time his journey will take. The greater the traffic flow, the longer this time. There is thus a rising cost curve, *MPC* (Figure 18.4). The demand curve, *D*, also takes account of this time factor: the greater the congestion, the longer the time journey, so that demand falls as the intensity of traffic-flow increases. Thus, left to the private motorists' decisions, the flow of traffic will be *OP*, where private marginal cost equals marginal benefit (price).

But while the private motorist allows for the time-cost of a heavy traffic-flow, the very fact of his taking his car on the road will add to the time-cost of others. Congestion can be defined as occurring when the private use of his car by a motorist 'impedes' the movement of other road-users, that is, at *OC* (Figure 18.4). There is a marginal social cost which, if added to the marginal private cost, gives the curve *MSC*. Applying the principle that output should take place where marginal social benefit equals marginal social cost the economically efficient flow of traffic would be *OS*.

This could be achieved by imposing a charge equal to *LM*. Ideally such a charge should reflect the time, miles covered on the road, the degree of congestion, the size of car and the location and direction of the journey in relation to the city centre. The difficulty lies in devising a single tax which covers all these requirements and is practical.

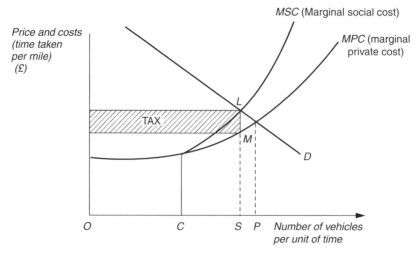

Figure 18.4 Allowing for the external cost of congestion

Imposing tolls on certain roads discriminates against the essential motorist, especially where no suitable alternative route is available. A high motor vehicle licence, by raising fixed costs, simply penalises car ownership rather than congestion costs. A petrol tax reflects only mileage and size of car, and is thus unfair to the country-dweller. Requiring the motorist to buy a permit to enter a congested area does not take account of the degree of congestion or the extent of use within the congested area. The London congestion charge, introduced in 2003, is a fee for some motorists entering the central London area.

The most appropriate method of charging is to fit each car with a meter which would electronically register 'units' as certain control points were passed. These control points could be located more closely to each other as the city centre was approached, and the number of units could be varied according to the time of day.

Some economists consider that an additional advantage of such road-pricing is that it would establish 'road values' and thus rates of return to guide future road investment. But metering faces difficulties.

(a) Though it is economically valid and technically possible, it is only practical if the cost of installation, the periodic reading of the meter and the payment of charges are accepted by the motorist. The costs of administration and enforcement could be high.

(b) Since this meter does not catch the parker, there would have to be additional parking charges.

(c) It raises a distributional problem in that the wealthier motorist would be able to travel on the now uncongested roads, while the poorer *non*-motorist would enjoy better public transport. The relatively-low-income motorist, who would now have to resort to public transport, would lose most. But why should the price mechanism be unacceptable on account of income differences in the road price market and not elsewhere in the economy?

(d) Unless *MC* pricing is imposed in all sectors of the economy and, in particular, on all modes of transport, an optimal allocation of road use will not be achieved.

(e) It has to be decided how the tax yield should be disposed of. Returning it to motorists would simply increase their income so that they could reclaim the road-use they have given up.

(6) Pricing policies to improve the split between the private car and public transport

We have to consider the respective merits of the private car and public transport from both the demand and supply sides.

On the demand side, the car affords a convenient door-to-door means of transport and, in comparison with public transport, is comfortable. Even traffic jams can be made tolerable by listening to the radio or cassette player. In contrast, public transport may be irregular and incur the discomfort of standing. Its great merit is speed, especially with rail travel for the long-distance commuter. Moreover, the method of charging for car travel as opposed to public transport favours the former. Much of the car's costs are fixed costs – the initial purchase price, the motor vehicle tax, insurance, and so on. The cost of actually using the car – the variable cost – is the cost of fuel and wear and tear (though motorists are inclined to ignore the latter). Thus the private motorist adopts a marginal-cost basis of pricing.

In contrast, apart from any subsidies given, fares on public transport have to cover both fixed and variable costs; that is, the fare per mile tends to equal *average total cost*. The price system cannot yield an efficient allocation of resources between private and public transport when different principles are adopted as the basis of pricing.

Moreover, since fixed costs, particularly for the railways, are high, public transport tends to operate under conditions of decreasing cost. This means that the principle of marginal-cost pricing cannot be used if total costs are to be covered (Figure 18.5). Instead public transport seeks to cover total costs by price discrimination, charging higher fares to passengers whose demand is least elastic. Such passengers tend to be commuters and business people – and higher fares simply induce them to switch to travelling by car. The alternative is to make good the shortfall by government subsidy.

On the supply side, consideration has to be given to the respective cost patterns of the car and public transport. Figure 18.6 shows that when a relatively small number of passengers have to be coped with, the car has a cost advantage. Since the initial fixed costs to put a car on the road are so small compared with the bus and train, for exposition purposes average cost per passenger can be regarded as constant.

However, as the number of passengers increases, the higher fixed costs of the bus are spread more thinly, so that eventually at *OB* average cost per passenger

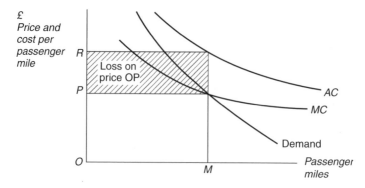

Figure 18.5   The effect of high fixed cost on public transport

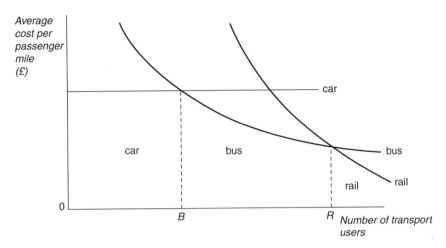

Figure 18.6 Difference in average costs per passenger mile of car, bus and rail transport

mile falls below that of the car. Rail transport has to incur even higher fixed costs in maintaining tracks, stations, expensive rolling stock, and so on, and so costs per passenger mile are only below those of the bus at a high level of passenger use, *OR*. In addition, development density should be high so that the number travelling from a single station is large. Hence urban rail travel is limited to very large cities.

One further point should be noted: the bus is more flexible in use than the train both in routeing and in dealing with small variations in the number of passengers. In its turn, the car is more flexible than the bus, especially for cross-commuting to employment in suburban offices, and so on.

It must again be emphasised that while the bus and train have a *cost* advantage over the car in dealing with passenger-users above *OB* and *OR* respectively, relative prices for each mode of travel will also depend upon demand. It may be that people's preference for car travel is so high its price would indicate that this mode should prevail even when the number of transport-users is high.

A policy for traffic congestion

The above analysis suggests that on *cost* considerations rush-hour travel is most economically provided by public transport, since this follows the predominantly radial flow to the centre and causes less congestion per passenger carried than the private car.

The logical first step, therefore, would be to tax the private car-user as described earlier. This tax, supplemented by funds from general taxation, could be used to subsidise public transport. The subsidy would:

(i)   enable public transport to cover its fixed costs;
(ii) recognise the 'fall-back' or 'option' benefit which everybody enjoys simply from there being available public transport facilities;
(iii) reward public transport users for the external benefits conferred by not increasing road congestion and other environmental costs, and
(iv) redistribute income in favour of the poorer sections of the community who are most dependent on public transport.

In addition, price discrimination could be introduced into the fare structure to allow for differences in the time and direction of travel so that passengers travelling in the direction of the traffic flow during the rush hours pay more.

But there are difficulties. First, the policy is dependent upon the extent to which travellers would respond to the change in relative prices and switch to public transport. People seem wedded to their cars, and public transport is regarded as an inferior good. In other words, there is a low price-elasticity of demand for the private car and a high income-elasticity of demand. Indeed, it can be argued that the decline in the use of public transport is a result more of inconvenience and discomfort (such as draughty bus-stops and overcrowding) than of cost. If this is so, in fairly affluent societies, more convenient and better transport even at *higher* prices would. attract more customers than cheaper transport of the traditional type.

Second, the efficiency and equity of public transport subsidies have to be considered. If one aim is to make public transport cheaper for poor persons, then some form of income supplement would be more efficient. Further-more, a subsidy financed by general taxation is unfair to the person who does not use public transport.

Conclusions

There are many approaches to the traffic problem and considerable controversy as to the most appropriate 'mix' of policies. A system which relies on any *one* mode of transport, or on one single approach, is unlikely to be satisfactory. There is a need for facilities which permit all types of transport: walking, cycling (through the provision of cycle tracks or lanes), car, minibus, bus and rail transport.

The cost of providing new roads to cater for the increasing number of private motorists may be such that some form of congestion tax may have to be imposed. But eventually an integrated city system could be introduced, with some flexibility to allow for individual preferences. The car would be used to get people from places where demand was insufficient to justify the fixed costs of providing public transport. Such people would be taken to collecting points from which they could transfer to public transport, as with 'park and ride.' In the absence of adjustments through the price system, methods of diverting travellers to public transport will have to be effected by physical controls, such as banning cars and goods vehicles from certain areas, extending and enforcing rigorously parking restrictions and creating bus lanes. In the long term, large cities may find that the solution to their traffic problems lies in building new underground railways.

Finally, the traffic problem cannot be solved in isolation from the location of urban activities. In the long run, one of the most effective ways of dealing with it may be to reduce the need for travel by so organising cities that work-places and residences are nearer each other or by embracing the revolution in information technology so that many more people can work from home.

18.7 CONCLUDING OBSERVATIONS

In suggesting measures to protect the environment, the economist is bound by certain fundamental considerations.

First, it has to be recognised that the market usually fails to allow fully for externalities. Indeed external costs may be increased by the extension of the market. Thus one of the reasons why Britain has lost 50 per cent of her ancient woodland over the last fifty years is that it is no longer profitable to retain them as a source of timber. Their oak and ash cannot compete with the cheaper, hardwoods imported from countries who are destroying their own rainforests!

Second, the environment is indivisible, and piecemeal 'micro' solutions may be inadequate for dealing with the delicate balance of the ecological system. For example, it was found that putting lime into lakes to counter act the effect of acid rain did restore the trout. But the lime, by damaging bog and moorland plants, harmed the insects and thus the birds, such as the golden plover, which fed on them. Even more important, adding lime merely distracts attention from the fundamental problem – acid rain.

Third, a 'sustainable earth' requires international agreement to deal with pollution e.g. from 'greenhouse' gases, acid rain and nuclear fallout. Unfortunately national interests intrude, usually for economic reasons, e.g. the USA's low tax on petrol, or Japan's whaling. It really needs a United Nations organisation to be established as an 'environment protection agency'. Since it is the richest nations who have the greatest interest in preserving the environment, they should provide funds which can be used in different ways to compensate the adversely-affected poorer countries, e.g. by leasing the Serengeti from Tanzania to ensure that its unique ecosystem is preserved.

CHAPTER SUMMARY

- Economics can provide solutions to environmental problems such as resource depletion, pollution and traffic congestion.
- Overfishing is likely in most deep sea fishing grounds because of the absence of property rights and the resultant open access to the fishing.
- Pollution is a negative externality arising from economic activity.
- Traffic congestion is a negative externality which is largely the result of the increased use of private cars for the journey to work.
- Economics can provide the tools to analyse these environmental problems in order to find the most efficient solutions to them.

REVIEW QUESTIONS

- What services does the natural environment provide?
- Why is overfishing a common problem?
- Illustrate the case for preserving a historic building.
- Explain why pollution occurs in a market economy.
- How can the price system be used to reduce urban traffic congestion?

 Visit the companion website for further questions

19 THE PROVISION OF GOODS AND SERVICES BY THE PUBLIC SECTOR

LEARNING OBJECTIVES

After studying this chapter you should be able to:
- explain why the government becomes involved in the provision of goods and services;
- identify the problems that can arise with public sector provision;
- describe pricing policies for publicly provided goods and services;
- explain the reasons for, and the difficulties of, privatisation in the UK.

19.1 THE CASE FOR PUBLIC SECTOR PROVISION

Community goods

In competitive markets: (a) the individual has to pay a price (the opportunity cost) in order to benefit from the consumption of a good; (b) the more the individual consumes, the less is available for others.

But as noted earlier (p. 167) with some goods these conditions do not hold, and so the government itself has to undertake the provision of such goods.

With *community goods*, e.g. defence, police, street lighting, flood control, there is indivisibility in that there must be a complete supply or none at all. Above all, 'free-riders' cannot be excluded. This *'non-excludability'* means that individuals cannot be charged a price on the basis of use.

Collective goods

In practice the government often provides *collective goods*, such as parks, beaches, motorways, bridges and drainage, which, although indivisible differ from community goods in that it is possible be exclude 'free-riders' by levying fees, charges or tolls. One reason for not doing so is that the costs of collection are regarded as being disproportionate to the revenue raised. A more fundamental reason is that with most indivisible goods, the use by one extra person does not impose a sacrifice on others since there is no addition to the cost of provision. This 'non-rivalry' means that, because MC is nil, the maximum benefits can only be enjoyed if no charge is made (MC = MR = O), the full cost being met by the State from taxation.

Merit goods

Merit goods, such as education and health care, are provided by the State because it is felt that they would be inadequately consumed (either through lack of income or simply spending preferences) if left entirely to market forces. Undesirable external costs, such as an untrained or physically poor labour force, could result. In subsidising the consumption of such goods, the government redistributes income and so makes a subjective judgment.

Other economic reasons for State provision are: the need to embrace widespread external costs and benefits, e.g. urban renewal, a new airport; an exceptionally large initial capital requirement, e.g. new town development, nuclear energy, Airbus.

Problems of public provision

Public provision of goods and services gives rise to its own particular problems. These concern:

(a) reconciling the principles of accountability and economic efficiency;
(b) assessing 'needs';
(c) a pricing policy if charges can be made;
(d) the pros and cons of possible privatisation.

We shall consider each in turn.

19.2 ACCOUNTABILITY V. ECONOMIC EFFICIENCY

Even after it has been decided that the State should provide goods and services, consideration has still to be given to two fundamental principles which pull in opposite directions.

The first, *'public accountability'*, arises because the citizen requires some assurance that powers granted to the State to produce goods and services are not abused by authoritarianism, inefficiency or monopolistic exploitation.

The second principle is *'economic efficiency'*. The difficulty is that, by insisting on strict public accountability, we may so tie the hands of those running the state services that they cannot operate efficiently, e.g. by parliamentary questions on day-to-day operations and restrictive Treasury control of finance.

The *government department* form of organisation achieves a high degree of public accountability through ministerial responsibility, parliamentary questioning and Treasury control of finance. But such accountability can undermine economic efficiency. Thus the *government department* is most appropriate for dealing with community and public goods which are of national importance and where local differences in the standard of provision would be unacceptable, e.g. defence, trunk roads, health care. Their cost is covered, therefore, by taxation.

Because the strict accountability of the government department form of organisation may conflict with economic efficiency, the *nationalised industries* were organised as *public corporations*. The minister concerned exercised control over their broad policies, but not their day-to-day operations. They were fairly free to choose their own pricing policies but had to submit an annual report to Parliament. Thus some accountability was sacrificed in the interests of economic efficiency.

Where goods are still produced under the auspices of the government, e.g. the coinage, the current practice is where possible to give the enterprise, e.g. the Royal Mint, the status of an executive *agency*, thereby affording management greater freedom to develop its business, e.g. by producing coins for other countries. Nevertheless its commercial performance is still subject to periodic official review.

Quasi-government bodies have usually been formed to operate particular services where only minimum accountability is required, e.g. the National Parks Commission, the Countryside Commission. In practice the degree of accountability varies.

Local authorities carry out functions, delegated by Parliament, chiefly where economies of scale and spill-over effects are relatively weak, e.g. education, police, roads, fire services, refuse collection, local planning control. Such local administration can respond to local needs.

19.3 THE PROBLEM OF ASSESSING 'NEEDS'

Differences between 'demand' and 'needs'

Whereas goods and services are supplied by private-sector firms in response to effective demand, government departments and local authorities provide goods and services according to 'needs', a social rather than an economic concept since it cannot be defined objectively. As a result 'needs' are more difficult to assess than demand.

For example, in the private sector owner-occupied houses are built according to the price which people are able and willing to pay for them. *Demand* will depend upon the price of the house, the prices of other goods and services (particularly near-substitutes), the level of income, the distribution of wealth and all the other factors mentioned in Chapter 4 as influencing the conditions of demand. Supply responds automatically to this demand; the number and type of houses supplied depends ultimately on the equilibrium price determined in the market.

In contrast, in providing housing according to *needs* the public-sector authorities regard housing as a social obligation. Consequently, price signals are either inadequate or non-existent. This increases the difficulties of decision-making. Consider the factors which have to be borne in mind in planning a housing programme based on needs. First, the authorities have to estimate the number of households seeking accommodation according to the sizes of the family units, the ages of their members, their location, their preferences as between houses and high-rise flats, and so on. Moreover, since houses are very durable, some consideration has to be given to future requirements. Second, the authorities have to decide arbitrarily on the standard of an adequate housing unit. Third, they have to get the dwellings built, either through a private contractor or by their own direct-labour building organisations.

Subjective assessment of 'needs'

The task of estimating needs is made more difficult because there is no price system in operation to provide reliable criteria. Thus rents charged by local authorities are less than the open-market rent. This means that demand exceeds supply, and the only indication of needs thrown up by this restricted-price system is the number of households waiting their turn on the housing list.

And, all the time, the authorities must be conscious of dealing with limited resources – more spent on housing may mean less available for the health services. In the last resort, therefore, the standard of goods and services provided on the basis of needs is determined by the political views of the central government and local councils.

19.4 PRICING POLICY

The problem arises as to how goods and services are to be paid for. There are three sources of funds: borrowing, taxation and user-charges.

Borrowing

In principle, long-term *government borrowing* should cover only spending on capital items, e.g. motorways, bridges. In practice, however, the government's yearly expenditure is so vast that what would normally be regarded as capital items are included in current expenditure, e.g. the cost of warships. In any case, from the point of view of control of the economy, it is the *total* spending of the government relative to revenue which is of major significance.

What happens, therefore, is that any excess of public sector expenditure over current income is covered by borrowing – the Public Sector Net Cash Requirement (PSNCR), formerly the Public Sector Borrowing Requirement (PSBR). For most of the past ten years the size of the PSBR has proved embarrassing for government economic policy (see p. 533).

Taxation

With *community goods*, where free-riders cannot be excluded, no price can be charged, since nobody will pay when private rights to them cannot be granted, e.g. with defence and flood control. Here the cost has to be covered entirely from taxation.

Charges can be levied on *collective goods* (see p. 235). But if their marginal cost is nil, e.g. for crossing bridges, visiting museums, welfare can only be maximised if no charge is levied, with taxation covering the cost.

With *merit* goods in particular, it may be desirable to recognise the uneven distribution of income when considering charges. For instance, charges for essential education would be highly regressive on low-income families with children of school-age. Alternatively, the regressive impact of charges can be modified by price discrimination. Thus low-income families are given housing benefits, while persons over retirement age do not pay prescription charges.

Where demand for a public service is not likely to be too high at zero price, the choice between tax financing and user-charging could reasonably rest on the question, who benefits from the service? Where the community as a whole benefits – e.g. street lighting and by-pass roads – tax-financing is appropriate. In contrast, if certain individuals benefit, the cost is best, and more fairly, covered by individual fees (e.g. public tennis courts and swimming pools).

User-charges

For goods other than community goods, the choice between charges, taxation or a combination of both is governed by technical, economic and political considerations. Thus while motorways could be financed by toll charges, the effect on the traffic flow, especially during rush hours, has led the UK to pay for them from general taxation. However, users contribute heavily through motor-vehicle licences and petrol duties. On the other hand, while public transport could be financed from taxation, economic factors favour charges, for elasticity of demand is such that, at a zero price (financed wholly from taxation), demand would be so high that a misallocation of resources would result. This applies to many other services, e.g. postal services. National Health prescriptions, dental treatment, sight testing and spectacles.

One other advantage of charges is that they can throw up a valuable guideline for investment. For example, metered water charges reveal demand at the current price and from this some estimate can be made of future demand.

In practice, the choice between charges and taxation is likely to be decided politically, especially where income redistribution figures prominently. But there are economic constraints on charging less than the free market price for an extended demand may impose a heavy burden on taxation generally. The result is that some form of administrative rationing according to need may have to be imposed, e.g. the 'points' system for allocating Council dwellings. More seriously, hidden rationing may prevail through depreciation of the quality of service provided, e.g. state medical services and education. Indeed this could apply to BBC television, where a 'community good' has been converted to a 'collective good' by a legal licence which creates excludability so that the cost falls on TV owners.

Determining user-charges

Even when it has been decided to cover the cost of a service by charges, difficulties may arise where there are relatively very high fixed costs, e.g. as with public transport, electricity, and natural gas, for supply by competing firms would mean that no one firm could be financially viable. In any case, for technical reasons, a monopoly may be necessary. For instance, only one firm can be given the right to acquire land for laying a gas main, while, for public transport, competing firms cannot be allowed to 'skim' the profitable commuter traffic with none providing a service at other times or on other routes.

This necessity of having to create a monopoly because of decreasing costs or of special technical conditions of supply strengthens the case for the provision of certain services by local authorities, e.g. passenger transport, or by nationalised industries.

Two major difficulties arise. First, the criterion may be laid down (as with the nationalised industries) that over time revenue should cover costs. It then becomes impossible to produce up to the point where price equals marginal cost (see Figure 14.1).

Second, fixed costs may be so high that total cost can never be covered by a single price.

In practice the problem has been overcome in three ways:

(i) The difference has been covered by a *subsidy*, either directly, e.g. for city transport, or indirectly, through writing off accumulated deficits from time to time, e.g. for coal and railways.

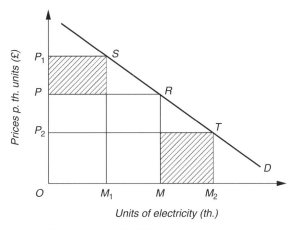

Figure 19.1   Increasing revenue by 'block pricing'

(ii)   A *standing charge* is levied irrespective of units consumed, e.g. for electricity. The standing charge goes to meet fixed costs; the price per unit consumed covers variable costs.

(iii)   The industry is allowed to exploit its monopoly position by *price discrimination*. This is possible where different customers, having a different elasticity of demand for the product, can be kept separate, each being charged the price he is willing to pay. By 'charging what the traffic will bear', total revenue is increased. Such price discrimination by consumer category is used by railways where, for example, cheap-day trippers, senior citizens and students are charged lower fares than commuters.

The highest degree of charging 'what the traffic will bear' is where the undertaking could discriminate perfectly between every consumer and charge different prices to each. While this is impractical, a modified form, 'block pricing', separates additional amounts of the product and charges them at decreasing prices.

Thus in Figure 19.1 total revenue from a single electricity price OP would be $POMR$. But if a consumer is charged OP_1 for the first OM_1 units, OP for the second block of M_1M units, and OP_2 for the third block of MM_2 units, the extra revenue realised is shown by the two shaded areas.

19.5   THE NATIONALISED INDUSTRIES AND PRIVATISATION

The nationalised industries

State provision of community, collective and merit goods is widely accepted, provided that where provision is possible through the market, e.g. health care, education, people are free to prefer this source.

But when the state takes over major industries from the private sector, its reasons for doing so must be justified by results. In other words, is such state interference an improvement on the market's allocation of resources or is it merely the application of a political dogma?

The stark fact is that neither Communism in the USSR nor the 'middle way' socialism of the UK have fulfilled the advantages claimed. The resurgence of the market economy through Mrs. Thatcher's privatisation measures beginning in 1983 and the demise of Communism in Eastern Europe from 1990 were the ultimate recognition of the failure of the 'command economy'.

Since at present there seems little likelihood of any resurgence of nationalisation in the UK, we concentrate on the reasons advanced for 'privatisation'.

Nature of privatisation

'Privatisation' implies more than the movement of assets from the public to the private sector. Rather it embraces all the different means by which the disciplines of the free market in the provision of goods and services can be applied to the public sector. Thus this 'pushing back the frontiers of the state' covers:

(a) the transfer of the nationalised industries to private ownership, e.g. British Telecom, British Gas, British Airways, British Airports Authority;

(b) selling other state assets, either completely (e.g. Britoil, Rolls-Royce, motorway service areas) or partially (e.g. woodlands owned by the Forestry Authority, British Petroleum shares, council housing);

(c) opening-up state monopolies to outside competition, e.g. relaxing licensing restrictions to allow private bus firms to compete with publicly owned services;

(d) 'contracting-out' to the private sector services paid for out of public funds, e.g. refuse collection, street cleaning, hospital ancillary services;

(e) charging beneficiaries for publicly provided goods and services, e.g. medical prescriptions, school meals, council housing;

(f) the private finance initiative, where the private sector is induced to fund and see through projects in which the government has a strong interest (see below).

The success of privatisation

While Mrs. Thatcher's first term of office concentrated on reducing the PSBR, privatisation took the form of returning to the private sector firms which had been recently acquried (e.g. British Aerospace and Cable and Wireless) and by encouraging contracting-out of services. But during her second term beginning in 1983 privatisation measures were extended and integrated in line with her private enterprise views and supply-side policies (see pp. 404–6). The advantages claimed for the privatisation policy were that it would:

(a) reduce the burden of providing continual subsidies to cover the operating deficits of many State industries;
(b) enable the sale proceeds to reduce a worrying PSBR;
(c) remove detailed political control and permit managers to pursue their own pricing and long-term investment strategies;
(d) improve efficiency through competition in the market;
(e) provide more resistance to trade unions' inflationary wage demands;
(f) create a property-owning democracy by wider share ownership.

Problems of privatisation

Difficulty was experienced in fixing a satisfactory price at which an industry's shares were to be offered to the public. If the offer were oversubscribed, the government would be accused of not realising the full potential of public assets; if shares were left with the underwriters, the object of achieving wide ownership would be defeated since eventually they would be bought by the institutions. A different method (British Airports Authority) was to offer a proportion of the shares at a fixed price, and the rest by tender. The device of offering a bonus royalty share for every ten shares held for the first three years was less successful than hoped for, since many small purchasers soon took their profits by selling. In the event, most offer prices undervalued assets, and recognition of this enabled the new Labour government of 1997 to impose windfall taxes on the privatised utilities amounting in all to £5.2 billion.

Steps also had to be taken to provide some form of competition for many of the industries and to introduce devices which would ensure regard was paid to the 'public interest'. The major difficulty is that while privatisation eliminates direct government involvement in decision-making and operating responsibility for particular industries, many, especially the 'natural monopolies' (chiefly public utilities) have retained their monopolist and monopsonist positions. This can result in exploitation of consumers by monopoly pricing and inefficiency through lack of competition.

Consequently, where possible, indirect competition has been fostered. For example, gas still has to compete with coal, oil and electricity, while new firms have been granted a licence to compete in telecommunications with British Telecom. Similarly, Vodafone is a major competitor in mobile telephones with British Telecom's Cellnet. The most striking progress has been in the rapid growth of express coach services with reduced fares after competition with the National Bus Company was allowed.

An alternative arrangement has been to grant independence to firms on a franchise basis for a limited period, e.g. regional television companies. Provision is made to prevent mergers and, in reviewing the franchise, consideration can be given to past conduct as regards quality of service and sensitivity to the wishes of the public as well as to the price tendered. The difficulty with this method is that investment may be inhibited by lack of certainty of long-term future operations.

Where some form of competition is difficult to devise, the responsibility for protecting the public interest may rest with a regulatory body. Thus the Office for Telecommunications (OFTEL) acts as a watchdog to ensure fair competition by restraining British Telecom from behaviour to weaken competing firms, e.g. by delaying the installation of other firm's equipment. Furthermore, price rises are limited to 7 per cent *less* than the rate of inflation. This ensures that the consumer receives some benefit of technical improvements, but encourages efficiency in that the company is allowed to retain any additional cost savings. An aggrieved firm can appeal to the Monopolies and Mergers Commission. But in 1997 the Commission supported OFGAS which had imposed on TransCo, British Gas' pipeline business, a 21 per cent one-off price cut for the next year followed by price rises limited to 2.5 per cent *less* than the rate of inflation for each of the next four years.

In spite of these difficulties, however, we must recognise the radical nature and achievement of the Thatcher government. Until 1977 the public sector was growing and this seemed to be generally accepted. What the Thatcher government did was to reopen the debate on the proper role of the State in the economy, and other countries, e.g. France, with mixed economies are privatising their State-run industries. Even Russia, with the breakdown of the communist regime, has followed the same path.

Yet not all government activities can be satisfactorily privatised, e.g. education and medical treatment for the majority of people. For these there must be a continuing process of improving their management and account-ability by efficiency scrutinies and by monitoring their progress within the financial limits imposed.

The Private Finance Initiative (PFI)/Public–Private Partnerships (PPP)

The return of rail services to the private sector virtually completed the programme of privatisation. But the PFI, formally launched in 1992, emphasised how the strengths of the private sector could be introduced to other activities traditionally regarded as within the province of the State.

The logic of the PFI (also known as PPP) is as follows. What people really want is services, for example quick transport, custody of prisoners, care of the aged, etc. But to provide these services there has to be investment e.g. roads, railways, prisons, old peoples's homes. Such investment involves assessing the financial risk, obtaining the necessary funds, and constructing and subsequently managing the project. Since these functions, it is held, are performed better by the private sector than by the State, there would be an improvement in efficiency if they were undertaken by the former. The State would then be able to obtain the services it required simply by purchasing or leasing them from the private sector provider.

In practice, the PFI covers three types of project:

(a) *Financially free standing*, in that the contractor covers his costs (including normal profit) from charges on users, e.g. the Channel Tunnel, the Heathrow–Paddington Express rail link. Here the State's contribution to the project is simply that of planning and determining the route, the private sector being responsible for its construction and management.

(b) *Services leased to the public sector by a private contractor*, e.g. prison places, new government offices.

(c) *Joint ventures*, where part of the cost is met from public funds to take account of the social benefits (externalities) of the scheme, e.g. less road congestion, urban regeneration. But risk-bearing, construction and subsequent management would still remain with the private sector contractor.

It is considered that involving private participation in the above ways could mean an overall increase in investment in such projects, for it would lie outside any public sector borrowing restraint.

Latest privatisations and future policy

In 2001, after a prolonged controversy, the UK National Air Traffic Services (NATS), which is responsible for air traffic control, was part-privatised. This was a public private partnership (PPP) raising £750m for the government who retained a 49 per cent stake in the new company (46 per cent being bought by the Airline Group and 5 per cent by the staff). In February 2006, the government's defence research service QinetiQ was sold. Somewhat controversially, the major share buyer was a US investment firm.

Future UK privatisation plans include the nuclear power group British Energy. The government's 65 per cent stake could be worth £10bn, especially if the firm gets permission (from the government) to operate new power stations in the UK. Also, Tote bookmakers could be sold for £500m.

The Wider Markets Initiative is a government policy designed to encourage more intensive use of public assets such as land, buildings, people and intellectual property through the development of new, non-statutory goods and services which are sold on a commercial basis. Utilising those assets more fully can involve selling existing goods and services, developing new goods and services from existing assets, licensing and leasing arrangements, and sponsorship activities. The more efficient use of public assets that results helps the public sector to reduce its cost base and improve its skills base.

CHAPTER SUMMARY

- Community goods such as defence and street lighting are non-excludable and so the government itself has to provide them.
- Collective goods, such as parks and drainage, are excludable by levying charges, but they are non-rival, meaning that their use by one person does not affect costs. Because MC is zero, maximum benefits arise if the state provides them free of charge.
- Goods and services provided by the state can be paid for from taxation, government borrowing or user-charges.
- Privatisation is the process of transferring nationalised industries to private ownership and selling other state assets, such as council houses, to the private sector. It also involves increasing competition to state-run enterprises and contracting out to the private sector services paid for by public funds.

REVIEW QUESTIONS

- What problems arise when the state provides goods and services?
- Explain how 'block pricing' can increase the revenue received for a nationalised industry.
- Describe, giving examples, the advantages of privatisation.

 Visit the companion website for further questions

THE FACTORS OF PRODUCTION AND THEIR REWARDS

CHAPTER 20

LABOUR AND WAGES

LEARNING OBJECTIVES

After studying this chapter you should be able to:
- describe recent changes in the workforce of the UK;
- explain why labour is treated as a separate factor of production;
- describe the process of collective bargaining;
- analyse how wage rates are determined.

20.1 THE WORKFORCE OF THE UK

Table 20.1 shows that in 2006 the UK had a workforce of nearly 31 million in employment. In addition there were nearly a million workers unemployed (as measured by the number of people claiming unemployment-related benefits), giving a total working population of around 32 million.

This represents an increase over the last 20 years of 7 million, of whom many have been women. For women employment rates have generally been rising from 59 per cent in 1984 to 70 per cent in 2003. This influx of women has been brought about by the expansion of the service industries (Table 20.2) and the increase in part-time working. 45 per cent of women workers are part-time, compared with only 8 per cent of men, and today the activity rate of all women 16–60 years of age is 66 per cent, higher than all other countries except for Japan and the Scandinavian countries.

Over the last 20 years self-employment has also increased by 2.2 million (79 per cent), largely through the encouragement of the government. It occurs mostly in agriculture, construction, distribution, catering and professional services.

As regards the industrial distribution of employees (Table 20.2) the most significant change has been the increase in the service industries. This, however, is merely a reflection of a long-term trend. Thus, between 1975 and 2005 services increased

Table 20.1 Workforce in employment in the UK (000s)

	1986	1991	1996	2006
Employees in employment	21,377	22,250	22,116	26,705
Self-employed	2,792	3,413	3,282	3,988
HM Forces	322	297	221	206
Government-supported trainees	226	353	200	80
Total workforce in employment	24,717	26,313	25,819	30,979

Table 20.2 The industrial distribution of employees

	1991		1996		2005	
	000s	per cent	000s	per cent	000s	per cent
Service industries	16,187	72.8	16,783	75.9	24,711	80.2
Manufacturing	4,319	19.4	4,017	18.2	3,383	11
Other industries*	1,744	7.8	1,316	5.9	2,716	8.8
Total all industries	22,250	100	22,116	100	30,810	100

* These include energy, water supply, agriculture and construction.

from 52 per cent of all employees to 80 per cent, while in comparison and over the same period manufacturing has declined from 36 per cent to 11 per cent.

The basic reason for these changes has been the increase in real income. As a result spending moves to those goods having a high income elasticity of demand. But the decrease in manufacturing has also been brought about by the uncompetitiveness of UK products in world markets, largely owing to the inability to contain wage costs relative to competitors. Technical advances and increased mechanisation also contributed (as also the decline in energy and agriculture). In contrast, services are more labour intensive although some – such as financial services, computers and telecommunications – have economised in labour employment.

20.2 THE NATURE OF THE LABOUR FORCE

Why labour is treated as a separate factor of production

Labour is the effort, both physical and mental, made by human beings in production. It is the 'human' element which is important.

Because people have feelings and emotions their response to economic forces is different from that of machines. First, whereas a machine which proves profitable can be reproduced fairly easily and quickly, the overall supply of labour does not depend upon its earnings. Other factors are more important in deciding how many children parents have. Second, the effort of labour is not determined solely by the reward offered. The method of payment may affect effort, while raising wages may result in less work being offered. Above all, a contented worker will produce more than an unhappy one; thus job satisfaction or loyalty to a firm, rather than a high rate of pay, may be decisive in inducing an employee to work overtime. Third, people have to go where the work is. But labour does not move readily, either occupationally or geographically, in response to job opportunities or the offer of a higher reward. Often such 'immobility' results from strong human contacts. Fourth, workers can combine together in trade unions. Finally, if unemployed for long periods, workers deteriorate physically and mentally.

Both firms and government must have policies which take account of these special characteristics. Training schemes are essential to improve the skill of workers and thus their productivity. Firms must pay particular attention to psychological and social factors in order to motivate workers, e.g. by profit-sharing schemes. Furthermore, they must endeavour to co-operate with the workers' trade-union representatives. Above all, firms have to comply with the constraints imposed by government policy (see p. 267).

The overall supply of labour

By the supply of labour we mean the number of hours of work offered. There are two separate problems to be considered: the total overall supply of labour available, and the supply of labour to a particular industry, occupation or locality. Here we consider the first.

The total supply of labour in an economy depends upon:

1. The size of the population

The size of the population sets an obvious limit to the total supply of labour. But while it is influenced by economic factors, e.g. through their effect on the birth rate and immigration, it is doubtful, especially in more advanced economies, whether they are of paramount importance.

2. The proportion of the population which works

In Britain, the proportion of the population which works is 50 per cent of the total population (somewhat higher than most European countries). It is determined chiefly by:

(a)   The numbers within the 16–65 age group.
(b)   The activity rates within this group, especially as regards young people and

female workers. The tendency over the last twenty years has been for a higher proportion of young people to remain in further education, thus reducing their activity rate. On the other hand, higher proportion of women are now entering the working population. The expansion of the service and light manufacturing industries has provided increased job opportunities for women, while the changed attitude to women workers is reflected in the Equal Pay Act 1970 and the Sex Discrimination Act 1975. Above all, the smaller family, the availability of crèches and school dinners, the development of part-time employment opportunities and new labour-saving domestic appliances have allowed married women to work.

(c) The extent to which people over retiring age continue to work, something which is largely influenced by the level of pensions.

(d) The numbers who can live on unearned incomes.

(e) The employment opportunities available – the tendency being for the working population to contract in a depression (mainly through withdrawal of married women).

3. The amount of work offered by each individual labourer

Higher rates of pay usually induce a person to work overtime, the increased reward encouraging a substitution of work for leisure. But this is not always so. In addition to the substitution effect, there is also the income effect, and the latter may outweigh the former (see p. 59). A higher wage rate enables the worker to maintain the existing material standard of living with less work, and extra leisure may be preferred to more goods. Thus while it is usual to depict the supply curve of labour as in Figure 20.1a, it is possible that, in the short period, it may follow the shape of the curve in Figure 20.1b (see p. 256).

Nevertheless, as we shall see, more significant than the overall supply of labour are the obstacles to mobility which divide up the labour market.

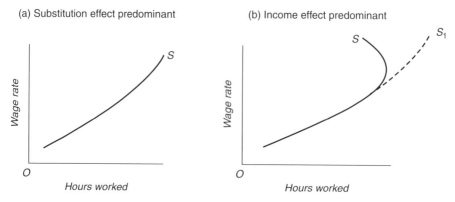

Figure 20.1   The relationship between the wage-rate and hours worked

20.3   METHODS OF REWARDING LABOUR

The wage-rate and earnings

Some people are self-employed – window-cleaners, plumbers, solicitors, etc. As such they are really entrepreneurs, securing the rewards when demand is high but accepting the risks of being unemployed or working for a low return. Nevertheless, most workers contract out of risk, accepting a wage which is received whether or not the product of their labour is sold – although some element of risk-bearing may be incorporated in the wage agreement, e.g. by commission payments, bonus schemes, profit-sharing arrangements and employee share plans introduced in 2000.

In what follows, reference will be mainly to the *wage-rate* – the sum of money which an employer contracts to pay a worker in return for services rendered. This definition includes salaries as well as wages, and makes no distinction between time- and piece-rates.

Earnings are what the worker actually receives in his pay-packet (his 'take-home' pay) *plus* deductions which have been made for national insurance, income tax, superannuation, etc. In practice earnings over a period often exceed the agreed wage-rate, additions being received for overtime working, piece-rates and bonus payments.

Where the nature of the work allows workers to be paid on a piece-rate basis as an alternative to time-rates, the firm has to consider their respective merits.

Time-rates

Time-rates are more satisfactory than piece-rates where:

(1)   A high quality of work is essential, e.g. computer programming.
(2)   The work cannot be speeded up, e.g. bus driving, milking cows.
(3)   There is no standard type of work, e.g. car repairs.
(4)   Care has to be taken of delicate machinery, e.g. hospital medical tests.
(5)   Output cannot be easily measured, e.g. teaching, nursing.
(6)   Working long hours may undermine health, e.g. laundry work.
(7)   The labour is by nature a fixed factor which has to be engaged whatever the output, e.g. secretarial and selling staff.
(8)   Periods of temporary idleness necessarily occur, e.g. repair work.

On the other hand, time-rates have certain disadvantages:

(1)   There is a lack of incentive for better workers.
(2)   Supervision of workers is usually necessary.
(3)   Agreements can be undermined by working to rule and 'go-slow' tactics.

253

Piece-rates

Where output is both measurable and more or less proportionate to the amount of effort expended, piece-rates are possible. It is not essential that each individual worker's output can be measured exactly. So long as the output of the group can be assessed the worker can share in the group's earnings.

The advantages of piece-rates are:

(1) Effort is stimulated.
(2) The more efficient workers obtain higher rewards.
(3) Constant supervision and irksome time-keeping can be eliminated.
(4) Interest is added to dull, routine work.
(5) Workers can proceed at their own pace.
(6) A team spirit is developed where workers operate in small groups.
(7) Workers are encouraged to suggest methods of improving production.
(8) The employer's costing calculations are simplified.
(9) Output is increased, and the more intensive use of capital equipment spreads overheads.

We see, therefore, that piece-rates have advantages for both employee and employer. Moreover, the lower prices which result benefit the community as a whole. Nevertheless, for the following reasons they are often disliked by trade unions:

(1) Workers may over-exert themselves.
(2) Where piece-rates have to be varied according to local conditions or different circumstances, e.g. capital per employee, negotiations for a national wage-rate are difficult.
(3) Variations in piece-rates from one place to another undermine union solidarity.
(4) The union may lose control over the supply of labour, and this makes it difficult to take strike action or to apportion work in periods of unemployment.
(5) Piece-rates are subject to misunderstanding, e.g. a firm which instals a better machine may be accused of cutting the rate if it does not attribute all the increased output to the effort of labour.
(6) Workers may resist being shifted from tasks in which they have acquired dexterity (and which therefore produce high piece earnings) even though the current needs of the factory organisation require such a transfer. Thus employers find that piece-rates lead to a loss of control over their employees, and many prefer to pay high time-rates to avoid this.

Combined time- and piece-rates

When deciding the basis of the wage-rate, both employees and employers want certain guarantees. Workers have a minimum standard of living to maintain, and they desire protection against variations in output which lie outside their control, e.g. weather conditions. On the other hand, employers providing expensive equipment must ensure that it is used for a minimum period of time. Thus piece-rates are usually incorporated in a wider contract which provides for some basic wage and a stipulated minimum number of hours.

20.4 THE DETERMINATION OF THE WAGE-RATE IN A PARTICULAR INDUSTRY, OCCUPATION OR LOCALITY

In theory, the wage-rate in a particular industry, occupation or locality will be determined as shown in Chapter 10 by demand and supply. Demand is shown by the MRP curve. Its position can shift with changes in: (a) the price of the final product, (b) the price of substitute or complementary factors, and (c) the productivity of labour (e.g. owing to a change in the amount of capital supplied). Supply depends upon the wage-rate offered compared with that in other industries.

In practice this merely provides a first approach. In the real world the actual wage-rate and conditions of employment are influenced by immobilities which split up supply, worker's psychological attitudes, imperfect competition in both the product and labour markets, the strength of the relevant trade union and government intervention.

Workers' resistance to a cut in the money wage-rate, their desire to preserve time-honoured wage differentials and notions regarding the status of their occupation all serve to prevent 'market clearing' with the workers preferring unemployment at least in the short run.

The wage-rate and the immobility of labour

The main weakness of the MRP theory is that, in concentrating on what determines the demand for labour, it underplays conditions on the supply side.

The supply of labour to an industry depends on:

1. The response of existing labour to a higher wage-rate

In the short period an industry may find that the supply curve of labour corresponds to curve *S* in Figure 20.1b. This was once the case in coalmining, where, as wages have increased, miners preferred to enjoy more leisure. In the long period, however, higher wage-rates should attract labour from other industries, with the result that the long-period supply curve follows the dashed line, S_1.

2. The cost of attracting labour from alternative uses or localities

Unless there is unemployment, the supply of labour in a particular use can be expanded only by increasing the wage offered. This will attract labour of the same or of a nearly similar kind from other industries, occupations or localities. The extent to which this happens depends upon the elasticity of demand for the products in these alternative uses. If demand is inelastic, higher wages can be offered to hold on to labour, and thus the supply of labour will expand little in response to the wage rise (see p. 265).

3. The mobility of labour

A rise in the price of a factor should attract it from alternative uses or localities. This may take time, but it is achieved in the 'long period'. With labour, however, there are particular obstacles to moving, and these may mean that the long period is delayed indefinitely. Such obstacles provide frictions to the full and efficient operation of the price system.

Take the wages of plasterers, for instance. The demand for plasterers depends upon the price at which houses sell (a derived demand) and the productivity of plasterers. The supply of plasterers is the number offering their services at different wage-rates. This will vary with the length of time under consideration. But in the long period more will be forthcoming the higher the wage-rate, since they will be attracted from lower-paid areas or occupations.

For example, if the conditions of demand and supply are different in different parts of the country, the wages of plasterers will differ. If there were perfect geographical mobility, plasterers would move from low-wage districts to high-wage districts, until eventually a common equilibrium wage-rate would be established. Similarly, where different wage-rates exist for different occupations, perfect occupational mobility would eventually eliminate these differences.

In practice, geographical and occupational mobility are not perfect, so that differences in wage-rates persist. A typist earns more in London than in Norwich; a doctor earns more than a docker. In short, immobilities result in the labour market's being divided into a number of separate smaller markets according to locality and occupation.

Thus differences in the wage-rates between occupations, or between localities for the same occupation, can frequently be explained by differences in the supply rather than by differences in demand. We are dealing not with one market for labour but with a number of fairly distinct markets.

What are these major barriers? What are the causes of the 'immobility of labour', as it is usually termed?

Workers may be required: (a) to shift from one industry to another; (b) to change occupation; (c) to move home to a different district. Often conditions dictate that all three types of change take place at the same time, but this is not necessarily so. Each presents its own obstacles to workers in their efforts to change jobs.

(a) Obstacles between industries

Provided that it does not involve a change of occupation or district, a worker can usually move job from one industry to another fairly easily. Secretaries, lorry drivers and porters, for example, are found in most industries. But middle-aged and older workers may experience difficulty. Prejudice or tradition in certain industries may also prove to be obstacles. Women drivers, for instance, would find it difficult to become taxi drivers in London. Moreover, a worker's loyalty to a particular firm may prevent him or her from looking for another job, even though a cut in wages has been suffered (though obviously this does not apply if the worker is made redundant).

(b) Obstacles to a change of occupation

In changing occupations, obstacles may be encountered in both moving out of the old occupation or in entering a new one. They arise because:

   (i)   a high natural ability is required in certain occupations;
   (ii)   training may be costly and take time;
   (iii) stringent entry conditions are sometimes prescribed by trade unions and professional associations;
   (iv)   the new job may be repugnant; and, equally, some occupations, e.g. the Church, art and acting, are so pleasant that workers are not drawn into another occupation by the offer of a higher wage rate;
   (v)   through a high division of labour, only limited skills have been acquired;
   (vi)   workers may be reluctant or too old to learn a new job;
   (vii) workers may prefer to remain unemployed rather than accept a wage below a 'recognised minimum' in an alternative occupation;
   (viii) in spite of prohibiting legislation, there is discrimination on account of sex, colour, social class or religion;
   (ix)   workers are ignorant of wage-rates and opportunities in other occupations.

Of the above, the greatest obstacle to occupational mobility is natural ability. In this respect it should be noted that there can be more mobility between occupations, e.g. storeman and clerk, requiring the same level of innate ability than between doctors and dockers, where there are marked differences in the natural ability and training required. The first is sometimes termed 'horizontal' occupational mobility; the second, where there are non-competing groups of workers, 'vertical' mobility.

(c) Obstacles to a change of district

When it comes to moving from one part of the country to another, workers have to overcome both real and psychological obstacles. These include:

(i) the costs of moving, which to many workers represent a considerable capital sum and are incurred even if workers own their own homes;

(ii) the difficulty of securing accommodation elsewhere on comparable terms, particularly for council and rent-controlled tenants but also for owner-occupiers having to move into the more expensive housing in southern England;

(iii) social ties of friends, clubs, Church, etc.;

(iv) family ties, such as the children's education;

(v) imperfect knowledge of vacancies or wages paid in other localities;

(vi) prejudice against certain parts of the country, e.g. people at present generally prefer to live in the south-east rather than in the industrial north.

Such immobility of labour means that wage-rates can often be more easily explained by supply conditions rather than by demand and is one of the major causes of unemployment. In Chapter 35, we consider some of the ways in which the government tries to reduce occupational and geographical immobility.

Imperfection in the labour market also arises where one firm is the major employer in a locality (see above). But mainly it is due to trade unions, which (through the closed shop) can establish what is virtually a monopoly in the supply of a given type of labour. We therefore analyse the economic background to trade-union activity with reference to its strength in negotiating wage increases.

20.5 TRADE UNIONS: THE PROCESS OF COLLECTIVE BARGAINING

It would be wrong to regard trade unions primarily as a disruptive influence in the economy. For one thing there must be a means by which workers can communicate with employers. For another, by making the worker more contented, they enhance productivity. We can summarise their most important functions as: (i) improving working conditions; (ii) providing educational, social and legal benefits for members; (iii) improving standards of work; (iv) obtaining pay increases; and (v) cooperating with governments in order to secure a workable economic policy and to improve working and living conditions generally. The remainder of this chapter is concerned with (iv).

The process of collective bargaining

Collective bargaining is the settlement of conditions of employment by employers negotiating with the workers' trade unions. For its smooth working, certain conditions should be fulfilled. First, it must be pursued with good sense on both sides. This is enhanced where the industry has a tradition of good labour relations and where there is some accepted objective measure to which wage-rates can be linked (e.g. the Retail Prices Index, wage-rates paid in similar trades, the level of profits in the industry). Second, both sides should be represented by strong organisations. Where all employers are linked in an association, there is no fear of outsiders gaining advantage by negotiating independent wage bargains, while, if the union can speak for all its members, employers know an agreement will be honoured. Unofficial stoppages damage the union's reputation, and to avoid them there must be regular contact between employer and union and prompt investigation of grievances on the shop-floor. Third, there must be an understood procedure for settling disputes. While this must not be so prolonged as to fray patience, it should exhaust all possibilities of reaching agreement before a strike or lock-out is called.

In short the procedure of collective bargaining covers (i) negotiation and (ii) the settlement of disputes.

1. Negotiation

Broadly speaking the machinery for negotiation falls into three categories:

(1) Voluntary negotiation

Generally, the government has left it to the unions and employers' organisations to work out their own procedures, and today voluntary machinery covers nearly 48 per cent of the insured workers of the UK. Because union organisation varies, the recognised procedure differs between industries and trades.

(2) Joint industrial councils

Most industries have some national joint council or committee which, without outside assistance, thrashes out agreements. Usually it follows the system of Joint Industrial Councils, composed of representatives of employers and workers in the industry. These consider regularly such matters as the better use of the practical knowledge and experience of the work-people, general principles governing the conditions of employment, means of ensuring workers the greatest possible security of earnings and employment, methods of fixing and adjusting earnings, technical education and training, industrial research, improvement of processes and proposed legislation affecting the industry. Although Joint Industrial Councils are sponsored by the government, they are not forced upon any industry, and some important industries, such as iron and steel, engineering, shipbuilding and cotton, which had already developed their own procedure for negotiation, have not formed Joint Industrial Councils. Nevertheless, the tendency today is towards wage-rates being determined by local rather than by national agreements.

(3)   Government appointed wage-fixing boards

In 1909 the government set up over 20 Trade Boards (renamed Wages Councils) to fix minimum wage-rates for the 'sweated' trades, such as retailing, catering, hair dressing and clothing manufacture. These were abolished in 1993.

However, the Agricultural Wages Board survived, largely because it was liked by employers. It consists of employers' and workers' representatives and some independent members, including the chairman. Each year it fixes minimum wage rates and holiday entitlements, and its orders are enforceable by law.

2.   Settlement of disputes

Where the negotiating machinery fails to produce an agreement, it is a help if agreed procedures exist for ending the deadlock. Three methods can be employed: conciliation, arbitration or special inquiry.

(1)   Conciliation

In 1974 the Secretary of State for Employment set up an *independent* Advisory, Conciliation and Arbitration Service (ACAS), controlled by a council whose members are experienced in industrial relations. When efforts to obtain settlement of a dispute through normal procedures have failed, ACAS can provide conciliation if the parties concerned agree.

(2)   Arbitration

ACAS can, at the joint request of the parties to a dispute, appoint single arbitrators or boards of arbitration chosen from a register of people experienced in industrial relations to determine differences on the basis of agreed terms of reference.

Alternatively the Terms and Conditions of Employment Act 1959 allows claims that a particular employer is not observing the terms or conditions of employment established for the industry to be referred compulsorily to an industrial court for a legally binding award.

(3)   Inquiry and investigation

The Secretary of State for Employment has legal power to inquire into the causes and circumstances of any trade dispute and, if he thinks fit, to appoint a court of inquiry with power to call for evidence. Such action, however, is chiefly a means of informing parliament and the public of the facts and causes of a major dispute, and is taken only when no agreed settlement seems possible.

The minister's power of inquiry also allows for less formal action, by way of setting up committees of investigation, when the public interest is not so general.

Neither a court of inquiry nor a committee of investigation is a conciliation or arbitration body, but both may make recommendations upon which a reasonable settlement of a dispute can be based.

Trade union arguments for wage increases

A trade union is likely to base its claim for a wage increase on one or more of the following grounds.

1. A rise in the cost of living

Because inflation reduces their real incomes, workers seek an increase in money wages. But difficulties have arisen. First, wage demands could become an annual event. Second, they were often pitched higher than the rate of inflation, thereby fuelling further inflation (see Chapter 32).

2. A higher wage-rate in comparable grades and occupations

The trouble here is that wage differentials are often ingrained in workers' attitudes, whereas they should reflect changes in the demand for and supply of particular types of labour. Furthermore, it is often difficult, indeed impossible, to assess 'comparability', e.g. between a social worker and a computer programmer. On the other hand, if there is a shortage of nurses in national health hospitals owing to the higher pay offered in private hospitals, there is a strong argument for increasing the wage of the state-paid nurse.

3. Profits have increased

Trade unions feel that they should share in extra profits and here they may be in a strong position (see pp. 262–7).

4. Productivity has increased

Where output per worker is increasing, there is a rise in the MRP curve, and firms can grant a wage increase (see below). But there may be difficulty in apportioning the increased productivity between the workers' efforts and investment in new machines, research, etc. Capital has to receive its share if investment is to continue.

Trade union bargaining limitations

The question must now be answered – how, and to what extent, can trade unions secure increases in the wage rate for their members in conditions of free collective bargaining? We shall assume that the trade union is a 'closed shop' with 100 per cent membership, making it virtually a monopolist in selling its particular type of labour. (Closed-shop agreements are not unlawful. However, the cost of enforcing them has been made impossibly high by the Employment Act 1988 and the Employment Act 1989. One of the last examples of the closed shop in the UK was the acting profession where actors were required to be a member of the actors' union Equity.)

Broadly speaking, there are three ways in which a trade union can secure a wage increase:

1. It can support measures which will increase the demand for labour

An increase in the demand for labour will come about if the MRP curve rises, either through an improvement in the physical productivity of the workers or through an increase in the price of the product.

The situation is illustrated in Figure 20.2. As marginal revenue productivity rises from MRP to MRP_1, wages of existing workers, ON, rise from OW to OW_1. Alternatively, if there were unemployment, extra men, NN_1, could be employed at the previous wage-rate.

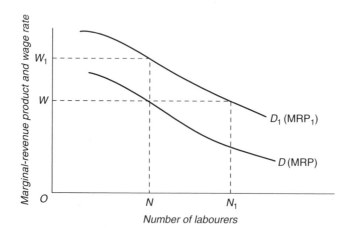

Figure 20.2 The effect on the wage-rate of a change in marginal revenue productivity

2. *It can restrict the supply of labour, allowing members to compete freely in fixing remuneration with employers*

A trade union or professional association may be sufficiently strong to restrict entry by apprenticeship regulations (e.g. plumbers and electricians) or high professional qualifications (e.g. solicitors, doctors, accountants and survey-ors). While a minimum wage-rate or scale of fees may be suggested, many members work on their own account and these are left to negotiate their own rewards.

We can therefore analyse this method of securing a wage increase by the simple demand-and-supply approach (Figure 20.3). If the trade union reduces the supply of workers in an occupation from S to S_1, the wage-rate rises from OW to OW_1.

3. *It can fix a minimum wage-rate*

Trades union members can be instructed not to work at rates below those set by the union. This is difficult to enforce, however, because of regional and local variations in rates of pay. Furthermore, this can act as an encouragement to employers to use non-union labour.

Where wages are raised by restricting entry, the trade union does not have to worry about unemployed members. It works simply on the principle that, assuming demand remains unchanged, greater scarcity leads to a higher reward.

Most trade unions, however, are faced with a more difficult problem. While they may secure higher wage-rates for their members, their success may be double-edged if, as a result, many members are sacked. What we really have to ask,

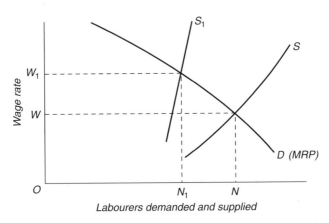

Figure 20.3 The effect on the wage-rate of trade-union restriction of the supply of labour

therefore, is: *Under what conditions can a trade union obtain higher wages for its members without decreasing the numbers employed?*

This means that we have to consider conditions of competition in both the product and factor markets. There are four main combinations:

(a) *Perfect competition in both selling the product and buying labour*. In the short period, even if there is perfect competition, a firm may be making supernormal profits. Here a strong trade union could, by threatening to withhold all its labour, force the employer to increase wages to the point where the whole of his supernormal profits disappear.

But this could not be permanent. The long-period equilibrium position is one in which there are no supernormal profits and the wage rate is equal to the MRP. A higher wage will represent a rise in costs. Some employers will now be forced out of business (see p. 144) and remaining firms will have to reduce their demand for labour until once again the MC of labour (the wage rate) is equal to the marginal-revenue product. Thus, in Figure 20.3 we will assume that OW is the original wage rate fixed by competition and ON the number of men employed – the trade-union membership. Suppose the trade union stipulates a minimum wage of OW_1. In the long-period, employment will then be reduced to ON_1. Given a downward-sloping MRP curve, this will always be true. Where there is perfect competition both in selling the product and in buying labour, a trade union can successfully negotiate an increase in wages only if there has been increased productivity; any increase without this will merely lead to members becoming unemployed.

The amount of unemployment resulting from such a rise in wages depends upon the elasticity of demand for labour. This will vary according to:

(i) *The physical possibility of substituting alternative factors.* As the price of one factor rises, other factors become relatively cheaper and the tendency is to substitute them for the dearer factor. Thus, if wages rise, firms try to install more machinery and labour-saving devices; that is, they replace labour by capital. But because different factors are imperfect substitutes for each other, such substitution is limited physically. Indeed, if they have to be employed in fairly fixed proportions, little or no substitution is possible. As we saw in Chapter 5, the extent to which substitution can take place largely determines the elasticity of demand.

The degree of substitution is shown by the slope of the MRP curve. Where labour is added to another factor, but is a poor substitute for it, marginal productivity falls steeply; where it is a fairly good substitute, marginal productivity falls more gently. Thus in Figure 20.4a, a labour is not a good substitute for land, and marginal-revenue productivity falls steeply as the number of men employed increases. Demand for labour is therefore inelastic, and a wage rise of WW_1 leads to only NN_1 extra men being unemployed. Compare this with Figure 20.4b, where labour and land are better substitutes. Here the same wage rise leads to a much larger number of men being unemployed.

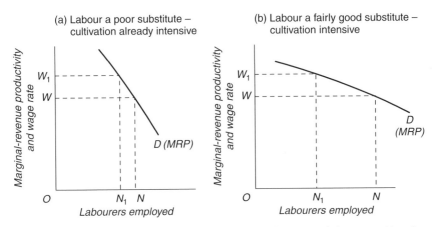

Figure 20.4 The relationship of substitutability between labour and land and numbers employed

It should be noted that, since the possibility of substitution increases over time, the longer the period under consideration, the greater will be the change in the labour force.

(ii) *The elasticity of supply of alternative factors.* Under conditions of perfect competition, the cost of a factor to an individual firm will not rise as the firm's demand for that factor increases (see p. 130). But when we are analysing a rise in the wage-rate of the workers of an *industry*, we must recognise that the whole industry will now be demanding the alternative factors in order to substitute them for labour. This increased demand will affect the price of the alternative factors, and a higher price will have to be paid in order to attract a greater supply. This increase in price of the alternative factors also limits the extent to which substitution is carried out. Thus if the supply of the alternative factor is perfectly elastic, only the physical considerations referred to above will affect the demand for it; if, on the other hand, supply is inelastic, then it is likely that the quick rise in its price will soon make it uneconomic to substitute it for labour. Once again, the elasticity of supply of the alternative factors will be greater the longer the period of time under consideration.

Where unemployed labour exists, two conditions prevail that make it difficult for a trade union to obtain a wage increase without reducing the level of employment: (i) a high degree of substitution existing between the union labour and the alternative factor, unemployed labour, particularly if the work performed is unskilled; (ii) an infinite elasticity of supply of the alternative factor, unemployed labour, at least for a time. Hence trade unions are relatively weaker in periods of unemployment.

(iii) *The proportion of labour costs to total costs.* The proportion of labour costs to total costs has two effects. First, if labour costs form only a small percentage of

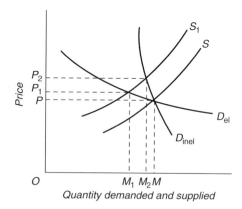

Figure 20.5   The extent to which demand for the product contracts as a result of a wage increase

total costs, demand for labour will tend to be inelastic, for there is less urgency in seeking substitutes (see p. 66). Second, if labour costs form a small percentage of total costs, as in steel production, a rise in wages will produce only a small movement of the supply curve of the product to the left. The opposite applies in each case, e.g. with government services, which are labour intensive.

(iv) *The elasticity of demand for the final product.* The effect of a rise in the wage-rate will be to decrease the supply of a good at each price; that is, the supply curve moves to the left. Hence the market price of the good rises. We have to ask, therefore: 'How much will the demand for the good contract as a result of this rise in price?' Once again we are back to the practical application of elasticity of demand.

If demand is elastic (D_{el}), the quantity of the good demanded will contract considerably, from OM to OM_1 (Figure 20.5). This will mean a large reduction in the numbers employed. On the other hand, if demand is inelastic (D_{inel}), there will be no great contraction in the quantity demanded – only to OM_2. Here people are willing to pay a higher price for the good (OP_2), and this will cover the increase in wages. In other words, the marginal-revenue productivity of labour has risen.

Elasticity of demand depends mainly on the availability of substitutes. Thus demand in export markets is usually more elastic than in the home market, for with the former there are often many competing alternative sources of supply from firms in other countries. Consequently, if an industry sells a high percentage of its output abroad, e.g. electronic equipment and aero engines, the trade union is limited in its ability to secure a wage increase.

(b)   *Imperfect competition.* If there is imperfect competition in selling the product or in hiring labour, the firm is likely to be making supernormal profits. Here it may be possible for the trade union to wring increased wages from the employer without loss of employment. Since it is a monopolist in the supply of labour, the union can insist that the firm shall employ *all* or none of its members at the new wage rate. Thus the firm may be forced to employ workers beyond the point where the MRP = MC. The difference would come from supernormal profits, with the firm working on the principle that it will share the profits with the workers.

In these circumstances there is a whole range of possible wage-rates between the minimum which workers will accept and the maximum which employers are prepared to give rather than lose all their labour. The success of the trade union will depend, therefore, upon (1) the extent to which it can maintain its monopoly position by preventing employers from engaging blacklegs – non-union workers, or other substitute labour – and (2) the bargaining ability of its leaders relative to that of the employers. On the one side, the union leaders have to estimate how high they can push the wage rate without employers allowing a strike to take place; on the other, the employers must judge the lowest rate acceptable without a strike. As each is by no means certain of the other's strength, bluff will play a large part in the negotiations. Such factors as a large order-book for the firm's products, costly equipment standing idle, a wealthy strike fund or increased profits, will obviously strengthen the union's hand. Considerations which could enlist public sympathy are a rise in the cost of living, a higher wage paid elsewhere in comparable occupations and an increase in productivity. Should a strike actually take place, it is usually because of mis-judgement by one side; it is doubtful whether either really gains in the long run by strike action. Thus the strike is a form of 'blood-letting', allowing one or both sides to reassess the position before further negotiations take place.

20.6 THE GOVERNMENT AND WAGES

Influence on wage determination

The government influences the wage-rate in four ways: (i) Minimum-wage regulations. The national minimum wage is a legal right covering almost all workers in the UK. It became law on 1 April 1999 to prevent unduly low pay and also to provide a level playing field for employers. In theory a minimum wage leads to unemployment or excess supply of labour if the minimum is set above the equilibrium or market wage-rate (Figure 20.6). The minimum wage is set above the equilibrium at MW and, as a result, demand for labour falls back to N_1 while supply of labour is increased at the new higher wage rate to N_2. But this is a static analysis and a more dynamic analysis is needed if other things change. So, when the minimum wage was introduced at a time of economic expansion, the demand for labour was increasing (shifting the demand curve for labour to the right (D_1) and absorbing the excess supply). Also, the increased spending power of the workforce increased their demand for goods and services, also increasing demand for labour. As a result, the predictions of unemployment resulting from the introduction of a minimum wage in the UK were proved wrong.

From 1 October 2006 the minimum-wage levels for the UK are: £5.35 per hour for adults; £4.45 per hour for workers aged 18–21; £3.30 per hour for workers aged less than 18.

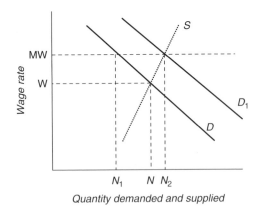

Figure 20.6 Minimum wage legislation

Other government influences on the wage-rate are: (ii) the legal protection it affords to workers with regard to conditions of work, e.g. stipulating a written statement of the conditions of employment, prohibiting discrimination on account of sex or race, protecting employees against unfair dismissal, providing for redundancy payments and regulating conditions for health and safety at work; (iii) its efforts to break down illogicalities, etc. sanctioned by custom; (iv) guidelines for wage settlements which it may lay down from time to time in its efforts to combat inflation (see p. 422).

Curbing trade-union power

With one main exception trade unions are similar to other pressure groups which seek to influence the government to further the interests of their particular causes. The exception is that trade unions can reinforce political means by economic sanctions. Moreover, in the case of key industries, just a small group of workers may, by strikes, go-slow tactics or working-to-rule, disrupt the whole economy.

Successive Conservative governments 1979–97 took the view, therefore, that to achieve the major role of stabilising the economy they could not allow policies to be undermined by trade unions misusing their current extensive legal advantages. Thus a succession of legislation progressively removed trade-union privileges.

In brief, the main changes effected are:

(a) Trade unions may be fined and their assets seized for offences committed by them or their members.

(b) Before industrial action can be taken, approval must be obtained by means of a fully-postal ballot of its members, to be independently scrutinised.

(c) Picketing by employees must be confined to their place of work.

(d) Sympathetic strikes by workers not directly involved in the particular strike are illegal.

(e) A majority of members of a trade union must approve by secret ballot: (i) the setting up or continuance of a closed shop; (ii) any use of funds for any political purposes; (iii) the election of executive committees at least every five years.

(f) Employers must be provided with at least 7 days' notice of official industrial action.

(g) Union subscriptions can only be deducted from employees' pay with their express consent.

Although the powers of trade unions in the UK have been eroded in the last 20 years, in 2005 6.39 million employees were members of a trade union. This represents 29 per cent of employees. Membership appears to be rising for women while falling slightly for men. Membership is also much greater in the public sector than the private sector.

CHAPTER SUMMARY

- UK employment in the service sector has expanded rapidly in the past 30 years while reducing just as rapidly in manufacturing. A large part of the increase in workforce numbers has been in employment of women.
- The size of the labour force is affected by a number of factors, including the population size, the proportion of the population which works and the amount of work offered by each worker.
- Wage-rates are determined by demand and supply, and demand is determined by the MRP of labour. Supply is very important, however, and is influenced by immobility of labour and the trade unions.
- Government legislation also affects the earnings of labour, notably the introduction of a national minimum wage.

REVIEW QUESTIONS

- Why should labour be treated as a separate factor of production?
- Does an increase in the wage-rate necessarily increase the supply of labour?
- What sort of work can be remunerated by 'piece-rates'?
- How can trade unions secure wage increases for their members?
- Explain why the introduction of a minimum wage in the UK in 1999 did not lead to increased unemployment.

 Visit the companion website for further questions

CHAPTER 21

CAPITAL AND INTEREST

LEARNING OBJECTIVES

After studying this chapter you should be able to:
- give different explanations of the meaning of capital;
- explain the nature of opportunity cost in relation to investment for increased future production;
- explain the demand for capital in relation to the marginal-revenue product of capital and the rate of interest.

21.1 CAPITAL

What is 'capital'?

A school teacher earns, say, £600 a week. He also has £1,300 in the National Savings Bank, yielding him £52 per annum interest (or £1 a week). We can say, therefore, that his total *income* is £601 *a week*, or £31,252 *per annum*; his *capital* assets are £1,300.

Thus we see that, whereas *income* is a *flow of wealth* over a *period of time, capital is a stock of wealth* existing at any one *moment of time*.

This broad definition of capital, however, has slightly different meanings when used by different people. The ordinary individual, when speaking of his or her 'capital', would include money assets, holdings of securities, the house, and possibly many durable goods, such as the car, television set, camera, etc. (sometimes referred to as 'consumer's capital'). The businessman would count not only his real assets (such as his factory, machinery, land, stocks of goods, etc.), but add any money reserves ('liquid capital') held in the bank and titles to wealth (such as share certificates, tax-reserve certificates and government bonds).

But the economist considers capital chiefly as a form of wealth which contributes to production. In other words, he is concerned with capital as a *factor of production*, i.e. as something real and not merely a piece of paper. It is the factory and machines, not the share certificates (the individual's entitlement to a part of them), which are vital to him.

This has two effects. First, in defining capital, the economist concentrates on pro-ducer goods and any stocks of finished consumer goods not yet in the hands of the final consumer. Second, in calculating the 'national capital', the economist has to be careful to avoid double-counting. Titles to capital – shares, bonds, savings certifi-cates, National Savings, Treasury Bills and other government securities – must be excluded. Share certificates merely represent the factories, machinery, etc., which have already been counted. Government debt refers to few real assets, for most has been expended on shells, ships, and aircraft in previous wars. The only exception regarding titles to wealth is where a share or bond is held by a foreign national, or conversely, where a British national holds a share or bond representing an asset in a foreign country. We then have to subtract the former and add the latter when cal-culating national capital. Foreign shares or bonds held by British nationals, for example, can always be sold to increase our real resources.

Naturally, 'social capital' (roads, schools, hospitals, municipal buildings, etc.) which belongs to the community at large is just as much capital as factories, offices, etc. And, in order to be consistent, owner-occupied houses have to be included, for they must be treated in the same way as houses owned by property companies (Figure 21.1).

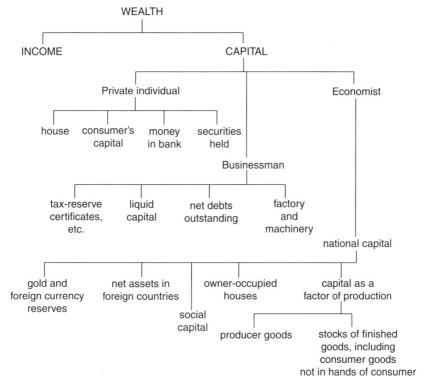

Figure 21.1 'Capital' in the economy

Capital as a factor of production

When the economist refers to 'capital', it is usually in the sense of *wealth which has been made by people for the production of further wealth*. This is because capital plays such an important part in increasing production, and therefore in improving living standards. It is in this sense that the term is used from now on.

Increased production occurs because capital – tools, machines, irrigation works, communications, etc. – greatly assists people in their work. Indeed, with modern electronic equipment, machines often take over the actual work. As the use of capital increases, there are three possible gains. First, more current goods can be produced. Between 1991 and 1996 net output of agriculture increased by 24 per cent. But over that period the number of employees *fell* by 9 per cent. There was thus an increased output per worker, due largely to more efficient machines and improved techniques resulting from capital investment in research. Second, instead of simply producing more current goods, people can be released to produce new goods. And, third, people can, as an alternative to more goods, enjoy increased leisure.

The accumulation of capital

If capital is so important in adding to our well-being, why do we not have more of it? The answer is simply that we can accumulate capital only by postponing current consumption. In everyday language, more jam tomorrow means less jam today. The accumulation of capital represents an opportunity cost over time – consumption now or greater consumption later? A simple example will make this 'trade-off' clear.

Suppose a peasant farmer has been tilling the ground with a primitive spade. By working twelve hours a day he can cultivate one hectare in a year. Obviously, if he had a plough which could be drawn by his oxen it would help him considerably. How can he obtain it? Three ways are open to him:

1. He could reduce the land he cultivates to 3/4 hectare. This would reduce his tilling time by three hours, and he could use this time to make the plough.
2. He could reduce his leisure and sleeping time from twelve to eight hours a day. This would give him an extra four hours for making the plough.
3. He might decide not to consume some of the produce already harvested, exchanging it instead for a plough.

Whichever method is chosen, some present sacrifice is necessary. With (1) and (3) he has to reduce his standard of living by having less to eat. With (2) he has to forgo some leisure – in short, he has either to draw in his belt or work harder. But the reward of such sacrifice comes when he has the plough at work. Then, with twelve hours' work a day he can cultivate 2 ha; his standard of living has doubled.

One other point emerges from this illustration. If, owing to the poverty of the soil, sixteen hours were required to dig his hectare, our farmer would have found it much more difficult to find time to make his plough. He could not reduce his food consumption below subsistence level, nor go without essential sleep. In other words, the more fertile his land, the easier it is for him to increase his income. In economics the maxim 'to him that hath shall be given' often holds. Thus a country with a very low standard of living finds it difficult to build up the capital which would improve its living standards and it is for this reason that any aid which can be given to poor countries is so valuable.

Maintaining capital intact

Naturally our farmer will have to devote time to repairing the plough. So long as his capital equipment is capable of cultivating 2 ha, we can say that it is being 'maintained intact'. If it is being increased or replaced in a more efficient form so that more hectares are cultivated, capital is 'being accumulated'. Where it is not being maintained (as in wartime), capital is being 'run down' or 'depreciated'.

In practice, it is unusual for the same people to devote so much time to producing consumer goods and so much to the production of capital. Instead, production is organised by applying the principle of the division of labour – some people specialise in consumer goods and others in capital goods.

We can now see why most governments encourage investment, the process of producing capital. Where the proportion of productive capacity devoted to investment falls, there may be serious consequences for living standards in the future. More important, the poverty of many countries is chiefly the result of their lack of capital. Hence India, China, Thailand and Cuba have directly restricted present consumption so that capital development may proceed rapidly under 'five-year-plans'.

21.2 INTEREST

Investment, i.e. adding to capital goods or stocks, usually first involves obtaining liquid capital. Interest, expressed as a rate, is the price which has to be paid for this liquid capital. What we shall examine here is the rate of interest which has to be paid for liquid capital in a *particular* use or industry.

The *demand for liquid capital* arises because it is necessary or advantageous to use capital in production. The farmer who sows seed in the autumn and harvests the crop in the summer is using capital in the form of seed. Similarly, a manufacturer needs capital in the form of a factory and machines because it is cheaper to produce in this way.

Now, as we saw when examining the peasant's decision to make a plough, the accumulation of capital can come about only by postponing present consumption. This can be done directly by the producer himself. The farmer could have obtained seed by putting aside a part of the previous year's harvest; the manufacturer could have secured capital by retaining rather than distributing profits.

However, such retentions may be inadequate. In this case funds may be borrowed from other persons who have so saved (that is, forgone current consumption), repaying them later when the product is sold.

The actual demand of the farmer or manufacturer will depend upon the MRP of capital – the addition to profit which, for instance, a farmer thinks will result from adding an additional cow to his herd. Suppose he calculates that profit can be increased by spending £800 on a cow now. To avoid complications, let us also assume that he considers that in eight years' time, when the cow ceases to be worth milking, he will be able to sell it for beef for £800. Assume that the increase in profit (yield from the extra milk less labour and feeding costs) is estimated to be £200 for the year. He would then be willing to borrow the money to buy that cow so long as the interest he had to pay was not more than £200, i.e. not more than 25 per cent. If he bought another cow, the net addition to receipts might be only £190, for the third cow £180, and so on. It is possible, therefore, to draw a curve showing the expected addition to profit which results from adding one more cow. We can term this the 'marginal revenue productivity of capital' curve, and the farmer will go on borrowing capital until the rate of interest equals the marginal-revenue product. Hence at different rates of interest, different quantities of capital will be demanded. In Figure 21.2, when the rate of interest is OR, the farmer will borrow capital to buy 8 cows. If the rate falls to OR_1, he will borrow sufficient capital to buy 11 cows. One point must be emphasised. Because he is producing in advance, the farmer has to base his demand for capital on the *prospective* money yield resulting from its use. His expectations are thus all-important, and we shall have more to say on this subject later.

The sum of the demand curves for liquid capital from all the firms in the industry gives the demand curve for the industry, though some allowance could be made for a fall in the price of the good produced by the capital equipment (see p. 157).

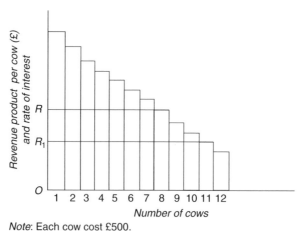

Note: Each cow cost £500.

Figure 21.2 Demand for capital, the marginal-revenue product of capital and the rate of interest

The *supply* of liquid funds for *one* use can only be obtained by bidding them away from alternative uses. How much has to be paid for a given quantity relative to other uses will depend upon (a) lenders' estimate of the risk involved, (b) the period of the loan, and (c) the elasticity of demand for the alternative products to which capital contributes.

Generally speaking, however, we can expect more liquid capital to be forthcoming for a particular use the higher the rate of interest offered. We therefore have an upward-sloping supply curve. Thus the rate of interest is fixed by the interaction of the demand and supply curves (as in Figure 13.2).

Once again, however, we must point out that this is only a *partial* explanation of the determination of a rate of interest. It does not tell us how the *general* level of the rate of interest is determined. To discover what determines this benchmark we have to look at the nature of money and government policy (see Chapters 24 and 27).

CHAPTER SUMMARY

....

- Capital is a stock of wealth existing at a point in time. To an economist, capital, such as factories and machines, is wealth which has been made by people to contribute to future production.
- There is an opportunity cost of capital which is the sacrifice of current consumption necessary in order to provide it.
- The demand for capital will depend on its marginal-revenue product (the addition to profit from a unit of capital).
- The cost of borrowing liquid capital is the rate of interest, and the investor will borrow until the MRP equals the rate of interest.
- For all units of capital where the MRP is greater than the rate of interest the investor makes a profit.

REVIEW QUESTIONS

....

- Why would it be difficult for a subsistence society to accumulate capital?
- Identify the determinants of the rate of interest.
- Explain how a factory owner would decide how many production machines to buy using borrowed money.

 Visit the companion website for further questions

LAND AND RENT

LEARNING OBJECTIVES

After studying this chapter you should be able to:
- explain the meaning of economic rent as a surplus resulting from the fixed nature of land;
- analyse the determinants of the economic rent earned by a factor of production;
- explain 'quasi-rent'.

22.1 'LAND' AND 'RENT' IN GENERAL TERMS

The everyday meaning of 'land' and 'rent'

To the economist the terms 'land' and 'rent' have a special meaning. This is just as well, for in everyday speech each can imply different things. Thus if I buy land for farming, it will probably include buildings, fences, a water supply and a drainage system, all of which are really capital. Similarly, I can rent things other than land – a house, television set, gas-meter, building equipment, shooting rights, etc. Rent in this sense simply means a periodic payment for the use of something. It can be termed 'commercial rent.'

Usually, however, rent does refer to payment for the use of a piece of land and, before we consider 'land' and 'rent' in their special economic sense, we must ask what determines how much rent is paid to a landlord.

The rent of land in a particular use – commercial rent

The problem is similar to the determination of the return on any factor service. The demand for land depends on its marginal-revenue productivity. The curve slopes downwards from left to right for the reasons given in Chapter 13. On the supply side, land, like labour, can usually be put to alternative uses – building factories or houses, growing wheat or barley, raising cattle or sheep, and so on. A given piece of land will be transferred to its most profitable use. If, for instance, the price of cattle rises and that of wheat falls, some land will be transferred from arable to pasture farming. Should the price of cattle rise still further, more land will be transferred, and so on. We can thus draw a supply curve for land in a particular use. It slopes upwards from left to right. The interaction of the demand and supply curves will give the rent actually paid (Figure 22.1).

Of course, this assumes: (a) that landlords can vary the rent charged any time the demand for and supply of their particular type of land alters; and (b) that land can be transferred fairly quickly to a different use. The first assumption is complicated by the fact that rents are usually fixed for a period of years. Only when the lease expires is the landlord free to adjust the rent. The second assumption implies that we are concerned only with the long period in our analysis. But what of the short period when land is a fixed factor? An analysis of this situation is what we are concerned with in the remainder of this chapter.

22.2 ECONOMIC RENT – LAND AND RENT TO THE ECONOMIST

Ricardo's views on 'land' and 'rent'

To explain the special meaning which economists today give to the terms 'land' and 'rent', we have to examine the views of David Ricardo, a classical economist of the early nineteenth century. He was concerned, not with the rent paid to land for a particular purpose, but with the rent paid to land as a whole. Moreover, just as in Chapter 6 we defined land as 'the resources provided freely by nature'

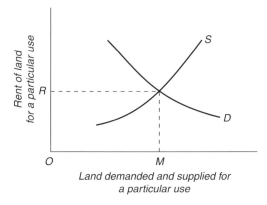

Figure 22.1   The determination of the rent of a plot of land

(thereby eliminating improvements by man through the addition of capital), so too it was the 'original and indestructible powers of the soil' that Ricardo emphasised. As such its total supply was fixed once and for all.

In this respect, he argued, land was different from the other factors of production, capital and labour. When the price of capital rose, people would be induced to postpone present consumption; the supply of capital would expand. Similarly, a rise in wages would be an inducement to rear and train more children. On the other hand, should the price of capital and labour fall, supply would contract. If no price at all were offered, there would be no supply. Both of these factors have a supply price, more being supplied the higher the price.

But with land as a whole – in the sense of space and natural resources – the same amount is available whatever the price offered. An increase in price cannot bring about an expansion of supply; on the other hand, if the price fell to zero, the same amount would still be available. Land as a whole, therefore, has no supply price. Its return was simply a residual surplus – the difference between receipts and payments of wages for labour and interest for capital. If the price received for the product were high, there would be more left over as rent; if the price were low, there would be less for rent. Rent did not determine the price of the good produced; instead, the opposite was true – rent was determined by price.

'Land' and 'rent' in economic theory today

On the ambiguities of Ricardo's reasoning we need not dwell. First, it can be argued that the total supply of land is fixed only in the short period; in the long run improved farming techniques and developments in transport are constantly increasing the amount of land which can be put to economic use. Indeed, in this respect there is little difference between land and other factors of production, which likewise can only be increased in the long period. Over a certain period of time – the short period, whatever that may be in months or years – all are fixed in total supply. Second, land, like other factors of production, has alternative uses. It can be used to produce different crops, or as a site for different buildings. The cost of putting it to one use is the yield that could have been obtained had it been employed in another way. Thus, in order to secure it for one purpose, a producer will have to pay a sufficient price to attract it from its best alternative use. It is this allocation of land between its different uses which is the main concern of the economist.

The nature of the return to a fixed factor

But Ricardo did point out an essential truth – that the return to a factor fixed in supply, i.e. whose supply is absolutely inelastic, will vary directly with variations in the price of the good produced by it. We can illustrate this more clearly by a simple example.

Let us assume: (a) a given plot of land on which only potatoes can be grown; (b) only land and labour are necessary to grow potatoes; (c) the supply of labour for growing potatoes is perfectly elastic because only a small proportion of the total labour force is required.

The return to this plot of land will depend entirely on the price of potatoes. This can be seen from Figure 22.2. When the marginal-revenue product of labour is shown by the curve QN, at a wage of OP, OM workers are employed. The value of the total product is $OMNQ$; the wage bill is $OMNP$ and the return to the plot of land PNQ. If now the price of potatoes increases, the marginal-revenue product of labour rises, in Figure 22.2, to Q_1N_1. OM_1 labourers are now employed at a wage bill of $OM_1N_1P_1$. (Each worker still receives the same wage, OP, because the supply of this type of labour is perfectly elastic.) But the return to the given plot of land has increased to PN_1Q_1. The opposite would apply if the price of potatoes fell.

Certain practical conclusions follow from the above analysis:

(i) Because the plot of land will grow only potatoes, it will be cultivated so long as the value of the total product is sufficient to pay the wage-bill. In other words, at the lower price a lump-sum tax on the plot up to QPN could be levied without affecting the output. This is the theoretical basis of the often proposed tax on land. Unfortunately, in practice it is impossible to distinguish precisely between economic rent and other factor earnings.

(ii) The return to land as we have analysed it above – rent in its economic sense – is purely a surplus. It arose because, by definition, our plot of land was confined to one particular use – growing potatoes. The supply of this land offered for sale or hire will not be affected by a price, simply because nobody has any other use for it. In short, it has no opportunity or transfer cost.

(iii) Once land has been built on, it is largely specific to a given use, and the return to the land and building will be dependent on future demand.

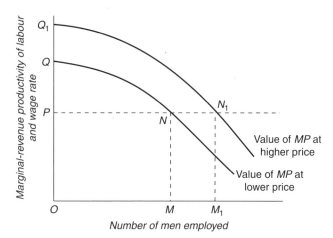

Figure 22.2 The effect of a change in the price of a product on the rent of land

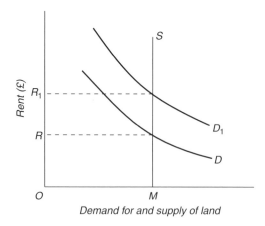

Demand for and supply of land

Figure 22.3   The determination of rent when land is fixed in supply

(iv)   Because land is really space, it is impossible to increase the area of sites in city centres except by building upwards, e.g. as in Oxford Street and the City of London. Such fixity of supply means that rent is largely determined by current demand. Thus in Figure 22.3 it is assumed that the supply of land is fixed at OM. This means that the rent is determined by demand: an increase from D to D_1 raises rent from OR to OR_1. For instance, rents in Oxford Street depend upon the demand for shops there (which in its turn depends upon people's spending) and rents in the City of London depend on the demand for offices there (which in turn depend upon the level of business activity).

Economic rent

The principle of rent being a surplus resulting from the fixed nature of land has a more general application. Economists have adopted Ricardo's concept of land as being symbolic of all factors which, in some way or another, are fixed in supply. The return to such factors is usually discussed under the headings of 'economic rent' and 'quasi-rent'.

'Economic rent' is the term used to describe *the earnings of any factor over and above its supply price*. Put in another way, it is any surplus over its transfer earnings – what it could obtain in its next most profitable use (its 'opportunity cost', in our earlier terminology). How this idea can be applied generally will now be explained.

The actual rate of return to a factor is the price per period of time at which it is now selling its services. For example, the return to a plasterer is his wage, say £360 per week.

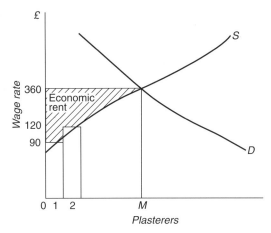

Figure 22.4 Economic rent

But what is the opportunity cost? Simply what has to be paid to retain it in its present use – that is, sufficient to keep it from going to the best alternative use. Take our plasterer, for instance. His next best occupation may simply be plasterer's labourer, earning £180 per week. He would offer his services as a plasterer, therefore, at anything above £180 per week.

A second plasterer, however, may be a competent bricklayer, and as such earn £240 per week. Therefore, at least £240 per week must be offered for the services of the plasterer. And so we could go on. The supply curve of plasterers to the industry is thus an 'opportunity cost' curve (Figure 22.4).

If in Figure 22.4 we now insert the demand curve, we can obtain the current wage rate to the industry, £360 when *OM* plasterers will be employed. But all plasterers receive this wage rate. Thus the first plasterer receives an economic rent of £180, the second £120, and so on. The total economic rent received by plasterers as a whole is shown by the shaded area.

What determines the size of economic rent?

The size of economic rent earned by a particular type of factor depends not only on demand but also upon the elasticity of supply of that factor and how the particular type of factor is defined.

1.   The elasticity of supply

Elasticity of supply is determined largely by the period of time under consideration and immobilities, some of which cannot be eliminated even in the long period. Both will affect economic rent.

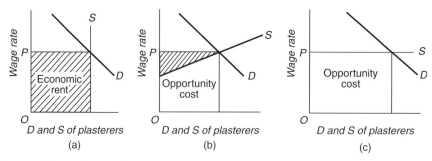

Figure 22.5 Economic rent and elasticity of supply

Let us assume that, in the short period, the supply of plasterers is fixed; there is insufficient time for them to move into alternative occupations or for others to move in. In short, there is no alternative occupation – they can either work as plasterers or not at all. Thus all their earnings are economic rent (Figure 22.5a).

In the long period, however, other occupations can be trained as plasterers, and existing plasterers can move elsewhere. Sufficient has to be paid – the opportunity cost – to retain plasterers. Thus we have a long-period supply curve of plasterers, and economic rent is smaller (Figure 22.5b).

If the supply of plasterers became perfectly elastic, then economic rent would disappear (Figure 22.5c). Thus economic rent depends upon a less than perfectly elastic supply curve to the industry.

Sometimes the degree of immobility between different uses or occupations persists indefinitely. Building sites for offices in the City of London, for instance, earn rents far in excess of what they could obtain in their best alternative use, say for houses. Simply because such sites are very limited in supply, competition for office accommodation has forced up the rents of these sites far beyond the possible price which houses could offer. A large part of their earnings is therefore 'economic rent'.

Occasionally, too, we refer to the 'rent of ability'. Many pop singers, film stars, barristers and surgeons have a talent which, to all intents and purposes, is unique, for it cannot be duplicated by training others. Their high earnings, therefore, are almost wholly in the nature of 'economic rent'.

2. The definition of an 'occupation' etc.

If we adopt a wide definition of our factor, e.g. land as a whole, the distinction is between employing it or idleness, and thus the whole of its earnings is economic rent. This is what Ricardo had in mind.

If, however, our definition is narrower, e.g. land for a particular use, such as for growing wheat, then the opportunity cost will be larger (e.g. growing barley) and economic rent smaller. Similarly, we could distinguish between cabinet-makers and carpenters, surgeons and doctors, etc. Each would give a smaller 'economic rent' than if the distinction were simply between cabinet-makers and labourers, surgeons and nurses, etc.

Likewise, economic rent will be different whether we are looking at it from the point of view of the industry or the firm. The industry is unlikely to have a perfectly elastic supply curve; thus there will be some element of economic rent in its payment to the factors it hires. The firm, however, will face, in perfect competition, a perfectly elastic supply curve. In this case it will pay the transfer cost to all factors (whose best alternative is another firm); there is thus no economic rent.

Quasi-rent

For fixed factors, particularly capital equipment, what the firm has to pay to retain them will vary according to the period of time.

In the short period, capital equipment is, by definition, fixed in supply. There is no transfer price. More capital equipment cannot be added; nor can existing equipment be diminished. The firm, as we have seen, will continue to work its capital equipment so long as total earnings just cover the cost of variable factors (see Chapter 11). Any earnings above variable costs will be in the nature of a residual which helps towards the cost of the fixed factors. The size of this residual depends upon the price at which the product sells.

This can be seen immediately if we refer to Figure 11.6. Were the demand for mowers to increase, the price would rise, say to £600, and production would be expanded to the point where once again price equalled marginal cost, i.e. to 100 units. The increased cost of such production would be equal to the increase in total cost, i.e. £5,100. But total receipts would have increased by £19,500, and so the fixed factors earn an additional return – the increase in 'supernormal profit', equal to £14,400.

As time passes, however, we move into the 'long period'. If the product has been selling at a high price, the high return to the capital equipment will induce firms to install additional equipment. On the other hand, if the price of the product were low, existing capital equipment will either be transferred to its next most profitable use, or, when it wears out, simply not be replaced. In the long period, therefore, earnings of fixed factors are, under perfect competition, equal to their transfer cost; economic rent is eliminated.

To distinguish between economic rent which is more or less permanent and that which disappears over time, the latter is often referred to as 'quasi-rent'. It is not a true rent, for the high return earned by such factors leads to an increase in their supply, and this eliminates the economic rent they earn. True rent refers only to factors which are fixed in supply; even if their earnings are high, identical factors are not forthcoming, and so economic rent persists.

CHAPTER SUMMARY

- The return to a factor fixed in supply will vary directly with variations in the price of the good produced by it.
- Economic rent is the earnings of any factor above its supply price or transfer earnings (what it could earn in an alternative use).
- The size of the economic rent of a factor is determined by the demand for it and the elasticity of supply of the factor, and how widely or narrowly the factor is defined.
- Quasi-rent is temporary economic rent (surplus) earned in the short-run but competed away in the long-run.

REVIEW QUESTIONS

- Use a diagram to analyse the earnings of a highly paid celebrity or foot-baller.
- Why does land in the City of London command a high price?
- Show how the return to land growing wheat will change as the price of wheat increases.
- Why should the price of building land increase if the price of houses increases?

 Visit the companion website for further questions

ENTREPRENEURSHIP
AND PROFIT

23.1 ENTREPRENEURSHIP

The identity of entrepreneurship and risk-bearing

For production to take place, resources must be brought together and set to work. Whoever undertakes this task is often described as 'the entrepreneur'. Usually, however, a somewhat narrower meaning is given to the term.

Organising production can be broken down into two parts. First, there is the task of co-ordination – bringing factors of production together and setting them to work. Second, there is accepting the risk of buying factors to produce goods which will not be sold until some time in the future – when receipts may not cover costs.

In practice, it is not always easy to separate coordination and risk. A farmer, for instance, not only manages and runs the farm, but also accepts the risk involved in deciding what to produce. On the other hand, in a joint-stock company most of the work of coordination is left to a paid board of directors, with a manager playing the major role. Here the risks of the business are borne by the ordinary shareholders. With a public sector agency, such as the Forestry Commission, they are carried by the taxpayers. But neither shareholders nor taxpayers take part in running the business except remotely.

The function of co-ordination, therefore, can be fulfilled by a paid manager. In this respect, management is simply an exceptionally highly skilled form of labour.

Thus we narrow our concept of enterprise to cover only bearing those risks of the business associated with ownership.

The nature of risks

A firm is always open to the risk of fire, accidents, theft, damage by storm, etc. But these risks are calculable. A mathematician can work out, for instance, the chances of a building catching fire during the course of the year. One cannot say which building will be destroyed in this way, but information is available which states that on average, say, 1 out of every 10,000 will be. Such risks can therefore be insured against. They are thus reduced to a normal cost – what the firm has to pay to contract out of the risk involved.

Certain risks, however, cannot be calculated according to a law of averages. Nobody, for instance, can forecast with certainty how many cold drinks will be sold in Britain next summer. That will depend upon the weather. Similarly, it might be thought that a new 'mini' car would sell profitably. But again there is a chance that this will not be so. The risk of demand being different from that estimated cannot be reduced to a mathematical probability. Such a risk, therefore, cannot be insured against; it must be accepted by those persons whose money is tied up in producing goods for an uncertain demand.

These uninsurable risks are inherent in a dynamic economy. Modern methods of production take time. When an entrepreneur engages factors of production, therefore, it is an act of faith – faith in his estimate of the demand for the product some time ahead. But demand can never be completely certain. People have freedom of choice, and their tastes may change. Many of the factors affecting demand fluctuate even over a relatively short period of time. It is similar on the supply side. Techniques do not stand still; new methods discovered by a rival may mean that, by the time a firm's product comes on the market, it is undersold by a cheaper or better substitute.

Thus there is always some degree of uncertainty, and this involves risk. It is a risk which must be shouldered by those who back with their money the decision as to what shall be produced. The true entrepreneurs, therefore, are those who accept the risks of *uncertainty-bearing*.

23.2 PROFIT

How profit differs in nature from other rewards

The reward of uncertainty-bearing is 'profit'. But profit differs from the earnings of other factors of production. First, profit may be negative. Whereas wages, rent and interest are paid as part of a contract at the time of hiring, profit is received in the future, and then only if expected demand has materialised. Where the entrepreneur has been far too optimistic, a loss is made. Second, profit fluctuates more than other rewards. Thus its size is uncertain, for it feels the immediate impact of booms and slumps. In a boom profits rise faster than wages, while in a slump they fall more severely. Third, unlike wages, interest, and rent, which are contractual and certain payments, profit is simply a residual.

Differences in the concept of the term 'profit'

We must be careful to distinguish four different concepts of 'profit':

1. Profit in its everyday meaning

To the accountant, profit means simply the difference between total receipts and total costs (see p. 124). But because the economist defines costs in terms of alternatives forgone, this idea of profit is amended by deducting, first, the return which would have been received on capital had it been used elsewhere, and second, the value of the entrepreneur's skill in the best alternative line of business (see also p. 124).

2. Normal profit under perfect competition

Because uncertainty cannot be eliminated from a dynamic economy, there must be a return to induce people to bear uncertainty. This is true even in the long period. Thus there must be a rate of profit – the price which equates the demand for and supply of entrepreneurship. In the long period under perfect competition, any rent element from profit is eliminated. We then have 'normal profit' – the cost which has to be met if the supply of uncertainty-bearing is to be maintained.

Two modifications should be noted. First, industries differ as regards the uncertainty involved. Where fashions or techniques change frequently, for instance, uncertainty is greater. Entrepreneurs in these riskier industries, therefore, would require a higher level of normal profit. Second, the elimination of the rent element in profit in the long period is only possible if one assumes that entrepreneurs of equal ability are available. In practice, this is not so. Thus there will always be some entrepreneurs earning a rent of ability (supernormal profit) even in the long period (see p. 144).

3. Supernormal profit

Under perfect competition the entrepreneur is able to make supernormal profit for a period because new firms cannot enter the industry. Certain factors such as key workers and machines are for a time fixed in supply, and entrepreneurs already possessing them will make supernormal profit. In other words such profit is really the return to fixed factors in the short period; it is the 'quasi-rent' earned by such factors.

4. *Monopoly profit*

With monopoly, competitors can be excluded. Certain factors, e.g. diamond mines, know-how, patents and copyrights, are fixed to the monopolist. Even in the long period, competitors cannot engage such factors, and so supernormal profits persist. The profits of the monopolist are therefore closer to economic rent than to quasi-rent.

23.3 THE ROLE OF PROFIT IN THE MARKET ECONOMY

'Profit' tends to be an emotive word, and firms which make large profits are often frowned upon. But usually there is little justification for this, since it is through profits – and losses – that the market economy works. We must emphasise, however, that we are discussing only profits under competitive conditions. But, given such conditions, profit fulfils the following functions:

1. Normal profit induces people to accept the risks of uncertainty

Because uncertainty is implicit in a dynamic economy, a reward – normal profit – is essential for entrepreneurs to undertake production. Thus normal profit is a cost, as essential as the payment of wages. The level will vary with the industry; thus it will be higher for oil exploration than for selling petrol.

2. Supernormal profit indicates whether an industry should expand or should contract

When a firm produces a good which proves to be popular with consumers, it probably makes supernormal profit. This indicates that output should be expanded. On the other hand losses show that consumers do not want the good, and production should contract.

3. Supernormal profit encourages firms to increase production

Profits not only indicate that consumers want more of a good: they are also the inducement to firms to produce those goods. As we saw in Chapter 11, supernormal profits act as the spur for existing firms to increase capacity and for other firms to enter the industry. On the other hand, when losses are being incurred, firms go out of production and the industry contracts. Thus losses are as important as profits in the operation of the market economy.

4. Supernormal profit provides the resources for expansion

An industry making supernormal profit can secure the factors necessary to expand. First, profits can be ploughed back, while shareholders will respond to requests for further capital, usually through rights issues. New firms can enter the industry, because investors will subscribe to a company intending to operate where the level of profits is relatively high. Second, profits allow expanding firms to offer higher rewards to attract factors. In this way resources are moved according to the wishes of consumers.

5. Supernormal profit encourages research, innovation and exploration

Research, e.g. for new drugs, and exploration e.g. for oil, carry a high risk of failure and therefore of wasted capital expenditure. But the possibility of high returns if successful induces firms to engage in research, especially if new developments are protected for a period from competitors by patents.

6. Profits ensure that production is carried on by the most efficient firms

In a competitive industry the firm making the largest profit is the one whose costs are lowest. It will have an incentive to expand production and, if necessary, can afford to pay more for factors to do so. Less efficient firms must copy its methods to retain factors. In any case the increased output of the more efficient firm will eventually lower the price of the product. As a result inefficient firms make losses: profits have become negative.

To sum up, profits and losses are the means by which the process of natural selection occurs in the market economy. The drive is provided by profits – and the fear of losses. Whether the desire for personal gain is the best of motives may be open to doubt. But, human nature being what it is, it is still the most effective. Uncertainty exists in any dynamic economy, and so there is bound to be scope for profits whether production is organised by private enterprise or by the State. What we have to ask, therefore, is: 'When no personal gain or loss is involved, is there the same incentive to maximise profits or to avoid losses?'

It must be pointed out, too, that under perfect competition, profits are self-destructive. Thus where there is competition it is wrong to regard profits as being somehow immoral. The exception is monopoly profits, which are not eliminated even in the long period. Entry into the industry is not free; consequently profits are not competed away. It may be that such monopoly profits stimulate research and allow an industry to expand. But where scarcity has been deliberately brought about, they simply represent an economic rent earned at the expense of consumers by the monopolist owners. Moreover, an efficient allocation of resources according to the wishes of consumers does not take place.

CHAPTER SUMMARY
....

- Entrepreneurs coordinate the factors of production and bear the risks of business.
- Profit is their reward for risk-taking or uncertainty-bearing.
- There are different concepts of profit, with supernormal profits (economic rent) being competed away in competition, but persisting in monopoly.
- Profits and losses of firms lead to their survival or decline and provide dynamism in the economy.

REVIEW QUESTIONS
....

- Is a company managing director an entrepreneur? Explain your answer.
- How does profit differ from the rewards to other factors of production?
- How do profits and losses drive change in the market economy?

 Visit the companion website for further questions

PART

VI

MONEY AND FINANCIAL INSTITUTIONS

MONEY AND THE RATE OF INTEREST

LEARNING OBJECTIVES

After studying this chapter you should be able to:
- describe the functions of money;
- explain why there is a demand for liquid money;
- identify the narrow and broad components of the money supply;
- show how interest rates are determined.

24.1 THE FUNCTIONS OF MONEY

What is money?

It is possible to exchange goods by a direct swap. But barter, as direct exchange is usually termed, is comparatively rare in the modern world. Consider this advertisement in the *Exchange and Mart*: 'Ever Ready battery portable in exchange for any pedigree bitch up to two years.' The formidable difficulties in the way of such an exchange are obvious.

In an economy where there is a high degree of specialisation, exchanges must take place quickly and smoothly. Hence we have a 'go-between' – money – a common denominator for all goods. The product of specialised labour is sold, that is, exchanged for money, and this money is then used to buy the many different goods and services required.

Anything which is generally acceptable in purchasing goods or settling debts can be said to be money. It need not consist of coins and notes. Oxen, salt, amber, woodpecker scalps, and cotton cloth have at times all been used as money.

In fact, the precise substance, its size and shape, are largely a matter of convenience and custom. But whatever is used, it should be immediately and unquestionably accepted in exchange for goods and services.

Legal tender

Sometimes an attempt is made to confer acceptability by law. In the United Kingdom, notes have full 'legal tender', in that a creditor must accept them in payment of a debt. But a commodity does not have to be legal tender for it to be money. A commodity will only be accepted as money if people feel confident it will retain its value.

Precious metals as money

Most commodities used as money in the past have proved unsatisfactory. Oxen, for instance, were bulky to transport, deteriorated over time, and were costly to store. Moreover, not only were they rarely uniform in size or quality, but they could not easily be divided to purchase goods of small value.

Hence, precious metals eventually replaced other goods as money. Later, in order to simplify transactions, metals were minted into coins of different weights and shapes. The exact amount of money required could now be found by counting (see Genesis 37 v. 25) instead of by weighing (Genesis 23 v. 16).

Paper money

In England, precious metals and coins were used almost exclusively as money until the middle of the seventeenth century. However, in 1640, Charles I appropriated £130,000 worth of gold held for merchants in the Tower of London. Thereafter gold and silver bullion plate were kept in the strong rooms of the goldsmiths. Eventually receipts for these deposits were accepted in exchange for goods, and so withdrawal of the actual gold and silver became unnecessary.

This was the origin of the bank-note and paper currency soon began to form an increasing proportion of British money. Because people who receive notes are confident that others too will accept them, notes possess the essential characteristic of money – general acceptability. This is true even though, since 1931, it has not been possible in the UK to exchange notes for gold at the Bank of England.

The functions of money

Money, it is usually stated, performs four functions:

(1) It is *a medium of exchange*, the oil, as it were, which allows the machinery of modern buying and selling to run smoothly.

(2) It is *a measure of value and a unit of account*, making possible the operation of a price system and automatically providing the basis for keeping accounts, calculating profit and loss, costing, etc.

(3) It is *a standard of deferred payments*, the unit in which, given stability in its value, loans are made and future contracts fixed. Without money, there would be no common basis to allow for dealing in debts – the work of such institutions as insurance companies, building societies, banks, pension funds and discount-houses. By providing a standard for repayment, money makes borrowing and lending much easier.

(4) It is *a store of wealth*, the most convenient way of keeping any income which is surplus to immediate requirements. More than that, because money is also the medium of exchange, wealth stored in this form is completely liquid: it can be converted into other goods immediately and without cost. Or, in the words of the Bible: 'Wine maketh merry; but money answereth all things' (Ecclesiastes 10:19). Since this 'liquidity' is the most distinctive characteristic of money, we can also define money as anything which confers complete liquidity on its holder. As we shall see, such liquidity results in money's playing an active rather than a merely neutral part in the operation of the economy.

24.2   THE DEMAND FOR MONEY

What do we mean by the 'demand for money'?

Most people would regard a miser as a crank. To the ordinary person, money is wanted not just for counting or to be gloated over, but to be spent on food, clothes, holidays, a car, and all the other things which can be enjoyed. In short, it would seem that money is useful only when we are getting rid of it.

But there is somewhat more to it than that. Money was defined as anything generally acceptable in settling debts. But why is it 'generally acceptable'? Simply because everybody has confidence that other people will accept it *immediately* whenever they wish to buy something. In other words, money is perfectly liquid.

Moreover, no other form of wealth is liquid to the same degree as money. Assets kept in a deposit account at a bank are subject to seven days' notice of withdrawal. Equities and bonds have to be sold before anything else can be bought, and this involves payment of broker's commission and maybe a capital loss. Or, if a house, car, or piano are to be exchanged for something else, it usually means first finding a cash purchaser. Only money can be changed into some other form of wealth without cost or delay.

People want money, therefore, because it is a perfectly liquid asset. It is in this sense that there is a 'demand' for money – *to hold perfectly liquid reserves*. We must now examine more closely why people should want such reserves.

Why people demand money

John Maynard Keynes gave three main reasons for holding money (in his 1936 *General Theory*):

1. The transactions motive

Both consumers and businessmen hold money to facilitate current transactions.

Most consumers receive the bulk of their income weekly or monthly. On the other hand, payments for food, travel, and pleasure have to be made each day. Thus a part of money income has to be held throughout the week or month to cover these everyday purchases. How much will this be?

Suppose that a man's take-home pay is £280 a week, all of which is being spent. He receives £280 on the Friday which begins the week, and by the following Friday he will have nothing left. Thus his average holding of money is £140. Should it now be decided to pay him monthly, and his spending habits remain the same, his average holding of money, either in cash or in his current account at the bank, would rise to £560. In the same way, if his income doubled but was still fully spent, the amount of money he held would double.

Similarly, a businessman requires a money balance because he has to pay wages, purchase raw materials, and meet other current expenses before he sells his goods, i.e. he has a 'cash flow' requirement.

There may be special reasons why the demand for money for the transactions motive may suddenly increase; it does, for instance, at Christmas and holiday periods, or if there is a flurry of activity on the Stock Exchange. Usually the underlying determinants are fairly stable. With consumers, these are the length of the time between successive pay-days and the level of income and prices; with businessmen, it is the size of turnover. It can be seen, therefore, that the community's demand for money for transactions purposes will be roughly in proportion to the size of national income.

It should be noted that the value of transactions for which money is required is much greater than the value of money national income. For instance, if the cost of goods to a shopkeeper (including shop expenses) is £100, and these goods are sold for £110, the income from the transaction is £10, whereas £210 in money was required to effect the necessary exchanges. In addition, money is required for what are basically non-income creating transactions, e.g. switching securities.

2. The precautionary motive

Apart from expenditure on regular, everyday purchases, money is also required to cover events of a more uncertain nature which may easily occur – illness, accident, unemployment, defects in the car or household appliances, and snap decisions to obtain a cash bargain. Similarly business-men usually keep some extra reserve of cash in case of bad debts or to make a favourable purchase.

The amount held will depend mainly on the outlook of the individual, how optimistic he is both as regards events and the possibility of borrowing at short notice should the need arise e.g. through an overdraft facility. But, taking the community as a whole, the amount set aside for the precautionary motive is, in normal times, likely to be tied fairly closely to the level of national income.

Keynes termed the money held for the transactions and precautionary motives as 'active' balances. The size of such balances is chiefly dependent on the level of income.

3. The speculative motive

Usually the amount of money in existence exceeds that necessary to satisfy the demand for active balances. But any surplus must be held by somebody, for it must be somewhere! Why, however, should people wish to hold 'idle' balances?

The immediate response of the reader might be 'why not?' As we have seen, money has no carrying costs (e.g. storage, maintenance) and is perfectly liquid. Of all assets, only money confers complete manoeuvrability.

But holding wealth in the form of money has the disadvantage that *it does not provide a yield*. (In periods of inflation, there is the added disadvantage that the value of money is falling, but we can ignore this complication for the time being.) Furniture, jewellery, works of art, etc., afford pleasure; a house can be lived in or rented out. With shares, there is usually a dividend; with bonds, a fixed rate of interest. There is thus an opportunity cost of being liquid – the yield forgone. To simplify, let us refer to this yield as 'the rate of interest'.

Thus, while people might desire liquidity, they have also to think of the cost involved. The higher the rate of interest, the greater the cost of remaining liquid. As the rate rises, so fewer people will be prepared to pay the 'price'; in other words, they will be tempted out of holding money. Thus demand for idle balances is closely related to the rate of interest – the higher the rate, the greater the cost of holding money and so the less will money be demanded.

But the complete answer is less simple than this. Keynes considered that the main reason why people hold idle balances is to guard against a possible capital loss. He termed this the 'speculative' motive.

On any given day it is quite usual for the prices of some securities to rise while those of others fall. But there are periods when the prices of almost all securities move in more or less the same direction. To simplify our explanation, however, we shall concentrate our attention on undated government bonds (fixed-interest-bearing securities); this eliminates time and risk complications.

If people think that the price of bonds is going to rise, they will buy bonds now. Should their forecast prove correct, they will make a capital gain. Similarly, if they think that the price of bonds is going to fall, they will sell bonds because money is now a better store of value. Now as the price of bonds falls, so more people will think that the next likely move will be upwards. As the price rises, so more people will start coming round to the view that the price is so high that a fall is likely to occur. It follows, therefore, that when the price of bonds is low, people prefer bonds to liquidity; but as the price rises, people move out of bonds in order to hold money.

However, the price of bonds varies proportionately but inversely with the rate of interest. Thus if the current rate of interest is 2.5 per cent (that is, the government can sell bonds on a 2.5 per cent yield), investors would be willing to pay £140 for a 3.5 per cent War Loan since this would reflect an equivalent yield. Similarly, if the current rate of interest were 14 per cent, the 3.5 per cent War Loan would fetch only £25.

Thus it is possible to relate the demand for money, not only to the price of bonds, but also to the rate of interest. When people are speculating against the future price of bonds they are speculating against the future rate of interest. Hence we can rewrite our original proposition as follows: when the rate of interest is low (the price of bonds is high), people will prefer to hold money; when the rate of interest is high (the price of bonds is low), people will not wish to hold money. This relationship between the current rate of interest and the demand for idle money balances is shown in Figure 24.1.

Keynes's term 'speculative' in this situation is rather unfortunate in that it tends to misrepresent the asset-holder's objective. Some 'speculation' must occur where there is an element of uncertainty, and persons in charge of funds, e.g. pension funds, have, as a minimum, to take precautions to avoid capital loss. In doing so they have to take a view as to the future movement of 'bond' prices generally. The bond-holder will compare the interest likely to be earned on the bond over a period with the possibility of any loss in its capital value. If the latter outweighs the former, the bond-holder will prefer to hold money.

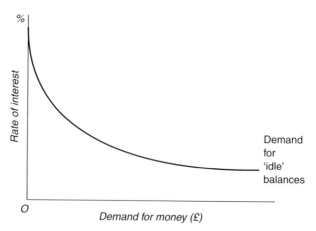

Figure 24.1 The relationship between the rate of interest and the demand for money

Whereas the level of income, the main factor influencing the demand for money for the transactions and precautionary motives, is fairly stable, people's expectations of the future rate of interest, the determinant of liquidity preference for the speculative motive, is far more liable to change. It is this speculation, therefore, which Lord Keynes considers exercises the dominating influence on the level of the rate of interest.

More recently however, economists have cast doubts on the justification for separating the three motives. Above all, criticism has been levelled at the view that increases in the supply of money will be absorbed in idle speculative balances rather than be spent (see p. 418).

The demand for money and saving

It must be emphasized that the demand for money and saving are quite different things. Saving is simply that part of income which is not spent, and the influences determining it are analysed in Chapter 30. Saving adds to a person's wealth. Liquidity preference is concerned with the form in which that wealth is held. The motives for liquidity preference explain why there is a desire to hold some wealth in the form of cash rather than in goods affording utility or in securities earning income.

24.3   THE SUPPLY OF MONEY

The supply of money consists of the following:

1.   Coins

These are insignificant in volume, being issued for the convenience of small, everyday transactions.

2.   Notes

From the seventeenth century, paper currency began to form an increasing proportion of British money and eventually Parliament had to exercise a strict control over the 'fiduciary issue' – the note issue in excess of the value of gold held by the Bank of England. Today, however, notes, like coins, are regarded as the small change of the monetary system, and so sufficient are always made available for the practical convenience of the public.

3.   Bank deposits

While purchases of everyday goods – bus rides, newspapers, drinks etc. – are usually paid for in coins or notes, about 80 per cent (in value) of all transactions are effected by cheque, standing order, direct debit, bank transfer or credit card. When a person writes a cheque, the bank is instructed to transfer deposits standing in his or her account to the person to whom money is owed. Bank deposits therefore act as money.

A large part of these deposits are 'created' by the bank. How banks create deposits and how they can be controlled is described in Chapters 26 and 27.

Other forms of money

There is really no hard and fast dividing line between what is money and what is not. 'True money' confers complete *liquidity* on its holder and, in the last resort, only banknotes and sovereigns do this, for other coins are limited in legal tender. But when considering what serves as money in our economy, the more practical approach is to start from the idea that 'money is what money does'. Is it accepted in payment for goods? If so, it is acting as money. Cheques, as we have seen, are money for this reason, though they represent nothing more than current deposits in a bank. Yet, in advanced economies, cheques form the major part of 'money' in use.

Indeed, although deposits held by bank customers in deposit accounts are subject to a specified notice of withdrawal, such notice will in practice be waived by the bank with the loss of some interest. Thus sums in deposit accounts can be regarded as 'near' money.

And, in pursuing our argument in the same direction, we find other instruments of credit which, although not 'true money' in the sense that they can be spent anywhere in their present form, nevertheless fulfil the functions of money, if only within a limited sphere. But we must be careful to see clearly how and when they add to the money supply. Deposits can be 'created' by banks only because their clearing system enables them to economise in cash (see Chapter 26). In this the banks hold a unique position; other forms of credit add to the money supply only when they are not covered by cash held idle to an equal amount. Thus, when a person buys a postal order to cover his 'pools' entry, the cash he pays in may be put into circulation again by the Post Office before the order is presented by the pools firm. Thus, to some extent, postal orders can form an addition to the money supply, for they are doing the work of money. This is true, too of other instruments of credit – credit cards (until the bank account is settled), bills of exchange (especially those 'negotiated', i.e. passed on to a third party to settle a debt), trade credit (particularly when deals between firms are allowed to cancel credit, or if the entitlement to payment is transferred to a third party) and book-entry settlements replacing cash (as occurs, for example, when there is a vertical amalgamation of firms).

'Near' money

We can carry the above idea further. Any assets possessed can usually be turned into money eventually. Liquidity, therefore, is largely a matter of degree, often depending upon the organisations which exist to make such assets as building society deposits, government securities, shares in public companies and insurance policies liquid. Thus in recent years traders have become more liquid by the development of factor houses to which trade debts can be sold immediate for cash. While assets may have to be sold at some capital loss, they do afford some degree of liquidity to the holder. People possessing first-class shares, for instance, would not need to keep so large a cash balance for the precautionary motive, for they could always sell some in an emergency. Indeed ownership of a house can serve to raise cash through a second mortgage. In short, the existence of 'near' money means that the demand for 'true' money can be correspondingly less. We shall assume that this has been allowed for in our demand for money curves, which therefore depict the demand for 'true' money.

The official definition of the supply of money

While there may be no hard and fast dividing line between money and certain other assets, the acceptance by the government of the view that the money supply is an important influence in the economy required that it be defined so that it can be measured and monitored as a guide to policy. To allow for varying degrees of 'moneyness', there were a number of definitions, but today there are two broad classifications.

Narrow money refers to money balances which are readily available to finance current spending, that is, as a medium of exchange for transactions purposes. The chosen monetary target is now M0 which consists of notes and coin in circulation, plus banks' holding of cash (till money) and their operational balances at the Bank of England.

But, as pointed out above, the distinction between current and deposit accounts is blurred by the ease with which funds can be switched from one to the other. This has to be allowed for if we want an indicator of aggregate monetary expansion in the economy. Thus *broad money* reflects the overall liquidity in the economy through the private sector's holdings of assets which, while a store of value, can be converted with relative ease and without capital loss into spending on goods and services. Here the chosen target is M4 which consists of notes and coins in circulation with the public plus all private sector sterling deposits (sight and time) held in UK banks and building societies (see also p. 532).

24.4 THE RATE OF INTEREST

We are now in a position to consider the problem postponed in Chapter 15: 'What determines the overall level of interest rates in the economy?' Or, as it is more usually put: 'What determines the *pure* rate of interest, the benchmark around which interest rates fluctuate?'

The rate of interest as a monetary phenomenon

Income not spent by an individual is said to be 'saved'. But even after some income has been saved, the choice still has to be made as to what assets will be held. This is because assets differ in the qualities they possess, particularly as regards lender's risk, liquidity and yield.

The greater the lender's risk, the higher the yield required, other things being equal. The exact difference in yield between different types of risk will be decided in the market. We can eliminate this complication by concentrating attention at the extreme end – government securities – where risk of non-payment of interest and capital is nil.

Liquidity and yield, too, are usually related inversely. Illiquidity has to be compensated for by a high yield. Complete liquidity, conferred only by money, involves total loss of yield.

But since liquidity is a desirable attribute of an asset, money can be regarded as an acceptable way of holding wealth in comparison with interest-yielding assets. Individuals, therefore, have to arrange their portfolios of assets according to the emphasis they put on liquidity. To eliminate the complication of loans of different periods, we shall assume that all securities are undated government stock, which we shall term 'bonds'. Thus there are only two kinds of asset which individuals may hold in storing their wealth – bonds and money (Figure 24.2). The price of bonds will also give us the rate of interest on riskless, undated securities, the 'representative' or benchmark rate of interest.

On the capital market there will be bonds offered for sale. Some will come out of the existing stock held by people; others will be new bonds arising from current government borrowing, but the former far outnumber the latter. Their price will be determined by demand and supply, just as the price of rubber, tin, wool, cotton and any other commodity is in their respective markets.

People holding money bid on the capital market for the bonds offered. How much money they have will depend upon the total supply of money in the economy and how much they want to hold for the transactions, precautionary and speculative motives (see pp. 295–9). At the end of a day's dealing, all bonds may have changed hands. But this need not be so. If the price of bonds is low, some

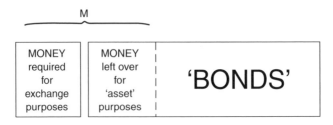

Figure 24.2   The alternative of holding wealth as money or 'bonds'

would-be sellers may prefer to hold on to them. On the other hand, if the price of bonds is high, some would-be purchasers may prefer to retain their money.

But, at the end of the day's dealings, a price will have been found at which people have finished dealing – nobody will wish to exchange more bonds against money, and nobody will wish to exchange more money against bonds. There is equilibrium at this price. This price is the inverse of the current 'pure' rate of interest – the benchmark referred to earlier.

The Keynesian emphasis on particular determining factors

It can be seen from the above that a change in the demand for money relative to bonds, given the stock of money and of bonds, will bring about a change in the rate of interest. Thus if it becomes less attractive to hold money, the rate of interest will fall.

But changes in the relative quantities of money and bonds, i.e. in the sizes of the stocks of each, will also produce variations in the rate of interest. If, for instance, the quantity of money increased and the demand for money and the stock of bonds remained unchanged, it would mean that more money was being offered against bonds, with the result that the price of bonds would rise. Looked at in an alternative way, the owners of wealth could not, at the given rate of interest, be induced to hold the whole stock of money. Thus there would have to be a reduction in the inducement *not* to hold money, i.e. in the rate of interest. Similarly, if the quantity of bonds increased, the demand for bonds and the supply of money remaining unchanged, the price of bonds would fall. Looked at in an alternative way, at the given rate of interest owners of wealth could not be induced to hold the whole stock of bonds. Hence the inducement to hold bonds, i.e. the rate of interest, would have to rise. In practice, stocks, both of money and of bonds, are not subject to great variations except over fairly considerable periods of time.

The supply of money is controlled by the government through the banking authorities (see Chapter 27). The supply of bonds coming on to the market comes chiefly from existing stocks of old bonds. In comparison, the flow of new bonds on to the market is small. Current government borrowing, unless it were very large, would therefore have little impact on the rate of interest. Thus, Keynes considered, it is much more realistic to analyse the rate of interest from the point of view of the variable most likely to change over the short period – the demand for money. And here he stressed the role of speculation.

In the market for bonds there will be many people whose main interest will be in their future price. Indeed, as we have seen, Keynes thought that the *speculative motive* dominated all others. If so, the demand for bonds is largely the result of the *present* price of bonds. Or, viewing it from the other angle, the *demand for money is primarily a function of the rate of interest* (see p. 298).

Instead of approaching the rate of interest through the demand and supply of bonds, therefore, it is possible to approach it through the demand for and supply of money, the alternative asset.

The demand for money depends upon the level of income (transactions and precautionary motives) and the rate of interest (speculative motive), though modern thought would not separate them completely, for people can economise on active balances when the rate of interest is high. But we can combine the demand for each in a single demand curve, adding the demand for active balances (which is largely unaffected by the rate of interest) to the demand for idle balances (which is influenced by the current rate of interest).

This is shown in Figure 24.3. The demand for money for active balances is shown by the distance of the vertical sections of the demand curve from the y-axis. Thus if income increases from Y to Y_1, the increase in the demand for active balances is equal to the horizontal difference between the two. To this demand for active balances must be added the demand for idle balances – the sloping portion of the curve.

Suppose the supply of money is equal to ON. If the level of income, Y, is low, there is less demand for active balances and thus more available for idle balances. The rate of interest is therefore only 8 per cent. With a higher level of income, Y_1, more money is demanded for active balances. This leaves less for idle balances and the rate of interest rises to 12 per cent. And so on.

A smaller supply of money, ON_1 would produce a rate of interest of 12 per cent with Y.

The demand curve can also change its position because of a change in expectations regarding the future rate of interest. For instance, people could expect this to rise in response to such economic events as increases in the PSNCR, in the rate

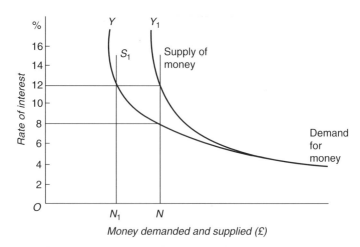

Figure 24.3   The determination of the rate of interest

of inflation, in the balance of payments deficit, in the eurozone rate of interest or in the sterling exchange rate on the market.

The structure of interest rates

It merely remains to remove our earlier simplification that the only type of security in existence is bonds. In practice, people can put their money into a range of securities each varying in the degree of liquidity and lender's risk involved. These securities can, however, be regarded as fairly close substitutes for one another, and there will be a rate of return on each depending on the demand for that type of security and the supply of it. These rates will be interrelated because, since they are close substitutes, the demand for one type of security will be affected by the rate of return on the security most similar to it. For instance, a rise in the rate of return on short-dated government stock will cause a movement of funds to it from its immediate close substitutes, such as Treasury bills. This sets up a ripple running through the whole structure of interest rates until eventually equilibrium has been restored. Of course, this ripple could easily start by a change in the demand for or supply of money. It is likely to have its first effect on short-term (three-month) securities, and eventually the long-term rate is brought into line, though this may occur only over a considerable period of time.

Allowing for inflation

By assuming a stable price level, Keynes was able to concentrate on liquidity and the choice between money and bonds. But when inflation enters into people's expectations, a dynamic element is injected into the situation.

First, we must distinguish between a once-for-all increase in the money supply and a continuous increase. The former lowers the rate of interest, as the analysis suggests. The latter, however, will eventually cause people to expect further inflation. It can occur, for example, by the need to finance a recurrent high PSNCR.

Second, the expectation of inflation leads people to widen their choice of wealth-holding assets. Apart from bonds, they can hold equities (shares in companies), real property or simply goods. Like bonds, all these incur a loss of liquidity. But whereas bonds valued in terms of money are bound to fall in real terms with inflation, equities, real property and goods have some degree of inflation-hedge. Thus people are likely to switch to holding these alternatives. Equities and real property also afford a yield, but if there is inflation this could be *below* the rate of interest on bonds because investors bid up their prices to obtain the advantage of the inflation-hedge. This difference is referred to as the 'reverse yield gap'.

Smaller holders of wealth are likely to invest in owner-occupied houses, antiques, works of art and, to some extent, goods in general, for these too are expected to carry a 'yield' through inflation. Thus prices of goods rise; in such circumstances, money *does* matter, as the monetarists claim.

In contrast, bonds are not wanted, and their price falls, people requiring a margin to allow for inflation, i.e. a higher yield.

The weakness of Keynes's 'idle balances' concept

In his theory of interest Keynes implicitly assumed that, given no change in income, any increase in the supply of money would automatically be absorbed in 'idle' balances where it would be available for spending on capital assets.

But what if, as above, extra money encouraged spending on actual goods and services rather than on bonds, because people regard all money simply as a temporary abode of purchasing power? In recent years this has proved to be a distinct possibility and we return to it in Chapter 33.

CHAPTER SUMMARY
....

- Money acts as a medium of exchange, a measure of value, a standard for deferred payments and as a store of wealth.
- People and firms hold money for transactions, for precautionary reasons and for speculation.
- Narrow money refers to money readily available for transactions while broad money is less liquid but still a store of value that can be converted into spending on goods and services.
- The rate of interest is determined by the interaction of the demand for money for active balances and the money supply.
- Other rates of interest will be related to the pure rate of interest but will vary according to the degree of liquidity and the lender's risk.

REVIEW QUESTIONS
....

- Explain the advantages and limitations of coins as a form of money.
- What is the opportunity cost of holding idle-money balances?
- A house can be sold by its owner and the money spent. Is a house, therefore, a form of money?
- Illustrate the determination of the rate of interest.

 Visit the companion website for further questions

FINANCIAL MARKETS

25.1 THE PROVISION OF LIQUID CAPITAL

The need for liquid capital

Where expenditure exceeds the receipts of firms or of the government, the deficit has to be bridged by borrowing. Such funds come from the community, which lends savings. Saving represents refraining from spending on consumer goods, thereby setting free resources for the production of capital goods required by firms or for additional expenditure by the government.

Markets for liquid capital

The market is the institution which brings borrowers and lenders together, making funds available to firms and the government at a price – the rate of interest. But, because finance is required by different types of firm and by the government, for different purposes and for different periods of time, there is a great variety in the types of loan available and in the institutions providing or arranging such loans. Nevertheless, markets can be classified into two broad groups: (i) the *money markets* (dealing in short-term loans) and (ii) the *capital market* (where medium- and long-term capital is raised). The clearing banks (the major source of firms' working capital) and the Bank of England (which exercises a general control over the availability of finance) are discussed in Chapters 26 and 27.

None of the money markets nor the capital market are formal organisations in that buyers and sellers meet regularly in a particular building to conduct business. Instead they are merely a collection of institutions which are connected, in the case of the money markets by dealing in bills of exchange and short-term loans, and in the case of the capital market more loosely – through channelling medium- and long-term finance to those requiring it. Moreover, as we shall see later, within each market there is a high degree of specialisation.

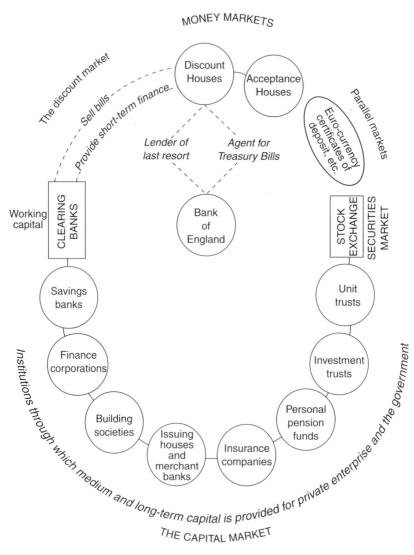

Figure 25.1 The provision of finance in the United Kingdom

Because it is such a large borrower, the government's requirements tend to dominate these markets, affecting the rates which have to be paid on short- and long-term loans. The complete structure is shown in simplified form in Figure 25.1.

25.2 MONEY MARKETS

The discount market

Bills of exchange are an important source of short-term finance – the commercial bill for firms, the Treasury bill for the government. The discount market comprises the institutions linked by dealings in bills – discount houses, merchant banks acting as acceptance houses, commercial banks and the Bank of England (Figure 25.3, p. 310).

It is customary in foreign trade for an importer to be allowed a period of grace, usually three months, to pay for goods. This is arranged through a *commercial bill of exchange*.

Suppose A in London is exporting cars worth £100,000 to B in New York. When he is ready to ship the cars, he draws up a bill of exchange, as shown in Figure 25.2. This is sent to B, together with copies of the shipping documents to prove that the cars are on the ship. B accepts the bill by writing 'Accepted' and his signature across the face of the bill, and then returns it to A. This acceptance of the bill by B is necessary before the original *bill of lading*, the documentary title to the cars, is handed over.

A can now do one of three things: (i) hold the bill until it matures; (ii) endorse the bill and then get a merchant to whom he is indebted to take it in settlement; or (iii) sell the bill, usually to a discount house.

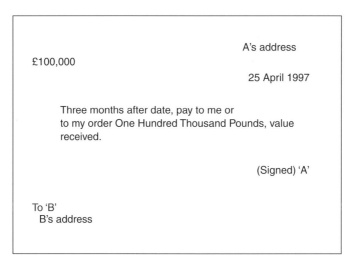

Figure 25.2 A commercial bill of exchange

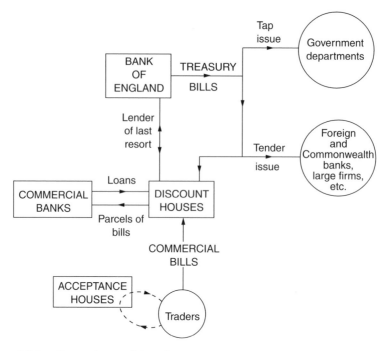

Figure 25.3   Operations of the discount market

1.   *Discount houses*

Probably A will choose the latter course. So, after endorsing it, he takes it to one of the *London discount houses*. The exact amount paid for the bill will depend on the length of time to maturity, the prevailing short-term rate of interest and the opinion of the discount house as to B's financial standing. If the bill still has three months to run and the prevailing rate of interest on that class of bill is 12 per cent, the discount house will pay just over £97,000 for it. The process is known as 'discounting'. Thus, while A quickly regains liquidity by selling the bill, B obtains three months' credit, during which time he will probably sell the cars.

Bills are not usually held for the full three months. Instead after about a month, they are sold in 'parcels' to the commercial banks, who like to have so many maturing each day.

2.   *Acceptance houses*

If B is a well-known firm of high financial standing, the accepted bill is, from the risk point of view, almost as good as cash. However, as bills are drawn on firms in all parts of the world, little may be known about B. Thus the discount house is either reluctant to discount the bill or will only do so at a high rate of interest.

The difficulty can be overcome by getting a firm of international repute to 'accept' responsibility for payment should B default. It is obvious that any firm accepting such a bill must have adequate knowledge of the creditworthiness of the trader upon whom the bill is drawn. Such knowledge is possessed by the *merchant banks*, such as Lazard and Rothschild, who commenced as traders but later specialised in financing trade in particular parts of the world. In their capacity of accepting bills such merchant banks are known as *acceptance houses*. For the service, they charge a small commission of about $\frac{3}{4}$ per cent, which is paid willingly because the rate of discount on a 'bank bill', i.e. one bearing the name of an acceptance house, is lower than on a 'trade bill' (a bill accepted only by a trader) or on a 'fine trade bill' (where the merchant is of good standing).

The business of accepting has now declined. Originally this was the result of the diminished use of the trade bill in international trade as the commercial banks competed through the cheaper method of the 'reimbursement credit'. With this, B, an importer in New York, asks his own bank to obtain an acceptance credit in London by making itself responsible for payment. Thus the London bank or acceptor there has only to satisfy itself as to the financial standing of the New York bank. This simpler procedure means that reimbursement credits can be granted at very low rates. Today the commercial bill is mainly used as a means of raising finance internally (see below).

The decline in the use of the commercial bill in international trade initially coincided with a large increase in government borrowing through Treasury bills. A *Treasury bill* is really a bill of exchange drawn by the Treasury on itself, usually for a period of three months (91 days), though occasionally two-month bills (63 days) are issued. Treasury bills are only issued in high denominations and so are primarily for institutional investors.

Recent developments have had repercussions on both the discount houses and merchant banks. The restrictions on the lending powers of the banks before 1971 led to the development of other means of short-term borrowing, e.g. internal commercial bills, local authority bills, certificates of deposit, etc. Furthermore, the government has reduced its dependence on short-term borrowing through Treasury bills (see p. 533).

Dealings in these short-term instruments are now, therefore, the mainstay of the *discount houses*, though they still tender for the reduced weekly offering of Treasury bills.

The functions of the *merchant banks* have also changed. The work of accepting is not required for Treasury bills or for most of the new short-term instruments since the standing of the borrower is generally known to be first class. Instead, they arrange and underwrite new issues, advise on the terms of 'take-overs' and mergers, and pay dividends to stockholders as they fall due. They compete in specialist fields, e.g. property development, in domestic banking business, and also act as trustees and manage investment portfolios. Some, e.g. S. G. Warburg and Morgan Grenfell, have become dealers in securities. Other functions have resulted from their overseas trading connections. Thus they have important business in the bullion and foreign exchange markets.

3. The commercial banks

The commercial banks fulfil two main functions in the discount market – providing the discount houses with funds and holding bills to maturity.

The discount houses do not themselves have sufficient finance to buy all the bills, commercial and Treasury, offered them. They overcome this difficulty, however, by borrowing money from the commercial banks at a comparatively low rate of interest. Then, by discounting at a slightly higher rate, they make a small profit. The banks are willing to lend at a low rate because the loans are of short duration, often for only a day, and need not be renewed if there is a heavy demand for cash from their ordinary customers. For the discount houses, the trouble involved in the daily renewal of this money at call and the slight risk of its non-renewal are compensated for by the comparatively low rate of interest charged.

The commercial banks can earn a higher rate of interest by themselves holding bills for a part of their currency. However, except on rare occasions, they do not bid for them directly but buy them from the discount houses when they still have about two months to run.

4. The Bank of England

The Bank of England enters the discount market as follows.

First, it is the agency by which the government issues Treasury bills. This issue is achieved by two methods, 'tap' and 'tender'. Government departments, the National Savings Bank, the Exchange Equalisation Account, the National Insurance Fund and the Bank of England Issue Department, all of which have funds to invest for a short period, can buy what bills they want at a fixed price, i.e. 'on tap'. This price is not published.

The discount houses and other purchasers (such as Commonwealth and foreign banks) can obtain their issue by 'tender'. Every Friday, the Treasury, acting through the Bank of England, invites tenders for a specified amount of bills, usually £100 million each week.

Second, the Bank of England is the 'lender of last resort'. When the discount houses are pressed for money because the commercial banks will not renew their 'call money', the Bank of England will make finance available to them at a price (see p. 339).

Parallel money markets

As a result of restrictions placed on bank lending, new secondary markets in short-term loans developed to meet the specific requirements of particular borrowers and lenders. Indeed the existence of such markets has encouraged funds to be lent short-term, since they have made it easier for lenders to regain liquidity. Such loans, however have only the integrity of the borrowing institution as security and so enjoy no lender of last resort facility.

The following are the most important of these markets:

1. Sterling interbank market

This is a market bringing together all banks, including merchant banks. British overseas banks and foreign banks, so that those having considerable funds surplus to their immediate requirements can lend to those having outlets for short-term loans or requiring greater liquidity. It is described as a 'wholesale' market, as opposed to a 'retail' market where funds are collected directly from the public, e.g. by building societies and clearing banks.

The going London Inter-Bank Offered Rate (LIBOR) is the key rate for other short-term loans.

2. Local authority market

Local authorities borrow on the open market. Short-term loans bridge the time difference between expenditure and revenue. Brokers now exist for placing with them short-term funds of banks, industrial and commercial companies, charitable funds, etc. Such brokers also deal in longer-term local authority bonds.

Today the market is integrated very closely with the interbank market, as funds from the latter are often deposited with local authorities.

3. Negotiable certificates of deposit market

Certificates of deposit enable the banks and building societies to obtain 'wholesale deposits' for periods from three months to five years. They are like bills of exchange but drawn on themselves. Since they are for a longer period than an ordinary time deposit, they facilitate medium-term lending. For the lender they offer a higher rate of interest, while the market in them means that they can be sold whenever cash is required.

4. Eurocurrency market

Eurocurrency deposits are simply funds which are deposited with banks outside the country of origin but which continue to be designated in terms of the original currency. The most important Eurocurrency is the dollar. As a result of the USA's continuing adverse balance of payments, branches of European banks have built up dollar balances as customers were paid for exports. These balances are offered to brokers in London (where interest rates have been higher than in New York), and are placed mainly with companies or banks (e.g. Japanese) operating on an international scale to finance foreign trade or investment. The Eurocurrency market allows for more convenient borrowing, which improves the international flow of capital for trade between countries and companies. For example, a Japanese company borrowing US dollars from a bank in France is using the Eurocurrency market. While the dollar still dominates the market, other European currencies are now dealt in, chiefly the euro, the Swiss franc and the Japanese yen.

5. Eurobond market

Financial transactions are based on market information which, through computers, is assembled rapidly and displayed on screens worldwide. This has meant that dealings in long-term capital – bonds, equities and foreign exchange – now take place globally 24 hours a day. New markets have developed, for example, in bonds raised in different parts of the world (the Eurobond Market), in foreign exchange and in 'futures' and 'options' (derivatives).

6. Other markets

Smaller specialist markets have developed in *finance-house deposits* and *intercompany deposits*. Thus finance houses have obtained funds by issuing bills which are accepted by banks and discount houses. Similarly, in periods of tight credit, firms which are short of finance turn to other companies which temporarily have funds to spare.

25.3 THE CAPITAL MARKET

Whereas the money markets developed to supply short-term finance to trade and the government, industry obtains most of its 'working' capital from the clearing banks (see Chapter 26). But long-term capital for both the public and private sectors is obtained through the capital market. As can be seen from Figure 25.4, this consists of, on the one hand, the suppliers of long-term capital and, on the other, those requiring such capital, the two being connected by a number of intermediaries, usually of a specialist nature. Some of these intermediaries have already been described; here we look briefly at the others.

(a) Insurance companies

Insurance companies receive premiums for insuring against various risks. Some of these premiums, such as those for insuring ships and property, are held only

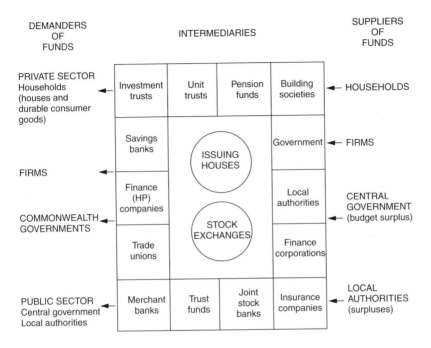

DEMANDERS OF FUNDS	INTERMEDIARIES				SUPPLIERS OF FUNDS

Figure 25.4   The capital market

Notes:
1 Arrows merely indicate direction, not particular intermediaries.
2 Intermediaries collect relatively small amounts of capital, which are channelled to where they are wanted.
3 Some intermediaries are mainly concerned with old issues.
4 Issuing houses assist the movement of funds; Stock Exchanges provide a market in old securities and thus encourage the provision of new funds.

for relatively short periods – having, apart from the profit made, to be paid out against claims. But with life insurance, endowments and annuities, premiums are usually held for a long time before payments are made. Hence insurance companies have large sums of money to invest in long-term securities. These investments are spread over government and other public stocks, the shares and debentures of companies, property and mortgages. Today 'institutional investors', of which insurance companies are the most important, supply the bulk of savings required for new issues.

(b)   Investment trusts

Investors usually try to avoid 'putting all their eggs in one basket' and therefore buy securities in different types of enterprise. However, this requires knowledge of investment possibilities and, above all, sufficient resources. The small investor can overcome these difficulties by buying shares in an investment trust. This invests over a wide range of securities, and after paying management expenses the net yields from these investments are distributed as a dividend on its own shares. Thus investment trusts are not 'trusts' in the legal sense but merely companies formed for the purpose of investment.

(c)   Unit trusts

Unit trusts are a development of the investment-trust idea, but they differ in two main respects. First, they are trusts in the legal sense of the term. Trustees are appointed, while the trust deed often limits investments to a specified range of securities. Second, the aggregate holding is split into many 'units' of low nominal value. Thus even a small investment covers a range of securities, though it is possible to concentrate on a particular group, e.g. minerals, financial securities, property, energy, European growth, capital accumulation, high income, etc.

Many unit trusts have schemes linked with insurance, to which savers subscribe on a regular basis. While most of the funds are used to purchase existing securities, trusts do make capital available for new investment, particularly when they take up 'rights' issues of companies whose shares are already held.

(d)   The National Savings Bank

The National Savings Bank operates mainly through Post Offices. It is the government's 'retail' means of collecting relatively small deposits from the public by providing savings facilities of different kinds, e.g. a Savings Book, National Savings Certificates, Savings Bonds and Premium Bonds. Although holdings are limited, these sums, when aggregated, make a significant contribution towards covering the PSNCR.

(e)   The Girobank

The Girobank, now part of the Alliance and Leicester Bank, carries out all essential banking services, mostly for private customers. Its strength is that it operates through the countrywide network of Post Offices. All records are kept at the computerised centre in Bootle, Lancashire.

(f)   Foreign banks

Branches of over 400 foreign banks are now located in London. Early on they thrived because they were free of the strict credit controls imposed by the government on the clearing banks. Their more recent expansion reflects the development of the international banking and financial system. While they carry out normal banking functions, their work is heavily concentrated on foreign exchange dealing.

(g) Trust, pension and trade-union funds

All these accumulate income which is re-invested in government securities, shares, property, etc.

(h) Building societies

The main functions of building societies are still the collection of retail deposits from the general public and the granting of long-term loans for the purchase of dwellings for owner-occupation. In recent years they have supplied cheque-books, credit cards and other services to depositors, thereby competing with the banks.

The Building Society Act 1987 allowed them to convert into companies (e.g. Abbey National), own property (mostly residential), grant second mortgages and unsecured loans up to 10 per cent of their total lending and to provide a variety of financial services connected with house purchase, e.g. arrange surveys, insurance. Some, such as the Halifax and Woolwich, have now converted into banks.

(i) Finance corporations

There are a number of consortiums, e.g. the Agricultural Mortgage Corporation, the Export Credits Guarantee Department of the Department of Trade, and the British Screen Finance Consortium which provide finance in their specialist fields.

(j) Finance houses

These were originally independent companies set up to borrow from the public and banks in order to finance hire purchase of both consumer goods and machinery. Today the industry is dominated by the larger commercial banks. For instance, Mercantile Credit is now part of Barclays Bank, and the United Dominion Trust a part of the Trustee Savings Bank.

25.4   MARKETS IN SECURITIES: THE STOCK EXCHANGE

History

By the second half of the seventeenth century there was a recognisable market for dealing in securities. This was gradually formalised and in 1773 the Stock Exchange occupied its first settled premises and from 1803 published its *Official List* of prices. From 1908 its organisation was based on a separation between 'brokers' and 'jobbers'. Brokers acted on behalf of their clients buying from and selling shares to jobbers, the dealers in the shares. This 'single capacity' requirement was designed to protect clients. Whereas brokers worked on a commission basis, jobbers relied on profits from their dealings.

Steps to 'Big Bang'

This cosy arrangement was jolted in the early 1980s by two developments. First, in 1970 government policy put greater emphasis on extending competition throughout the economy, and the Office of Fair Trading frowned upon fixed commissions as a monopolistic practice. Furthermore, the government was keen to maintain and even develop London's invisible earnings capacity (see p. 490). The abolition of fixed commissions in New York in 1979 made dealing costs for British institutions lower there than in London, while the ending of exchange control in the same year meant that British investors were unhampered in investing in foreign securities.

The second development was technological – the introduction of electronic information and communication systems. This meant that changes in security prices in a dealing centre in one part of the world could be transmitted and indicated visually on screens in other centres. Thus the three leading centres, Tokyo, London and New York, became one market in which, because of the time difference, dealing took place over almost the twenty-four hours of the day.

Thus the pressure was on the Stock Exchange to revise its fixed commission arrangements and to adopt a less parochial outlook. The actual changes took place on 27 October 1986 and produced such an immediate upheaval that it was referred to as 'Big Bang'.

The Stock Exchange agreed to end fixed commissions. But since this would have forced many brokers out of business it was necessary to end the 'single capacity' rule and allow members to act in a dual capacity as agents for both clients and dealers. The main dealers are termed 'market-makers'.

Market-makers negotiate their own commissions for buying and selling shares, and on the larger orders put through by the institutions can offer attractive terms. While private investors can also negotiate terms, the size of their business is not deemed profitable by the market-makers and commission rates remain much as they were before 'Big Bang'. This leaves room for brokers to earn a respectable living by acting as the retailer for the private investor, providing a personal contact and offering advice and even research.

Further developments

'Big Bang' proved to be the catalyst for even more far-reaching developments. The government's desire to establish London as an international trading centre necessitated making dealing costs more competitive and so stamp duty on buying shares was reduced to $\frac{1}{2}$ per cent. But to trade in competition with the larger Japanese and American firms UK dealers had to have access to considerably more capital in order to carry stocks of securities. Thus firms had to merge or, more usually, were taken over by larger financial institutions, such as the merchant banks.

In this, however, 'Big Bang' simply gave impetus to the movement which was already taking place of linking related services in one firm. The major clearing banks, for example, are now interested in hire purchase finance, granting mortgages and even acquiring estate agents. The idea has been extended into stockbroking. Market-making, however, has been left to the merchant banks who are less interested in the retail side of finance.

We still refer to the 'Stock Exchange' although dealing is no longer on the 'floor of the House'. Instead there is the Stock Exchange Automated Quotation system (SEAQ) which is the electronic market-place of the London stock market. Information from the sixty-four market-makers on prices and deals made is fed into SEAQ and displayed on screens. This enables the market-maker to quote a selling price and a lower buying price. This 'spread' will be larger when the shares are only dealt in infrequently or where the sale of comparatively few shares can lead to a large fall in price. Unfavourable news, such as a poor monthly balance of payments figure, will cause him to lower prices as a precautionary measure. These new prices would be recorded on the SEAQ screen for the rest of the market.

In 1995 the London Stock Exchange launched the Alternative Investment Market (AIM). While the financial standing of applicant companies is still vetted, the cost of joining is much lower than that of the main market. It is therefore particularly attractive to smaller, and often young and growing, companies who wish to have a quotation for their shares with the aim of raising further capital.

There have also been recent changes in *share trading arrangements*. To eliminate most of the paperwork involved in changes in share ownership, a new computerised system (CREST) has been introduced. Moreover, when shares are bought or sold, settlement must now take place within 10 days.

The government has a strong interest in the integrity of financial markets but opted for allowing the City to regulate itself rather than impose centralised control. The Secretary of State for Trade and Industry appointed a Securities and Investments Board (SIB) which oversees these Self-Regulating Organisations (SROs) and City dealers have to belong to one of these. The Stock Exchange, as a SRO, issues guidelines to members and ensures that these rules are adhered to.

Economic functions

While some short-term speculation does take place on the Stock Exchange, most securities are held on a long-term basis by investment trusts, insurance companies, pension funds, building societies and private individuals.

The truth is that, for the following reasons, an organised market in securities is an indispensable part of the mechanism of a capitalist economy.

1. It facilitates borrowing by the government and industry

If people are to be encouraged to lend to industry and the government by the purchase of securities, they must be satisfied that they will subsequently be able to sell easily those investments which they no longer wish to hold. Such an assurance is afforded to any holder of a fairly well-known security by the Stock Exchange, for it provides a permanent market bringing together sellers and buyers.

Thus, indirectly, the Stock Exchange encourages savers to lend to the government or to invest in industry. Indeed, if a new issue receives a Stock Exchange quotation, the chances of its success are considerably enhanced.

2. Through the market-makers, it helps to even out short-run price fluctuations in securities

By holding stocks of shares, a dealer provides in the short run a buffer against speculation by outsiders. This is because he does not merely 'match' a buyer with a seller but acts like a wholesaler, holding stocks of securities. Since he usually specialises in dealing in certain securities, he obtains an intimate knowledge of them. Thus when the public is pessimistic and selling, he may be more optimistic in his outlook and consider that the drop in price is not likely to continue. He therefore takes these securities on to his book. Similarly, when the public is rushing to buy he will, when he considers the price has reached its zenith, sell from his stocks. The effect in both cases is to even out the fluctuations in price, for, in the first case, he increases his demand as supply increases, and, in the second, he increases supply as demand increases.

3. It advertises security prices

The publication of current Stock Exchange prices enables the public to follow the fortunes of their investment and to channel their savings into profitable enterprises.

320

4. *It protects the public against malpractices and fraud*

With dealers acting in a dual capacity, the previous safeguard of a client that his broker acted solely on his behalf was lost. Under the new arrangements there are two safeguards, the open display of prices on the SEAQ screen and the regulations of the Stock Exchange Council as a SRO. The Council insists on a high standard of professional conduct from its members. Should any authorised member default, the investor is indemnified out of the Securities Association Compensation Fund.

The *Official List* of securities indicates that the Stock Exchange considers shares are reputable. Permission to deal is withdrawn if any doubts arise about the conduct of a company's affairs.

5. *It provides a mechanism for the raising of capital by the issue of securities*

While the Stock Exchange is essentially a market for dealing in 'old' securities, the success of a new issue to raise capital is enhanced if a promise can be made of a Stock Exchange quotation for it. More directly, brokers and dealers will actively arrange for certain clients to provide capital for firms wishing to expand (see p. 87).

6. *It reflects the country's economic prospects*

The movement of the market acts as a barometer which points to the economic prospects of the country – the Financial Times Stock Exchange index (FTSE) gives a good indication of economic prospects in 12 months' time.

CHAPTER SUMMARY

- Money markets deal in short-term loans while the capital market raises medium- and long-term capital.
- Money markets include the activities of discount houses, acceptance houses, commercial banks and the Bank of England (which exercises control over the availability of finance).
- The capital market comprises insurance companies, investment trusts, unit trusts, national savings, girobank, foreign banks, pension funds, building societies and finance corporations.
- The Stock Exchange facilitates borrowing by the government and industry and is an indicator of economic prospects.

REVIEW QUESTIONS

• Explain the purpose and operations of the money market.
• What do discount houses do?
• What are the economic functions of the Stock Exchange?

 Visit the companion website for further questions

26

CLEARING BANKS

LEARNING OBJECTIVES

After studying this chapter you should be able to:
- describe the structure of a clearing bank's assets;
- explain how banks create credit;
- show how the clearing banks have responded to increased competition.

26.1 TYPES OF BANKS IN THE UK

Banks vary, both in the type of function they perform and in size. They can be classified as:

1. The central bank

This is the Bank of England, which, on behalf of the government, exercises a general control over the banking system (see Chapter 27).

2. The clearing banks

These banks, once dominated by the 'Big Four' (Lloyds TSB, Barclays, Natwest and the Midland) now include former Building Societies, such as the Halifax, Abbey National, Woolwich and the Alliance and Leicester. Even so, unlike the systems of other countries, such as the USA, which are composed of a large number of unitary small banks, Britain has only a few large banks, each having a network of branches throughout the country.

This system of branch banking has two main merits. The first is that the larger unit of operation can enjoy the advantages of large-scale production. The second, and more important, is that there is less risk of failure when financial reserves are concentrated in a large bank than where the banking activities for a locality are conducted by a small bank. The fortunes of the small bank are tied up with the fortunes of the locality which, especially if the main activity is farming, may be liable to periodic fluctuations. In short, with a large bank, risks are spread geographically. On the other hand, the large unit has to suffer disadvantages on the managerial side, for usually loans of any size have to be sanctioned by Head Office. This is in sharp contrast to the manager of the small unit who can grant even large loans on the spot according to his own judgement.

It is mostly with the branches of the clearing banks that people in general come into contact, and so they are often termed 'retail banks'.

3.   Merchant banks (see p. 311)

4.   Foreign and commonwealth banks having branches in the UK (see p. 316)

5.   The National Savings Bank (see p. 316)

The joint-stock clearing banks are the subject of the rest of this chapter. Their importance in the financial system stems from the fact that most of their business is conducted by way of cheques which, through their central clearing arrangements, enables them to economise in cash and so 'create' credit. In particular, for an understanding of the supply of money we have to explain how they can do this.

26.2   THE CREATION OF CREDIT

The cheque system

Banks are companies which exist to make profits for their shareholders. They do this by borrowing money from 'depositors' and relending it at a higher rate of interest to other people. Borrowers are private persons, companies, public corporations, the money market and the government. The more a bank can lend, the greater will be its profits.

People who hold a current account at a bank can settle their debts by cheque. This is a very convenient form of payment. Cheques may be sent safely through the post, can be written for the exact amount, obviate carrying around large sums of money and form a permanent record of payment.

Credit cards possess somewhat similar attributes, and in addition can be used to pay for goods ordered over the phone but usually only up to a stipulated limit.

But the use of cheques and credit cards, is, as we shall see, advantageous to banks. Thus, to advertise their business, to induce customers to pay by cheque rather than by cash, and to encourage people to keep sums of money with them, banks perform many services outside their main business of borrowing and lending money – keeping accounts, making regular payments by direct debit, providing night-safe and cash dispenser facilities, paying bills by credit transfers, purchasing securities, transacting foreign work, storing valuables, acting as executors, granting mortgages, arranging insurance and so on.

The cheque as a substitute for cash

Cheques lead to a reduction in the use of cash. Suppose that I have paid £1,000 into my banking account. Imagine, too, that my builder banks at the same branch and that I owe him £500. I simply write him a cheque for that amount, and he pays this into the bank. To complete the transaction, my account is debited by £500, and his account is credited by that amount. What it is important to observe, however, is that in the settlement of the debt no actual *cash* changes hands. A mere book entry in both accounts had completed the transaction.

Perhaps my builder will, towards the end of the week, withdraw some cash to pay workers' wages. But it is likely that most payments, e.g. for building materials, petrol and lorry servicing, will be by cheque. Similarly, while from the £500 still standing to my account I may withdraw some cash to cover everyday expenses, the probability is that many of my bills, e.g. club subscription, council tax, hire-purchase instalments on the car, mortgage repayments, will be settled by cheque or by transfer directly from my account. Furthermore, even where cash is withdrawn by one customer, it is often compensated for by cash being paid in by other customers.

With the development of the cheque system, the proportion of cash which is required for transactions has decreased. Let us assume a simple model in which the banks operate free of government control but have discovered that in practice only 10 per cent of their total deposits need be retained in cash to cover all cash withdrawals. In short, only £100 of my original deposit of £1000 is needed to form an adequate cash reserve.

The creation of credit

It is obvious, therefore, that £900 of my original cash deposit of £1,000 could be lent by the bank to a third party without me or anybody else being the wiser. What is not quite so obvious is that the bank can go much further than this – and does!

Let us assume that there is only one bank and that all lending is in the form of advances (see p. 330). When a person is granted a loan by a bank manager, all that happens is that the borrower's account is credited with the amount of the loan, or, alternatively, he is authorised to overdraw his account up to the stipulated limit. In other words, a deposit is created by the bank in the name of the borrower.

When the loan is spent, the borrower will probably pay by cheque. If this happens, there is no immediate demand for cash. There is no reason, therefore, why the whole of my cash deposit of £1,000 should not act as the safe cash reserve for deposits of a much larger sum created by the bank's lending activities. But the bank must not overdo this credit creation. To be safe, our model has assumed, cash must always form one-tenth of total deposits. This means that the bank can grant a loan of up to £9,000. Because it is the only bank, there is no need to fear that cheques drawn on it will be paid into another bank and eventually presented for cash. In general, the deposit to cash multiplier equals

$$\frac{1}{\text{the reserve asset ratio}}$$

The process of credit creation is illustrated in Figure 26.1. X pays £1,000 in cash into the bank. This allows the bank to make a loan of £9,000 to B who now settles debts to C and D of £4,000 and £5,000 respectively by sending them cheques. These cheques are paid into the bank. C withdraws cash rather heavily, £700; but this is compensated for by D, who only withdraws £200 in cash. This leaves £100 cash – enough to cover the average withdrawal which X is likely to make. At the

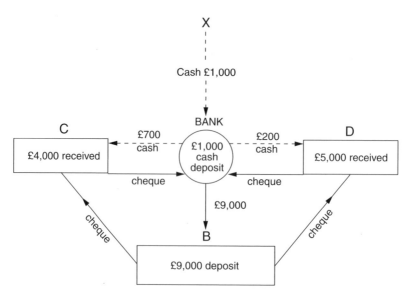

Figure 26.1   How a bank creates credit

same time as these cash withdrawals are being made, other cash is being paid in, thereby maintaining the 10 per cent ratio.

In practice, there are many banks, but for the purpose of credit creation they are virtually one bank, because they are able to eliminate a large demand for cash from each other by their central clearing arrangements. Moreover, banks keep in line with one another as regards their credit creation. Were one bank to adopt, say a 6 per cent cash ratio, it would find that because its customers were making such a large volume of payments to persons who banked elsewhere, it would be continually called upon to settle a debt with the other banks in cash at the end of the day's clearing, so that its cash reserve would fall below the safe level.

The effect of lending on the bank's balance-sheet

Suppose that the receipt of the £1,000 in cash and the loan to B are the sole activities of the bank so far. We ignore shareholders' capital. Its balance sheet would then be as follows:

Liabilities	£	Assets	£
Deposits:			
deposit account	1,000	Cash in till	1,000
current account	9,000	Advances	9,000
	10,000		10,000

The advance to B is an asset; it is an outstanding debt. On the other hand, B's account has been credited with a deposit of £9,000 – just as though B had paid it in. It can be seen, therefore that *every loan creates a deposit*.

B would pay the £1,000 into his current account if he himself had an overdraft. But if he had a sufficient credit balance there, he could pay it into a deposit account where it would earn some interest. Such deposits are referred to as 'time deposits' since technically they are subject to an agreed withdrawal notice (though banks usually waive this subject to loss of interest). The loan to B would be credited to B's current account and, since it is available for immediate spending, is known as a 'sight deposit'.

26.3 BANK LENDING

Considerations determining a bank's lending policy

In practice, the structure of the bank's assets is more varied than that above. This can be explained as follows.

Creating deposits in order to lend at a profit entails certain risks. In the first place, the loan may not be repaid. Second, and more important, there may be a run on the bank for cash, *X* (the original depositor) wishing to withdraw the £1,000, or *B*, *C* and *D* requiring between them an abnormally large amount of cash. Any suggestion that the bank could not meet these demands would lead to such a loss of confidence that other depositors would ask for cash, and the bank would have to close its doors.

Hence, although a permanent cash reserve ratio must always be retained, a bank must have a second and third line of defence so that in an emergency it can raise cash easily and quickly. This means, therefore, that it must not lend entirely by means of advances, for these are usually required by the borrower for a minimum of six months and even longer. Some loans must, if possible, be made for a shorter period – even for as little as a day at a time.

On the other hand, the shorter the period of the loan, the lower will be the rate of interest that the bank can charge. Yet it wants profits for its shareholders to be as high as possible.

The bank is therefore limited in its lending policy both quantitatively and qualitatively. Not only must credit be restricted to a multiple of the liquid reserves, but it must afford adequate *security*, *liquidity* and *profitability*.

As regards security, the bank endeavours not to lend if there is any risk of inability to repay. While it usually requires collateral, e.g. an insurance policy, the deeds of a house, or share certificates, this is regarded more as a weapon to strengthen its demand for repayment against an evasive borrower than as a safeguard against default. Collateral therefore really assists liquidity. Nevertheless, lending does involve some risk, especially if economic conditions worsen through recession.

Liquidity and profitability pull in opposite directions – the shorter the period of the loan, the greater the bank's liquidity, but the less it will earn by way of interest. The difficulty is resolved by a compromise: (a) loans are divided among different types of borrower and for different periods of time; (b) the different types of loan are kept fairly close to carefully worked out proportions. In short, the bank, for financial prudence, maintains a 'portfolio' of assets.

The distribution of a bank's assets

How in practice a bank reconciles the aim of liquidity and profitability can be seen by studying its sterling assets. This is possible because, apart from its cash, buildings and goodwill, loans represent its sole assets. Just as 'sundry debtors' appears on the asset side of a firm's balance sheet, so debt outstanding to a bank represent assets to it. The position is shown in Figures 26.2 and 26.3.

Cash covers: (a) till money, to meet customers' demand for coin and notes; (b) the working balance at the Bank of England to cover any liability on the day's

Figure 26.2   The nature and distribution of a bank's main assets

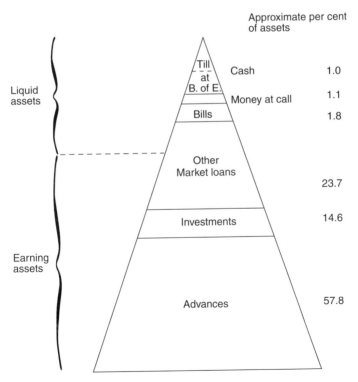

Approximate per cent of assets

Cash	1.0
Money at call	1.1
Bills	1.8
Other Market loans	23.7
Investments	14.6
Advances	57.8

Source: *Annual Abstract of Statistics*.

Figure 26.3   The pyramid of bank credit

clearing; (c) the non-operational balance of 0.15 per cent of total liabilities which has to be deposited with the Bank of England (see p. 335).

Bills, which are Treasury bills, local authority and trade bills, are obtained chiefly from the discount houses (though some may be discounted directly for customers) and are held for the remainder of their currency – usually two months.

Market loans consist mainly of: (a) money at call and short notice which enables the discount houses to discount bills and hold them for a month or so before passing them on to the banks (see p. 310); (b) loans of less than a year to local authorities; (c) certificates of deposit (see p. 313); (d) short-term loans to other monetary authorities.

Investments are medium- and long-term government securities bought on the open market.

Advances, to companies, partnerships and personal borrowers, are the most profitable (1 to 3 per cent above base rate) but also the least liquid of all the bank's assets. The main object of advances is to provide the working capital for industry and commerce. The type of loan preferred is 'self-liquidating' within a period of about six months. A good example is a loan made to a farmer, who borrows to buy seed and fertilisers and to pay wages, and repays the loan when the harvest is sold. Similarly, a manufacturer may borrow to employ additional labour and raw materials just prior to Christmas in order to increase production. When payment is received for those goods the overdraft can be repaid. Borrowers are often allowed to 'roll over' their overdrafts.

Banks also make a large number of 'personal loans', usually modest sums to cover exceptional items of personal expenditure. Repayments are spread over the term of the loan, though interest is charged at an agreed rate on the full amount of the loan for the whole of the period.

At one time banks refrained from providing long-term capital leaving this to the capital market. In recent years, however, they have competed in financing such long-term projects as commercial buildings and the purchase of farms and owner-occupied houses. These fixed assets are the security required, though the bank's main consideration is whether or not the venture is likely to succeed.

It must be emphasised that, apart from cash and bank buildings, these assets are covered only by credit created by the bank to make a loan or to buy securities. For example, Treasury bills and government securities are paid for by cheques which will increase the accounts of the sellers. If they are new issues, there is an addition to the government account at the Bank of England; if they are old issues, the bank is virtually taking over from somebody a loan already made to the government. In writing these cheques, the bank increases its liabilities, for only book-entry deposits cover them. This 'pyramid of credit', created to buy earning assets and to make loans upon a minimum liquid assets basis, is shown in Figure 26.3.

Furthermore, apart from maintaining its prudent cash ratio to attract deposits, the bank can only expand credit up to the limit in response to a new cash deposit if: (a) existing cash is already fully used to create credit; (b) no cash leaks out of the clearing banks as a result of a loan; (c) there is a demand for loans from willing borrowers.

26.4   MODIFICATION OF THE CASH-RATIO APPROACH

The importance of liquid assets as a whole

Our explanation of how a bank creates credit has followed traditional lines: credit bears a fixed relationship to the cash reserves. This approach is the easiest to understand and underlines the main principles involved.

However, while the basic principles of credit creation still hold true, some modification is necessary to allow for modern banking practice.

Today, banks are more concerned with the general liquidity position when lending rather than with one item, cash. This tendency of cash to lose significance originally stemmed from the introduction of the Treasury bill, which, through government support, became almost as good as cash. Improved markets for loans e.g. the parallel money markets described in Chapter 25, also increase liquidity and, as a result, such loans can be regarded as 'near money'.

External limitations on the banks' lending policy

Indeed, the monetary authorities (that is, the Bank of England acting as agent for the Treasury) now regard cash simply as the small change of the monetary system, and so they vary it according to the needs of trade.

It follows, therefore, that, if the authorities wish to control the amount of credit which can be created by banks, their attention will have to be directed to the size of the total assets which the banks hold. It is these external limitations on the banks' lending ability which we examine in the following chapter.

26.5   THE EFFECTS OF RECENT INCREASED COMPETITION

The above describes the fundamental credit-creation principle of banking. But the role of the clearing banks in the financial structure of the UK has been revolutionised since 1960 as they have had to respond to increased competition. This has come in five stages:

(1) Overseas banks (now over 400) came to London in the 1960s to share the Eurocurrency market there. In addition to dominating foreign currency lending, they now have some 30 per cent of lending in sterling to British companies and financial institutions.

(2) The Competition and Credit Control policy of 1971 removed restrictions on lending, thereby ending the clearing banks' 'interest rate' cartel. No longer could they simply rely on recycling personal deposits into loans to business. Now each bank had to compete for personal customers, e.g. by extending banking hours, increasing lending (especially through mortgages) and offering higher interest on deposits.

(3) The ending of exchange controls in 1979 removed the remaining restrictions on foreign lending institutions.

(4) The development of information technology has made possible credit cards, point of sales transfers and dealing in securities on an international scale.

(5) When in 1997 three large building societies converted into banks they retained their excellent network of high street offices, thereby enabling them to collect retail deposits at a comparatively low rate of interest and to supplement their basic mortgage business with other banking activities, such as personal loans and arranging insurance. This presented a serious challenge to the 'Big Four' who, following their losses in 1992 on Third World debt and property development financing, had secured excellent profits by reducing their dependence on corporate lending and concentrating on the personal sector where margins were wider, e.g. personal loans, credit cards. Increased competition has meant that bank margins between borrowing and lending rates have been squeezed and many personal customers' services which were previously given free are now charged for. In their turn the banks have had to improve customer relations.

Even so, with the growth of financial services and freer competition, the major banks have diversified into other operations, owning finance houses, leasing and factoring companies, merchant banks, securities dealers, insurance companies and venture capital companies.

CHAPTER SUMMARY

- The UK has a few large 'clearing' or 'retail' banks with a network of branches across the country.
- The banks can create credit by lending multiples of their deposits and keeping only a fraction of them in the form of cash to satisfy customers' limited cash requirements.
- Increased competition has led to major changes in the banking system in recent decades including more overseas banks, more competition on interest rates, building societies operating as banks and a proliferation of companies offering credit cards.

REVIEW QUESTIONS

•••

- What is meant by the 'clearing banks'?
- Explain how a low reserve asset ratio (or cash ratio) will lead to a large amount of credit creation.
- What are the main effects of increased competition on the clearing banks?

 Visit the companion website for further questions

27

THE BANK OF ENGLAND

For the past 200 years, the Bank of England has followed policies which have placed the needs of the country as a whole before its own financial interests. Nationalisation in 1946 merely formalised its position as a 'central bank' – the institution which, *on behalf of the government*, exercises the ultimate control over the policies of the commercial banks and other financial institutions. In the words of the Radcliffe Report, 'The Bank of England stands as the market operator between the public sector (to which it belongs) and the private sector'.

27.1 FUNCTIONS OF THE BANK OF ENGLAND

We need deal only briefly with most of the Bank's functions.

1. It issues notes

The Bank of England is the ultimate source of cash. If more cash is wanted for transactions, e.g. at Christmas, the Bank simply buys bills in the discount market, giving cash in exchange; if less is wanted, it sells bills.

The *Fiduciary Issue* (the amount by which the note issue is allowed to exceed the Bank's holding of gold) has ceased to have any relevance. Since 1939, the gold reserves of the Bank have been held in the Exchange Equalisation Account, and thus today the notes issued are backed by Treasury bills, other marketable government securities and commercial bills.

While in England and Wales the Bank of England is the sole note-issuing authority, certain Scottish and Northern Ireland banks can issue their own notes, though these have to be backed by Bank of England notes.

2. It is the government's banker

The government has always been the most important customer of the Bank of England. As a result the Bank has acquired the functions of a 'central bank' (see later). But it also performs many tasks for the government which spring from the normal banker–customer relationship:

(a) It keeps the central government account (the Consolidated Fund and the National Loans Fund) and the accounts of many government departments.
(b) It gives overnight assistance by means of 'Ways and Means' advances if the account goes temporarily 'into the red'.
(c) It manages the government's borrowing through the sale of Treasury bills and government stock in order to cover any time-lag between expenditure and revenue. This involves arranging new issues and conversions, paying interest, keeping the registers, and recording transfers.
(d) It advises the government on financial matters.

3. It is the banker's bank

The next most important customers of the Bank of England are the joint stock banks who use the Bank very much as a private customer uses his bank. In particular, they:

(a) hold about half their cash reserves at the Bank in order to: (i) provide a working balance to cover the day's clearing; and (ii) to conform with the Bank's 0.15 per cent cash to liabilities requirement (see p. 328);
(b) draw cash from their balances at the Bank as required;
(c) take advice on financial matters from the Bank.

4. It manages the exchange equalisation account (see p. 507)

5. It holds the government's gold and foreign currency reserves

The importance of these reserves is that they can be used in the foreign exchange market to maintain the stability of sterling. Until 1979 the reserves were protected by exchange control administered by the Bank of England. Today, to prevent the reserves from being depleted, the Bank raises the UK short-term interest rate (see p. 526). Where necessary, it will also arrange loans from other central banks.

6. It has financial responsibilities internationally

(a) The Bank of England maintains close contact with other central banks and monetary authorities and cooperates with them chiefly with the aim of bringing greater stability to international monetary affairs.
(b) It provides banking services for the central banks of non-sterling countries, e.g. holds and manages their holdings of sterling.
(c) It participates in the work of certain international financial institutions, such as the Bank for International Settlements, the International Monetary Fund, the International Bank for Reconstruction and Development.

7. It has overall responsibility for the integrity of the banking system

Regulations of the Bank of England are designed to ensure stability in the banking system. Thus, only bills accepted by approved banks – eligible banks – are discounted by the Bank (see below).

Until May 1997 the Bank also had the task of regularly examining the accounts of all British banks to ensure they were maintaining adequate liquidity and a safe exposure to risk. This supervision has now become the responsibility of a new unitary city regulator, the Financial Services Authority.

8. It manages the monetary system of the UK in accordance with government policy

The Bank of England is the central bank of the UK. It is therefore responsible for seeing that the monetary system of the country is working in harmony with government economic policy. In broad terms, this means varying the cost and availability of credit.

Where households and firms can obtain credit on relatively easy terms, the demand for goods (both consumer and producer goods) will normally increase.

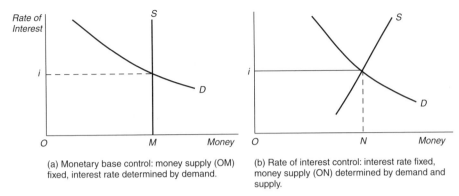

(a) Monetary base control: money supply (OM) fixed, interest rate determined by demand.

(b) Rate of interest control: interest rate fixed, money supply (ON) determined by demand and supply.

Figure 27.1   Monetary control alternatives

If there is unemployment, this is a good thing, for the economy will expand and idle resources be put to work. But expansion may be accompanied by rising prices and this becomes a problem as we approach full employment.

The Bank of England, therefore, may have to adjust the supply of credit to the prevailing economic situation. There are two broad ways in which the Bank can go about this: (1) by controlling the *supply* of credit quantitatively – that is, restraining lending by financial institutions; (2) restricting the *demand* for credit through its price – that is, varying the rate of interest (Figure 27.1).

27.2   MONETARY CONTROL THROUGH THE RATE OF INTEREST

The discarding of monetary base control

Between 1971 and 1979 the emphasis was on controlling the supply of credit quantitatively. The banks' ability to create credit was restricted by a variety of weapons chiefly aimed at reducing their liquid assets and by raising the *minimum lending rate* at which the Bank of England would discount bills as *lender of last resort*.

The main purpose of this quantitative control of credit was to reduce the need to raise interest rates, at least in the short term, by causing banks to ration their lending. In practice, quantitative controls only postponed the rise in interest rates needed. At the same time, they not only tended to reduce competition but caused funds to move from the controlled banking sector to uncontrolled institutions, such as the merchant banks, foreign banks and finance houses. Furthermore, the creation of money substitutes, e.g. the commercial bill of exchange, weakened the role of sterling M3 as a monitor of the money supply. Above all, quantitative controls became inoperable in 1979 when exchange controls were abolished, for funds could now be obtained from overseas sources, e.g. through the Eurocurrency market.

The control of inflation through the rate of interest

When the control of inflation became a major objective of the Thatcher government's policy, money aggregates were initially targetted as the appropriate method of control. But as measures they were defective (see p. 532) and the rate of interest become increasingly the weapon of control.

Until 6 May 1997, changes in base rate were decided by consultation between the Bank and the Chancellor of the Exchequer, with the latter having the final word when there was disagreement. But from that date onwards the Bank of England was given sole operational responsibility for setting interest rates with the specific objective of keeping the rate of inflation within the target (at present 2.5 per cent) set by the government.

On the Wednesday and Thursday morning following the first Monday in each month, a 9-member Monetary Policy Committee (which includes the Governor) meets to discuss whether any change in the interest rate is necessary. Decisions are reached on a majority vote and announced on the Thursday afternoon, with minutes of the meeting being published six weeks later (see also p. 534).

The Bank of England's dealing technique

A decision to raise the base rate signals that the Bank wants short-term interest rates to rise, and this happens because the Bank has the whip-hand as lender of last resort when it operates in the market to keep the banks short of cash. This is done by *open market operations* as follows:

- Each day the Bank of England estimates the cash position of the banking system. The amount of cash available will be affected by the operational balances the banks will aim at holding at the Bank of England and their cash flow, and also by net proceeds of Treasury bills and tax payments to the Treasury. With this knowledge the Bank can use open market operations to keep the banks on a tight rein. This is possible because the banking system is so competitive that the banks have to work on slim margins and keep their non-earning operational cash balances to a minimum. They are therefore always fully lent.
- If now the Bank puts Treasury bills on the market and they are bought initially outside the banks, the cash balances of the bank's customers, and thus the cash held by the banks both fall. As a result, the banks first of all call in their overnight loans (money at call) from the discount houses, and then, if necessary, sell bills through the discount market.

- When pressed for cash by the banks, the discount houses turn to the Bank of England. As lender of last resort, the Bank provides finance by buying Treasury bills or eligible bank bills from them. But it does not quote its terms for that would loosen its grip on the reins. Instead the discount houses have to suggest a price. If the Bank does not like this price, they are forced to lower the price, thereby giving an upward nudge to the seven-day interest rate.
- The Bank of England deals in other short-term loans; by its dealing rates for 91-day loans, it gives the market a signal as to what it considers the level of interest rates will be over the next three months. But while the Bank of England can *influence* the very short-term rate, the market may take a different view over longer-term rates. In any case, the longer the period, the more likely is the level of interest rates to be affected by outside shocks, such as a change in the eurozone rate of interest, or a severe fall in the sterling exchange rate.

CHAPTER SUMMARY

- The Bank of England issues banknotes, acts as the government's banker, acts as the clearing banks' banker, has international and domestic financial responsibilities and manages the monetary system of the UK.
- Monetary control has moved from money supply (quantitative control) to money demand (through interest rates).
- The Bank of England now has responsibility for setting interest rates with the objective of keeping the rate of inflation on target.

REVIEW QUESTIONS

- How does the Bank of England act as the government's banker?
- Briefly explain the difference between quantitative controls on money supply and monetary control through the rate of interest.
- What are 'open market operations'?

 Visit the companion website for further questions

PART VII

THE GOVERNMENT AND STABILISATION POLICY

MEASURING THE LEVEL OF ACTIVITY: NATIONAL INCOME CALCULATIONS

LEARNING OBJECTIVES

....

After studying this chapter you should be able to:
- show how the national income can be calculated in different ways;
- describe the difficulties of calculating national income;
- show the steps necessary to adjust from one measure of national income to another;
- describe the uses of national income statistics;
- explain the factors determining a country's standard of living.

28.1 THE PRINCIPLE OF NATIONAL INCOME CALCULATIONS

Fluctuations in the level of activity are monitored by quantitative information on the national income. Although the collection of statistics proceeds continuously, the principal figures are published annually in *The United Kingdom National Accounts (The Blue Book)*. See www.statistics.gov.uk.

The principle of calculating national income is as follows. Income is a flow of goods and services over time: if our income rises, we can enjoy more goods and services. But for goods to be enjoyed they must first be produced. A nation's income over a period, then, is basically the same as its output over a period. Thus, as a first approach, we can say that national income is the total money value of all goods and services produced by a country during the year. The question is how we can measure this money value.

We can tackle the problem by studying the different ways in which we can arrive at the value of a table.

Figure 28.1 shows that the value of the table can be obtained by taking the value of the final product (£100) or by totalling the value added by each firm in the

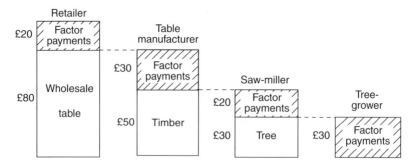

Figure 28.1 The value of the total product equals the sum of the values added by each firm

different stages of production. The output of the tree-grower is what he receives for the tree (£30) which, we will assume, cost £20 in wages to produce, leaving £10 profit. The output of the sawmiller is what he receives for the timber (£50) less what he paid for the tree. Again, this output (£20) is made up of wages and profit. And so on. The total of these added values equals the value of the final table. Thus we could obtain the value of the table by adding the *net outputs* of the tree-grower (forestry), the sawmiller and the table-maker (manufacturing) and the retailer (distribution).

Alternatively, instead of putting these individual outputs in industry categories, we could have added them according to the type of factor payment – wages, salaries, rent or profit. This gives us the *income* method of measuring output.

Thus, if we assume (i) no government taxation or spending and (ii) no economic connections with the outside world, we can obtain the national income either by totalling the value of final output during the year (i.e. the total of the value added to the goods and services by each firm) or by totalling the various factor payments during the year – wages, rent and profit.

There is, however, a third method of calculating the national income. The value of the table in Figure 28.1 is what was spent on it. If the table had sold for only £90, that would have been the value of the final output, with the final factor payment – profit to the retailer – reduced to £10. Thus we can obtain the national income by totalling *expenditure* on final products over the year.

It must be emphasised that the money values of output, income and expenditure are *identical by definition*. They simply *measure* the national income in different ways. This was shown by the fact that factor payments were automatically reduced by £10 when the table sold for £90 instead of £100.

Before we proceed to examine in more detail the actual process of measuring these three identities, it is convenient if we first consider some of the inherent difficulties.

28.2 NATIONAL INCOME CALCULATIONS IN PRACTICE

General difficulties

Complications arise through:

1. Arbitrary definitions

(1) Production

In calculating the national income, only those goods and services which are paid for are normally included. Because calculations have to be made in money terms, the inclusion of other goods and services would involve imputing a value to them. But where would you draw the line? If you give a value to jobs which a person does for himself – growing vegetables in the garden or cleaning the car – then why not include shaving himself, driving to work, and so on? On the other hand, excluding such jobs distorts national-income figures, for, as an economy becomes more dependent on exchanges, the income figure increases although there has been no addition to real output (see p. 353)!

An *imputed* money value is included for certain payments in kind which are recognised as a regular part of a person's income earnings, e.g. cars provided by a company to directors and employees.

(2) The value of the services rendered by consumer durable goods

A TV set, dishwasher, car, etc., render services for many years. But where would we stop if we imputed a value to such services? A toothbrush, pots and pans, for example, all render services over their lives. All consumer durable goods are therefore included at their price when bought, subsequent services being ignored.

The one exception is owner-occupied houses. These are given a notional rent to keep them in line with property owned for letting, whose rents are included, either directly or as profits of property companies. This also prevents national income falling as more people become owner–occupiers!

(3) Government services

Education and health services, although provided by the State, are no different from similar services for which some persons pay. Consequently, they are included in national income at cost. But what of certain other government services? A policeman, for instance, when helping children to cross the road is providing a consumer service. But at night his chief task may be guarding banks and factories, and in doing so he is really furthering the productive process. To avoid double-counting, this part ought to be excluded from output calculations.

In practice, however, it would be impossible to differentiate between the two activities, and so all the policeman's services – indeed all government services (including defence) – are included at cost in calculating national output (see p. 353).

2. Inadequate information

The sources from which data are obtained were not specifically designed for national-income calculations. For instance, the Census of Production and the Census of Distribution are only taken at approximately five-year intervals. As a result many figures are estimates based on samples.

Information, too, may be incomplete. Thus not only do income tax returns fail to cover the small-income groups, but they err on the side of understatement.

But it is 'depreciation' which presents the major problem, for what firms show in their profit and loss accounts is affected by tax regulations. Since there is no accurate assessment of real depreciation, it is now usual to refer to gross national product (GNP) rather than to national income (see Figure 28.3).

3. The danger of double-counting

Care must be taken to exclude transfer incomes when adding up national income (see p. 348), the contribution to production of intermediary firms when calculating national output (see Table 28.1) and indirect taxes when measuring national expenditure (see p. 350).

A fourth way in which a form of double-counting can occur is through 'stock appreciation'. Inflation increases the value of stocks, but although this adds to firms' profits it represents no increase in real income. Such gains must therefore be deducted from the income figure.

4. Relationship with other countries

(1) Trade

British people spend on foreign goods, while foreigners buy British goods. In calculating national *expenditure*, therefore, we have to deduct the value of goods and services imported (since they have not been produced by Britain) and add the value of goods and services exported (where income has been earned in Britain).

(2) International indebtedness

If a father increases his son's pocket-money, it does not increase the family income. Instead it merely achieves a redistribution, the father having less and the son more. But if the boy's aunt makes him a regular allowance, the family income is increased. Similarly, with the nation: while transfer incomes, e.g. retirement

Table 28.1   Calculations of Gross National Product of the UK, 1995

INCOME	£m
Income from employment	377,895
Income from self-employment	67,685
Gross trading profits of companies	91,027
Gross trading surplus, public corporations	4,634
Gross trading surplus, general government enterprises	613
Rent	62,758
Imputed charge for consumption of non-trading capital	3,898
Total domestic income	608,510
less stock appreciation	−4,902
Statistical discrepancy	−113
GROSS DOMESTIC PRODUCT	603,495
Net property income from abroad	9,572
GROSS NATIONAL PRODUCT	613,067

EXPENDITURE	£m
Consumers' expenditure	447,247
General government final consumption	148,643
Gross domestic fixed capital formation	105,385
Value of physical increase in stocks and works in progress	3,851
Total domestic expenditure	705,126
Export of goods and services	197,600
Total final expenditure	902,726
less imports of goods and services	203,086
Statistical discrepancy	486
GROSS DOMESTIC PRODUCT (at *market prices*)	700,126
less taxes on expenditure	−103,597
plus subsidies	6,966
GROSS DOMESTIC PRODUCT (at *factor cost*)	603,495
Net property income from abroad	9,572
GROSS NATIONAL PRODUCT	613,067

OUTPUT	£m
Agriculture, forestry, and fishing	11,896
Mining, quarrying, oil and gas extraction	14,575
Manufacturing	131,658
Electricity, gas and water supply	15,787
Construction	31,815
Distribution, hotels and catering: repairs	84,706
Transport and communication	50,835
Banking, finance, insurance, business services and leasing	158,224
Public administration, national defence and compulsory social security	39,510
Education and health social work	72,972
Other services	23,255
Total	634,402
Adjustment for financial services, etc.	30,794
Statistical discrepancy (income adjustment)	−113
GROSS DOMESTIC PRODUCT	603,495
Net property income from abroad	9,572
GROSS NATIONAL PRODUCT	613,067

Source: Annual Abstract of Statistics.

pensions and student grants, do not increase national income, payments by foreigners do. These payments arise chiefly as interest on loans and dividends from investments made abroad. In the same way, foreigners receive payments for investments in Britain. Net property income from abroad (receipts less payments) must therefore be added to both domestic expenditure and output.

Government calculations of the national income

We start off by measuring Gross Domestic Product (GDP). The GDP is simply the money value of the final output of all resources located within a country irrespective of whether their owners live there or abroad. Hence in order to obtain Gross National Product (GNP) we have to add the balance of *net* property income from abroad (Figure 28.2).

Figures for GNP are calculated for income, expenditure and output. Because information is incomplete and derived from a variety of sources, results are not identical. Hence from the residuals a 'statistical discrepancy' is calculated.

1. National income

National income is the total money value of all incomes received by persons and enterprises in the country during the year. Such incomes may be in the form of wages, salaries, rent, or profit.

In practice income figures are obtained mostly from income tax returns, but estimates are necessary for small incomes. Two major adjustments have to be made:

(1) Transfer incomes

Sometimes an income is received although there has been no corresponding contribution to the output of goods and services, e.g. unemployment-insurance benefit and interest on the National Debt. Such incomes are really only a redistribution of income within the nation – chiefly from taxpayers to the recipients. Transfer incomes must therefore be deducted from the total. Other forms of transfer income which must be excluded are private money gifts and receipts from the sale of financial assets and of second-hand goods, e.g. a house, furniture, a car.

(2) Income from government activities

Personal incomes and the profits of companies are obtained from tax returns. But since dividends and interest payments are already included in profits, to avoid double-counting they are not shown separately.

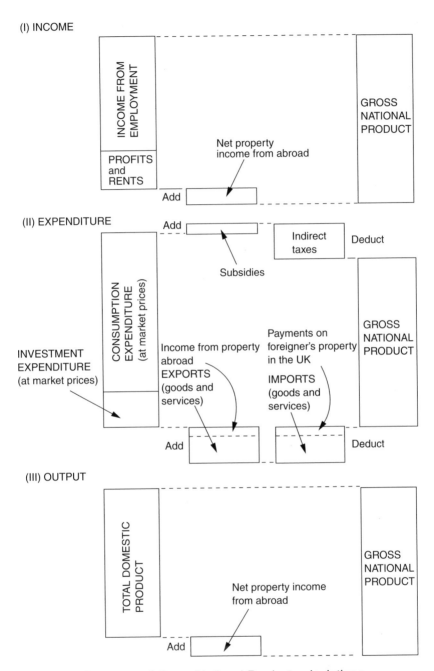

Figure 28.2 Summary of Gross National Product calculations

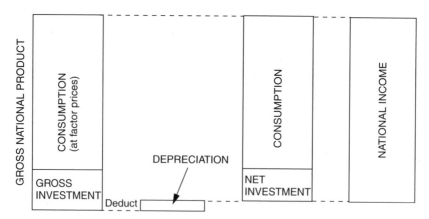

Figure 28.3   Gross National Product and national income

Trading-activities of public corporations, e.g. the Post Office, the BBC, and of local authorities e.g. housing, transport, may also show surpluses which have to be added in, while an imputed rental value is given to the property owned and occupied by the government and local authorities (non-trading income).

2.   National expenditure

National expenditure is the total amount spent on final goods and services by households and central and local government and by firms on net additions to capital goods and stocks in the course of the year.

Figures for calculating national expenditure are obtained from a variety of sources. The *Census of Distribution* records the value of shop sales, while the *Census of Production* gives the value of capital goods produced and additions to stocks. But these censuses are not taken every year, and gaps are filled by estimates from data provided by the *National Food Survey*, and the *Family Expenditure Survey*.

Market prices are swollen by indirect taxes on goods and services, e.g. VAT, and reduced by subsidies, e.g. on council housing. What we are trying to measure is the value of the national expenditure which corresponds to the cost of the factors of production (including profits) used in producing the national product. This is known as 'national expenditure at factor cost' and is obtained by deducting indirect taxes from and adding subsidies to national expenditure at market prices.

Adjustments necessary for exports and imports have already been referred to (see p. 346).

3.   *National output*

National output is the total of consumer goods and services and investment goods (including additions to stocks) produced by the country during the year. It can be measured by totalling either the value of the *final* goods and services produced or the *value added* to the goods and services by each firm, including the government.

Gross National Product and national income

In the course of production, machinery wears out and stocks are used up. This represents depreciation of capital. If we make no allowance for this but simply add in the value of new investment goods produced, we have *gross national product*. But, to be accurate, the calculation of total output should include only net investment – that is, the value of new investment goods and stocks *less depreciation* on existing capital and stocks used up. Because depreciation is difficult to measure, GNP is more generally used. For 1995 we have (in £million) GNP = 613,067 – depreciation 72,424 = Net National Product = National Income = 540,643.

Summary

GDP at market prices

$$- \text{ indirect taxes}$$
$$\underline{+ \text{ subsidies}}$$
$$= \text{ GDP at factor cost}$$
$$\underline{+ \text{ net property income from abroad}}$$
$$= \text{ GNP}$$
$$\underline{- \text{ depreciation}}$$
$$\underline{= \text{ NI}}$$

Personal disposable income

For some purposes, e.g. as an indication of people's current living standards, a measurement of personal disposable income, that is, what people actually have to spend, is more significant. The necessary adjustments to gross national product to obtain personal disposable income are shown in Figure 28.4, giving a figure of £502,433 mn for 1995.

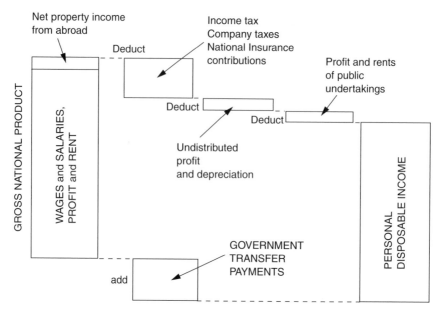

Figure 28.4   The relationship between Gross National Product and personal disposable income

28.3   USES OF NATIONAL INCOME STATISTICS

1.   To indicate the overall standard of living

Welfare is not identical with wealth (see p. 9), but wealth bears the closest single relationship to it. Income, the flow of wealth, is therefore the nearest indication of welfare.

Nevertheless, the national income figure cannot be accepted solely at its face value. Thus, although the national income of the UK was £268,315 million in 1985 and £540,643 million in 1995, it does not automatically follow that everybody had doubled his standard of living over that period. The following qualifications have to be made:

(a)   Some of the increase may be due to inflation (see Chapter 32), whereas what is relevant is real national income. One way of handling the difficulty is to re-value all money national incomes at 'constant prices' by applying the prices prevailing in a common base year.

(b)   The national income figure must be related to the size of population; thus average income per head is a better indication of well-being.

(c)   A person's standard of living depends upon the quantity of consumer goods and services he enjoys. But the increase in national income may have come about mainly through an increase in the production of producer goods. While these goods enable a higher standard of living to be enjoyed in the future, they do not increase *present* welfare. Thus average personal disposable income might provide a better indication of current living standards, though national income per head is the more satisfactory in the long run.

(d) The increase in national income may have come about through a surplus of exports over imports. This represents investment overseas, and thus (c) above applies.

(e) The average-income-per-head figure is merely a statistical average. It does not indicate how any increase in national income is distributed; it may go mostly to a few rich people (as in the oil sheikhdoms), perhaps leaving the others little better off.

(f) National income figures do not reflect the 'quality' of life. An increase in national income may be the result of longer working hours, inferior working conditions, longer journeys to work, or the presence of more home-workers at work (with less comfort in the home). The national income does not value leisure time.

(g) The quality of goods may have improved without any increase in price, e.g. mobile phones, razors, personal computers.

(h) All government spending is included at cost in national income calculations, no distinction being made between expenditure on consumer services and expenditure on defence. As a result, if spending on the social services were cut to pay for rearmament, national income would be unchanged!

(i) The national income figure is swollen when people pay for services which they previously performed themselves. Thus a married woman who returns to teaching but pays a woman to do her housework adds to the national income twice – although the only net addition is her teaching services. Indeed, even an oil spillage can increase national income by the costs of cleaning up, unless these are covered by the polluting shipping company.

(j) Because national income figures are based on private costs and benefits, external costs or benefits do not enter into the calculations. Thus the erection of electricity pylons would be included at cost, no allowance being made for the social cost of spoiling the landscape.

(k) The increase in national income may have incurred an excessive consumption of irreplaceable resources, e.g. fossil fuels.

(l) National income figures do not include the 'black' economy (some estimates would add 10 per cent) where services are exchanged for cash in order to evade taxes.

(m) National income includes payments for services necessitated by the stress of modern living, e.g. anti-depressant drugs, clinics for alcoholics.

2. To compare the standards of living of different countries

Comparisons of the national incomes of different countries are often necessary for practical purposes. How much help should be given by the rich countries to the very poor? Which are the very poor countries? What contribution should be made by a country to an international body, such as the United Nations, the Red Cross and NATO? What is the war potential of a country?

But, when used to compare countries' standards of living, national income figures must be subjected to qualifications *additional* to those mentioned in 1 above.

(a) Because figures are expressed in different currencies they have to be converted into a common denominator. Using the exchange rate for this purpose is not entirely satisfactory, for the rate is determined by factors other than the internal purchasing powers of currencies, e.g. capital movements. More satisfactory is the use of a conversion rate based on the purchasing power parity for a common basket of goods.

(b) Different people have different needs. The Englishman has to spend more on heating than the Indian. Obviously, the Englishman is no better off in this respect – though the national income figures, by valuing goods at cost, would indicate that he is.

(c) The proportion of national income spent by different countries on defence varies. Countries which spend less can enjoy consumer goods instead, but average national income does not indicate the difference.

(d) Countries vary as regards the length of the average working week, the proportion of women who work, the number of jobs which people do for themselves, the degree to which goods are exchanged against money, the size of the 'black economy' and the accuracy of tax returns. Some allowance must be made for each of these factors.

(e) Differences exist in the distribution of income (see p. 353).

(f) The availability of educational and medical facilities per head may differ although these affect welfare.

3. To calculate the rate at which a nation's income is growing

Is the national income growing? Is it growing as fast as it should? Are the incomes of other countries growing faster? Is there sufficient investment to maintain future living standards? The answers to these and similar questions can be found by comparing national income figures, though for the reasons given above some caution must be observed.

4. To establish relationships which arise between various parts of the economy

If, for example, national income figures revealed a relationship between the level of investment and growth, or between educational expenditure and growth, or between profits and the level of investment, such information would be useful in planning the economy.

The figures might also indicate trends, e.g. the proportion of national income which is taken by the government.

5. To assist the government in managing the economy

Some central government planning is now regarded as essential for achieving full employment, a stable currency and a satisfactory rate of growth. But this requires having figures for the various components of the national income, such as consumption spending, investment, exports and imports. How they can be used will be explained later.

6. To assist businesses, trade unions, financial journalists, etc. to ascertain economic trends and forecast future movements

7. To indicate changes in the distribution of income

While, as a scientist, the economist is not concerned with the 'fairness' of the distribution of income, the government is, for taxation and political considerations. National income figures provide the statistical basis when deciding on such matters.

28.4 FACTORS DETERMINING A COUNTRY'S MATERIAL STANDARD OF LIVING

Since people can enjoy only what they produce with their limited resources, the production-possibility curve shows the limit to their material standard of living. Because income is not evenly distributed, however, what we are talking about is an average standard of living, usually measured by the national income per head of the population.

The factors which limit the standard of living can be classified as internal and external, the latter resulting from economic relationships with the rest of the world.

The most important *internal* factors are:

1.   Original natural resources

Obviously, 'natural resources' cover such things as mineral deposits, sources of fuel and power, climate and the fertility of the soil and fisheries around the coast, but also included are geographical advantages, such as navigable rivers or lakes, which help communications.

While national output increases as new techniques or transport developments allow national resources to be exploited, the exhaustion of mineral resources works in the opposite direction. Moreover, where a country's economy is predominantly agricultural, variations in weather may cause its output to fluctuate from year to year.

2.   The nature of the people, particularly of the labour force

Other things being equal, the standard of living will be higher the greater the proportion of workers to the total population and the longer their working hours.

But the quality of the labour force is also important. This will depend upon the basic characteristics of the people – their health, energy, adaptability, inventiveness, judgement and ability to organise themselves and to cooperate in production – together with the skills they have acquired through education and training.

3.   Capital equipment

The effectiveness of natural resources and of labour depends almost entirely upon capital equipment. Thus machinery is necessary to extract oil and minerals, a turbine generator to harness a waterfall, and hotels to exploit Spanish sun and beaches. Similarly, the output of workers varies almost in direct proportion to the capital equipment and power at their disposal. Investment, the addition to capital, is one of the most important causes of material progress.

4.   The organisation of resources

To achieve the maximum output from scarce factors of production, they must be organised efficiently. Have we the correct proportion of machinery to each worker? Is the production of the particular good being carried on in the best possible locality? Could the factors be better deployed within the factory? Such questions have to be answered by those organising production.

5. Knowledge of techniques

Technical knowledge is acquired through capital expenditure on research and invention. Further capital expenditure is necessary to develop discoveries, e.g. to utilise our present knowledge of renewable energy. Nevertheless, the rapid increase of the standard of living of the UK over the last hundred years has largely been due to the development and application of new inventions such as the steam engine, the internal combustion engine, electrical power and electronics.

6. Political organisation

A stable government promotes confidence and thereby encourages saving and investment in long-term capital projects.

To the above we have to add what can be termed *external* factors:

7. Foreign loans and investments

A net income from foreign investments means that a country obtains goods or services from other countries without having to give goods and services in return, and vice versa. Generally speaking, welfare from this source is only likely to fluctuate over a long period.

8. The terms of trade

In the short run, fluctuations in the terms of trade are likely to be far more important in changing material welfare, especially if the country has, like the UK, a high level of imports and exports.

By the *terms of trade* we mean the quantity of another country's products which a nation gets in exchange for a given quantity of its own products. Thus, if the terms of trade move in a nation's favour, it means that it gets a larger quantity of imports for a given quantity of its own exports. This happens because the prices of the goods that are imported have fallen relative to the prices of those exported. Thus the 1979 increase in the price of oil reduced the standard of living of the importing countries and raised that of the oil producers.

9. Gifts from abroad

Aid to countries for purposes of economic development and defence improve the standard of living of the receiving countries.

REVIEW QUESTIONS
....

- Explain why national income, national expenditure and national output are measures of the same thing.
- What is the difference between Gross National Product and Net National Product (national income)?
- Why does Gross National Product give only a rough guide to standards of living?
- What are the main determinants of standards of living in a country?

 Visit the companion website for further questions

29

UNEMPLOYMENT

LEARNING OBJECTIVES

After studying this chapter you should be able to:
- describe the nature of unemployment;
- explain the causes of unemployment.

29.1 THE NATURE OF UNEMPLOYMENT

Although today (mid 2006) 5.4 per cent of the working population are unemployed, this compares favourably with the situation in pre-war Britain, where in the worst year – 1932 – the national unemployment rate was 22.1 per cent. Unemployment means that labour, machines, land and buildings stand idle; as a result, the standard of living is lower than it need be. But the real curse is the human misery that results. Many people, without work for years, lose hope of ever finding a job; in any case skills deteriorate as the period of unemployment lengthens. Thus unemployment is usually discussed in terms of labour.

Unemployment is said to occur when persons capable of and willing to work are unable to find suitable paid employment. Important points concerning and arising out of this definition, however, need to be stressed:

1. Unemployment must be involuntary; persons on strike are not reckoned as being unemployed.
2. 'Persons capable of work' must exclude the 'unemployable' – those not capable of work through mental or physical disability. On the other hand, unemployables are usually in the pool of unemployed labour seeking jobs and, where labour is scarce, more use will be made of them – provided that minimum wage regulations do not prevent this.
3. Full employment does not mean that workers will never be required to switch jobs or occupations. Changes in the conditions of demand and supply are

bound to occur, and such changes will be more frequent the more dynamic the economy and the more a country is dependent on international trade.

Thus there will always be some workers unemployed. A full employment policy must identify and deal with the particular cause of the unemployment.

Interpreting unemployment figures

Measuring unemployment involves problems of definition. How, for example, should part-time workers be treated? Is registration at a Jobcentre to be the test for inclusion? In comparing changes in the rate of unemployment over time, has the official definition of unemployment changed? Since 1982 official unemployment figures have counted only those persons actually claiming benefit.

But interpretation of the figures also necessitates subjective judgements as to the extent to which they are over or understated. When employment is buoyant, does the figure conceal 'disguised' unemployment in that firms are reluctant to release redundant workers or because some employees are working at less than their full potential? Is a high rate of job turnover adding to frictional unemployment? Are minimum wage regulations leading to unemployment? Is the rate of unemployment benefit, especially the 'poverty trap', discouraging an active search for work? In comparing unemployment rates over time should not some allowance be made for a changing age structure?

29.2   CAUSES OF UNEMPLOYMENT

1.   Frictional

Unless the economy is completely static, there will always be people changing their jobs. Some merely desire a change of employment or a move to a different part of the country. In certain occupations, e.g. unskilled labour in the construction industry, workers are not employed regularly by any one employer: when a particular contract is completed, labour is made redundant. Occasionally, too, workers are discharged when a factory is being reorganised.

Unemployed workers usually register at the local Jobcentre, forming a pool of labour from which employers can fill vacancies. But how large should this pool be? If it is too large, workers remain unemployed for long periods. If it is too small, production is dislocated by bottlenecks in filling vacancies (with employers holding on to labour not currently needed), by job-switching just for the sake of change and, above all, by strikes in support of claims for higher wages.

Frictional unemployment is partly unavoidable, and the grant of unemployment benefit affords the worker some protection against its effects. Moreover, the installation of expensive machinery which must be kept fully employed has quite often had the indirect effect of 'decasualising' labour.

2. Seasonal

Employment in some industries, e.g. building, fruit-picking and holiday catering, is seasonal in character. The difficulty is that the skills required by different seasonal jobs are not 'substitutable'. To what extent, for example, can hotel workers become shop assistants in the January sales? Seasonal employment is not completely avoidable. But it can be reduced if a small, regular labour force will work overtime during the 'season' and admit, say, students during the busy periods. Moreover, the price system may help. By offering off-season rates, hotels at holiday resorts can attract autumn conferences.

3. International

Because the UK is so dependent on international trade, she is particularly vulnerable to unemployment brought about by a fall in the demand for her exports. Such a fall may occur because:

(1) The prices of UK goods are too high to be competitive in world markets

If home prices rise, for example because of wage increases, the export market is likely to be hit severely. The demand for exports is usually highly elastic, since substitutes are often available from competing countries. The effect on employment is shown in Figure 29.1. The wage increase moves the supply curve from S to S_1. Because demand is elastic there is a considerable fall in the demand for the good, from OM to OM_1. The industry, and therefore employment, contract.

(2) Incomes of major importing countries may be reduced by a recession or a deterioration in the terms of trade

If incomes of importing countries fall, their demand for UK goods, especially those having a high income-elasticity of demand, will be likely to decrease. This is what happened following the increases in the price of oil in 1973 and 1979.

4. Structural

Structural unemployment, like frictional, results largely from the immobility of labour. Ignorance of opportunities elsewhere or, more likely, obstacles to moving mean that workers do not move to available jobs in other parts of the country. Thus employers in the south of England found it difficult, because of the higher cost of housing there, to recruit from high unemployment regions.

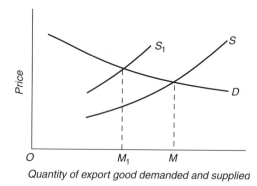

Figure 29.1 The effect on employment of a wage increase in an export industry

More serious, however, is occupational immobility resulting from long-term changes in the conditions of demand and supply in certain industries, especially exporting industries.

On the demand side, there may be a change in any of the factors influencing the conditions of demand. The price of substitutes may fall (Dundee jute products have largely been replaced by plastics), or foreign buyers may switch to competitors' goods (British shipyards have been hit by competition from other countries). On the supply side, new techniques or the exhaustion of mineral deposits may make labour redundant. Automation has reduced ICI's demand for workers at Stockton; exhaustion of the better coal seams has led to the closure of pits in South Wales and mid-Scotland.

Where an industry is highly localised in a particular area, the resulting unemployment may be particularly serious (see Chapter 35).

5. Cyclical

The term 'cyclical unemployment' refers to the alternate booms and slumps in the level of industrial activity which have occurred over the last hundred years. It was the major cause of the high unemployment of the 1930s, and while we no longer speak of a 'trade cycle', we do still move between boom and recession.

This is the most serious form of unemployment and is the subject matter of Chapters 30 and 31.

6. The search theory of unemployment

A different approach to frictional unemployment views it as primarily search unemployment. According to this view individuals may not take the first available job but will continue to search for a job which may offer a higher income stream in the future. Since search is costly and time-consuming, both firms and workers must use some of their resources to find a good match.

When a worker gets a wage offer, for instance, he or she must decide whether to accept it or continue searching for a better offer. Accepting the offer means forgoing the chance of a higher wage offer later, while continuing the search means losing the wages that would have been earned if he or she had accepted the offer and started working. Since the cost of search is often reduced by the payment of unemployment benefit, an appropriate policy response would be to reduce the amount of this payment (the 'replacement ratio') or tighten eligibility criteria. Then the higher cost of search would encourage individuals to accept job offers earlier.

An improvement in technology could have a long-lasting effect on the unemployment rate if it led to a permanent increase in the rate at which searching firms and workers 'find' the right match. This may be what the Internet has done. Firms now routinely post vacancies on the Internet, so that workers can look for jobs in multiple (perhaps remote) locations at almost no cost. Several million CVs are now estimated to be online and the Internet is available to half the UK population. These developments should help reduce the amount of time spent searching for the right match, and so should help lower the equilibrium unemployment rate.

CHAPTER SUMMARY

- Unemployment occurs when persons able to work are unable to find suitable paid employment.
- Unemployment figures can be misinterpreted because of problems of definition.
- Frictional unemployment occurs when workers are between jobs, although the length of time they spend searching for a suitable job may be extended if the replacement ratio – the ratio of benefits to earnings – is high.
- Seasonal unemployment occurs in certain industries such as tourism.
- Some unemployment occurs because of reduced international demand for UK exports.
- Structural unemployment occurs because of changes in the long-term structure of industry, with some industries declining as others develop.
- Cyclical unemployment increases as the economy moves from growth into recession.

REVIEW QUESTIONS

....

- Identify the costs of unemployment.
- Why might the ratio of unemployment benefits to earnings in work affect the level of unemployment?
- How can international conditions affect the level of UK unemployment?

 Visit the companion website for further questions

30

THE LEVEL OF OUTPUT AND AGGREGATE DEMAND: THE KEYNESIAN EXPLANATION

LEARNING OBJECTIVES

After studying this chapter you should be able to:
- describe and illustrate the circular flow of income in an economy with households, firms, government and international trade (a four-sector or 'open' economy);
- explain the relationship between consumption and income;
- explain the determinants of investment;
- analyse the working of the economy using the multiplier.

30.1 THE LINK BETWEEN SPENDING AND PRODUCTION

The circular flow of income

We begin by repeating in simplified form the identity which exists between income and expenditure. Take a simple example. A teacher buys a table from a carpenter. With the money he receives, the carpenter pays the timber merchant for the wood, who in turn pays the man who cut the wood. But where did the teacher obtain the original money to buy the table? Simply from the carpenter, the timber merchant and the tree-feller, who each from their receipts pay fees to the teacher for instructing their children. Similarly with the other goods the teacher buys. Thus there is a circular flow of income – one person's spending becomes another person's income. Spending is therefore necessary for earnings.

The same applies to the economy as a whole; at any one time spending equals income. This was the principle upon which we measured national income.

Since spending on goods determines the receipts and thus the profits of firms, it is of vital importance in deciding the level of their output and thus of the aggregate level of activity. To explain more fully, we use Figure 30.1, which shows the *money* flows which correspond to the movement of factors and goods in

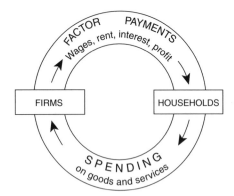

Figure 30.1   The circular flow of income

Figure 2.2 – payments by firms for factors and expenditure of households on goods. The first represents income of households; the second represents receipts of firms.

If spending on goods and services is maintained, factor payments can be maintained; in other words the profitability of production is unchanged and thus firms have no cause to vary output. If, however, for some reason or another, spending should fall, some of the goods produced by firms will not be sold, and stocks accumulate. As a result output is curtailed. On the other hand, if spending on goods and services increases, stocks will be run down. Production has become more profitable and output is expanded.

Three important points emerge from our discussion so far:

1. There is no impetus towards a contraction or expansion of production if spending on goods and services equals spending (including normal profits) by firms on factors of production. In short, the economy is in equilibrium.
2. The level of production, and therefore of employment, is closely related to the level of spending.
3. There is nothing to guarantee that spending will be sufficient to ensure a level of production where all factors are fully employed.

Definitions and assumptions

Before we show how changes in spending occur, we must make simplifying assumptions:

1. All retentions for depreciation are actually spent on replacement investment

Thus, when in future we speak of 'investment' it refers solely to net additions to fixed capital and stocks, i.e. net investment.

2. Net profit equals gross profit less retentions for depreciation: all net profit is distributed to the owners of the risk capital

This means that there is no 'saving' by firms.

3. There is no government taxation or spending

4. There are no economic connections with the outside world; it is a 'closed' economy

From the above assumptions it follows that: (1) the sum of the factor payments is equal to national income (equals national output) as defined in Chapter 28; and (2) income equals disposable income.

5. There are no changes in the price level

Thus any changes in the money value of national income reflect changes in real output.

6. The level of employment is directly proportionate to the level of output

In practice this may not be strictly true: existing machinery, for example, may be able to produce extra output without additional labour. But until these is full employment the simplification does allow employment to vary directly with the level of national income.

30.2 REASONS FOR CHANGES IN AGGREGATE DEMAND

Aggregate demand

Our task, therefore, is to discover why changes occur in the national income (hereafter symbolised by Y). Now, as we have just shown, Y depends upon the level of spending, which we shall refer to as aggregate demand (abbreviated to AD). Thus we can find out why Y changes by discovering why AD changes.

Changes in AD

Let us return to our example of the teacher who earns £31,252 in a given year. Most of it will be spent on consumer goods and services – but not all. Some will probably be put aside for a 'rainy day'. That part of income which is not spent we can say is 'saved'. What happens to it? The money could be hidden under the mattress; in that case it is obviously lost to the circular flow of income. But the teacher is more likely to put it in a bank, where it is safer and earns interest.

Nevertheless, at this point it is still lost to the circular flow. Saving represents a 'leak' from the flow of income.

So far we have looked only at spending on consumer goods. But spending may also be on capital goods. Firms borrow money from their banks (and other institutions) for such purchases. Thus the sum deposited by the teacher stands a good chance of being returned to the circular flow of income by being 'invested', i.e. spent on capital goods or additions to stocks. Investment, therefore, can be regarded as an 'injection'. And, if exactly the amount of money saved by households is spent by firms on investment, the level of *AD* is maintained (Figure 30.2) and *Y* is unchanged.

But suppose that the amount saved does not coincide with what firms wish to invest. This can come about either by a change in the amount invested or by a change in the amount spent by consumers.

Let us first assume that households' spending on consumer goods remains constant. If now firms reduce the amount they borrow for investment, *AD* is smaller. On the other hand, if firms increase their investment, *AD* will be larger.

Alternatively, the amount of income spent on consumer goods may alter. Investment, we will now assume, remains unchanged. Here, if more is spent out of a given income, *AD* will increase; if less, *AD* decreases.

What it is important to recognise is that in an economy where people are free to dispose of their income as they please, and where firms make their own investment decisions, a difference can easily exist between the amount of income which people plan to 'save' (i.e. which they do not wish to spend) and the amount which firms wish to invest. This is because, in their spending, households and firms act for different reasons. Two questions have therefore to be asked: (i) What determines spending on consumer goods and therefore saving (at position *A*)? (ii) What determines investment spending (at position *B*)?

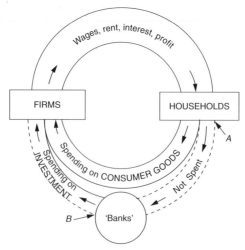

Figure 30.2   The level of income maintained through investment

In our analysis, consumption, that is spending on consumer goods and services, will be given the symbol C; saving, i.e. income not spent on consumption, S: investment, i.e. spending on *net additions* to capital goods and stocks, I.

30.3 CONSUMPTION SPENDING

Consumption and saving by households: 'personal saving'

Income is received as wages or salaries, rent, interest and profits. With it households buy the consumer goods they need. The part of income which is not spent has been defined as 'saving'. Hence $Y = C + S$, $C = Y - S$, and $S = Y - C$.

C and S, therefore, are merely two sides of the same coin. Thus, whenever we consider C or S, we must examine the factors which influence both spending and thrift.

Spending decisions are more important in the short run, for people's first concern is to maintain their standard of living. They are influenced by:

1. Size of income

A small income leaves no margin for saving. Only when basic needs have been satisfied will a part of income be saved. Indeed, if current income falls below this level, past savings or borrowing may be used to maintain the standard of living accustomed to.

But we can go further. As income increases, the proportion spent tends to decrease; or, as it is often put, there is a *diminishing marginal propensity to consume* (C). Thus Figure 30.3 shows that below an income of *OD* there is 'dis-saving'. At *OD* all income is consumed, the difference being covered by spending past

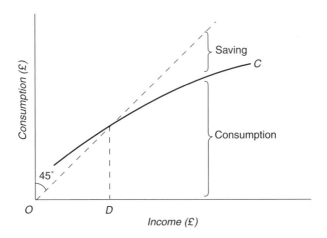

Figure 30.3 The relationship between consumption and income

savings or by borrowing. At higher incomes the proportion spent of any increase falls and saving occurs. This *diminishing marginal propensity to consume* is shown by the decreasing slope of the consumption curve: for any given increase in income, the extra amount spent grows successively smaller.

But the evidence suggests that while diminishing marginal propensity to consume applies to individuals, when we consider national income as a whole the average propensity to consume remains fairly constant. This suggests that everybody is raising their *level* of consumption in order to 'keep up with the Joneses'.

2. The time-lag in adjusting spending habits

It takes time for people to adjust their standard of living to changes in income either through inertia or because they relate their saving to what they regard as their permanent income. But if they *expect* a higher permanent income, consumption may increase accordingly. In fact consumption patterns may be related to the different levels of income which pertain over their life cycle.

The above explains the *shape* of the consumption curve – how spending changes as income changes. But we still have to consider the autonomous factors which determine the proportion of any given income which is spent, that is, the *position* of the curve. These include:

3. Changes in disposable income

We have assumed that firms have distributed all net profits and that there are no government taxation or transfers. In practice both profit distribution and government taxation will affect the size of income available for spending. Increasing direct taxation, for instance, would, by reducing disposable income, lower the C curve.

4. The size of the wealth owned by an individual

Wealth can increase consumption because it can be borrowed against, e.g. by mortgaging property.

5. The invention of new consumer goods

In recent years family cars, TV sets, iPods, camcorders, central heating and holidays abroad have all induced spending, especially when backed by intensive advertising.

6. Hire-purchase and other credit facilities

Easier hire-purchase or bank credit terms encourage spending.

7.   An anticipated fall in the value of money

If people considered that the prices of goods were likely to rise, they would bring forward their spending rather than save for the future.

8.   Inflation

Uncertainty regarding possible government measures to reduce inflation may lead to increased saving. Furthermore, the real value of assets fixed in money terms falls. People may be induced to save more to restore the real value of their assets. This happened in 1990–2.

9.   The age distribution of the population

Since most saving is done by people over 35 years of age, an ageing population will tend to reduce the propensity to consume of the community as a whole.

In the longer run, people have some concern for their future standard of living, and *thrift* exercises a greater influence on their spending. The main factors determining thrift are:

1.   Size of income

Saving tends to increase as income increases at an increasing rate.

2.   The life cycle

For most people spending tends to exceed income early in life but income exceeds spending later in life as they save for retirement.

3.   Psychological attitudes

Some communities are by nature more thrifty than others, providing against sickness, unemployment and old age. On the other hand, ostentation – the desire to 'keep up with the Joneses' – may motivate a high rate of spending.

4.   Social environment

Apart from influencing the general attitude to saving, environment can be a major factor in other ways. Such institutions as savings banks, building societies, insurance companies and unit trusts encourage regular saving out of income.

Political conditions, too, influence saving habits. Countries continually threatened by war or revolution do not provide the stable background necessary to encourage thrift.

5. Government policy

The government can influence people's attitude to saving in a variety of ways. In the UK it tries to stimulate personal saving through the rate of interest offered, tax concessions (e.g. ISAs or Individual Savings Accounts: tax-free annual investment allowances) and special devices (e.g. Premium Bonds). On the other hand, a comprehensive state social-insurance and pension scheme may reduce personal saving.

At one time it was thought that people could only be induced to postpone consumption, i.e. to save, by offering interest as compensation (see p. 273). This view, however, is now largely rejected, chiefly because much saving is contractual, e.g. pension and mortgage payments. The dominant factor is the *ability* to save, i.e. the level of income.

Under our simplifying assumptions that all net profits are distributed and that there is no government taxation or spending, all saving is done by households. But saving can be achieved through retentions by firms and the government (Figure 30.4). In order to consider these, we will temporarily relax assumptions (2) and (3) above.

Business saving

Saving by businesses (which in volume remains fairly stable) is achieved by not distributing to shareholders all the profits made in a year. Some profits are usually retained, either to be 'ploughed back' for the expansion of the business, or to

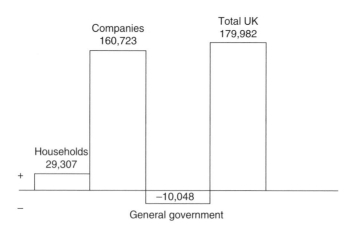

Figure 30.4   Saving in the UK, 2004 (£million)

be held as liquid reserves in order to meet tax liabilities or maintain dividends when profits fluctuate. The chief factors affecting this type of saving are:

1. Profits

Transfers to reserves are dependent upon and stimulated by the level of current profits. In practice, therefore, business saving is determined principally by the level of *AD*.

2. Subjective factors

Profits are likely to be retained when directors are expansion-minded or financially prudent.

3. Government policy

An increased tax on *distributed* profits would tend to increase company saving.

Government saving

Central government saving depends upon the relationship between current government revenue and expenditure. The surplus may be desirable: (i) to provide for the government's own investment and loans; and (ii) to ensure that, with personal and business saving, total saving will be sufficient to prevent an inflationary *AD* from developing. A deficit may be embarrassing for monetary policy (see p. 392), but where there is severe unemployment it can serve to boost *AD*.

Public corporations are similar in many ways to ordinary businesses. But, as their operations are more directly under government control and their capital requirements are largely covered by the Treasury, their savings and investments are included under the public sector. Local authorities could also have savings in the form of a budget surplus.

Thus in the public sector, saving is determined chiefly by government policy, economic and political.

Conclusion

In the private sector, spending (and therefore saving) depend upon (i) the level of *Y*, i.e. the size of *AD*, and (ii) other factors influencing the amount spent out of income. In comparison with changes in *AD* these other factors are fairly stable.

Hence the main factor affecting short-term changes in consumption spending is the size of *AD*!

We have therefore to look elsewhere for the reason why *AD* changes. It is to be found in the comparative instability of the other form of spending – investment.

30.4   INVESTMENT SPENDING

What do we mean by 'investment'?

Investment is spending over a given period on the production of capital goods (houses, factories, machinery, etc.) or on net additions to stocks (raw materials, consumer goods in shops, etc.).

It is important to distinguish between this definition of *real* investment and *asset* investment, which is the one usually referred to as 'investment' by lay people. In national income analysis, investment takes place only when there is an actual net addition to capital goods or stocks. It cannot be applied to putting money in the bank or to the purchase of securities.

It should be noted that the definition above would cover 'gross investment', since it makes no allowance for the depreciation of existing capital assets. But, as already explained, we are analysing in terms of national income (net national product) *not* gross national product. Investment in our model, therefore, must be limited to *net* investment, i.e. gross investment less depreciation.

Investment in the private sector of the economy

While in the private sector some investment in housing is undertaken by owner-occupiers who add garages, rooms, etc., to their property, most personal investment is by sole traders and partnerships. However, such investment is less than half that of companies (see Figure 30.5).

The level of investment by firms is governed by the expected yield relative to cost, changes in techniques, changes in the rate of consumption and government policy.

1.   Expected yield relative to cost

Firms spend on new capital equipment when they think that the cost will be justified by the addition to revenue which will directly result. In short, marginal-revenue productivity must at least equal marginal cost.

Whereas marginal-revenue productivity in the case of labour can be estimated fairly accurately, it is not so with capital. Capital equipment lasts a long time, and its return is spread over many years. This involves uncertainty. Is demand for the product likely to change? Are competitors likely to enter the market? Will

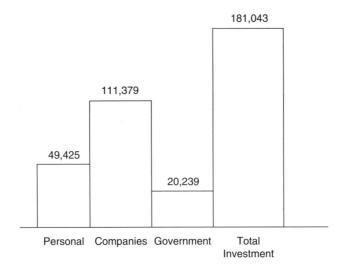

Figure 30.5 Investment in the UK, 2004 (domestic fixed capital formation, £million)

the present methods of production become obsolete? The return to the capital equipment over its life, therefore, can be no more definite than a series of yearly yields which the entrepreneur reasonably *expects*. It is usual to discount these yields to their present value and to express the return over the initial cost as a rate. This rate will be referred to as the *marginal efficiency of investment* (symbol MEI).

We can give more precision to this term by a simple example. Suppose a machine costs £1,000. It has a working life of four years, during which the entrepreneur expects that it will add £400 each year to receipts. We could find a single rate of discount which would make the £400 received during the first year plus the £400 received during the second year plus the £400 received during the third year plus the £400 received during the fourth year just equal to the initial cost of £1,000. This rate of discount is the MEI. (In our example, it is about 22 per cent.) If the MEI is greater than the rate of interest – the cost of borrowing the original £1,000 – the entrepreneur will buy the machine; if it is less, he will not.

In the above example, we have shown how the marginal efficiency of a *particular* machine is determined. But what of the marginal efficiency of new capital *in general*? How will this vary as the capital equipment of the community increases or decreases?

For two reasons it can be expected that the MEI will fall as the stock of the community's capital increases. First, as more machines are produced, so will the products made by those machines increase in supply. Thus the price of those products falls, and so the expected yield of the machine will also fall. Second, producing more machines will increase the demand for the factors of production making those machines. This will increase the price of those factors, and so the supply price of the machines is likely to rise as more are produced. From the first, we have smaller expected yields to be discounted; from the second, a larger initial supply price as capital increases. Both lead to a smaller MEI as the supply of capital increases.

In other words, the curve relating MEI to the level of investment slopes downwards from left to right (Figure 30.6).

With a marginal efficiency of investment as depicted by the curve MEI and a rate of interest of *OR*, the level of investment will be *OM*.

The level of investment may alter through any change in (a) the expected yield, or (b) the rate of interest. Thus if expected yield rises to MEI$_1$, investment will increase to *OM*$_1$. On the other hand, if the rate of interest rises to *OR*$_2$, investment will fall to *OM*$_2$. What we now have to do, therefore, is to examine the possible extent and frequency of changes in expected yield, and to see whether those changes are likely to overshadow changes in the rate of interest.

Let us consider the *expected yield*. We have already shown that this is clouded in uncertainty because the firm will have to look far into the future to estimate changes in the demand for its product and to allow for possible changes in costs and methods of production. Upon what can it base its estimates?

The simple answer is that it has little definite to go on. Its estimate of the earning power of an investment over, say, the next five years can be only tentative, and allowance will have to be made for its confidence in its accuracy. The main factors influencing its decisions are: the level of current income; the course of Stock Exchange prices; the future price level; and government policy. Let us consider each in turn.

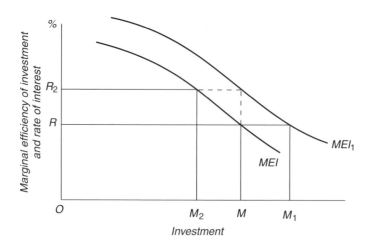

Figure 30.6 The determination of the level of investment

In making its estimate, the firm will most likely commence from the position about which it does have some definite knowledge – the present. If current demand for its goods is buoyant, and has been so for some time, future prospects will probably look rosy. On the other hand, if present demand is low, it will think twice before adding to its productive capacity. But the current demand for goods as a whole depends chiefly upon the current level of *AD*. Investment is likely to be higher, therefore, the higher is *AD*.

Prices of shares on the Stock Exchange influence investment decisions in two ways. First, a firm will be unwilling to extend its factory if current Stock Exchange prices value businesses, particularly those similar to its own, unfavourably. Second, when its share price is high, a company will find it easier and cheaper to raise capital through a 'rights' issue.

As regards the price level, if the firm thinks that prices in future will be higher, then more investment is likely now. Not only will the value of the factory or machine appreciate, but expected yield will be higher through the rise in the price of the product.

Political instability and changes in government policy add to uncertainty. The former discourages investment, particularly by foreign companies operating in the country. The possibility of the latter influences expectations. Is corporation tax likely to be increased? Will the Bank of England raise the rate of interest to reduce the rate of inflation?

This brings us to the *rate of interest*, the cost of investment. If it rises, marginal projects cease to be viable, and so the level of investment falls. This applies even if funds come from internal reserves, for the opportunity cost – the return on the best alternative, e.g. government securities – has to be considered. To Keynes, therefore, the long-term rate of interest was a major factor in determining the level of investment.

However, we must not assume a *precise* relationship. While the prevailing rate of interest could be decisive for projects where the yields extend far into the future, e.g. houses, shops and offices, and for investment by small firms, practical considerations may loom large with other investment.

For one thing investment decisions, especially for large firms, are mainly the result of a planned long-term programme. For another, firms allow a safety margin when deciding on investment, and this may be sufficient to absorb a relatively small rise in the rate of interest. Even the holding of stocks may not be affected by the rate of interest, as this may form only a small part of the cost of holding stocks, with warehousing, etc., being relatively far more important. Finally, a part of any increase in interest charges would be covered by reduced tax liability.

Nevertheless, when in 1989 interest rates rose sharply, many investment projects became sub-marginal, and recession followed.

Even so, pessimistic expectations were probably the prime cause of investment stagnation. Thus in the 1989–92 recession a progressive lowering of the base rate from 15 per cent to 7 per cent failed to stimulate investment.

This implies that, *compared with firms' expectations*, the rate of interest plays a secondary role in determining the level of investment. Moreover, uncertainty means that expected yield is subject to frequent reappraisal. In other words, changes in expectations may cause the MEI curve to change so frequently and by so much that it outweighs the effect which a movement in the rate of interest may have on the level of investment. We can illustrate from Figure 30.6. A rate of interest OR and a marginal efficiency of investment curve MEI would give a rate of investment OM. A rise in the rate of interest to OR_2 should reduce investment to OM_2. But this assumes that there is no change in the position of the MEI curve. If, for example, as the rate of interest rises to OR_2, revised expectations cause the MEI curve to move to MEI_1, investment will remain at OM. Expectations may be such that, in a slump, a low rate of interest does little to stimulate investment. It is the fickleness of business expectations which gives investment a central role in the determination of the level of employment.

2.   Changes in techniques

Technical innovation, such as the internal combustion engine, nuclear energy, the microchip and North Sea gas and oil, give an added impetus to investment. Against this the possibility of important new products and of new techniques rendering existing capital equipment obsolete must be allowed for when estimating the MEI.

3.   Changes in the rate of consumption: the 'accelerator'

Our conclusion in (1) above, that the rate of investment was tied fairly closely to the size of aggregate demand, is capable of further refinement. Changes in the rate of investment are closely linked, not to the absolute level of consumption, but to changes in the *rate* of consumption. A simple example will explain.

Suppose that 1,000 machines are fully employed in producing bicycle tyres and that the life of each machine is ten years. This means that 100 machines have to be replaced each year and the industry making this type of capital good must have a yearly capacity of 100.

Now suppose demand for bicycles increases so that the demand for tyres increases by 10 per cent. If there is no excess capacity for producing tyres, it can be seen that 100 new machines, in addition to the replacement requirement, are needed immediately. In this year, therefore, 200 tyre-making machines must be produced. Thus although the increased demand for consumer goods was only 10 per cent, it led to a doubling of the capacity of the industry making the machines.

If consumption of tyres now remains constant at the new level, production of the machines will have to contract sharply, for until the extra machines wear out in ten years' time, only the annual replacement of 100 machines will be required.

Taking this example as it stands, three conclusions can be drawn.

(a) Variations in the rate of consumption will produce changes in investment on a magnified scale. Usually changes in consumption are the result of variations in the level of *AD* (known today as recessions and recoveries). But they may also be brought about by such factors as changes in hire-purchase facilities, the boom in hire-purchase commitments being followed by stagnation for two or three years while repayments are made.

(b) Swings in the level of production are much greater in the producer-goods industries than in the consumer-goods industries. The longer the life of a machine, the greater will be the swing. Thus in our example, if the machine for making tyres lasts for twenty years, the 10 per cent increase in demand for tyres would necessitate a trebling of the capacity of the tyre-machine industry.

(c) A single change in the level of consumption can produce a built-in mechanism whereby changes in the level of investment will be repeated subsequently at fairly regular intervals.

Nevertheless, when we look at the assumptions which are implicit in our example, it loses some of its precision. In the first place, although we stated that there was no excess capacity in the tyre-producing industry, the opposite was assumed in the tyre-machine-making industry where the 100 per cent increase in demand was met by the production of 100 extra machines. If extra tyres can be produced by using idle machines, working overtime or by double-shift working, then there will be no need to increase the number of machines. On the other hand, if there is no surplus capacity in the tyre-machine-making industry, the increased demand for bicycles may simply find its outlet in higher prices, and investment will not increase. Second, the model fails to allow for the expectations of entrepreneurs. An increase in the demand for bicycle tyres may have been anticipated by building up stocks or by holding excess capacity in reserve. On the other hand, it may be thought that the increase in demand is unlikely to be permanent, in which case the extra machines would not be bought.

In practice, induced investment may result, not only from an increase in consumption, but from an autonomous increase in investment. Thus it is more accurate to say that the accelerator depends upon changes in *AD* rather than simply on changes in the level of consumption.

4. Government policy

To be complete we must again relax our assumption of no government taxation or spending. Government policy may directly influence private investment. Banks have been instructed from time to time to restrict credit for certain types of investment. Should it desire to stimulate private investment, the government may give subsidies (e.g. for restoring old houses, or improving farm buildings), raise investment or depreciation allowances in tax assessment, and revive the optimism of firms by lowering the rate of interest and, more important, by increasing its own spending.

Investment in the public sector

This includes not only the capital expenditure of the central government, but also that of public corporations and agencies and of local authorities.

Much of central government investment is fairly stable, depending chiefly on policy commitments – road construction, school and hospital building, etc.

Local authority investment, however, may react to changes in the rate of interest, especially where finance is raised on the open market.

The real importance of public sector investment is that, for the purpose of adjusting *AD*, it is under direct government control. Indeed, it is mostly included within the global figure of 'government spending' which can be varied to adjust *AD*.

Summary on investment

Employment depends upon the level of *AD* – the total of spending on the goods produced. *AD* fluctuates according to the relationship between intended saving and investment.

(i) *AD* expands if:
    (1) investment increases but saving remains unchanged;
    (2) saving decreases but investment remains unchanged.
(ii) *AD* contracts if:
    (1) investment decreases but saving remains unchanged;
    (2) saving increases but investment remains unchanged.

In practice investment is more liable to frequent change than is saving. Whereas firms' expectations are highly sensitive to new conditions, people's spending habits are fairly stable. Fluctuations in the level of *AD*, and therefore of income, are thus mainly the result of changes in the level of investment.

There is another important way in which saving differs from investment in the process of income creation. Whereas an increase in investment will, other things being equal, automatically produce an increase in saving through an expansion of income, an addition to saving need not lead to an increase in investment. Indeed income merely contracts until what is saved from it equals investment.

By influencing expectations, the current level of income will play a part in determining the rate of private investment. Moreover, investment will bear some relationship to the rate of change of income.

But, in order to simplify our analysis, we shall ignore these connections between investment and the level of income and assume that all investment is autonomous. In other words, investment decisions of firms are based on a number of considerations, and changes in investment are not automatically induced by income changes.

30.5 EQUILIBRIUM THROUGH CHANGES IN THE LEVEL OF INCOME

The restoration of equilibrium

We must now follow through what happens when, for some reason, intended saving and investment become unequal. A simple arithmetical example will help. We shall assume:

1. $Y = 10,000$.
2. At this level of income there are unemployed resources.
3. Consumption spending by households is $(0.6)Y$ (disposable income) at all levels of Y. (In practice, consumption is more likely to be about 90 per cent of disposable income, but our assumption will make the diagrams clearer.)
4. Any increase in Y does not affect the proportion of Y spent by any change in the distribution of Y.
5. Investment spending by firms is autonomous: that is, it is independent of the level of income. Initially the rate of investment $(I) = 4,000$.
6. All figures are in £ million, and prices are constant.

Initially, in period 0, the economy is in equilibrium:

$$AD = C + I = 6000 + 4000 = 10\,000$$
$$Y = C + S = 6000 + 4000 = 10\,000.$$

Now suppose that, in period 1, the rate of I increases by 2,000 to 6,000. AD is now 12,000. The receipts of firms rise to 12,000, and stocks of goods decrease. As a result firms expand production – factor payments equal $12,000 = Y$ (Period 1). This expansion of Y has come about solely because I is greater than planned S. Similarly, a contraction of Y will occur if I is less than planned S.

The 'multiplier'

But this is not the end of the expansion. An increase in Y to 12,000 will mean that more workers are employed, and they, too, will have income to spend. Thus $C = 0.6\,(12,000) = 7,200$. Together with $I = 6,000$, this gives a new AD of 13,200. Thus, in period 2, Y increases to 13,200. And so it continues. How the process works in real life can be illustrated from Nevil Shute's *Ruined City*. The shipyard in the town obtained an order for three tankers. 'A shop, long closed, reopened to sell meat pies ... A man who gleaned a sack of holly in the country lanes disposed of it within an hour ... A hot roast chestnut barrow came upon the streets, and did good trade.' In our example the process will only come to an end when

Y has expanded to 15,000. At this level of income, $S = 6,000$ – sufficient to match $I = 6,000$. Because $S = I$, this is the new equilibrium level of Y.

The sequence outlined above is shown in Table 30.1 and in Figure 30.7.

It will be noted that the increase in Y is much larger than the original increase in I. The ratio

$$\frac{\text{Increase in } AD}{\text{Initial increase in } I}$$

is known as the 'multiplier'.

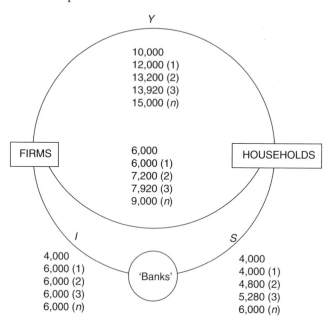

Figure 30.7 The effect of an increase in the rate of investment on the level of income

Table 30.1 The effect of an increase in the rate of *I* on the level of *Y*

Period	C	I	S	Y
0	6,000	4,000	4,000	10,000
1	6,000	6,000	4,000	12,000
2	7,200	6,000	4,800	13,200
3	7,920	6,000	5,280	13,920
4	8,352	6,000	5,568	14,352
.	.	.	.	.
.	.	.	.	.
.	.	.	.	.
n	9,000	6,000	6,000	15,000

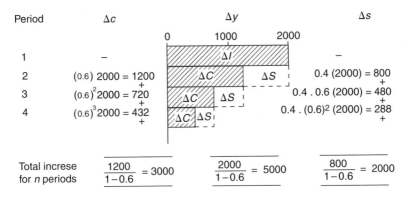

Period	Δc	Δy	Δs

Figure 30.8 Increases in consumption, saving and income resulting from an increase in the rate of investment

To see what the size of the multiplier depends upon, we can concentrate on changes in C, S and Y. As we are referring to changes, we shall prefix our symbols with the sign Δ. These changes are shown in Figure 30.8.

Figure 30.8 is explained as follows. The initial ΔI leads to an increase in Y. A proportion of these extra factor payments (for example, received by workers previously unemployed) is spent according to the marginal propensity to consume (0.6). The proportion not spent (0.4) is saved.

This extra spending increases AD, and therefore Y, still further. And so the process is repeated, extra increments of C going to swell the total increase in AD and therefore of Y.

These totals are shown at the foot of each column. Each is really a geometric progression of the form $a + ar + ar^2$, where r equals the marginal propensity to consume. Now the sum of a geometric progression to infinity where r is less than 1 equals $a/(1 - r)$. It follows, therefore, that:

$$\text{Total } \Delta Y = \frac{\Delta I}{1 - \text{marginal propensity to consume}} = \frac{\Delta I}{1-c} = \frac{\Delta I}{s}$$

The larger the marginal propensity to consume (c), the greater will be the total increase in Y. Since we defined the multiplier as $\Delta Y/\Delta I$, the value of the multiplier in this example is

$$\frac{1}{1-c} = \frac{1}{1-0.6} = 2.5$$

This can be verified visually in Figure 30.8, where the shaded area equals the total increase in Y. If the proportion of income spent fell to 0.5, the shaded areas would

383

be smaller. Our analysis points to the reason for this. When the fraction of income consumed falls, a higher proportion is saved. Thus income does not have to expand so much in order to bring intended saving into line with investment.

This brings us to the basic difference between saving and investment in the process of income creation. Whereas an increase in investment will, other things being equal, automatically produce an increase in saving, extra intended saving need not lead to an increase in investment. Instead income merely contracts until what is saved from it (realised saving) equals investment.

Diagrammatic representation of changes in the equilibrium level of income

Employment, we have assumed, varies directly with the level of income (AD), which itself depends upon spending on consumption and investment. If this total spending is equal to income, firms do not make losses and can continue employing the same amount of labour. If total spending is less than income, then firms make a loss because they are getting back less than their expenses of production, and so production is reduced. If total spending increases, then firms more than realise their expectations and production is expanded. This is explained in Figure 30.9.

The income–expenditure line, at an angle of 45°, traces all points where expenditure is equal to income (the same scale being chosen for both the x- and y-axes). Therefore, any point on this line will represent an equilibrium level of income.

The line C shows consumption expenditure at different levels of income. In our example $C = 0.6Y$. To this we have to add investment expenditure of 4,000 at all levels of income. Thus the line $C + I$ is vertically distant 4000 above the C line at all levels of income.

In equilibrium, $Y = AD = C + I$. The only point where this can occur is where the $C + I$ line cuts the 45° line. Here

$$AD = Y = 10\,000$$

When I increases to 6,000, the $C + I$ line moves vertically by 2,000 to $C + I'$. AD immediately increases to 12,000, and so does Y. Of this income, $C = 7,200$, which, with $I = 6,000$, means that AD and Y increase to 13,200. This expansionary process continues until AD and Y are equal to 15,000 where planned $S =$ realised $S = I = 6,000$.

Figure 30.9 (b) concentrates on leakages (S) and injections (I) as in our original approach (pp. 367–9). The equilibrium level of Y is 10,000. Below this, there is an unplanned running down of stocks and so Y expands. If Y exceeds 10,000, there is an unplanned accumulation of stocks, and Y contracts (eventually to 10,000) as workers are laid off.

If I increases by 2,000, Y expands to 15,000
Here the multiplier

$$\frac{\Delta Y}{\Delta I} = \frac{a}{b} = \frac{5000}{2000} = 2.5$$

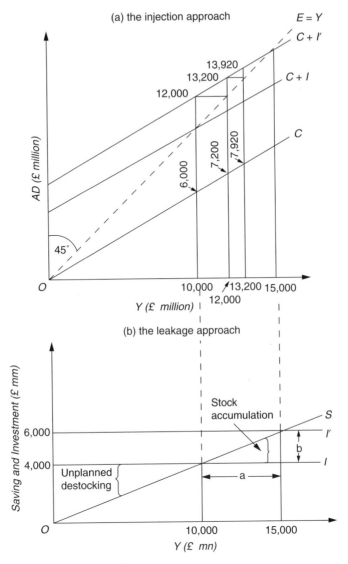

Figure 30.9 The effect on *Y* of a change in *I*

The effect of a diminishing marginal propensity to consume

So far we have assumed that the marginal propensity to consume is constant at all levels of income. But, even if the propensity to consume diminishes as income increases, the principle of the multiplier is the same. The only difference is that the calculations are more complicated because, for each period increment, we have to apply a smaller multiplier as income increases.

30.6   THE EFFECT OF CHANGES IN CONSUMPTION

An autonomous change in consumption

So far we have analysed what happens to *AD* when there is an increase in autonomous investment. But the result is exactly the same if there is an autonomous increase in consumption (that is, not related to *Y*), investment remaining unchanged.

Suppose, for instance, that *C* increases by 2,000 at all levels of *Y*. That is, $C = 2000 + 0.6Y$. This simply means that the original $C + I$ curve (Figure 30.9) would move vertically upwards by 2,000 to the $C + I'$ position (as with an autonomous increase in *I* equal to 2,000). The increase in *C* is subject to the same multiplier effect, and thus *Y* increases as before to 15,000.

The paradox of thrift

But what is the situation when there is a decrease in the propensity to consume, i.e. an increase in saving? Here we have what is often called the 'paradox of thrift'.

As we have seen, saving occurs because all income is not spent on consumption; people are limiting their demand for consumer goods. In real terms, they are saying that they will free factors from the production of goods for present consumption so that they can produce capital goods. In this respect, therefore, thrift is a virtue.

But when our peasant farmer reduced present consumption in order to make his plough (see p. 272), he automatically carried out investment with the time at his disposal. However, in a modern economy decisions to save and decisions to invest are carried out for different reasons by two different sets of persons – households and firms respectively. When intended saving is greater than investment, not all factors switch from producing consumption goods to producing capital goods. Some are unemployed. From the community's point of view saving can only be in capital goods or additions to stocks. When factors are unemployed there is no *real* saving – what they could have produced is lost to the community for ever.

What happens, as we have seen, is that income falls until it has reached that level where intended saving out of income just equals investment. Thus, if additional saving is not matched by additional investment, thrift is a curse, not a virtue, for it leads to a reduced standard of living as factors become unemployed and fewer consumer goods are produced.

Worse still, the fall in consumption could adversely affect firms' expectations. Therefore investment itself falls, causing an even greater fall in income. Thus the real paradox of thrift is that, in these circumstances, we can end up with less saving than we originally started with.

30.7   GOVERNMENT SPENDING AND TAXATION

We can now relax our assumption that there is no government activity. The government raises taxes (symbol T). T is a leak out of the circular flow of income, similar to saving.

But government spending (symbol G) is an injection into the flow of AD. Therefore, $AD = C + I + G$. This is shown in Figure 30.10.

G performs the same role as other forms of spending. Any increase in G will be subject to the multiplier. This can be illustrated from Figure 30.9. If, instead of the increase in I, the increase in AD took the form of $G = 2000$, the $C + I'$ line would be simply $C + I + G$, and the new level of Y would still be 15,000.

The effect of taxation is a little more difficult to analyse. However, we shall simplify by assuming: (a) taxes are not related to income (that is, they are imposed autonomously by the government as lump sums); (b) house-holds spread the burden of any change in the level of taxation between consumption and saving.

Suppose $AD = C + I + G = 9000 + 4000 + 2000 = 15\,000 = Y$; assume also that there is no T. Thus disposable income still equals Y, $C = 9000$ and $S = 6000$. The government now decides to raise 2,000 by taxation. Does this mean that Y falls back to 10,000? The answer is 'no'. As disposable income now equals $Y - T$, it falls to 13,000. As a result there is an initial fall in C of $(0.6 \times 13\,000) = 7800$. But this fall in C is subject to the multiplier; thus the total fall in Y equals $1200 \times 2.5 = 3000$, giving $Y = 12\,000$ with $C = 6000$, $I = 4000$ and $G = 2000$. The

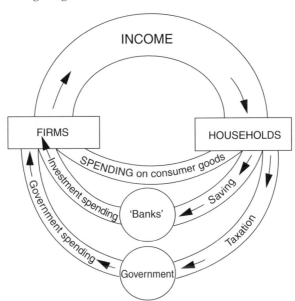

Figure 30.10   The circular flow of income and government spending and taxation

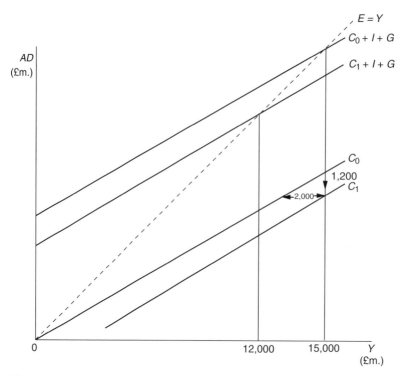

Figure 30.11   The effect of an increase in taxation on disposable income and consumption

reason why Y does not fall to 10,000 is that part of the burden of T falls on S, which is already a leak from the circular flow of income.

Figure 30.11 illustrates the above diagrammatically. A lump sum direct tax of 2,000 reduces disposable income. Consumption is therefore now only what it would be if disposable income were 2,000 smaller at all levels of income. Thus the C curve moves downward vertically from C_0 to C_1 by 1,200.

It should be noted that in moving from a budget deficit of 2,000 to a balanced budget, the government has reduced Y by 3,000. Similarly a budget deficit of 2000 from $Y = 12\ 000$ would increase Y by 3,000. *Budgetary policy*, therefore, influences the level of AD.

30.8   THE EFFECT OF FOREIGN TRADE

We can now relax our assumption of a closed economy.

Let us assume that the production of consumer and investment goods is at a given level, and that there is unemployment. Now imagine that British firms obtain orders to supply £2,000 worth of capital equipment to the USA. As a result, in the British economy *AD* and *Y* expand initially by 2,000 – paid out in wages, salaries and profits, the cost being covered by firms borrowing the money.

But this is not all. Of the initial 2,000 increase, 1,200 will be spent and 800 saved. The 1,200 spent now becomes income of other persons, who in their turn spend 720 and save 480. So we could go on. The position is exactly the same as with investment – additional spending on British exports has a multiplier effect depending upon the marginal propensity to consume. In this case, as a result of the initial additional spending of 2,000 on exports, *AD* increases by 5,000.

Increased spending on imports works in exactly the opposite way. There is now more spending on foreign goods, and less on British. As a result, foreign rather than British workers supply goods for the home market. Less expenditure on home-produced goods means that income is taken out of the circular flow, and *AD* contracts. As before, the initial loss of income is multiplied according to the marginal propensity to consume.

We can summarise the position as follows. Expenditure on exports is equivalent to an addition to investment – income is generated in producing goods which do not become available on the home market. Expenditure on imports, on the other hand, is a leak from the circular flow of income similar to a reduction of consumption (Figure 30.12).

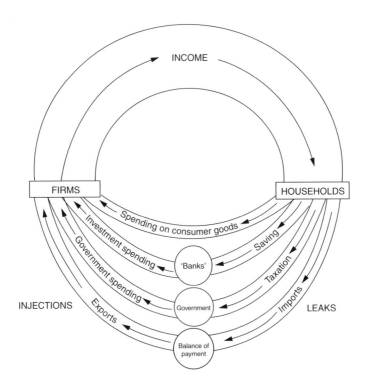

Figure 30.12   Total leaks and injections

Thus we can combine the effect on *AD* of changes in investment, exports and imports as follows:

$$\Delta AD = \frac{\Delta I + \Delta \text{Exports} - \Delta \text{Imports}}{s}$$

The above explanation, however, does assume that both exports and imports are autonomous, i.e. they bear no precise relationship to the level of income. We shall continue this assumption with exports, though it could be that these decline as income expands, since it is now easier to sell on the home market.

But imports are likely to form a proportion of consumer spending and therefore of income. Thus if we assume that imports form one-sixth of consumption or 0.167C, we can say that the 'propensity to import' is one-tenth of income or 0.1Y. We can now treat this import leakage in the same way as saving. Whatever the cause of the initial expansion in *Y*, leakages occur because some of this increased *Y* will be saved and some will be spent on imports. Thus, when *m* represents the *marginal* propensity to import, we have:

$$\Delta AD = \frac{\Delta I + \Delta \text{Exports}}{s + m}$$

Suppose, for instance, that income is an equilibrium at 10,000. Up to this there is no foreign trade, and *C* = 6000 and *S* = 4000. At any income above this the marginal propensity to import is 0.167C = 0.1Y. If there are now exports of 2,000, the increase in *Y* will be 2000 × 1/0.4 + 0.1 = 4000.

The analysis of this section indicates why, during the 1930s, many countries tried to solve their unemployment problems by pushing exports (which increase income and therefore employment) and by discouraging imports (which decrease income). A little reflection will show, however, that such a restrictionist policy merely 'exports' unemployment to other countries. Nowadays we realise that countries must cooperate with one another in fighting unemployment (see Chapter 37).

30.9   DEMAND MANAGEMENT

Policy implications of Keynes

Given its assumptions, the Keynesian model indicates that, since cyclical unemployment is brought about by inadequate *AD*, *AD* has to be maintained at a level which will achieve the full employment level of output. In terms of Figure 30.13, full employment requires *Y* to equal *OE*. An *AD* as shown by *C* + *I* + *G'*, however, will produce equilibrium where *Y* = *OF* = *OZ*. If we look at the situation from the full-employment level of *Y* at *E*, there is a deficiency of *AD* equal to *LM* – the 'deflationary' gap. The government has to raise the *AD* curve to *C* + *I* + *G*, chiefly

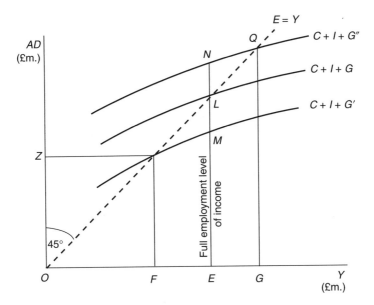

Figure 30.13 Equilibrium levels of income

by increasing its own spending. Should *AD* expand beyond this, the extra income of *EG* is unobtainable and this overheating would result in rising prices, increased imports and falling exports as home-produced goods became less price-competitive. An *AD* represented by *C + I + G"* would have to be reduced by the inflationary gap of *NL*.

The responsibility for maintaining an adequate level of *AD* must rest with the government. First, only the government can exercise the powers, particularly as regards collecting the statistics and information necessary for adequate planning. Second, the government's own spending forms such a large proportion of *AD* that, to a great extent, it can be used to balance variations in the private sector. Third, the knowledge that the government is committed to a full-employment policy will eliminate much of the uncertainty from which cyclical fluctuations begin. The means by which *AD* can be maintained are discussed on pp. 399–402.

Post-war demand management in the UK

Keynes's theory dominated economic policy during the 1950s and 1960s. Successive UK governments maintained an *AD* which until 1974 (apart from 1971–2) kept unemployment below 3 per cent. Whenever expansion of *AD* led to balance-of-payments difficulties, the government imposed temporary 'stop' policies. 'Fine-tuning' the economy in this way appeared to be working for the comparatively low inflation rate of 5 per cent seemed an acceptable price to pay for maintaining low unemployment.

But preoccupation with maintaining a high level of employment underemphasised other possible repercussions of the policy. 'Fine-tuning' the economy was in reality only dealing with the part of the iceberg showing above the surface. The high level of demand produced a state of 'overfull' employment, with vacancies consistently exceeding unemployed workers. The outcome was inflation, balance-of-payments difficulties, shortages of skilled workers, high labour turnover, firms holding on to surplus workers in case they should be required in the future ('disguised' unemployment), underinvestment in new equipment, a failure by industry to adopt new techniques or to switch to the production of high-technology products and an unsatisfactory rate of growth (see Chapter 34). As a result, British industry was in poor shape to withstand international competition during the world recessions of 1974–5 and 1979–82.

More than that, in the 1970s the rate of inflation and the level of unemployment increased together – a situation known as 'stagflation'. Hence Keynes's views came under increasing scrutiny.

Weaknesses of the Keynesian approach

It must be remembered that Keynes was writing his *General Theory* against the background of the high cyclical unemployment of the 1930s. For him, therefore, unemployment was the major problem. In reality, though, the many objectives of government stabilisation policy are interrelated and cannot be dropped into different boxes with separate measures to deal with each.

First, too little attention was given to how supply responds to increases in AD as full employment is approached. The analysis assumes a stable price level. This is justifiable at higher rates of unemployment. Firms have spare capacity and can increase output at constant costs. Increased *AD* is therefore covered by increased output and the price level remains stable. But eventually, as output increases, firms experience rising costs owing to more intensive use of existing capacity and bottlenecks in obtaining variable factors. As a result prices rise (see p. 397).

Keynes recognised that this rise in prices would occur: the remedy was to remove the inflationary gap NL (Figure 30.13) by reducing *AD*. But this ignores the dynamic forces which come into play once prices start to rise, chiefly the role of trade union inflationary expectations in the wage-bargaining process (see Chapter 33).

Second, Keynes's theory of the price level failed to recognise that increases in the money supply could have the effect of increasing *AD* directly (see pp. 418–19).

Third, Keynes underplayed the side effects of a large PSNCR which high government spending could give rise to. Keynes recognised that government deficit-spending would increase the National Debt, but since loans could be 'rolled over' as they matured, only interest had to be currently paid and, apart from overseas lenders, such payments were simply transfers from taxpayers to lenders within the UK. But Keynes did not foresee the big increase in government borrowing necessary to pay for the welfare state. Servicing a large PSNCR creates difficulties for both monetary and fiscal policy. If it is covered by borrowing from the banks, their extra liquidity allows them to increase the supply of money. If, alternatively, it is covered by non-bank borrowing, e.g. by institutions or persons buying government bonds, the price has to be sufficiently attractive to clear the market. Thus the rate of interest rises. This could cause private investment to fall – 'crowded out' by the increased government spending!

Fourth, changes in the level of *AD* and in the price level have repercussions on the balance-of-payments which may impose a constraint on the expansion of *AD*.

These are the interrelationships which are examined in Chapters 31 and 42.

CHAPTER SUMMARY

- Spending becomes someone else's income and so there is a circular flow of income in the economy.
- Aggregate demand in the economy comprises consumer spending C, investment spending I, government spending G and export spending X minus import spending M.
- The multiplier effect causes national income to increase (or decrease) by more than any initial increase (or decrease) in C, I, G or X − M.
- Leakages from the circular flow of income are savings S, taxes T and imports M. Generally speaking they will cause the economy to contract.
- Injections into the circular flow of income are investment I, government spending G and exports X. Generally speaking they will cause the economy to expand.
- The Keynesian analysis of the economy suggests that aggregate demand AD can be adjusted to achieve full-employment. The main weakness of this policy is that it ignores effects in other areas of the economy such as supply response, government debt and, particularly, inflation.

REVIEW QUESTIONS

....

- If the marginal propensity to consume is 0.5, what is the value of the multiplier?
- If investment were to increase by £100 million, what would be the final increase in national income if the marginal propensity to consume is 0.8?
- Why does expenditure on imports cause the economy to contract?
- What is meant by a 'deflationary gap'?
- What is meant by an 'inflationary gap'?

 Visit the companion website for further questions

CHAPTER 31

EMPLOYMENT AND THE PRICE LEVEL

LEARNING OBJECTIVES
....

After studying this chapter you should be able to:
- explain the meaning of 'full-employment';
- use aggregate demand and aggregate supply curves to analyse equilibrium in the economy and changes in the price level and the level of national income;
- describe fiscal and monetary policies;
- explain supply-side economics.

31.1   CHANGES IN THE APPROACH TO 'FULL EMPLOYMENT'

The meaning of full employment today

While our presentation (Chapter 30 and Figure 30.13) of the Keynesian theory of the level of activity has, for the sake of clarity, shown the full employment level of income as a single point, it is, in the real world, a too simplistic and static approach. The incompatibility of government objectives – particularly full employment and price stability – means that in practice there is no precise target full-employment level of income which can be achieved and maintained by 'fine-tuning'.

Instead the 'full-employment' position has to be decided politically according to the emphasis placed by the government on its other economic objectives. What is certain, however, is that the level of 3 per cent, which until the 1970s people regarded as the maximum unemployment acceptable, has been modified by subsequent events. High rates of inflation and of unemployment have meant that most political parties now recognise that unemployment of around 5 to 6 per cent is a more realistic target.

A revised analytical approach

Recognition of the fact that the objective of full employment has to be considered in conjunction at least with movements in the price level means that we need a somewhat different approach from the basic Keynesian aggregate demand model outlined in Chapter 30. We now have to relate changes in aggregate demand to changes in the price level. This is achieved by paying more attention to the supply side and aggregate supply *AS*.

Our task is to build a model which (1) shows how *AD* and *AS* change with respect to the price level, and (2) brings *AD* and *AS* together to determine both the level of activity and the appropriate price level.

31.2 AGGREGATE DEMAND AND AGGREGATE SUPPLY

The aggregate demand curve

In Chapter 30 it was shown that *AD* consisted of the total of all *planned* spending on final goods and services in the economy; that is, consumers' expenditure + investment + government spending + (exports − imports). In terms of the symbols previously used:

$$AD = C + I + G + (X - M)$$

The *AD* curve shows how this total spending changes in response to changes in the price level. It is assumed that the money supply, taxation rates and the marginal propensity to consume remain constant. Since we are dealing with final goods and services, *AD* is the demand for real output. To simplify we will concentrate on *C* and *I*.

The *AD* curve slopes downwards from left to right (Figure 31.1), showing that, as the price level falls, *AD* expands. In other words, the lower the price level, the greater will be the total real output demanded in the economy.

The reasons for this are:

1. Consumers are wealthier: the 'real balance effect'

Given no change in the money supply, a fall in the price level increases the purchasing power of all balances held in cash. In other words, cash held will buy more. Thus spending on goods and services increases.

2. The rate of interest falls

With no change in the money supply, a fall in prices means that there is less demand for money for transactions purposes, leaving more for the purchase of both goods and 'bonds'. This extra liquidity raises the price of 'bonds'. That is, the

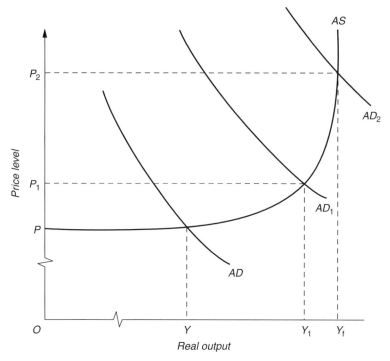

Figure 31.1   The relationship of output and the price level to *AD* and *AS*

rate of interest falls. As a result, spending which is financed mainly by borrowing – particularly houses and cars and, above all, firms' investment – increases.

3.   Home-produced goods are more competitive

When their price falls, home-produced goods become more competitive in foreign markets and so exports increase. Furthermore, because these goods are now relatively cheaper on the home market than imported substitutes, imports tend to decrease. Taken together, $X - M$ increases, thereby expanding AD.

Of course, the opposite effects apply for a rise in the price level.

The aggregate supply curve

The AS curve shows the relationship between the price level and the real output of the economy. It is, however, a short-run supply curve; that is, the capital capacity of the economy as a whole is fixed so that output can only be varied by increasing or decreasing inputs of the variable factors, chiefly labour.

In general, high prices enable firms to extend output. But for analytical purposes, we have to distinguish between three broadly different situations, as follows.

At a low level of output, firms have surplus capacity; they can therefore increase output at constant costs. Equally efficient labour can be taken on and other necessary variable inputs, such as basic materials and components, obtained at existing prices. In the economy as a whole, this increased spending by firms on resources is matched by a proportionate increase in output. Thus there is no pressure on prices to rise. The AS curve is perfectly elastic at the current price level, P, for the output OY (Figure 31.3).

Eventually, however, as the full employment output is approached, fixed capital equipment has to be used more intensively, and diminishing returns set in. In addition, what are usually termed 'bottlenecks' appear through skilled labour shortages, longer delivery dates for components, etc. Above all, trade unions are in a stronger position and obtain wage increases. Thus firms' marginal and average costs rise and the AS curve turns upwards.

The AS curve slopes upwards at an increasing rate the nearer output approaches OY_f, the maximum potential output which is attainable with given limited resources and current technology. The vertical portion is thus the equivalent of the long period AS curve. It can be shifted to the right only by factors which make for long-term growth (see Chapter 34). Given this absolutely inelastic AS curve, any attempt to expand output by increasing AD will be impossible and will simply find its outlet in steeply rising prices.

AD and *AS* combined

Equilibrium occurs at the intersection of the AD and AS curves because at this point the output which households and firms are willing to spend on C and I equals the output which firms will supply. Thus in Figure 31.1 when aggregate demand is AD_1, real national output is OY_1 per year (still less than full employment) and the price level is P_1. Full employment can only be achieved by increasing aggregate demand to AD_2, when the price level will rise to P_2. Such increases in AD have led to demand-pull inflation (see Chapter 30).

31.3 FULL EMPLOYMENT AND DEMAND MANAGEMENT

The significance of the Keynesian approach

One conclusion to be drawn from the above analysis is that an adequate level of AD is necessary if output is to be maintained somewhere near the full employment level. The importance of Keynes was that he highlighted this essential fact.

Since he was concentrating on the prevailing high level of unemployment, he was mainly concerned with the horizontal part of the AS curve up to Y. Thus the assumption of a stable price level was by and large permissible, and so policy had to be directed to increasing AD.

Keynes also showed *how* the government could increase AD. Our immediate task is to examine this. Its inadequacy as a complete policy is discussed below.

The nature of government intervention policies

There is no given formula for government intervention. Not only is the economic situation constantly changing but governments differ in the emphasis they place on the major objectives – full employment, a stable price level, growth – and on the measures which are appropriate to achieving them.

In any case, the role of the government in controlling the economy can be likened to that of the driver of a car going to work in a city. At no time can the car run on its own without some direction, and the driver has to make the necessary adjustments continuously. From time to time, too, he or she is concerned with more definite alterations, varying pressure on the accelerator and changing gear. The driver may even modify the route, making detours to avoid traffic congestion.

But in all these manoeuvres, different drivers act differently. Some use the gear lever rather than the accelerator in changing speed. Others estimate that the traffic congestion will not be so bad as to warrant a detour. Nor does the same person do exactly the same things each day. The driver knows many different routes to work and, being flexible, makes use of them as he or she thinks fit.

So it is with the government. Like the driver guessing the traffic congestion, the government has to work from incomplete information in estimating what changes in AD are necessary to produce the desired result and the extent to which the measures it adopts will produce that change.

It should be noted, however, that with all policies, timing and technique are crucial. If, for instance, reflationary action to pull the economy out of recession is taken when it has begun to turn up of its own accord, subsequent pressure on the price level may exceed that anticipated.

31.4 HOW THE GOVERNMENT CAN MANAGE AGGREGATE DEMAND

Although as we explain later, it is possible to construct a model which shows that, given certain assumptions, a change in AD will not, especially in the long run, affect the level of activity, the government has usually to assess whether the level of AD is appropriate to its chosen objectives. If not it must take measures to make the necessary adjustment. Such measures fall into two broad groups, fiscal and monetary, but it is important to ensure that one supports the other.

Fiscal policy

In the context of full employment, fiscal policy refers to changes in government expenditure and taxation designed to vary the level of *AD*. These changes are broadly of two types: (1) those which operate automatically; (2) those which are discretionary in that they are specifically initiated by the government.

1. Automatic stabilisers

To some extent there are stabilising forces which come into play to reverse changes in *AD*.

Taxation is important in this respect. As incomes increase, so does the yield from taxation especially if taxation is progressive, e.g. income tax, or, like VAT, is applied on an *ad valorem* basis to expensive goods having a high income elasticity of demand. One important point must be made. If the stabilising effects of taxation are to work, the government must not increase its own expenditure as tax receipts rise, and vice versa.

Government spending on unemployment benefits and agricultural price support also has stabilising effects for, as unemployment increases, so do benefit payments, while there are likely to be increased subsidies to maintain farmers' incomes.

2. Discretionary fiscal changes

Indirectly, fiscal policy can influence private consumption and investment by simply changing the *type* of taxes levied. Thus a switch from indirect taxation would tend to increase consumption, for it would mean greater spending power for poorer people (those having a high propensity to consume). Similarly, a movement away from taxes on companies would tend to increase investment through improved profitability. But altering the structure of taxation simply to effect short-term adjustments in *AD* is too cumbersome a weapon.

Changes in government spending increase *AD* directly. Much government spending, however, is more or less contractual (e.g. social welfare benefits, interest on the National Debt), while public projects, such as motorways, schools and hospitals cannot be put on ice until there is a deficiency in *AD*. Long-term government policy, not short-term marginal adjustments according to the level of activity, must decide priorities for such projects.

Because of these disadvantages, public spending programmes are unlikely to be sufficiently flexible for 'fine-tuning' *AD*. In any case the government will be more concerned about the relationship between its spending and revenue, usually referred to as 'budgetary policy'.

Here the aim is to influence private consumption (*C*) by varying personal disposable income through changes in taxation. Thus a simple decrease in a direct lump-sum tax of ΔT increases disposable income by ΔT. As a result *C* is increased according to the marginal propensity to consume (c) by $c\Delta T$. This produces, via the multiplier, an increase in Y equal to $c\Delta I/(1-c)$. In terms of Figure 30.11, the C curve will rise. Thus, if government spending remains unchanged, the curve $C_1 + I + G$ will rise to $C_0 + I + G$.

Attention must be paid to the phrase 'if government spending remains unchanged'. Budgetary policy is essentially one of adjusting the relationship between government taxation and expenditure. As we have seen, taxation represents an appropriation by the government of a part of private incomes. The amount so appropriated is retained in the circular flow of income only in so far as it is spent by the government. Hence *AD* will be increased if taxation is less than government spending and vice versa. If previously the budget were balanced, there will now be a budget deficit, and vice versa.

In other words, if *AD* has to be expanded, the government can run a budget deficit and thus stimulate spending which, if continued from year to year will, through the multiplier, increase the national income flow. Conversely, to reduce *AD*, the government can run a budget surplus.

Thus today the budget is regarded not simply as the means of raising revenue to meet the year's estimated expenditure, but as a weapon to adjust spending. Since, as explained above, the ability to vary public expenditure is limited, it is taxation which tends to take the strain.

Such a policy is not without its difficulties. First, the convention of annual budgets tends to dictate the timing of major adjustments. However, 'mini' budgets are possible, while the 'regulator' does allow the Chancellor to vary indirect taxes by up to 25 per cent either way between budgets. Second, reducing taxes may, because of administrative difficulties, take time to be effective. With PAYE, for instance, new tax tables have to be distributed. Thus reliefs will often have to concentrate on putting extra purchasing power quickly into the hands of consumers, e.g. by reducing indirect taxes. Taxation, too, has objectives other than that of adjusting *AD* – redistributing income, for instance. But a rise in taxation may have to be achieved by increasing indirect taxes because of possible disincentive effects of high income tax. Thus policies can conflict. Third, overall budgetary policy cannot direct demand into those districts and industries where unemployment is highest and has to be supplemented by a regional policy (see Chapter 35). Finally, the deficit may be so large and persistent that the size of the PSNCR creates problems elsewhere. Not only does it increase the National Debt and thus the revenue which has to be raised to service interest payments but, and more important, if it is covered by borrowing from the banks, it increases the money supply and adds to inflationary pressure (see p. 392). Thus fiscal policy can only be used in conjunction with monetary policy.

Nevertheless, budgetary policy does allow the national product to be allocated between the private and public sectors according to their relative priorities. Certain tasks can be undertaken better by the State – road-building, defence, health care, etc. – and the government must decide on the proportion of the national product which shall be devoted to each. Taxes adjust private demand in order to release resources for the public sector.

Monetary policy

Monetary policy now operates through the cost of money, the rate of interest, influencing the amount demanded. Reducing the supply by monetary base control or selective controls, e.g. on hire purchase, is difficult with the development of international wholesale deposit markets.

Using the rate of interest to adjust AD depends on the fact that both households and firms rely on borrowing for much of their expenditure. Another advantage is that it can be applied quickly and to a fine degree and, if implemented early, can provide advance warning of the authorities' intentions. Indeed the psychological effects of changes are probably as important as any direct effect on investment spending.

But there are weaknesses. Only when the rate of interest is high will it, as we have seen, affect long-term investment programmes. Nor does it discriminate in its operation, e.g. as between firms which export a high proportion of their output and those which do not; projects of high social value (e.g. slum clearance) and those of less certain merit (e.g. gaming casinos); and between industries the demand for whose products is particularly dependent on borrowed funds (e.g. housing construction, property development, consumer durable goods) and those having a strong cash flow (e.g. advertising). Most serious of all is that interest policy cannot be operated in isolation from the general level of world rates. If, for instance, the UK retains interest rates which are low in relation to those of the rest of the world, there will be an outflow of short-term capital and a consequent lowering of the sterling exchange rate (see Chapter 39).

The inadequacy of demand management

In Figure 31.1 demand is adequate for expanding the level of output up to OY. But the crucial part of the AS curve is output greater than OY, for the increase will be accompanied by rising prices. We concentrate on this section in Figure 31.2.

Ignoring the dynamics of rising prices, let us trace what happens when AD is increased beyond OY.

(a) The short-run equilibrium

Given the current conditions of supply (e.g. the cost of inputs, particularly wage-rates) resulting in the AS_s curve, and the aggregate demand curve AD, the equilibrium level of output is OY and the price level OP.

Suppose AD is increased to AD_1. Output prices will now rise to OP_1, but a time-lag means that input prices remain constant for the time being. Thus what firms receive for their products now exceeds their costs. These windfall profits lead them to expand output to Y'.

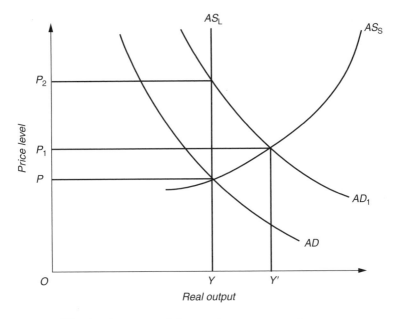

Figure 31.2 The inadequacy of demand management

(b) The long-run equilibrium

In time, however, workers require higher money wages to compensate for the rise in the cost of living (as indicated by the Retail Prices Index). Furthermore, higher wages bring about a rise in the prices of other inputs, including components. As a result profits revert to the original situation, and firms respond by cutting output to the original OY – but the new equilibrium price level is OP_2. Since this argument applies to all movements of the AD curve to the right, the long-run AS curve is vertical at AS_L. This is termed the 'natural rate of output'.

Some economists go further. The only reason why an increase in AD resulted in a short-run expansion of output was that it took time for wages, etc. to adjust to the rise in output prices because this rise had not been *anticipated*. But it is likely that workers, learning from experience and with increasing access to better relevant information, are able to anticipate future price rises accurately. In short, they take note of the rise from AD to AD_1 and with 'rational expectations' allowing them to forecast immediately that the resulting equilibrium price level will be P_2, obtain the compensating increase in money wages forthwith.

If 'rational expectations' apply, therefore, there is no time-lag and the short-run and long-run curves are one and the same – AS_L. In these circumstances an increase in AD is completely powerless to expand the level of output. The only effect is to raise the price level.

The supply-side approach

From this dilemma there has developed another strategy which has gained strength in recent years. Instead of concentrating entirely on *AD*, why not try to lower the short-run supply curve? If, as in Figure 31.3, policies could lower the aggregate supply curve from AS_1 to AS_2 with aggregate demand of AD_1, employment could be increased to OY_1 at a lower price level P_1. Even if aggregate demand were increased to AD_2 to reduce unemployment to Y_2Y_f, the price level need then only rise to P_2.

31.5 SUPPLY-SIDE ECONOMICS

The objective of supply-side measures

The objective of supply-side measures is to shift the short-run aggregate supply curve from AS_1 to AS_2 (Figure 31.3). If this succeeds the government can follow policies to expand *AD* without incurring an unacceptable rise in the price level.

It should be noted that the equilibrium natural rate of output may fall short of the full employment output OY_f in Figures 31.1 and 31.3, and of the production possibility curve *I* in Figure 34.1. Since we are dealing with comparatively short period

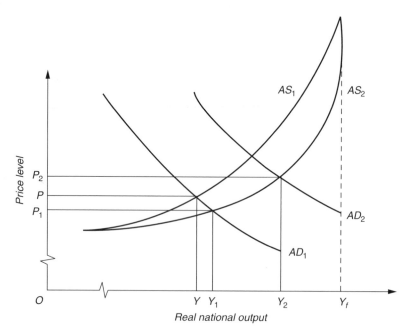

Figure 31.3 Supply-side strategy

fluctuations in output, the supply-side measures available are only those which are effective within a fairly short period, e.g. better use of equipment. We must not confuse them with measures which account for growth (Chapter 34). These will shift the *AS* curve, including the vertical portion, to the right, and the production possibility curve outward. But they take time and the most that can be expected through secular growth is a rate of increase in output of about 3 per cent a year.

In Figure 31.4, output of the economy is originally *OM* and the price level at *P*. In order to reduce unemployment the government increases aggregate demand from *AD* to *AD₁*. At the same time, however, supply-side measures move the aggregate supply curve from *AS* to *AS₁*. Thus while unemployment is reduced by *MM₁*, the price level remains at *P*.

The advocates of supply-side economics hold that this movement of the short-run *AS* curve can be achieved by freeing controls over markets, introducing positive measures to lower costs and by providing incentives for greater effort and for releasing enterprise and initiative. In essence, these proposals reflect their belief in the basic efficiency of the free market system. They introduce largely microeconomic measures to deal with macroeconomic problems.

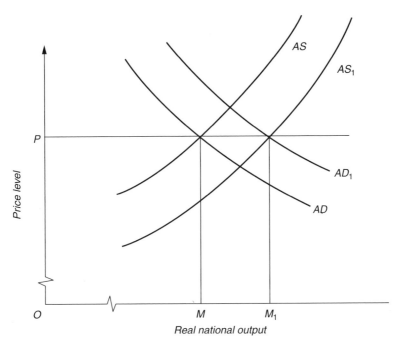

Figure 31.4 Supply-side policy

Market freedom

Markets must be allowed to work more freely and steps taken to improve this efficiency by:

(a) freeing them as far as possible from government controls (e.g. over wages and pricing policies);

(b) promoting competition (e.g. in real property conveyancing, optical and financial services);

(c) restricting the power of trade unions (e.g. as regards precipitate and sympathetic strike action, unofficial strikes, the closed shop);

(d) the privatisation programme (see pp. 242–3);

(e) introducing competition in the natural monopolies by new devices (see p. 243);

(f) removing institutional barriers in the capital market (e.g. exchange control, the Stock Exchange);

(g) using the rate of interest (the price of liquid capital) as the main weapon for adjusting aggregate demand.

Cost reduction

Positive measures to effect a lowering of costs include:

(a) reducing national insurance contributions (an *ad valorem* tax on employing labour);

(b) improving the supply and quality of labour, e.g. by developing training schemes, encouraging flexible working hours to attract part-time workers, improving mobility, granting subsidies to firms to locate in the Assisted Areas where surplus workers are available (see p. 441);

(c) providing advisory services (e.g. on the EU's Single Market 1993).

Incentives

Incentives designed to increase effort, reward enterprise and encourage saving and investment include:

(a) an emphasis on the effect of a reduction in the marginal rate of income tax on effort and incentives, even though it may reduce total tax revenue;

(b) a lower corporation tax to encourage investment and the taking of entrepreneurial risks;

(c) special help for new firms to obtain the initial capital, e.g. 'start-up' schemes, encouraging 'venture capital';

(d) profit-related pay (which gives employees a direct stake in the success of the company and enables pay to respond more readily to changing market conditions), share option schemes and wider share ownership generally.

The above represent a variety of measures to create conditions in which the free play of market forces can stimulate the economy to work more efficiently. They formed a major part of the Conservative government's economic programme between 1979 and 1997.

31.6 POSTSCRIPT

The foregoing analysis of the relationship of *AD* and *AS* and its effect on the level of output and the price level suffers from three main weaknesses.

First, it ignores the fact that, unlike ordinary demand and supply curves, the *AD* curve and the *AS* curve are not independent of each other.

Second, it largely ignores that there are institutional forces at work, chiefly trade unions, which cause a rising price level to gather momentum. These are the problems of maintaining a stable price level which we examine in Chapter 33.

Third, while supply-side measures are necessary, we have to ask are they sufficient. We should not allow them to jettison the possibility of obtaining from labour a workable agreement on moderating wage demands.

CHAPTER SUMMARY

- Since the 1970s, high rates of inflation and unemployment have led to a recognition of the difficulty of reducing unemployment below about 5 per cent.
- An aggregate supply curve shows the relationship between the price level and real output in the economy.
- Equilibrium in the economy occurs at the intersection of aggregate demand and aggregate supply because this is where households and firms expenditure equals the amount of output that firms will supply.
- Demand management may be inadequate in the long-run, only increasing the price level and not employment and output. As a result governments have turned to supply-side measures to stimulate the economy to work more efficiently.

REVIEW QUESTIONS

• Why does the aggregate demand curve slope downwards from left to right?
• Why is the aggregate supply curve vertical at the full employment level of output?
• What are automatic stabilisers?
• What is meant by rational expectations?
• Explain the objectives of supply-side policies.

 Visit the companion website for further questions

CHAPTER 32

INFLATION: ITS EFFECTS

LEARNING OBJECTIVES
....

After studying this chapter you should be able to:
- explain the disadvantages of inflation;
- show how a price index is calculated;
- outline the process of weighting an index.

32.1 WHY CONTROL INFLATION?

Inflation can be defined as a sustained rise in money prices generally. Today the control of inflation is given priority in government policy. To appreciate why, we have to look at the effects of rising prices or – what is the same thing – a fall in the value of money. In Chapter 33 we consider the causes of inflation and the possible remedies that can be applied.

Possible benefits

At one time, a gently rising price level was not viewed with too much concern. It improved the climate for investment and so helped to maintain aggregate demand. Moreover, it tended to reduce the real burden of servicing the National Debt through 'fiscal drag': while interest payments are fixed in money terms, receipts from taxation increase as money national income rises.

The snag, however, is that, once started, the rise in prices is difficult to contain. At first it becomes uncomfortable, producing undesirable results, both internal and external. Eventually the rate of inflation increases. The situation is then serious, for it is much more difficult to reverse the trend. Indeed it can develop into runaway inflation.

Internal disadvantages

1. Real income and wealth are redistributed arbitrarily, for inflation imposes a tax on those who hold money as opposed to those holding real assets. Moreover, not only does inflation reduce the standard of living of persons dependent on fixed incomes, e.g. pensions, but, unless 'inflation-proofed' it benefits debtors and penalises lenders. Thus the stability upon which all lending and borrowing depends is undermined.

2. The arbitrary redistribution of income could conflict with the government's policy on redistribution.

3. Interest rates rise, both because people require a higher reward for lending money which is falling in value and also because the government is forced to take disinflationary measures. Not only may this discourage investment but it can have social consequences, e.g. in meeting monthly mortgage payments.

4. Saving is discouraged because postponing consumption simply means that goods cost more if bought later. On the other hand, fear of possible unemployment as a result of government anti-inflation policy may induce caution in spending.

5. Inflation encourages borrowing to buy speculative paper assets rather than real investment for production.

6. The allocation of resources is distorted. Thus institutions, such as insurance companies, invest funds in assets having a strong inflation-hedge. As a result the capital value of such assets rises, encouraging developers, for instance to build office blocks rather than houses for letting.

7. Efficiency is reduced because:
    (a) a buoyant sellers' market blunts competition as higher selling prices allow even inefficient firms to survive;
    (b) uncertainty is increased;
    (c) market signals are less clear since some inflation-hedge may be included e.g. in contracts;
    (d) it strengthens the possibility of disruption of production until demands for wage increases are agreed;
    (e) financial services spring up to advise on protecting savings from losses through inflation.

8. Inflation generates industrial and social unrest since there is competition for higher incomes. Thus, because of rising prices, trade unions ask for annual wage rises. Often demands exceed the rate of inflation, anticipating future rises or seeking a larger share of the national cake to improve their members' real standard of living. Those with the most 'muscle' gain at the expense of weaker groups.

9. Additional administrative costs are incurred in off-setting go-slow and work to rule disruptions, allowing for inflation in negotiating contracts and wage rates, revising price lists and labels, etc. (the 'menu' cost of inflation).

10. The rate of inflation tends to increase, largely because high wage settlements in anticipation of higher future prices help to bring about the very rise which people fear.

11. Because money in a current account earns no interest and has no inflation-hedge, balances are kept to a minimum by frequent checks and trips to the bank (the 'shoe-leather' cost of inflation).

External effects

Inflation can create balance-of-payments difficulties for a country dependent on international trade, as Britain has discovered over the past forty years.

1. Exports tend to decline because they are relatively dearer in foreign markets. Firms exporting a large proportion of their output may therefore have to lay off workers.

2. Imports tend to increase because foreign goods are relatively cheaper on the British market.

3. Higher money incomes in the UK increase the demand for imports and tend to decrease exports because the buoyant home market makes it less vital for manufacturers to seek outlets abroad for their goods.

4. An outward movement of capital may take place if price rises continue since foreign traders and financiers lose confidence in the pound sterling maintaining its current rate of exchange.

While the above effects are uncomfortable, it is possible to live with a moderate rise in prices. The snag is that where rising prices are thought likely to continue, people bring forward their spending, thereby producing the very price rise feared – an example of 'self-justified expectations'. So the process gathers momentum, stimulated still further by demands for higher wage increases.

32.2 A NOTE ON MEASURING CHANGES IN THE GENERAL LEVEL OF PRICES

Changes in the value of money and the 'cost of living'

Suppose a man's take-home pay is £400 a week and his weekly shopping bill for food, rent, clothes, fares, cigarettes, etc., comes to £300. Now suppose his pay rises to £500 a week, but for the same goods his shopping bill increases to £420. Is he better off? In other words, has his standard of living improved?

The answer is 'no'. Although wages have increased by 25 per cent, expenditure on the same amount of goods has gone up by 40 per cent. It can be seen, therefore, that to compare *standards of living*, that is, the goods, services, and leisure enjoyed, it is necessary to adjust money income by any changes in the value of money, that is, by the cost of living.

Measuring changes in the value of money over a period

In theory, a change in the value of money would refer to a change in the level of prices in general. But different kinds of prices – wholesale prices, retail prices, capital goods prices, security prices, import prices, etc. – change differently. If we tried to measure changes in all prices, therefore, our task would be stupendous. But more than that, it would lack practical significance. Suppose, for instance, that security prices rose considerably, other prices remaining unchanged. But a rise in such a general level of prices would be of little interest to persons owning no securities.

When measuring changes in the value of money, therefore, it is usual to concentrate on changes in the prices of those goods which are of most general significance – the goods bought by the majority of people, for it is upon the prices of these that the cost of living really depends. But again, since different people spend their income differently, the value of money could be different for each.

Method of measuring changes in the value of money

Since we are mainly interested in the extent to which the value of money has altered between one date and another, it can be measured as a relative change by means of an *index number*. The steps are as follows:

1. A base year is selected. This is now referred to as the 'reference date'.
2. In order to ensure that the same goods are valued over the period under consideration, a 'basket' of goods, based on the current spending habits and income of the 'typical' family is chosen.
3. The basket is valued at reference date prices, and expressed as 100.
4. The same basket is revalued at current prices.
5. The cost of the current basket is then expressed as a percentage of the base year. Thus if the cost of living had risen by 5 per cent, the index for the current year would be 105.

In practice, the percentage price relatives of the selected goods are calculated, and are then 'weighted' according to the relative expenditure on the commodity at the reference date. Suppose, for instance, that there are only two commodities, bread and meat, upon which income is spent. The index between two years is calculated as in Table 32.1. The price in year II is expressed as a percentage of the

Table 32.1 Calculation of index number

	Price	Units bought	Expenditure	Weight	Price	Year II as % of Year I	Weighted Price relative
			YEAR I			*YEAR II*	
						Price relatives	
Bread	30p	5	150p	10	45p	150	1,500
Meat	150p	11	1650p	110	180p	120	13,200
				120			120)14,700
							= 122.5

Index

Year I (base)	100
Year II	122.5

price in year I. This is multiplied by the appropriate weight to give a 'weighted price relative'. These weighted price relatives are then totalled and divided by the total of the weights to give the new index number.

Difficulties in calculating index numbers

The method outlined above of calculating changes in the value of money has obvious snags:

(1) The basket and the weighting are merely an arbitrary average. Different income groups have widely different baskets, and even within the same group the amount spent on each good varies. Thus a change in the Retail Prices Index does not affect all people equally.

(2) The basket becomes more unreal the further we move from the reference date (at present 13 January 1987 = 100). For instance, an increase in income gives a different pattern of expenditure, new goods are produced and the quality of goods changes, and spending is varied according to relative price changes. The Retail Prices Index tries to overcome this defect by revising the weights each January on the basis of the *Family Expenditure Survey* for the previous year.

(3) Technical difficulties may arise both in choosing the reference date and in collecting information. For instance, the reference date may coincide with abnormally high prices, while the development of discount stores may upset standardised methods of collecting prices.

Thus a Retail Prices Index is merely an indication of changes in the cost of living. But if we bear its limitations in mind, it is the most useful measurement we have of changes in the value of money. It therefore provides the yardstick for calculating changes in real earnings and for 'inflation-proofing' public sector pay and pensions.

The Consumer Prices Index (CPI)

In his pre-Budget statement on 10 December 2003, the Chancellor announced that he was switching the definition of the target for UK inflation from the RPIX (retail prices excluding mortgage payments) to the CPI. CPIs are calculated in each member state of the EU for the purposes of European comparisons. It is used as a measure of price stability in the euro area by the European Central Bank. Although the methodology of the CPI is similar to the RPI there are differences in the way in which it is calculated and the composition of the index. For example the CPI excludes housing costs and in particular owner-occupiers' costs such as mortgage interest payments.

Household Index of Consumer Prices (HICP)

The HICP is a standardised measure of inflation used to compare changes in the cost of living between member nations of the European Union.

CHAPTER SUMMARY

- Although there can be some relatively minor gains from inflation for certain sectors of society, such as borrowers, there are many serious disadvantages. These include arbitrary redistribution of income, reductions in efficiency and adverse trading conditions.
- Measurement of the rate of change of prices is done using the Retail Price Index. This looks at the prices of the average basket of goods for the average family. The goods are weighted according to their significance in household budgets.

REVIEW QUESTIONS

- Why does inflation reduce efficiency in the economy?
- What are 'menu' costs of inflation?
- How does inflation impact upon international trade?
- Explain the procedure for constructing an index of prices.
- What are the limitations of a price index?

 Visit the companion website for further questions

33

POLICIES TO ACHIEVE PRICE STABILITY

LEARNING OBJECTIVES

After studying this chapter you should be able to:
- explain Keynesian and monetarist theories of the causes of inflation;
- illustrate and explain the relationship between inflation and unemployment;
- show how the theory of a natural rate of unemployment means that reducing unemployment by demand management will not be successful.

33.1 CAUSES OF INFLATION: A SIMPLIFIED STATEMENT

Prices rise when there is excess purchasing power for goods available at current prices. But what brings about the excess of purchasing power? We can begin by distinguishing initiating impulses on both the demand and supply sides.

1. Demand-pull

The Keynesian analysis suggests that, if there is cyclical unemployment, the situation can be improved by expanding aggregate demand, e.g. from AD to AD_1 (Figure 33.1). Prices would not rise as long as output increased correspondingly. Eventually as bottlenecks arose, prices would rise.

But the really inflationary situation occurred when aggregate demand continued to expand once the position of full employment had been reached, e.g. with AD_3. Henceforth any expansion of aggregate demand would find its outlet entirely in rising prices. Any excess aggregate demand at full employment thus represented an inflationary gap (see p. 391).

Today, however, we would say that inflation starts much earlier at Y, for thereafter any increase in aggregate demand, e.g. from AD to AD_1 would mean that it exceeded AS at the current price level, thus forcing up prices.

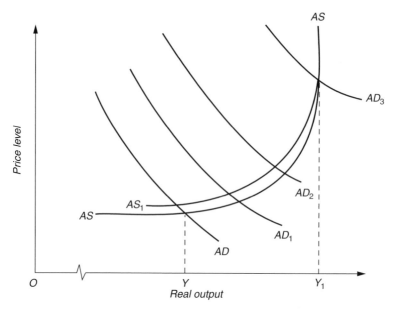

Figure 33.1   Demand-pull inflation

2.   Cost-push

The rise in prices can start on the supply side, e.g. through an increase in the price of imports. Thus the fivefold rise in oil prices in 1973–4 aggravated inflation in the UK, indeed worldwide. The AS curve rises from AS to AS_1 (Figure 33.1).

More usually, however, cost-push inflation has followed demand-pull. Once prices start to rise as the government pursues a full employment policy by increasing AD, trade unions seek compensating wage increases. Indeed, the scale of their demands tends to increase in order to allow for future price rises. Furthermore, it is common practice for such demands to be presented yearly, often in excess of the current rate of inflation and without any justifying increase in productivity.

Where the level of activity is high, employers tend not to resist such demands, feeling that product prices can be raised to cover them. In practice their expectations are justified, for unless the government imposes financial restraints to make it more difficult for firms to cover higher wages, the increased wages themselves provide the incomes and expenditure to justify higher prices. We have, therefore, what is termed 'cost-push' inflation – prices are being 'pushed up' by an initial increase in costs.

The Phillips curve

The simple Keynesian situation where expanding output is eventually accompanied by rising prices seemed to be supported in 1958 by Professor A.W. Phillips, whose

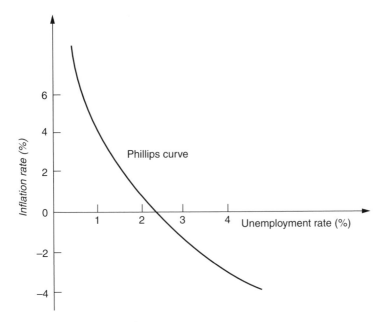

Figure 33.2 The Phillips curve

research showed that in the UK over the past century there was a strong statistical negative relationship between the annual rate of inflation and the annual rate of unemployment (Figure 33.2). The policy conclusion was that a reduction in the rate of unemployment could be 'traded off' against a rise in the rate of inflation.

It should be noted that we are here comparing the *rate* of inflation with the *rate* of unemployment (the usual form of measurement) as opposed to the output changes of Chapter 31. Also we are concentrating on the rate of *unemployment* instead of the level of real output.

Alternatively, where the basic cause is cost-push, the government could urge or impose wage restraint, backing this with restrictions on price rises.

Stagflation and the spiral of inflation

Until the mid-1960s the Phillips curve relationship held, but then both unemployment and inflation increased together, a situation described as 'stagflation'.

The weakness of our simplified statement on Keynesian lines is that it is too static, allowing nothing for *expectations*. Instead of inflation being merely a condition of excess demand at the full-employment level, it is a *process*. And the UK's post-war experience has shown that this process can start even at a fairly low *rate* of increase in the price level. An initial price rise generates demands for wage increases from trade unions in key industries even though there had been little increase in productivity and irrespective of the fact that some of their members may be already unemployed. Moreover, wage rises awarded in the growth industries have been in practice conceded in declining industries, e.g. shipbuilding, steel, cars, etc., through the annual process of wage bargaining. Indeed, it is asserted that any norm urged by the government merely reinforces an across-the-board increase since it is interpreted as a minimum for all workers.

But, unlike the demand and supply curves which we studied earlier, the *AD* and *AS* curves are not independent of each other. An increase in wage-rates not only moves the *AS* curve upwards but, by increasing purchasing power, moves the *AD* curve (for example, from AD_1 to AD_2). Thus prices rise still further, resulting in further wage demands, often geared to an *expected* higher rate of inflation. In short, there is an inflationary spiral. This means that, once the rate at which prices are rising has reached a certain level, the remedy is not a simple piece of surgery to remove excess fat, but rather a fight against a cancerous growth.

Therefore, an alternative theory of inflation embodying *expectations* was required. This has been built up by the 'monetarists', led by Professor Milton Friedman.

33.2 MONETARISM

The current monetarist explanation of inflation has three main elements: the direct connection between the money supply and *AD*; inflation expectations as a cause of the inflation process; and a 'natural rate of unemployment' hypothesis. We will explain each in turn.

The money supply and *AD*

It was observed that there was a positive correlation between increases in the money supply and the rate of inflation. But is there a causal connection? Does an increase in the money supply *directly* increase *AD*?

As we have seen (p. 306), Keynes considered that the supply of money does not enter directly into spending decisions. In the short run these are dependent upon the level of income; over time they will be affected by long-term factors, such as social example, thrift habits, contractual commitments to regular saving, etc. Any increase in the supply of money simply increases liquidity in the economy and the rate of interest – the price paid for liquidity – therefore falls. *AD* will expand only indirectly, through a lower rate of interest leading to more investment spending.

In contrast, Milton Friedman holds that the demand for money, instead of adjusting to the money supply by being automatically absorbed in 'idle' balances, has a degree of stability (see below). As a result an increase in the supply of money can lead *directly* to additional spending and thus *cause* inflation.

To a large extent it is a revival of the *Quantity Theory of Money* which attributes a rise in the general price level to an increase in the supply of money. Usually it is given precision by being expressed in the form of the Fisher equation $MV = PT$, where M is the amount of money available in the economy, V is the velocity of circulation, the average number of times each unit of money changes hands in carrying out transactions, P is the general level of prices, and T the volume of transactions, the total quantity of goods and services exchanged against money.

If we are concerned with the Fisher equation as a statement of fact, there is nothing to quarrel about, for the two sides are equal by definition. MV, the amount of money multiplied by the number of times each unit changes hands in a given period, is merely the expenditure by buyers of goods and services over the period. Similarly, PT, the average price of goods multiplied by the volume, is simply the receipts of sellers. Since expenditure must be the same as receipts, MV and PT are simply different ways of expressing the same thing.

But as an explanation of what *causes* changes in the price level, the Quantity Theory is only valid if T and V can be assumed to be constant. It is regarding V that Keynes and Friedman clash.

The monetarists consider that people maintain a fraction of their nominal income in cash balances. An increase in the money supply results in their having larger cash balances than they require, and so they run them down by spending. Such spending increases AD and money incomes until cash balances are equal to their former fraction. Nor does this surplus cash have to be spent on 'bonds', Keynes's omnibus term for non-money assets. Wealth can be held in many forms: cash which yields liquidity, 'bonds' which yield interest and possible capital appreciation and, the monetarists emphasise, *consumer goods* which yield utility. People distribute their spending according to their marginal preferences for those different forms of yield (which in turn can be influenced by their expectations of the future rate of inflation).

Thus any increase in the money supply is likely after a little while to lead to some increase in the demand for consumer goods resulting, at least in the long run when it comes up against the natural rate of output (p. 404), to a rise in prices.

Inflation expectations

Once inflation expectations enter into wage negotiations, the monetarists hold that increasing AD will not achieve a *long-term* decrease in the rate of unemployment but simply result in higher inflation. In short there is no trade-off between inflation and unemployment. We return to the Phillips curve.

In Figure 33.3 we assume that the rate of inflation is 4 per cent and the rate of unemployment is 5 per cent. This position at D is stable because wage-bargainers have expected 4 per cent to be the inflation rate.

The government now decides that it wants to reduce the unemployment rate to 4 per cent and accordingly increases AD. Prices rise to 6 per cent inflation at F, but

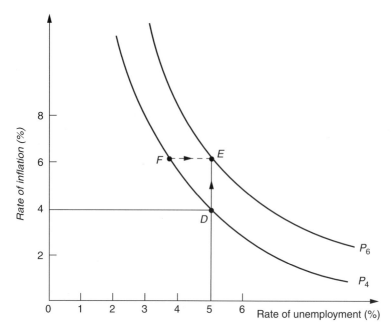

Figure 33.3   The effect of inflation-expectations on the rate of unemployment

money wage rates do not rise since workers expect only a 4 per cent rise in inflation. Thus firms, enjoying increased profitability, increase output so that initially unemployment falls to 4 per cent on curve P_4.

But this is only a short-term position depending on the fact that workers tend to concentrate on nominal money wages, which have not fallen, rather than on real wages, which have – the 'money illusion'. Eventually, however, they realise that real wages have fallen and in their next wage negotiations they obtain a 6 per cent rise in money wages (based on the previous year's inflation rate) to cover what they expect to be the rate of inflation. The recovery in real wage-rates increases costs, so that firms reduce output and unemployment reverts to 5 per cent. The Phillips curve has moved outwards to P_6 and there is a new equilibrium at E.

The 'natural rate of unemployment'

In the above example, D and E represent two long-term equilibrium positions. Thus the long-run Phillips curve is a vertical straight line at 5 per cent. The monetarists would term this 5 per cent the 'natural rate of unemployment' – the rate to which unemployment will eventually revert *given the current real wage-rate, imperfections in the labour market, immobility costs, etc.* If the expected rate is less than the actual rate, an increase in *AD* can lead to less unemployment; if it is more, the current rate of unemployment can only be sustained by a higher rate of inflation. There will be long-run equilibrium when the expected rate of inflation has been adapted to take account of and equals the actual rate. This is as far as Friedman goes.

But certain economists go further, disputing whether employment can be increased even in the short run by the Keynesian method of increasing *AD*. Wage-bargainers learn by experience and have available information by which they *predict* and allow for the future rate of inflation. Thus any increase in the money supply evokes the correct estimate of the rate of inflation which will result, and this is embodied immediately in the new wage-rate. This assertion of 'rational expectations' in place of a mere *adaptation* to an inflation rate based on the previous year's inflation rate means that there is now no short-run curve, only a long-run one, and thus no room for reducing unemployment by increasing *AD*.

This view corresponds very closely to that of the Classical economists who held that, given flexible real wage-rates, there would be market clearing at that wage-rate where the demand for and supply of labour are equal, *OW* (Figure 33.4). If the real wage-rate is above *OW*, the supply of labour exceeds the demand; there is voluntary unemployment. This is the case with the natural rate of unemployment with rational expectations. Those who hold this view, therefore, are known as the new classical economists.

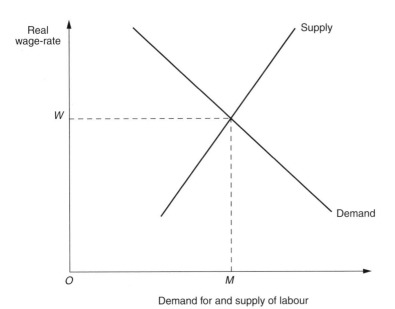

Figure 33.4 The real wage-rate and employment

33.3 POLICY IMPLICATIONS OF MONETARIST THEORY

Variations of the theoretical approach

Monetarist theory originated as an explanation of how increases in the supply of money led directly to increases in AD and thus to rising prices. Even with cost-push inflation, extra money is necessary to accommodate wage increases. Thus the first condition for keeping inflation in check is strict control over the money supply. A major difficulty here is that 'money' is difficult to define (see p. 301) and policy has to be based on an imperfect money index (p. 532).

But, as we have seen, the theory goes further to show that expanding AD to reduce unemployment will only be successful for as long as the government can maintain a discrepancy between the actual rate of inflation and the expected rate of inflation. This will produce a fall in real wage-rates in the short period, largely owing to the 'money illusion'. This is as far as Friedman goes: actual and expected rates of inflation become equal *eventually* as it takes time for labour to incorporate a revised higher expected rate of inflation in its wage negotiations. With the new classical economists, they become equal *immediately*. Most economists now accept some form of the natural rate of unemployment hypothesis; fewer would subscribe to the 'rational expectations' version.

But some even reject the view that the natural rate of unemployment determines unemployment. The evidence is inconclusive but they point to the fact that even when a high level of unemployment is *steady*, those in work still seek wage increases, but when the unemployment rate is *increasing*, workers moderate their wage demands so that real wages do not catch up with inflation. In short, actual unemployment has brought about a fall in the natural rate!

Influencing inflation expectations and wage settlements

How long the deviation from the natural rate of unemployment persists will depend upon: (a) how rapidly expectations adjust; and (b) how rapidly wages can adjust once expectations have been revised. An anti-inflation policy should seek to bring about a slow-down in both.

The government must aim at convincing the trade unions that the trend of the future rate of inflation is downwards. This is not easy for until wage negotiators can actually see a falling rate of inflation, they interpret a wage increase which falls short of their expected rate of inflation as a cut in real wages. Yet wage restraint is the 'least-cost' policy for controlling inflation. The difficulty is that voluntary restraint soon breaks down, and statutory wage and price freezes have to be imposed in an attempt to break the inflation spiral. But the rigidity in the economy which results means that even these cannot last long.

An alternative approach is to reduce inflation expectations by announcing strict monetary and fiscal targets for the medium-term future (see p. 532). The extent to which such a policy reduces inflation expectations largely depends on how far unions are convinced of the government's resolve to hold to its targets. In this respect it should be noted that if the government sets a limit to the PSNCR it virtually has to have a wages policy for the public sector, and its determination to restrict wage increases here will have its impact on the private sector.

Unfortunately, the change in the economic climate takes time to be realised especially when in the past trade union negotiators have been consistently successful in obtaining inflationary wage increases. In the meantime, there may be a sequence of unsuccessful strikes and prolonged period of unemployment. This is the 'high cost' alternative.

33.4 SUPPLY-SIDE MEASURES

The introduction of the hypothesis of a 'natural rate of unemployment' suggests that, since expanding *AD* is unreliable in reducing unemployment, more attention should be given to *AS*. Reducing the costs of production would mean that a greater output could be supplied at any given price level. Put in an alternative way, the objective is an eventual reduction in the natural rate of unemployment.

Policy to achieve this embraces a variety of incentives usually included under the umbrella term *'supply-side economics'*. It integrates longer-term micro measures within the overall macro policy (see pp. 404–7).

33.5 CONCLUDING OBSERVATIONS

This chapter has discussed the difficulty of achieving a low rate of unemployment without making the rate of inflation uncomfortable.

The Keynesian solution puts the emphasis on reducing unemployment by expanding *AD*. Its success depends largely on achieving an effective policy to restrain rises in real wages which are not matched by increases in productivity.

In contrast, monetarist policies centre on strict control of the money supply and *supply-side* economics. The monetarist approach rests on two hypotheses – a stable demand for money and a natural rate of unemployment – both of which still require empirical verification. However, the experience of Britain and other Western economies in recent years does seem to indicate a link between an increase in the supply of money and, after a time-lag, an increase in the rate of inflation. What is certain is that without increases in the supply of money, inflation cannot continue.

Few economists, however, would go so far as to say that the increase in the supply of money was the *cause* of an inflation. As we have seen, there is no *single* cause. Excess *AD* may be generated in a number of ways apart from spending newly created money. It may come from increased government spending, or arise on the cost side through wage demands or higher import prices. The tendency, therefore, is to favour a pragmatic approach combining control of the money supply with other policies, such as reducing government spending and supply-side economics.

This is consistent with the fact that inflation cannot be considered in isolation from employment, the balance of payments and economic growth. Control of inflation may be the prior condition for a healthy economy, especially for the UK which is so dependent on maintaining exports. But in the final analysis the extent to which priority is given to inflation is a political decision.

The ways that actual policies have varied and been implemented in the UK over the last twenty years are described in Chapter 42.

CHAPTER SUMMARY

- Inflation can be caused by excess demand and by increasing costs.
- The Phillips curve suggested that a reduction in the rate of unemployment could be traded off against a rise in the rate of inflation. This simple inverse relationship between unemployment and inflation clearly broke down in the 1970s when both rose together.
- Monetarist explanations of inflation suggest that an increase in the money supply will cause a rise in aggregate demand which will lead to inflation if the aggregate supply curve slopes upwards.
- The natural rate of unemployment is the rate to which unemployment will return despite any increase in aggregate demand in the short-run. To reduce the natural rate of unemployment, it is necessary to use supply-side measures.

REVIEW QUESTIONS

- Use aggregate demand and aggregate supply curves to illustrate demand-pull and cost-push inflation.
- Why might Professor Phillips have suspected a negative relationship between inflation and unemployment?
- What is the theoretical basis of monetarist explanations of inflation?

 Visit the companion website for further questions

ECONOMIC GROWTH

34.1   THE NATURE OF GROWTH

The meaning of 'growth'

When there are unemployed resources, the economy's *actual* output is below its *potential* output; in terms of Figure 34.1 the economy is producing inside the production-possibility curve, say at point *A*. Here output can be increased, even in the relatively short term, by measures which absorb unemployed resources.

But, by itself, full employment of an economy's resources does not necessarily mean that the economy will grow. Growth is essentially a long-run phenomenon – the *potential* full-employment output of the economy is *increasing* over time. Whereas full employment simply means that the economy is producing on a point on the production-possibility curve I, growth means that, over time, the curve is pushed outwards to II and III. Even with full employment of resources, advanced economies can achieve an *annual* growth rate of 3 per cent.

Increases in the productive capacity in the economy over time are usually measured by calculating the rate of change of real gross national product per head of the population (see Chapter 28). However, when people talk about 'growth' they are thinking chiefly of the difference it makes to the standard of living rather than to output itself. Allowances have to be made, therefore, for defects of GNP

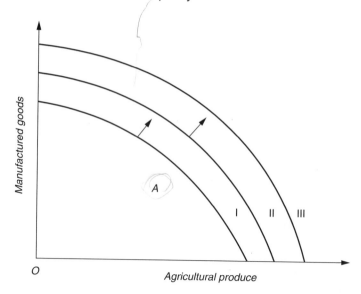

Figure 34.1 Economic growth

as an indication of the standard of living (see Chapter 28). Also, when measuring long-term *secular* growth by the change in real GNP per head between different years, we must recognise that initial unemployment rates may differ.

Advantages of growth

Economic growth is the major factor for achieving improvements in the standard of living – more consumer goods, better living conditions, a shorter working week, and so on. While such improvements occur gradually and almost imperceptibly from year to year, small differences in the *annual rate* of growth produce large differences: in the *speed* of growth. For instance, a rate of growth of 2.5 percent per annum will double real GNP in 28 years, whereas a 3 per cent rate doubles GNP in only 24 years.

In addition, growth makes it easier for the government to achieve its economic policy objectives. Revenue from taxation increases, allowing government services, e.g. education and health care, to be expanded without raising the *rates* of tax. Income can also be redistributed in favour of the poorer members of society while still allowing the standard of living of the better-off to show some improvement.

However, as noted earlier (Chapter 18) economic growth does have its costs (see also p. 429).

34.2 ACHIEVING GROWTH

Factors producing growth

There are five basic causes of growth:

1. A rise in the productivity of existing factors

In the short run, productivity may be raised by improvements in organisation, which secure, for example, more division of labour and economies of large-scale production, or a more intensive use of capital equipment (e.g. the adoption of shift-working). Physical improvements for the labour force, e.g. better food and working conditions, may also increase productivity.

In the longer run, more significant increases can come with education and the acquisition of skills through training. These really represent, however, an increase in the capital invested in labour.

It is also important to draw attention to the differences in personal incentives provided by the market economy and the command economy. Compare, for instance, the growth rates of Hong Kong and Poland over the last forty years.

2. An increase in the available stock of factors of production

(a) A rise in the labour input

The size of the labour input can increase relative to the total population through either an increase in the number of hours worked per worker, or an increase in the ratio of the working population to the total population. The first is hardly likely to be a cause of growth in normal conditions, for as living standards improve the tendency is to demand more leisure. The second, however, may come about if the percentage of the population in the working age group increases or if attitudes to work change (see pp. 251–2).

(b) Development of natural resources

North Sea natural gas and oil, for instance, have allowed Britain to obtain her fuel supplies from fewer factors of production, enabling resources to be transferred to other output and thus promoting growth.

(c) Additional capital equipment

Here we must distinguish between 'widening' and 'deepening' capital. Widening capital – adding similar capital equipment – is necessary if the labour force increases, in order to maintain the existing capital–labour ratio and thus

427

output per head. Suppose 10 men, digging a long ditch, have 5 spades between them. If the labour force is increased to 20 men the capital–labour ratio falls from 1:2 to 1:4 unless 'widening' takes place – that is, unless another 5 spades are provided to maintain the existing ratio. 'Widening' does not increase productivity; it simply prevents diminishing returns to labour setting in.

'Deepening' capital occurs when the capital–labour ratio is increased. If, for example, when there were 10 spades to 20 men, the men were given a further 10 spades, the capital–labour ratio would be raised to 1:1.

3. Technological change

All we have done in our example so far has been to increase the stock of a given kind of capital equipment, spades. Over time, however, productivity can be raised more significantly by innovation and technological improvements. Thus the twenty men and their spades may be replaced by a single trench-digger and its driver. Because this does the job more quickly and efficiently the remaining nineteen men are released for other kinds of work.

In practice, all three causes are usually operating at the same time to increase productivity. Thus, as the labour force or natural resources are expanded, new capital is required, and this allows for the introduction of new techniques.

The speed with which new capital and improvements are introduced also depends upon the price of capital equipment relative to the wages of the labour for which it can be substituted. Over the last fifty years, wages have tended to rise relative to the cost of capital equipment. The effect has been to increase the rate of technological change in such industries as agriculture, cargo handling, transport, shipbuilding and mining.

Other factors affecting growth are:

4. Fundamental changes in the composition of the national output

As a country's standard of living improves, so spending switches from agricultural to manufactured goods and then towards services. Since the opportunities for employing more capital and technical improvement are greatest in manufacturing, the growth rate increases as countries industrialise but then slows down as the relative demand for personal and government services increases.

5. A sustained improvement in the terms of trade (see p. 478)

Constraints upon growth

In practice the UK has not succeeded in sustaining a 3 per cent annual growth rate. Thus from 1960 to 1991 it averaged only 2.5 per cent. Why is this?

First, when employment was buoyant, consumer demand left fewer resources available for investment. Investment in capital goods involves saving, that is present sacrifice of consumer goods enjoyed (see p. 272) Figure 34.3 shows a production-possibility curve in terms of capital goods and consumer goods.

If society wants to move to curve II on Figure 34.1, it may choose point P (Figure 34.3). If, however, it wants the growth shown by curve III (Figure 34.1) over the same time-span, it must choose position F (Figure 34.3) giving up MM_1 consumer goods for NN_1 extra capital goods.

Second, inflation has proved inimical to investment (see p. 410). Government disinflationary measures undermine the confidence of entrepreneurs.

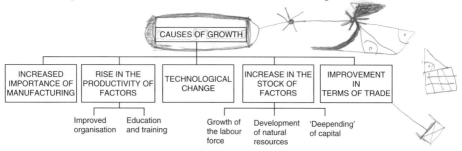

Figure 34.2 Factors leading to growth

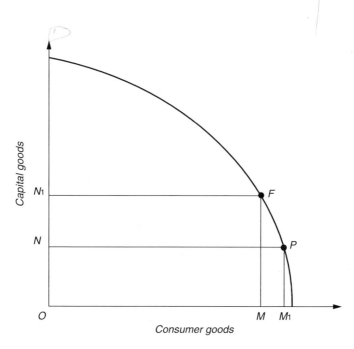

Figure 34.3 The choice between consumer goods and capital goods

Third, at times growth has been incompatible with other government objectives. For instance, 'stop' policies have been necessary because, as the economy expands, increasing imports can produce balance-of-payments difficulties (see p. 504).

Fourth, growth entails costs additional to the reduced current consumption necessary to accumulate capital. Growth usually requires change, and the more rapid the growth, the greater the change. Changes in the structure of the economy are, as we have seen, bound to lead to some unemployment, and if growth is to be achieved people must be willing to change jobs quite radically, three or four times in their working lives. This will entail retraining and probably moving around the country; and, as techniques change more rapidly, these processes will happen to a far greater extent than at present.

Fifth, growth is not achieved without environmental costs – pollution, noise, loss of natural beauty, destruction of wildlife habitat. And, as material wealth grows, people are inclined to question the full costs of growth with some consequent slowing down of the rate at which it can proceed.

Finally, and on the same theme, Britain's growth has been taken in forms not appearing in GNP calculations (see p. 353). Increasing welfare may mean preferring a quiet life and more leisure to the 'rat-race' and stress of accumulating material goods.

34.3 THE GOVERNMENT AND GROWTH

Difficulties in framing policy

Most people look for an improvement in their standard of living. Thus one objective of the government is to secure a satisfactory rate of growth. But there are difficulties in framing policy.

(1) How is growth to be measured? We have already drawn attention to the ambiguities of GNP figures as a measure of improved living standards. Is growth to take the form of more leisure, less spending on defence, a litter-free environment, the preservation of town and rural beauty, safer and more comfortable travel?

(2) Of all the factors producing growth, which plays the greatest part – education of the population, training of labour, additional capital equipment, technological advance? There is no real means of measuring.

(3) Growth does not proceed at a *steady* rate but rather by a series of take-offs and slow-downs around an upward trend. Small fluctuations in the pace of expansion are unavoidable, and firms are generally able to cope, e.g. by adjusting their stock levels. However, if these fluctuations are too wide, uncertainty can deter investment and thus have an adverse effect on the overall rate of growth (see below).

Government policy

Since there is no single satisfactory theory of growth, government action seeks to promote the various factors which are essential to growth.

Growth results mainly from capital investment in its different forms. But accumulating capital involves foregoing present consumption – saving. Thus a first requirement for the government is to ensure that its policies, especially as regards taxation, will provide the amount of real saving required.

Second, additions to capital take place in both the public and private sectors. The government itself is largely responsible for investment in the public sector – the infrastructure (such as roads, hospitals, schools), education of its people and the training of the labour force.

On the other hand while all these are important as regards growth, the scale of the government's priorities must not 'crowd out' desirable private sector investment. Decisions here are based on expected profitability. Private investment can be increased, therefore, by providing a stable economic background free from 'stop–go' policies so that fixed capital formation, research and development (R & D) are not inhibited.

While we must not ignore micro supply-side measures, the major spurts in growth have come through breakthroughs in technology by innovation and the application of inventions. Most of these, e.g. aircraft, computers, antibiotics and other drugs, plant-breeding, animal selection, pesticides, etc. are the result of long-term R & D. While about a half of R & D is carried out in the private sector, the other half, particularly as regards defence, is under the control of the government, largely through government-sponsored research bodies.

Finally, the government has to encourage the application of the fruits of R & D so that innovation and inventions are transformed into new marketable products.

CHAPTER SUMMARY

- Economic growth occurs when the potential full-employment output of the economy is increasing over time.
- Growth makes possible an increase in living standards.
- Growth can be achieved through increases in productivity, increases in the stock of factors of production, technological change, improvements in the terms of trade and changes in the composition of national output.
- The UK has had a long-term growth rate of about 2.5 per cent which, although less than comparable nations, is still sufficient to have brought about a doubling of GNP over 28 years.

REVIEW QUESTIONS

- What are the advantages of economic growth?
- What are the five basic causes of economic growth?
- Why has the post-war growth record of the UK been less than it might have been?
- Suggest ways in which government policy could promote economic growth.

 Visit the companion website for further questions

35

BALANCED REGIONAL
DEVELOPMENT

LEARNING OBJECTIVES

After studying this chapter you should be able to:
- explain why the UK has a regional development problem;
- describe the consequences of regional depression;
- explain government and EU policies for regional assistance.

35.1 THE REGIONAL PROBLEM

Unemployment and the immobility of labour

Even where there is considerable unemployment, there will be some job vacancies. Thus, while in mid-2006 the number of persons unemployed was 1,650,000 there were in existence 598,100 vacancies at Job-centres. Why are there these unfilled vacancies?

On the one hand, conditions of demand and supply change. Tastes change, incomes rise, foreign competitors produce at a lower price, etc. As a result, demand is buoyant for some goods and slack for others. On the supply side, technological change leads to redundancies. Thus in the UK since the Second World War, we have had a buoyant demand for consumer durable goods, services, electronic equipment, high technology products, etc., and a considerably reduced demand for coal, cotton goods, iron and steel, ships, etc. The demand for factors of production is a 'derived' demand; if the demand for a good decreases, the demand for the workers producing that good will also decrease.

On the other, there are obstacles to the movement of redundant labour to vacancies in expanding industries. This labour immobility, discussed in Chapter 20, gives rise to frictional, seasonal and structural unemployment. It is the latter which is the one most closely linked to the regional problem.

433

Yet while labour immobility must be recognised when formulating a regional policy, it must not be overestimated. Over time there is movement; studies have shown that over a period of ten years, nearly one-quarter of all male employees move from one part of the country to another.

The nature of the regional problem

In broad terms, a regional problem can arise because:

1. The particular region may be endowed with poor natural resources

This applies, for example, to the Highlands of Scotland. More generally, with the growth of national income, an agricultural region which does not attract expanding industries – e.g. Cornwall and Devon – cannot provide its population with living standards comparable with those of the rest of the country. Consequently, either any increased labour productivity is the result solely of emigration, or income per head simply remains below that of the rest of the country.

Where the region is too remote to introduce new industries, any improvement may have to depend largely upon a rise in incomes elsewhere, provided it is attractive to tourists – for example. North Wales, the Lake District.

2. The resources of the region may not be fully developed, usually through lack of capital

This applies particularly to the less developed countries. Here the more immediate solution is for capital to be provided on favourable terms by richer regions.

In the long term an improvement in the imbalance may depend mainly on rising incomes elsewhere. Exploitation of the area's resources may now become economically viable. For example, prosperity came to Aberdeen and the Shetlands only when the rise in the price of oil and the development of modern technology made extraction of North Sea oil an economic proposition. Alternatively, rising incomes in other regions may allow tourism to be developed, e.g. North Wales, the Lake District.

3. A region's basic industry is either stagnant or in decline

Such a region is usually characterised by: a rising rate of unemployment; a level of income which is falling relatively to other regions; a low activity rate, particularly of female workers; a high rate of outward migration; and an inadequate infrastructure. It is thus this type of regional imbalance which creates the problem

Table 35.1 Percentage rate of unemployment by government office region, July 2006

United Kingdom	5.4
Region:	
North East	6.0
North West	5.1
Yorkshire and Humber	5.5
East Midlands	5.5
West Midlands	5.3
South West	3.8
East	5.1
London	7.9
South East	4.5
Wales	5.0
Scotland	5.6
N. Ireland	4.5

Source: www.statistics.gov.uk.

for *national* governments; indeed the depressed regions are normally identified by their unemployment rates (Table 35.1).

In contrast, other regions may be expanding so rapidly that their further development results in congestion, inadequate social capital and inflationary pressures. Yet the problems of both are linked, and policies must take account of this.

The correction of regional imbalance through the market economy

The classical model considers that industries, like trees in the forest, grow, decline, and eventually rot away. But there will always be new industries growing to which the resources of the decaying industries can transfer. Theoretically the market should move workers who become unemployed to other jobs. The fall in the demand for a good, and the consequent unemployment, should result in a relative wage fall. On the other hand, where demand is buoyant wages should rise. Such changes in relative wages should: (a) move workers from low-wage to high-wage industries, and (b) industries from high-wage to low-wage areas.

Weaknesses of the market mechanism

The attraction of the above model is that correction of an imbalance can be brought about by the market. Yet in suggesting that a government regional policy is largely superfluous, the theory has serious weaknesses:

(a) Factor markets adjust much less perfectly than the theory implies. Not only
     is labour immobile, but factor prices, especially wage rates, tend to be resist-
     ant to any downward movement. Moreover, national wage-bargaining
     weakens the response to the price signals of regional imbalance. Finally, the
     information available to factor markets is often imperfect. Thus capital mar-
     kets tend to be centralised in the more prosperous regions of a country. If such
     markets operate with a bias against, or with imperfect knowledge of, invest-
     ment opportunities in the peripheral regions, there may well be no injection
     of investment to cover savings in these regions.

(b) The assumption of constant returns to scale which is implicit in the theory
     may not hold. Manufacturing in particular is characterised by increasing
     returns to scale over the relevant output range so that high-wage regions
     may also generate high returns to capital. Thus firms, like labour, may
     migrate to the prosperous high-wage regions. Indeed, as communications
     improve, these regions may gain with the progressive opening of trade at the
     expense of the decaying region. Thus the south-east region of England has
     benefited from its close connections with the EU.

Should movement be entirely outwards, the model has additional
weaknesses:

(c) The theory ignores the external costs to society of (i) the loss of social capital
     and the disintegration of communities in the depressed regions, and (ii) the
     congestion and inflationary pressures generated in the expanding areas
     (see below).

(d) Those workers who do move from the depressed regions are mainly the
     better educated, most highly skilled and more enterprising young adults.
     As such they are often the leaders of the community. The result is that
     the region becomes still further depressed *and* more unattractive to new
     industries.

(e) The model follows a purely partial equilibrium approach. It ignores the fact
     that migration from the depressed regions leads to a loss of income there.
     The multiplier effect of reduced consumer spending and investment serves
     to depress the area still further.

It should be noted that even if, as the theory predicts, economic efficiency could
be secured through market forces, government action may still be needed on the
grounds of equity. The model only predicts that interregional differences in factor
payments and employment *within a particular industry* will be automatically
removed. Per capita *regional incomes* may not be equalised simply because differences in resource endowments and industrial structure may give some regions
high-wage sectors and others low-wage sectors.

Consequences of regional depression

The existence of prolonged depression in certain regions has adverse consequences which can be summarised as follows:

1. An underutilisation of resources through unemployment

Not only does regional unemployment result in lost output for the community as a whole, but it can have serious social and psychological effects on the workers concerned. Moreover, significant differences in people's income between regions has equity implications.

2. A loss of social capital as towns and cities decay

Where the nation's population is static or falling, outward migration from depressed areas involves social costs in that schools, churches, etc. fall into decay while certain public services have to be operated below capacity. In contrast, new roads and public buildings, such as hospitals, have to be provided in the expanding areas.

However, the implied assumption that social capital should never be allowed to become obsolete has to be questioned. The stock of social capital in the high unemployment areas tends to be older and of lower quality than in the expanding areas of the south. In other words, it may be due for renewal and can be replaced as easily in another part of the country (subject to the qualification that there are no congestion or inflationary problems there).

3. External social costs

Migration from decaying regions results in a loss of welfare through the break-up of communities and the destruction of the 'social character' of an area. It could be, however, that having overcome their reluctance to moving away from friends, people find compensatory benefits, both economic and social, in a more pleasant environment. In any case, it is difficult to assess the loss resulting from this 'destruction of social character'.

Similarly, there may be external costs of excessive urbanisation (e.g. traffic congestion, noise, pollution and intensive housing) through migration to a prosperous region. Here again, however, the argument needs qualification. In recent years, population movement out of city centres into the surrounding countryside has exceeded other movements of population. Thus Greater London is losing population at a faster rate than any other area in the country, while areas gaining from migration, such as East Anglia, may be areas of relatively low congestion. Thus present migration may serve to reduce congestion costs as much as to increase them.

4. Differences in unemployment between regions make it more difficult to manage the economy

Prosperous regions tend to become 'overheated' through the pressure of demand. This is reflected in higher wage-rates and labour shortages. Higher wage-rates tend to be transmitted even to the depressed regions through national wage agreements, the insistence on traditional wage differentials, etc. But anti-inflationary measures, both monetary and fiscal, apply nationally, thus adding to the unemployment problems of the depressed regions. It is argued, therefore, that ironing out unemployment differences between regions would not only reduce the rate of inflation but do so at a lower overall level of unemployment.

5. Economic integration between nations may be undermined by the political opposition of depressed regions' pressure groups

The rationale of economic integration between nations, e.g. the EU, is to secure greater comparative advantages by the removal of trade barriers and increased factor mobility. However, it may exacerbate the problem of regional imbalance because certain industries, particularly in areas on the periphery, such as Northern Ireland and Scotland, find it more difficult to compete. Political pressure groups in such areas, therefore, may react by opposing integration.

35.2   GOVERNMENT POLICY

Objectives of government policy

The objectives of government policy have widened in the light of experience. In brief, current regional policy seeks to:

(i)   reduce the relatively high level of unemployment in certain regions;
(ii)   achieve a better balance between the population and the environment;
(iii)   preserve regional cultures and identities;
(iv)   relieve inflation by reducing the pressure of demand in the expanding regions;
(v)   counter possible adverse regional effects of greater international economic integration and of more open economies.

It has to be recognised, however, that these objectives are not always compatible with national economic policy. For instance, diverting firms from their optimum location to a depressed area may hamper growth, while it may be necessary to stimulate exports of goods and services produced in the more prosperous regions in order to improve the national balance of payments. Furthermore, where it is necessary to concentrate growth at particular locations within regions, greater equality between regions may only be achieved at the cost of greater inequality within regions. Finally, any regional employment policy has a better chance of success when there is full employment generally in the economy. Not only are unemployed workers encouraged to move to where there are unfilled vacancies, but firms will be more ready to go where labour is available provided it can be trained in the appropriate skills.

The main thrust of government policy

The regional problem in the UK has resulted from (a) the decline of certain major industries, particularly coal, shipbuilding and textiles, which were concentrated in specific geographical areas; and (b) the failure of the depressed regions to attract expanding industries, such as services, consumer durables, light engineering and chemicals; and (c) the geographical immobility of labour. Government policy must concentrate on these three weaknesses.

Where an area is depressed, the government can give first aid by placing its contracts there, e.g. for defence equipment, and awarding it priority for public-works programmes – schools, new roads, hospitals, the physical regeneration of urban areas, etc. Subsidies may also be granted to secure contracts, for example, to build ships.

In the long term, however, the government must take measures that will, on the one hand, encourage the outward movement of workers, and on the other induce firms to move in to employ those workers who find it difficult to move and also to halt further degeneration of the region. The first is usually referred to as 'workers to the work', the second as 'work to the workers'.

Workers to the work

Taking workers to the work is basically a micro approach to overcome market frictions, chiefly the immobility and imperfect knowledge of labour. In pursuing this policy, however, the government must bear in mind the following:

1. Unemployment arising through immobility is far more difficult to cure when cyclical unemployment also exists, for an unemployed person has little incentive to move if there is unemployment even in the relatively prosperous areas.
2. Other government interference in the economy may add to the problem of immobility. Thus high rates of income tax whittle away monetary inducements to move and unemployment benefit may reduce the incentive to seek a job elsewhere. Similarly, rent control and residential qualifications for local authority housing priorities lead to difficulties in finding accommodation.

3. Even owner-occupiers in depressed regions may be restricted in mobility by the much higher cost of housing in the prosperous areas.
4. Many changes of both occupation and area take place in a series of ripples. Thus an agricultural labourer may move to road construction to take the place of the labourer who transfers to the building industry.

The government's first task must be to improve occupational mobility. Entry into certain occupations should be made less difficult, e.g. by giving information on opportunities in other industries and occupations and by persuading trade unions to relax their apprenticeship rules. More important, people must be trained in the new skills required by expanding industries, e.g. through local Training and Enterprise Councils.

Improving the geographical mobility of workers to the more prosperous regions operates chiefly under the government's Employment Transfer Scheme. This consists of granting financial aid towards moving costs, providing information on prospects in other parts of the country and giving free fares to a place of work away from the home town.

Work to the workers

Although a 'workers-to-the-work' policy has a role to play in correcting regional imbalance, it suffers from: (i) an exclusive concern with unemployment to the neglect of other consequences of regional imbalance; (ii) a failure to recognise the macro effects of the outward movement of workers.

Thus taking work to the workers is now regarded as the policy most likely to effect a long-term solution to the problem for it reduces regional differences in income and the rate of growth as well as in unemployment. By helping the more immobile workers, such as older people and married women, it stimulates the activity rate. It also avoids forcing workers to leave areas to which they are attached, relieves the growing congestion in south-east England, and prevents the loss of social capital resulting from the depopulation of depressed areas. Above all, it works in harmony with Keynesian macro theory. The 'multiplier' operates for regional economies in much the same way as it does for the national economy. Moving unemployed workers and their families reduces spending in the area (e.g. because unemployment benefits are no longer being drawn) and this gives rise to a negative multiplier. In contrast, moving firms into the area generates spending power and produces a positive multiplier, variously calculated at between 1.25 and 1.50.

On the other hand, a policy of locating firms in depressed areas may involve them in higher costs. Their desire to establish plant in the South East is to secure location advantages, such as a supply of skilled workers, easier and less costly communications, contact with complementary firms and nearness to EU markets.

Regional assistance

Assisted area status now confers eligibility of aid from the EU as part of the EU policy of reducing the level of aid to industry and to prepare for the entry of new states. The Assisted Areas of Great Britain are based upon a map drawn up and agreed with the European Commission in July 2000. Assistance comprises Tier 1 (Article 87(3)a) and Tier 2 (Article 87(3)c Regional Selective Assistance Grants (RSA). Additionally, there are large areas of the UK where a lower level of grant aid can be made available to Small and Medium Enterprises (SME). These areas are classified as Tier 3 (additional enterprise grant areas). In the Assisted Areas *Regional Selective Assistance* is given on a discretionary basis, mainly through project grants based on the capital cost and the number of jobs created. The budget of over £100 million is under the control of the Invest in Britain Bureau (IBB) which has had outstanding success in inducing US, Japanese and South Korean firms to establish overseas centres in Britain, often in the depressed regions. From 1 January 2007, the Assisted Areas map will change (see Figure 35.1) and the areas qualifying will shrink because of Britain's relative economic success within Europe in the last six years. The following areas currently qualify for Assisted Area Status and will continue to do so due to their continued eligibility for European convergence funding (previously referred to as objective one funding): Cornwall; West Wales and the Valleys; and the Scottish Highlands and Islands.

In the dispersal of industry the government has set an example. Thus the Department of Health and Social Security is based in Newcastle, and the Driving and Vehicle Licensing Agency in Swansea, while much of the work of departments (such as Defence and HM Revenue and Customs) has been relocated to the Assisted Areas.

35.3 URBAN REGENERATION

Until the 1980s, regional policy tended to concentrate on attracting firms to the regions where structural change had led to high rates of unemployment. But there were weaknesses. In focussing aid on manufacturing industry it failed to take advantage of the growing service industries. Moreover, the objective of actual job creation was lost sight of through the concentration on *investment* grants to attract firms. This simply induced those firms relocating to substitute capital for labour and resulted in a high cost per job created – £26,000 in the case of attracting Samsung to the North East region. Also the emphasis on regional differences diverted attention from problems within regions where there were pockets of run-down areas. Nor are such areas confined to the industrial North West and North East regions. For instance within London's boundaries there are 15 of the 20 most deprived areas in the UK. Often these areas have a predominantly ethnic population needing to be taught new skills.

The government and stabilisation policy

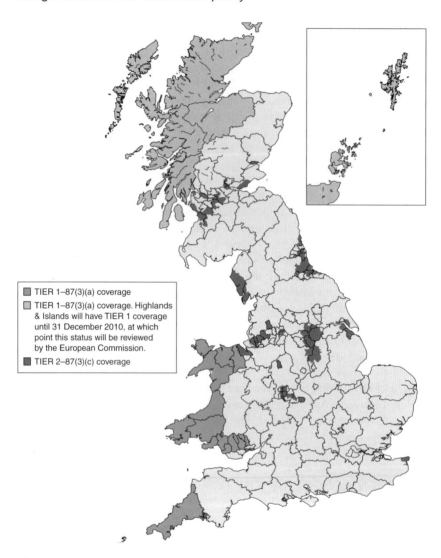

Note: Northern Ireland will have full 87(3)(c) coverage.
Source: www.dti.gov.uk/regional/assisted-areas.

Figure 35.1   Proposed Assisted Areas in Great Britain, 2007–13

It was recognised that regeneration was not simply tidying up derelict land. It had to rebuild communities by providing them with jobs and decent living conditions, chiefly by attracting investment from the private sector. As a result urban regeneration had to be coordinated with regional industrial policy. In fact funds were switched from regional assistance to the urban regeneration programme, though it must be recognised that much of the urban degeneration was in the Assisted Areas. With the object of regenerating these run-down areas the government introduced a variety of schemes – Enterprise Zones, Urban Development Corporations, City Grants, City Challenge – which were amended in the light of experience or the need to reduce the financial commitment.

These administrative and spending initiatives have now been replaced by English Partnerships, a Single Regeneration Budget and Regional Development Agencies (RDAs), all responsible to the Office of the Deputy Prime Minister (ODPM).

English Partnerships (EP), created in 1997, is a national government agency which has powers to acquire land and decide on planning in a designated area. Furthermore, unlike the previous City Grant where the Treasury required a stipulated rate of public to private funding, EP can itself decide on how it uses its investment fund, amounting to several hundred million pounds (in 2002–3, EP spent £230 million). This means that EP can shoulder risk, providing even 100 per cent of initial funds as a pump priming exercise to draw in developers. It was thus able, for example, to use its investment fund to put together a coordinated package which induced Samsung to locate a manufacturing base at Stockton-on-Tees in the North East. Its original fund can be augmented by any profits it makes on its initiative and by EU funding where spending occurs in an Assisted Area.

The Single Regeneration Budget (SRB) was set up to achieve overall control of spending on urban regeneration by providing a global sum to cover all the spending of the operating bodies. Its aim is to fund flexible and locally responsive forms of regeneration administered by the Regional Development Agencies. Much of this funding is competed for on a challenge basis, grants for regeneration schemes and even neighbourhood projects being awarded on an assessment of their merit.

For England, nine Regional Development Agencies (RDAs) have been set up to decide on local regeneration priorities, promote inward investment, help small businesses and coordinate regional economic development. Apart from the North West region, which now includes Merseyside, these have the same boundaries as the Government Office Regions, with which they will work closely. Scotland, Wales and Northern Ireland have their own agencies for similar functions.

The New Deal for Communities (NDC) aims to tackle multiple deprivation in the poorest areas. New Deal programmes are key to the government's strategy to tackle multiple deprivation in the poorest neighbourhoods, giving local people resources to tackle their problems in what the government emphasises is 'an intensive and coordinated way'. Like some other initiatives it grew out of the work of the Social Exclusion Unit and, specifically, its report BRINGING BRITAIN TOGETHER: A NATIONAL STRATEGY FOR NEIGHBOURHOOD RENEWAL. Together, local people, businesses, voluntary organisations and public agencies form a 'pathfinder' partnership in selected local authority districts to formulate proposals for the regeneration of neighbourhoods covering 1–4,000 households. In launching the New Deal for Communities, Prime Minister Tony Blair said it was 'a massive and desperately needed investment programme'. So far £2 billion has been allocated over a ten-year period.

35.4   REGIONAL POLICY IN THE CONTEXT OF THE EU

A healthy integrated EU – at both economic and political levels – is possible only if progress is made towards reducing disparities in economic opportunity between regions within the Community. Indeed, while the foregoing reasons for regional policy are all relevant at the Community level, additional considerations apply:

(a) Physical controls are more difficult to operate in the EU context. Not only are they at variance with the objective of greater mobility within the EU, but firms have the option of relocating in a prosperous region of another member state.

(b) The depressed peripheral regions of Scotland, Northern Ireland, Southern Italy, etc., are more distant from the expanding centre of the Community – south-east England through to north-east France and Germany – than they are from the centres of their own countries. This EU 'centre' forms a concentrated market to which industries are likely to be increasingly attracted, thereby adding to its dominance.

(c) The EU embraces regions exhibiting wider economic disparities than in any one member state. Moreover, regional problems are more heterogeneous – for example, whereas the UK depressed regions are mainly industrial, Italy has many depressed agricultural areas.

These additional considerations mean that the formulation of an effective EU regional policy is a difficult task. Not only must it respond quickly as new regional problems arise, but it has to be linked with, and be complementary to, the individual nation's regional policy. Indeed EU policy should also coordinate the regional policies of member states, for example a physical control in one country must not be undermined by a firm being able to locate in another country.

It follows, therefore, that regional policy must be handled to a substantial degree at the EU level and be wide-ranging in the measures employed so that one reinforces the others. Above all, to achieve greater equity, it must envisage substantial transfers of income through incentive funds which are additional to and not a substitute for those provided by the member states.

The emphasis of the EU's three Structural Funds is now on regional development programmes rather than on individual projects, and the EU Commission can insist that grants are actually spent in the specified region. These funds are as follows:

(1) The *European Regional Development Fund* (ERDF) funds the development and structural adjustment of less-developed regions (such as Spain, Italy, Portugal and Greece) and declining industrial regions (for example, within the UK, Spain and France). The UK's depressed regions are major beneficiaries of the ERDF.

(2) The *European Social Fund* (ESF) provides funds to organisations running vocational training and job-creation schemes.

(3) The *European Agricultural Guidance and Guarantee Fund* (EAGGF) supports farming in less-favoured or environmentally sensitive areas, and the modernisation of infrastructures.

(4) The *Financial Instrument for Fisheries* (FIFG) may support projects which modernise the structure of the fisheries sector and related industries, and encourage diversification of the workforce and fisheries industry into other sectors. It also aims to promote sustainability within the fishing industry by encouraging a balance between fisheries resources and their exploitation.

Loans are also available on favourable terms from the European Investment Bank (EIB) and the European Coal and Steel Community (ECSC).

CHAPTER SUMMARY

- Immobility of labour is an obstacle to the working of the free market to solve regional problems. Such problems can arise because regions have poor natural resources, a lack of capital and declining industries. Regional problems include unemployment, loss of social capital, external costs, such as pollution, and they may make the national economy more difficult to manage.
- The government tries to take 'workers to the work' by encouraging labour mobility, and it aims to take 'work to the workers' through a variety of schemes including Regional Development Agencies and the New Deal for Communities. In addition the EU operates Assisted Areas schemes which provide regional grants.

REVIEW QUESTIONS

- Why does the UK have a regional development problem?
- Why is it difficult for market forces to resolve the regional development problem?
- What are the consequences of regional depression?
- Explain government policy in relation to regional development problems.
- Why is regional policy a problem at the level of the European Union?

 Visit the companion website for further questions

PUBLIC FINANCE

36.1 THE DISTRIBUTION OF INCOME

Introduction

Public finance is concerned with government spending and revenue (chiefly taxation), and the relationship between the two (the PSNCR). Not only are the magnitudes of each relative to the size of GDP significant but their make-up has economic implications, and this is especially so with individual taxes.

While the government may have to regulate in order to secure certain economic objectives, e.g. monopoly control, conservation, restriction of pollution, much can be achieved by fiscal measures. Such objectives include greater efficiency in the allocation of resources; the stabilisation of employment, the price level and the balance of payments; the redistribution of income. In this chapter we are mainly concerned with a more detailed examination of the economic characteristics of the different types of tax.

Because welfare cannot be measured objectively, we are unable to treat the redistribution of income scientifically (see p. 9). But the subject cannot simply be brushed aside: both the objectives of government expenditure and how revenue is raised redistribute income and wealth. But even though decisions on redistribution are political, the economist can still point out the possible economic aspects and the choices open to the government.

The government and the distribution of income

At the micro level, the marginal productivity theory provides a theoretical explanation of how the owners of factors of production are rewarded. But it analyses rewards only on a functional basis – wages, interest, rent and profits. To explain the distribution of income between individual house-holds other influences – chiefly the *ownership* of factors of production resulting from the unequal distribution of wealth – have to be taken into account.

The government is interested in the distribution of income for four main reasons:

The first is 'fairness'. Especially in the richer Western economies, people's social conscience will not tolerate 'poverty in the midst of plenty'. Yet private giving through charitable institutions is irregular, unreliable and inadequate in dealing with the relative size of the problem of inequality in a 'caring society'.

Second, gross inequality of income is divisive of society and disruptive of economic life, e.g. through strikes for higher pay.

Third, the distribution of income affects the broad macro variables, e.g. saving and taxation yield, which the government has to take into account in formulating stabilisation policies.

Fourth, the extent to which the government is successful in its stabilisation policies will, in its turn, affect income distribution, e.g. through unemployment and rising prices. The government, therefore, has a moral obligation to compensate for any failure on its part, by providing unemployment benefit and 'indexing' social security benefits in line with inflation.

Lorenz curves

Inequalities in the distribution of income can be depicted by a Lorenz curve (Figure 36.1). This plots the cumulative percentage of income against the cumulative percentage of households.

The straight diagonal line *OA* shows a perfectly equal distribution of income: the first 10 per cent of households receive 10 per cent of national income, the first 20 per cent of households receive 20 per cent of national income, and so on.

The curved line *B* shows that the first 10 per cent of households receive only 4 per cent of income, while the first 20 per cent receive 8 per cent. On the other hand, the last 10 per cent enjoy 25 per cent of total income. If we join these and similar points we have a Lorenz curve. The more the curve bows away from straight line *OA*, the greater is the inequality of income. Thus curve *C* depicts an

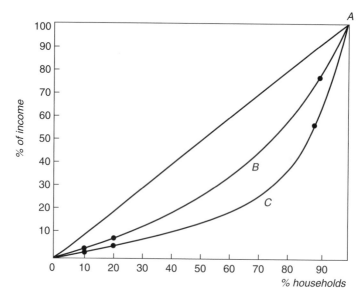

Figure 36.1 Lorenz curves

even greater inequality of income than curve *B*, the last 10 per cent of households having 45 per cent of income.

36.2 GOVERNMENT REVENUE AND EXPENDITURE

Figure 36.2 shows the main items of government revenue and expenditure. Total public spending is expected to be around £552 billion for 2006–7, around £9,200 for every man, woman and child in the UK. It is set to rise to £583 billion in 2007–8 and projected to rise to £610 billion in 2008–9.

The distribution of government expenditure

Government spending can be classified under the following headings:

(i)   *Defence,* where spending has fallen since the ending of the Cold War in 1989.
(ii) *Internal security* – the police, law enforcement and fire brigades.
(iii) *Social responsibilities* – education, and protection against the hazards of sickness, unemployment and old age.

(iv) *Economic policy*, covering subsidies to agriculture and industry, help for Assisted Areas, worker training and the provision of capital for urban regeneration.

(v) *Miscellaneous*, including expenditure on diplomatic services, grants to local authorities, overseas aid and – the largest single item – interest on the National Debt.

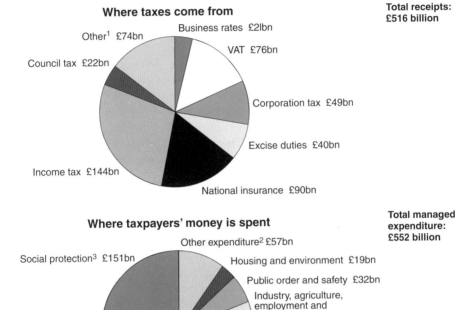

Where taxes come from

Total receipts: £516 billion

Other¹ £74bn
Business rates £2lbn
Council tax £22bn
VAT £76bn
Corporation tax £49bn
Excise duties £40bn
Income tax £144bn
National insurance £90bn

Where taxpayers' money is spent

Total managed expenditure: £552 billion

Other expenditure² £57bn
Social protection³ £151bn
Housing and environment £19bn
Public order and safety £32bn
Industry, agriculture, employment and training £21bn
Debt interest £27bn
Personal social services £26bn
Defence £29bn
Education £73bn
Health £96bn
Transport £21bn

Notes: ¹ Other includes capital taxes, stamp duties, vehicle excise duties, and some other tax and non-tax receipts (e.g. interest and dividends).
² Other expenditure includes spending on general public services; recreation, cultural media and sport, international cooperation and development; public service pensions; plus spending yet to be allocated and some accounting adjustments.
³ Social protection includes tax credit payments in excess of an individual's tax liability.
Source: HM Treasury, 2006–7 projections.

Figure 36.2 Public money 2006–7: where it comes from and where it goes

Today government expenditure takes about 40 per cent of gross domestic product – a remarkable increase since 1910, when the figure was only about 10 per cent. The government is now spending on a much wider range of activities. It should be noted, however, that, many items of government spending, e.g. pensions, National Debt interest and grants to local authorities, are unavoidable since by nature they are basically contractual.

Controlling general government expenditure

It may seem that the government has merely to estimate its expenditure and impose taxes to cover it. But this is not the case. Since goods and services in the economy are limited, the government has to cut its coat according to its cloth, asking such questions as: What can be afforded for the Arts Council? How much can be given to local authorities? Can nursery education be introduced? Can National Insurance Contributions be reduced? The economic problem confronts private persons and the government alike. The method of dealing with it is as follows.

General government expenditure covers spending by both the central government and local government. But to explain the present principle of control attention will be focused on the central government's expenditure.

Over the economic cycle, revenue and expenditure should be balanced. Where expenditure exceeds revenue there is a PSNCR which, if it exceeds 3 per cent of GNP makes it more difficult to sustain growth since it puts upward pressure on the rate of interest (see p. 533). Furthermore, in adding to the National Debt it increases the government's current interest payments.

The problem is that each spending government department regularly presses for more funds. In the past the overall level of public expenditure has tended to emerge from a series of compromises between the chief secretary to the Treasury and the departments. This 'bottom up' approach, however, tended to give too much weight to what expenditure was desirable rather than what was affordable.

Without extra taxation, an increase in government spending ought not in the long term to exceed what growth in the economy can provide by way of the additional revenue resulting from higher incomes, profits and consumer spending. Recognising this economic problem of scarcity, the government has now adopted a 'top down' approach, determining a global figure for total expenditure and keeping aggregate spending departments' allocations within this. In practice most adjustments are relatively marginal and ultimately rest on political considerations.

How government expenditure is financed

In the same way that firms have to pay for both variable and fixed factors, the government has to spend not only on single-use goods and services but also on goods which render services over long periods. The first, which involve regular yearly spending, should be paid for out of regular yearly income. But capital spending, on such items as roads, loans for urban regeneration and university building, is more fairly financed by borrowing, for the repayment of the capital then partly falls on future beneficiaries.

Regular yearly income comes from two main sources: (i) miscellaneous receipts, chiefly interest on loans, rents and charges on goods and services (such as medical prescriptions); and (ii) taxation, described in more detail below.

The difference between expenditure and revenue has to be covered by borrowing – the PSNCR. Yearly borrowing increases the National Debt, the capital sum of accumulated borrowing.

Government borrowing takes the form of:

(i) Short-term loans from the sale of Treasury bills. Originally these were used to bridge the time-gap between expenditure and receipts from taxation, but – because it is cheaper to borrow short than long – they eventually became a major means of government borrowing. Nevertheless, being liquid assets to the banks, there are possible inflationary effects.

(ii) Medium- and long-term loans are obtained by selling stock having a minimum currency of five years. Some, such as 3.5 per cent War Loan, are undated.

(iii) *'Non-market' borrowing*, through National Savings Certificates, Premium Savings Bonds, etc. and the National Savings Bank.

Since 1980 additional capital funds have been obtained by the 'privatisation' sales of publicly owned assets (see p. 242).

(see p. 242)

36.3 THE MODERN APPROACH TO TAXATION

The attributes of a good tax system

In his *Wealth of Nations* Adam Smith was able to confine his principles of taxation to four simple canons. Stated briefly, these were: persons should pay according to their ability; the tax should be certain and clear to everybody concerned; the convenience of the contributor should be studied as regards payment; the cost of collection should be small relative to yield.

While today the main purpose of any tax is usually to raise money, the additional uses of taxation have rendered Adam Smith's maxims inadequate. Indeed objectives other than revenue may take priority. Nevertheless, it is helpful to list the general attributes which a Chancellor of the Exchequer would wish his system of taxation to possess. As far as possible, taxes should be:

1. Productive of a worthwhile revenue which the Chancellor can estimate fairly accurately.
2. Certain to the taxpayer and difficult to evade.

3. Convenient to the taxpayer as regards the time and manner of payment.
4. Equitable in the sense that:
    (a) 'the most tax should be paid by those with the greatest ability to pay';
    (b) impartial between one person and another.
5. Adjustable to changes in policy.
6. Automatic in stabilising the economy. Thus while, in order to achieve full employment or a stable price level, the Chancellor can adjust taxes in his budget to influence consumer spending, it is helpful if they respond automatically in the desired direction.
7. Harmless to effort and initiative.
8. Consistent with other aspects of government policy. Although the tax structure should not change frequently, individual taxes must be constantly reviewed to promote current government policy. To encourage effort, should income from work be taxed at a lower rate than investment income? Will an indirect tax, by raising the cost of living, increase wage-push inflation?
9. Minimal in their effect on the optimum allocation of resources.
10. Equitable in its distribution of the tax burden. Taxes can be classified according to the proportion of a person's income which is deducted:
    (a) A *regressive* tax takes a higher proportion of the poorer person's income than of the richer. Indirect taxes, for instance, which are a fixed sum irrespective of income (e.g. television licences), are regressive.
    (b) A *proportional* tax takes a given proportion of one's income. Thus between £2,151 and £33,000 of taxable income, income tax is proportional, 23 per cent being taken from every pound of taxable income.
    (c) A *progressive* tax takes a higher proportion of income as income increases (Figure 36.3). Thus income tax, which has higher rates above certain limits (see p. 456), is progressive.

Justification for taxing the rich higher than the poor rests on the assumption that the law of diminishing utility applies to additional income, so that an

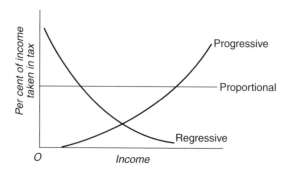

Figure 36.3 The difference between regressive, proportional and progressive taxes

extra £50 affords less pleasure to the rich person than to the poor person. Thus taking from the rich involves less hardship than taking from the poor. Generally this can be accepted as true, but we can never be sure, simply because there is no absolute measure of personal satisfaction.

36.4   THE STRUCTURE OF TAXATION

Because the objectives of taxation are now so varied and may even be incompatible, no single tax is completely perfect. Consequently, there must be a structure of taxation, combining different taxes which can be varied according to changes in emphasis on different objectives.

The following classification is based on their methods of payment.

Direct taxes

With these taxes the person makes payment direct to the revenue authorities – Her Majesty's Revenue and Customs (HMRC) or the local authority. Usually each individual's tax liability is assessed separately.

1.   Income tax

'Taxable income', which is subject to a 10 per cent rate on the first £2,150, a basic 22 per cent up to £33,300 and 40 per cent above £33,300 (2006), is arrived at after deductions for a personal allowance, marital status, etc.

2.   Corporation tax

Profits, whether distributed to shareholders or not, are taxed at 19 per cent up to £300,000 and at 30 per cent over £1,500,000. In-between these amounts there is 'marginal relief', which means that smaller companies do not have to pay the full 30 per cent rate. A part of corporation tax is imputed to shareholders and deducted in advance when the dividend is paid. This advance payment is allowed against the main 30 per cent corporation tax payment (which is always paid in arrears), while for the shareholder it counts as a 'tax credit' and is refundable if income tax is not paid because of low income.

3.   Capital gains tax

A tax is now levied at income tax rates on any capital gain when an asset is disposed of. Owner-occupied houses, cars, National Savings Certificates and goods and chattels worth less than £6,000 are excluded, and losses may be offset against gains.

Where the net gain does not exceed £7,700 (2006) in any year, no tax is payable.

4. Inheritance tax

Inheritance tax applies to lifetime gifts as well as to legacies, though the former generally bear only half the latter's rate of tax. The starting point is £285,000 (2006) and the rate of duty is 40 per cent. Gifts made more than seven years before death are exempt from tax.

5. Other taxes

These consist of stamp duties (payable on financial contracts), motor vehicle duties and a Petroleum Revenue Tax.

The Council Tax and Uniform Business Rate levied on business premises can also be regarded as direct taxes.

This also applies to National Insurance contributions – a pay-roll tax of up to 11 per cent on employers – with a slightly lower rate paid by employees and the self-employed.

Direct taxes yield nearly two-thirds of total revenue. Their great merit is that, being progressive and assessed according to the individual's circumstances, they ensure that the heaviest burdens are placed on the broadest backs. Their progressive character also gives additional weight to their role as built-in stabilisers.

Their main disadvantage is that when the rate of tax is high there may be disincentive effects. As a result indirect taxes also have to be levied.

Indirect taxes

Indirect taxes on goods and services are so called because the revenue authority (Her Majesty's Revenue and Customs) collects them from the seller, who, as far as possible, passes the burden on to the consumer by including the duty in the final selling price of the good (see p. 464). They may be *specific* (i.e. consisting of a fixed sum irrespective of the value of the good) or *ad valorem* (i.e. consisting of a given percentage of the value of the good).

Indirect taxes may be divided into:

(i) Customs duties levied at EU rates on goods imported from outside the EU.
(ii) Excise duties on home-produced goods and services, e.g. beer, whisky, petrol, cigarettes and gambling.

(iii) Value Added Tax (VAT): an *ad valorem* tax, levied on most goods and services at each stage of production at a basic rate. Using Figure 28.1 as an example, a VAT at 17.5 per cent paid by the consumer on the table in the shop would be £17.50 making a total purchase price of £117.50. The VAT, however, would have been paid at each stage of production: tree-grower £5.25; saw-miller £3.50 table manufacturer £5.25; retailer £3.50. In practice each producer would pay to the Customs and Excise the full 17.5 per cent tax of the goods as invoiced by him *less* the VAT paid by his suppliers of materials, etc. as shown on their invoices. Thus the retailer would pay the Customs and Excise £3.50, i.e. £17.50 minus the VAT of £14 charged to him.

Some goods, e.g. food (except meals out), childrens' clothing, houses, books, newspapers, public transport fares, medicines on prescription, etc. are zero rated. This means that the final seller charges no VAT *and* can reclaim any VAT invoiced by intermediary producers. Other goods, e.g. rents and medical services, are 'exempt'. Here no VAT is charged by the final seller, but any VAT paid by an intermediary, e.g. for building repairs, cannot be reclaimed.

The main merit of VAT is that it is broad based, the yield increasing almost proportionately to consumer spending. Moreover, since VAT covers most forms of spending, it does not distort consumer choice as much as a highly selective tax (p. 461).

36.5 THE ADVANTAGES AND DISADVANTAGES OF DIRECT TAXES

We can use our survey of the attributes of a good tax to analyse the merits and demerits of the different types of tax. As regards direct taxes, the main reference will be to the income tax, but most of the arguments will apply to the other direct taxes.

As Figure 36.2 shows, direct taxes account for approximately 55 per cent of the total tax revenue, with income tax providing 28 per cent. Taxes on capital account for only 1 per cent.

Advantages

1. A high and elastic yield

In the UK, a 1p increase in the income tax yields approximately £4 billion. In comparison with yield, costs of collection are low. Indeed, through the PAYE system, the government makes use of employers as collectors.

On account of its high yield, changes in the income tax are very effective in varying households' spending power.

2. Certainty

Income tax payers usually know how much tax they will be expected to pay out of a given income and when they must pay it. Moreover, it is difficult to evade payment. Workers draw their wages less PAYE deductions, while dividends and interest are received less the standard rate of income tax.

Similarly, on the government's side, the Chancellor can rely on the yield from income tax, but with inheritance tax, the yield may fluctuate.

3. Convenience

Weekly PAYE tax deductions enable the tax burden to be spread over the year. Companies and self-employed persons, such as doctors, surveyors, authors, and entertainers, receive a lump-sum demand which is paid in two half-yearly instalments.

Inheritance tax is a form of wealth tax but is convenient in that the owner is able to enjoy his property throughout his life.

4. Automatically stabilises the economy

Both income tax and corporation tax have an automatic effect in stabilising the economy (see p. 452).

5. Equity

In the case of income tax, equality of sacrifice is achieved in two ways:

(a) an allowance is given for being married and for other responsibilities, e.g. a dependent aged relative;
(b) the tax rate increases from 10 per cent to 22 per cent above £2,150 and 40 per cent above £33,300 taxable income (2006–7).

6. Redistributes income and wealth more equally

By being progressive and giving allowances for special needs, income tax brings about greater equality in incomes. Inheritance tax works similarly as regards wealth.

Disadvantages

The simplest and fairest method of increasing revenue is to raise the rate of income tax. But here there is a major obstacle. When the rate is already high, the disadvantages of direct taxes are magnified.

1. High rates act as a disincentive to effort

When income tax is around 40 per cent, people may prefer to take their income in the form of leisure (which is not taxed) rather than in money (which is taxed).

The extent to which this occurs, however, is uncertain. If a person has fixed money commitments, e.g. mortgage repayments and insurance premiums, he may have to work *harder* when his income is reduced. Furthermore, if we assume that a high rate of income tax is a disincentive to effort, we infer that people always look upon work as distasteful, and leisure as a pleasurable alternative. For many, this may be true but in the high-income brackets there are some who find their work enjoyable. Last, we have to remember that most people are not free to vary their hours of work except as regards overtime. The normal working week is often an agreement on a national basis between trade unions and employers.

The disincentive effect is more likely to occur when there is a jump in the rate of tax at a given income level for people may reduce their effort at this higher income. This is a psychological reaction, for there is no fall in their standard of living as happens when there is a general rise in the rate of tax. In other words, the disincentive occurs when the marginal rate of tax exceeds the average rate.

The disincentive effect may be reflected in other ways. People on social security may be reluctant to seek employment since taxed wages may leave them little better off, while highly skilled workers may emigrate to a lower tax country – the 'brain drain'.

2. High direct taxes stifle enterprise

A higher money reward is usually necessary to induce a person to devote time to training or to incur the cost of moving a home to secure promotion. It follows, therefore, that where the wage differential between skilled and unskilled labour is eroded by income tax, incentives are proportionately reduced. Similarly, firms are only prepared to accept risks if the rewards are commensurate.

3. High rates of tax do not encourage efficiency

Companies have 30 per cent of profits taken in taxation. Thus the penalty of inefficiency is not borne entirely by the firm. Because income is smaller, less tax is paid and so a part of the cost falls on the government.

457

4. High rates of direct taxation encourage tax avoidance

Although income tax may not directly reduce effort, it is likely that people will, wherever possible, seek to reduce their tax liability in other ways. Accountants are employed to advise on how tax may be legally avoided. Where possible, income is taken in kind – through share options, company cars, housing and even education for children – but the government is trying to tighten up.

Illegal tax evasion becomes more worthwhile, too, when the tax is high.

5. High direct taxes may prevent the optimum allocation of resources

Direct taxes may affect the supply of factors, particularly capital, to industry. It may be that high taxation discourages saving; it certainly reduces the power to save. This is not serious for large companies, but the major source of capital for the small private company or sole proprietor is the owner's personal savings out of income. Normally firms which are making the largest profits will be the more likely to want to expand. Thus income tax and corporation tax deprive small, risky, but often progressive companies of much needed capital.

Not only that, but high direct taxes may repel foreign capital. Since a company has to bear corporation tax on profits, the amount available for distribution to shareholders is therefore less. Consequently, people may prefer to invest in companies operating in countries where there is a higher return on capital – the result, not of superior efficiency, but simply of lower taxes.

36.6 THE ADVANTAGES AND DISADVANTAGES OF INDIRECT TAXES

Advantages

1. Revenue yield helps to avoid high direct taxes

The revenue need of the government is now so great that, without indirect taxes, such a high rate would have to be borne by direct taxes that there would be serious effects on effort and initiative.

In any case, some people feel that some indirect taxes, which affect everybody, are desirable in that they foster a responsible attitude to government spending.

2. Certain and immediate yield

Especially when the Chancellor concentrates tax changes on goods with a fairly inelastic demand, the revenue yield can be calculated fairly accurately. Indirect taxes are cheap to collect and difficult to evade.

Where the Chancellor requires immediate revenue, indirect taxes have a special advantage. Any increase produces extra revenue with little time-lag – quite different from a change in income tax.

3. Convenient to the taxpayer

Buyers are able to spread their payments as and when purchases are actually made. Indeed, if the tax does not change frequently, buyers soon regard the combined price and tax at which the good is sold as the usual price, thereby reducing the resentment which taxation normally incites.

4. Unharmful to effort and initiative

While direct taxes are linked to earning, indirect taxes fall on spending. With indirect taxes, therefore, there is little disincentive to effort. It may even be that higher prices will cause people to work harder in order to maintain their customary standard of living.

On the other hand, care must be taken that certain 'incentive goods' – cars, camcorders, dish washers, etc. – are not taxed so heavily that they are priced beyond the reach of persons who would otherwise work overtime in order to secure them.

5. They may automatically stabilise the economy

In as much as goods having a high income elasticity of demand (chiefly home-produced and imported luxuries) are taxed the most heavily, the yield from indirect taxes increases as incomes rise. This increase in the revenue helps to stabilise the economy in an inflationary situation (see p. 452).

Today, the Chancellor of the Exchequer is able to reinforce this automatic mechanism by the 'regulator'. He can alter an indirect tax either way by 25 per cent of the existing rate.

6. They are adjustable to specific objectives of policy

Selective taxes can be changed according to the particular needs of government policy. The following are examples:

(a) In order *to build up infant or vital defence industries*, protection from competitive foreign products may be afforded by an import duty. The British motor car, aircraft, paper, and chemicals industries have been built up in this way (see p. 482).
(b) The effects of *changes in the conditions of demand or supply on the long-term structure of an industry* may be mitigated by favourable tax concessions or by the imposition of duties on competing imports, e.g. cotton goods.

(c) The government may encourage the *use of certain goods* by VAT concessions, e.g. books are zero-rated.

(d) *Political links may be strengthened* by duties which give favourable treatment to particular countries, e.g. fellow-members of the EU.

(e) Citizens' health may be safeguarded by taxing certain goods, e.g. spirits, cigarettes.

(f) The *terms of trade may be improved* by taxing certain imports (see p. 477).

(g) The *balance of payments may be strengthened* by import duties on foreign goods (p. 482).

Disadvantages

1. Regressive

In so far as they buy the same goods, poor persons pay exactly the same tax as the rich. More than that, purchases are made out of income left after income tax has been paid. Thus not only are indirect taxes regressive, but they undo some of the redistributive effects of direct taxation.

To some extent, the regressive nature of indirect taxes can be offset by: (*a*) imposing *ad valorem taxes* instead of *specific taxes*; (*b*) exempting from VAT such items as food, housing and children's clothing.

2. Not completely impartial in their application

Although indirect taxes fulfil the requirement that all persons in the same position should pay the same tax, the concentration of taxes on a few goods – chiefly tobacco, alcoholic drink, and motoring – does penalise severely certain forms of spending. Thus a person who obtains his pleasure from walking, reading, cycling, and eating receives many benefits from state expenditure, benefits which are largely paid for by his smoking, drinking, and car-driving neighbour!

3. Possibly harmful to industry

Where taxes are subject to frequent variation, they may dislocate industry. This will be more marked the higher the elasticity of demand for the product (see p. 461).

4. Rigidity

Protective duties and subsidies (a 'negative tax') may originally be designed to give special assistance to an industry. But the Chancellor often finds his hands tied when he wishes to reduce this form of help. Industries such as agriculture, which have come to rely on protection or subsidies, strenuously resist any such move.

5. May have inflationary influences

Indirect taxes, by increasing the price of goods, raise the Retail Prices Index. This leads to a demand for wage increases.

6. Prevent resources from being distributed in the best possible way

The imposition of an indirect tax on a *particular* good results in resources not being perfectly allocated according to the real preferences of consumers. In the long period, under perfect competition, the cost of producing the good is just equal to people's valuation of it. Moreover, consumers have allocated their outlay so that marginal utility relative to the price of the good is equal in all cases. A tax on one good destroys this equilibrium, for the price of the good rises (unless supply is absolutely inelastic). This results in a redistribution of consumers' expenditure and thus of the factors of production. In addition, there will be some dislocation of the industry concerned (see p. 462).

7. Result in greater loss to the consumer than an income tax which raises an equivalent amount

Unlike an income tax, indirect taxes change the relative prices of goods so that consumers have to rearrange their pattern of expenditure. This substitution involves a loss of satisfaction in addition to that suffered through the reduction in income.

36.7 THE INCIDENCE OF TAXATION

What do we mean by the 'incidence' of a tax?

So far we have considered only the *formal* incidence of a tax – how the tax is distributed between the various taxpayers. Thus direct taxes, we saw, are progressive, falling heaviest on the higher income groups. Indirect taxes, on the other hand, are regressive as regards consumers, though the direct incidence falls on producers or distributors who actually pay the tax to Her Majesty's Revenue and Customs.

But the economist is chiefly concerned with the *effective* incidence – how the real burden of a tax is distributed after its full effects have worked through the economy.

In the case of *direct* taxes, we have seen that, with some qualifications, both income tax and corporation tax adversely affect effort, enterprise and risk-bearing, economy in expenditure, and saving (p. 457).

An increase in income tax can be passed on only by those workers who can secure some addition to their wages by way of compensation. For this to happen, they must be in a strong bargaining position. Certain conditions must be fulfilled (see p. 266), the chief one being that the demand for the good they produce is fairly inelastic. The increase in the price of the good which results from the higher wages will be borne mainly by consumers – which really means workers in other groups who are not in such a strong bargaining position.

Similarly, in the short period, when supply is fairly inelastic, an increase in a tax on profits will be borne chiefly by producers (see p. 466). But in the long period, when some entrepreneurs transfer from the riskier enterprises (which the tax hits hardest), there will be changes in the relative supply of goods, and consumers of those goods whose production involves the most risk will, according to their elasticity of demand, have to bear a part of the tax.

A tax which falls on monopoly profits, however, cannot be passed on. There has been no change in the demand or supply curves, and the monopolist is already producing where his profits are a maximum. Hence if he has to pay, say, a 20 per cent tax, his equilibrium position will be unchanged; four-fifths of maximum profits are still better than four-fifths of anything less.

With *indirect taxes*, the effective incidence can be analysed more precisely. An indirect tax may be *general* or *selective*. A sales tax levied across the board on all goods and services at a standard rate would be a *general* indirect tax. VAT comes closest to such a tax. The important point is that *relative* prices remain unchanged and the consumer cannot switch to a substitute which is relatively cheaper because it bears no tax. If the government wishes to reallocate resources, therefore, it must do so by using the proceeds of the tax to subsidise certain industries, or by imposing additional excise duties on goods whose consumption it would like to curtail, e.g. tobacco.

Any tax which is levied at a higher rate on certain goods is termed *selective*, e.g. tobacco, alcohol, cars, petrol. When a tax is selective, the following questions become important: what is the effect of imposing a selective tax on the size of the particular industry? How will the burden of such a tax be ultimately distributed between the producer and consumer?

We begin by explaining how the imposition of a tax can be shown diagrammatically.

The diagrammatic presentation of a tax

Theoretically, the effect of a tax can be analysed on either the demand or the supply side. No matter which is chosen, the same new equilibrium position for price and output will result. Later we shall prefer one method to the other according to the particular problem being analysed.

Consider the following demand and supply schedules for commodity X.

Price of X (pence)	Demand (units)	Supply (units)
12	60	150
11	70	130
10	80	110
9	90	90
8	100	70

The equilibrium price is 9p. Now suppose a tax of 3p is charged on the producer for each unit of X he puts on the market. This means that whereas before the tax he supplied 70,000 units at a price of 8p, he will now only supply this quantity at 11p (because 3p would go in tax). Similarly, 90,000 units will only be supplied at a price of 12p instead of 9p. Thus the effect of the 3p tax can be shown by the shift in the supply curve from S to S_1 (Figure 36.4). This gives a new equilibrium price of 11p, the buyer paying 2p more and the producer receiving 1p less, the quantity traded falling from 90,000 units to 70,000 units.

The result is the same if the 3p tax is levied on purchasers. Before the tax, 100,000 units were demanded at a price of 8p. If purchasers now have to pay a 3p tax, this is equivalent to a price of 11p including tax, and so they will demand only 70,000 units. Similarly, for a price of 9p they will demand only 60,000 units instead of 90,000. Thus the effect of the 3p tax imposed on buyers can be shown

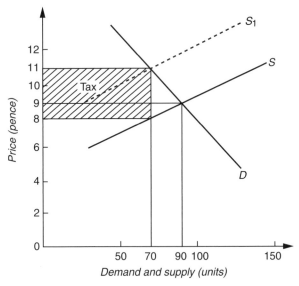

Figure 36.4 The diagrammatic representation of a tax on the supply side

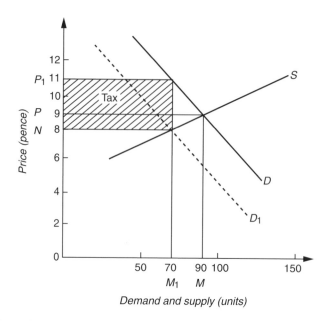

Figure 36.5 The diagrammatic representation of a tax on the demand side

by the move in the demand curve from D to D_1 (Figure 36.5). This gives a new equilibrium price of 11p (8p at which the market is cleared, plus 3p tax), and the quantity traded falls from 90,000 to 70,000.

The effect of an indirect tax on the size of an industry

The greater the elasticities of demand and supply, the greater will be the effect of a tax in reducing production. We can show this diagrammatically (Figure 36.6).

1. Elasticity of demand

Before the tax is imposed, total output is OM. The effect of the tax is to raise the supply curve from S to S_1. Two demand curves are shown, D_a being less elastic than D_b at price OP. The effect of the tax is to reduce output to OM_1 where demand is D_a, and to OM_2 where it is D_b. In the latter case consumers switch to buying substitutes.

2. Elasticity of supply

Before the tax is imposed, total output is OM (Figure 36.7). The effect of the tax is to lower the demand curve from D to D_1. Two supply curves are shown, S_a being less elastic than S_b at price OP. The effect of the tax is to reduce output to OM_1

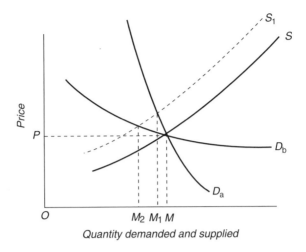

Figure 36.6 The relationship of elasticity of demand and production when a tax is imposed on a good

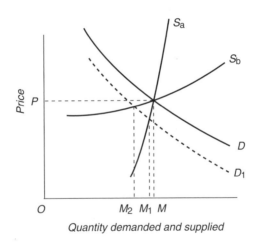

Figure 36.7 The relationship of elasticity of supply and production when a tax is imposed on a good

where supply is S_a, and to OM_2 where it is S_b. In the latter case producers can turn to producing alternative goods.

The proposition under this heading has important practical applications.

(a) The government may use a subsidy (which can be illustrated by moving the supply curve to the right – p. 467) to increase the production, and thus employment, of an industry. The effect will be more pronounced where demand and supply are elastic.

(b) Because the effect of a tax is to reduce production, even a temporary tax may be harmful to an industry. This is particularly so where home demand is elastic and production takes place under decreasing costs. Thus a higher selective tax on cars would not only reduce home demand, but, by doing so, lose economies of scale, thereby putting up prices to both home and foreign markets. Even when the tax is subsequently withdrawn, foreign markets may not be regained, for sales organisation, servicing arrangements and goodwill might all have suffered permanent harm.

The distribution of the burden of a selective tax between consumers and producers

When a good is subject to a selective tax, it does not mean that its price will rise by the full amount of the tax. Thus in Figure 36.5 the tax is 3p, but the price of X rises by only 2p. The proposition is that the amount of the tax falling on consumers as compared with that falling on producers is directly proportional to the elasticity of supply as compared with the elasticity of demand. That is:

$$\frac{\text{Consumers' share of tax}}{\text{Producers' share of tax}} = \frac{\text{Elasticity of supply}}{\text{Elasticity of demand}}$$

That this proposition is likely to be true can be seen from the following argument. When a tax is imposed, the reaction of the producer is to try to push the burden of the tax on to the consumer, while similarly the consumer tries to push it on to the producer. Who wins? Simply the one whose bargaining position is stronger. This will depend upon the ability to switch to producing substitutes if the price falls as compared with the ability to switch to buying substitutes if the price rises. Now the possibility of substitution largely determines elasticities of supply and demand. Thus the relative burden of the tax paid by producers and consumers depends upon relative elasticities of supply and demand.

The proposition can be proved geometrically as follows. As a result of the tax, price rises from OP to OP_1, and the quantity demanded and supplied falls from OM to OM_1 (Figure 36.5).

$$\text{Elasticity of supply at } OP = \frac{M_1M/OM}{NP/OP}$$

$$\text{Elasticity of demand at } OP = \frac{M_1M/OM}{PP_1/OP}$$

$$\therefore \ \frac{\text{Elasticity of supply}}{\text{Elasticity of demand}} = \frac{M_1M}{OM} \times \frac{OP}{NP} \times \frac{OM}{M_1M} \times \frac{PP_1}{OP}$$

$$= \frac{PP_1}{NP}$$

Increase in price (burden of the tax) to the consumer

Decrease in price (burden of the tax) to the producer

This proposition has a number of practical applications:

(a) A tax on a good having an inelastic demand, e.g. cigarettes, falls mainly on the consumer.

(b) Where supply is inelastic compared with demand, the tax falls mainly on the producer. Thus the imposition of VAT on the construction of new office blocks will have to be borne initially by the current land-owner.

(c) Because in the long period supply tends to be more elastic than in the short period, so, as time passes, the price will tend to rise as consumers are required to bear a greater share of the tax.

(d) Where supply is inelastic even in the long period, a tax will take longer to pass on to the consumer. Thus if there are any unoccupied offices, an increase in the Uniform Business Rate will have to be borne mainly by the owners of the property.

(e) An increase in price as a result of a tax will vary according to the relationship of elasticity of supply to elasticity of demand. The greater the elasticity of supply relative to the elasticity of demand, the greater will be the price rise.

The distribution of the benefit of a subsidy

The grant of a subsidy ('negative tax') can be analysed similarly by moving the demand or supply curve to the right, e.g. S to S_S (Figure 36.8).

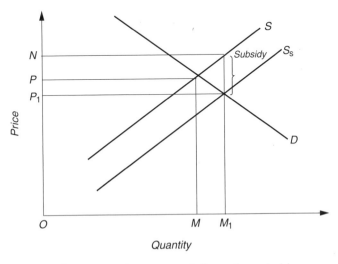

Figure 36.8 The diagrammatic representation of a subsidy

Price falls from OP to OP_1, and the quantity traded increases from OM to OM_1. As previously, it can be proved that the benefit of the subsidy to consumers as compared with that of producers is directly proportional to the elasticity of supply to the elasticity of demand. That is:

$$\frac{\text{Consumers' share of subsidy (fall in price paid)}}{\text{Producers' share of subsidy (increase in the price received)}} = \frac{\text{Elasticity of supply}}{\text{Elasticity of demand}}$$

CHAPTER SUMMARY

- Public finance is concerned with government spending and revenue. The aims of fiscal policy are much greater than simply raising revenue for government expenditure, however. They include: income redistribution, greater economic efficiency, stabilisation of the economy and stabilisation of the price level.
- Direct taxes, such as income tax, provide a high and elastic yield, but can be a disincentive to effort.
- Indirect taxes, such as VAT, help to reduce the burden of direct taxation, but are regressive in taking a larger share of lower incomes.

REVIEW QUESTIONS

- How can fiscal policy influence income distribution?
- What are the attributes of a good tax system?
- Illustrate the differences between regressive, proportional and progressive taxes.
- What are the disadvantages of direct taxes?
- What determines the incidence of a unit tax?

 Visit the companion website for further questions

PART VIII

INTERNATIONAL TRADE

37

THE NATURE OF
INTERNATIONAL TRADE

LEARNING OBJECTIVES
....

After studying this chapter you should be able to:
- use the principle of comparative advantage to explain why international trade takes place;
- explain how a nation's terms of trade are determined;
- describe the methods that nations can use to protect their trading position;
- evaluate the reasons given for protectionism.

37.1   WHY INTERNATIONAL TRADE?

How international trade arises

International trade arises simply because countries differ in their demand for goods and in their ability to produce them.

On the demand side, a country may be able to produce a particular good but not in the quantity it requires. The USA, for instance, is a net importer of oil. On the other hand, Kuwait does not require all the oil she can produce. Without international trade most of her deposits would remain untapped.

On the supply side, resources are not evenly distributed throughout the world. One country may have an abundance of land; another may have a skilled labour force. Capital, oil, mineral deposits, cheap unskilled labour and a tropical climate are other factors possessed by different countries in varying amounts.

Nor can these factors be transferred easily from one country to another. Climate, land and mineral deposits are obviously specific. Labour is far more immobile internationally than within its own national boundaries. Capital, too, moves less easily; exchange controls, political risks and simple ignorance of possibilities may prevent investors from moving funds abroad.

Because factors are difficult to shift, the alternative – moving goods made by those factors – is adopted. What happens is that countries, if the terms of trade are appropriate, specialise in producing those goods in which they have the greatest comparative advantage, exchanging them for the goods of other countries. Thus international trade arises.

Why make a separate study of international trade?

So far we have said nothing that is different in principle from trade between persons or between localities within a country. A carpenter who makes a chair exchanges it through the price mechanism for the food and other goods needed. Similarly, cars made at Sunderland are exchanged for washing machines made in South Wales. Why then, apart from the fact that longer distances are involved, do we treat separately the exchange of cars made in Britain for the wool produced in Australia?

The answer is that although the same theoretical principles apply, international trade gives rise to different problems. Exporters lack knowledge of foreign markets, find demand more difficult to predict, and have to cope with differences of language, weights and measures, government regulations, and changes of currency. Such factors tend to reduce the volume of international trade. Above all, since goods have to cross frontiers and be paid for in the currency of the country selling them, international trade may be regulated by governments for both economic and political reasons (see p. 481). What we have to do, therefore, is to show the theoretical gains which result from international trade and then indicate why our theoretical argument has to be modified in practice.

37.2 THE ADVANTAGES OF INTERNATIONAL TRADE

1. It enables countries to obtain the benefits of specialisation

Specialisation by countries improves the standard of living for all.

(a) It is obvious that, without international trade, many countries would have to go without certain products. Iceland, for instance, has no coal, Britain no gold or aluminium, and Sweden no oil.

(b) More important, many goods can be enjoyed which, if produced at home would be available only to the very wealthy, for instance bananas, spices, oranges and peaches in Britain. But this benefit can be applied generally to all imports. The 'law of comparative costs' shows that, provided countries differ in the relative costs of producing certain goods, they can probably gain by specialisation and trade. We can explain as follows.

Assume:

(i) assume constant unit costs (in terms here of opportunity costs);
(ii) no barriers to trade;

(iii)   no transport or trading costs;
(iv)   two countries, *A* and *B*, producing just two commodities, wheat and cars. Each has the same amount of capital and the same number of labourers, but *A* has a good climate and fertile soil compared with *B*. *B*'s workers, on the other hand, are far more skilful;
(v)   all factors are fully employed.

When both countries divide their factors equally between the production of wheat and cars, they can produce as follows:

Country	Wheat (units)	Cars (units)
A	500	100
B	100	500
Total production	600	600

But if *A* specialises in producing wheat and *B* in cars, total production would be 1,000 wheat and 1,000 cars. There is thus a net gain of 400 wheat and 400 cars to be shared between them.

Here the gains are obvious, because *A* has an *absolute* advantage in producing wheat and *B* in producing cars. But suppose *A* also has skilled labour and capital, and is better at producing both wheat and cars, as follows:

Country	Wheat (units)	Car (units)
A	500	300
B	400	100
Total production (no specialisation)	900	400

Are there still gains to be achieved by specialisation?

Provided the rate at which cars can be exchanged for wheat lies within certain limits (see p. 476), the answer is 'yes'. The reason for this is that *A*'s superiority in producing cars is far more marked than her superiority in producing wheat. In the production of the former she is three times as efficient, but with the latter only one-and-a-quarter times. *Comparative*, rather than absolute, advantage is what is really important. The result is that if *A* specialises in producing cars, leaving *B* to produce wheat, total production will be 800 wheat and 600 cars.

Suppose now that world conditions of demand and supply are such that 2 wheat exchange for 1 car: that is, the price of cars is exactly twice that of wheat. *A* now exchanges 200 cars for 400 wheat, giving her a total of 400 wheat and 400 cars, and *B* 400 wheat and 200 cars.

It can be seen, therefore, that through specialisation *B* is 100 cars better off. But has specialisation improved *A*'s position? She now has 400 cars but only 400 wheat, a gain of 100 cars but a loss of 100 wheat. But by her own production she

International trade

would have had to go without 166.66 wheat in order to obtain the extra 100 cars. Thus we can conclude that she too is better off.

The above arguments can be put in terms of opportunity costs. If there is no specialisation, *A* has to give up 3 cars in order to produce 5 units of wheat. On the international market, however, the terms of exchange are such that 3 cars can obtain 6 units of wheat. It will obviously pay *A*, therefore, to specialise in producing cars and to obtain her wheat by exchange. Similarly with *B*. For 4 units of wheat she can, by her own efforts, obtain only 1 car. On the world market she gets 2 cars. It will thus pay her to specialise in producing wheat and to obtain her cars by exchange.

The above explanation must be amplified to allow for:

(1) *Demand*

The law of comparative costs merely shows possibilities on the *supply* side – how two countries can specialise to advantage when their opportunity costs differ. But until we know the demand for goods we cannot say definitely whether specialisation will take place or, if it does, to what extent. Thus, although a country may be favourably placed to produce certain goods, a large home demand and thus a relatively high price may mean that it is a net importer of that good (as the USA is of oil).

(2) *Transport and trading costs*

These reduce possible gains and therefore make for less specialisation. Indeed, it is conceivable that transport costs could so offset *A*'s superiority in making cars that *B* found it better to produce her own requirements. Other costs are incurred in insurance and currency exchange.

(3) *Changes in the conditions of supply*

Few production advantages are permanent. Climate and, to a large extent, mineral deposits persist, but new techniques can make factors more productive. Thus India now exports cotton goods to Britain!

(4) *Interference by nations with the free movement of goods*

This occurs by customs duties etc. for such reasons as defence, maintaining employment and protection of an infant industry. (See p. 482.)

(5) *The possibility of diminishing returns setting in as the production of a good increases*

The theory as stated assumes that, at all stages of production, wheat can always be produced instead of cars by both *A* and *B* at a constant ratio. Thus at any output, *A* can have 5 wheat instead of 3 cars and *B* 4 wheat instead of 1 car. But it is

474

likely that as *B* increases her output of wheat, diminishing returns set in, for inferior land and labour have to be used. Thus instead of getting 4 additional wheat for 1 car, she receives only 3, and later only 2, and so on. The same applies, too, as the production of cars is increased by *A*. Eventually, therefore, it pays to specialise no longer. *A* can obtain her wheat cheaper by producing herself than by buying it on the world market, and the same applies to *B* as regards cars. Diminishing returns, and thus increasing costs, usually mean in practice that there is only partial specialisation – up to the point where opportunity costs are less than those offered by the terms of trade. Thereafter it is better for a country to produce the good itself.

2. By expanding the market, international trade enables the benefits of large-scale production to be obtained

Many products, e.g. computers, drugs, aircraft and cars, are produced under conditions of decreasing cost. Here the home market is too small to exploit fully the advantages of large-scale production. This applies particularly to small countries such as Switzerland. In such cases, international trade lowers costs per unit of output.

But it is the advantages of large-scale production which mainly account for the fact that more than half the world's trade takes place between countries similarly endowed and with the same income and patterns of demand. Thus with aircraft engines, Britain both exports to and imports from the USA, but each specialises in producing different types. In short, much international trade now takes the form of inter-industry trade between developed countries, e.g. EU trade.

3. International trade increases competition and thereby promotes efficiency in production

As we have seen, any restriction of the market makes it easier for one seller to gain control. In contrast, international trade increases competition. A government must always consider the risk of a monopoly developing when it gives protection to the home industry by tariffs, etc.

4. International trade promotes beneficial political links between countries

Examples of this are the EU and the Commonwealth, where trade is an important link.

37.3   THE TERMS OF TRADE

The limits of the exchange rate

In our example, A specialises in producing cars and B in producing wheat. By her own efforts, A could have 5 wheat for 3 cars. Obviously, therefore, she will not specialise in cars if, by exchange, she receives less wheat than this. Similarly, B will not specialise in producing wheat if she has to give up more than 4 wheat for 1 car.

Thus for specialisation to be beneficial to both A and B the rate at which wheat exchanges for cars must lie somewhere between the upper limit of $\frac{5}{3}$ and the lower limit of 4.

Determination of the exchange rate

But how is the actual rate of exchange (which we assumed to be 2 wheat for 1 car) determined?

The answer is quite simple. When we say that 2 wheat exchange for 1 car, we are really comparing relative values. Hence the price of cars will be twice that of wheat. Their relative prices will be fixed in the market, like all other prices, by demand and supply. We can explain by developing our simplified example still further.

Suppose A and B are the only two countries engaged in trade and that only two commodities, wheat and cars, are produced. Through specialisation, but before exchange, A has 600 cars and B 800 wheat. As the relative prices of wheat and cars change, so we have the following imaginary demand and supply schedules:

Price (exchange ratio) wheat:cars	A		B	
	Wheat demanded	Cars offered	Cars demanded	Wheat offered
3:1	1,500	500	100	300
$2\frac{1}{4}$:1	900	400	240	540
2:1	650	325	325	650
$1\frac{3}{4}$:1	350	200	400	700

It can be seen that, given the conditions of demand and supply as shown in the above schedules, only at a price of 2 wheat to 1 car is there market equilibrium. The example could be extended to cover more than two countries and more than two commodities.

For both A and B, the rate at which wheat exchanges for cars represents the *terms of trade*. If there are changes in demand or supply, so that more wheat has to be given for a car, then the terms of trade have improved so far as A is concerned, but have worsened for B. On the other hand, if less wheat has to be given for a car, the terms of trade have improved for B but worsened for A.

Changes in the terms of trade

The terms of trade, therefore, are the rate at which a country exchanges its exports for imports. Where goods are traded internationally, this rate is fixed by (a) world conditions of demand and supply, i.e. the real forces, and (b) the currency exchange rate, i.e. monetary influences.

Long-term changes in the terms of trade are brought about by changes in the conditions of either demand or supply. Thus, in our example, if there is a large increase in A's demand for wheat, the price of wheat will move nearer to the higher limit of 1.67:1. Likewise, if there is a decrease in A's demand for wheat, the price will move nearer to the lower limit of 4:1. Or, if the conditions of supply change so that A can produce 1000 cars instead of 600, she would probably be willing to supply more cars in exchange for a given quantity of wheat, and so the price of cars falls, the terms of trade moving in favour of B. On the other hand, if A's skilled labour emigrates and tends to be replaced by unskilled labour, she may be able to produce only 500 cars instead of 600, and the price of cars rises. The terms of trade move in favour of A.

Examples of how changes in the terms of trade can originate in the real world are:

1. Changes in the conditions of demand

(a) Demand may increase through industrial development. Thus a large increase in world demand for oil without any corresponding increase in production would improve the UK's terms of trade.

(b) A decrease in the demand for raw materials and basic minerals resulting from world recession when their supply is inelastic, brings about a large fall in the price. This was a factor helping to improve the UK's terms of trade in 1980.

2. Changes in the conditions of supply

(a) Technical improvements may increase supply, e.g. in agriculture during the 1970s and 1980s. Where demand is inelastic, the price of a good may, as a result, fall considerably, improving the terms of trade for net importers of foodstuffs.

(b) Political unrest or war in a country which is the main producer of a good, e.g. Kuwait (oil), may raise world prices and so improve the terms of trade for other major producers, e.g. the UK.

(c) Producing countries may form a successful monopoly to raise the price of their product, e.g. oil.

How *currency* exchange rates are determined is explained in Chapter 39. Basically they reflect the relative demand for exports and imports. Thus the improvement in the sterling exchange rate in 1980 was a reflection of Britain's becoming self-sufficient in oil, and even a net exporter.

But the currency exchange rate is also influenced by capital movements. Some of the 1996–7 improvement in the sterling exchange rate resulted from the movement of short-term capital to London because foreigners took advantage of higher interest rates as the Bank of England sought to control possible future inflation.

Thus a country's terms of trade can change even when there have been no real changes in the conditions of demand and supply simply because the value of its currency has altered on the foreign exchange market.

Measurement of the terms of trade

The terms of trade express the relationship between the price of imports and the price of exports. In practice, however, our interest is centred on this relationship not so much at any one time but rather as it changes over a period of time. We therefore measure relative changes in the terms of trade from one period to another.

Because countries import and export many goods, and the prices of different goods move in different ways and by varying amounts, we have to measure changes in the price of imports and exports as a whole by index numbers. And, it must be remembered, these are subject to defects (p. 413).

In practice, therefore the terms of trade are measured as follows:

$$\frac{\text{Index showing average price of exports}}{\text{Index showing average price of imports}} \times \frac{100}{1}$$

Actual figures are given in Table 37.1.

When a country's exports become cheaper relative to her imports, she will have to give more goods in exchange for a given quantity of imports. It is then said that the terms of trade have 'worsened', 'moved against her', or 'become less favourable'. If the opposite occurs, the terms of trade are said to have 'improved', 'moved in her favour', or 'become more favourable'. Table 37.1 shows that the terms of trade for the UK worsened in 2000–1, but have since improved.

Results of changes in the terms of trade

The direct effects of an improvement in a country's terms of trade are beneficial. First, she obtains more imports for a given quantity of exports. Second, her balance of payments may be improved. Suppose, for instance, that Britain's imports and exports are equal in value. Now suppose that the price of imports in sterling

Table 37.1 The terms of trade of the UK, 1995–2004 (base year 2002)

Year	Export unit-value index (1)	Import unit-value index (2)	Terms of trade (1) / (2)
1995	113.2	115.0	98.4
1996	113.9	114.8	99.2
1997	108.0	107.1	100.8
1998	102.7	100.7	102.0
1999	100.6	100.2	100.4
2000	101.7	103.5	98.3
2001	100.0	102.6	97.5
2002	100.0	100.0	100.0
2003	101.8	99.3	102.5
2004	102.0	98.7	103.3

Source: *Annual Abstract of Statistics.*

falls, but that the price of Britain's exports in sterling remains unchanged. If Britain's demand for imports is inelastic, the direct effect will be to improve her balance of payments, for less will be spent in sterling on imports. Similarly, if the demand for her exports were inelastic and their price in sterling rose, Britain's balance of payments would improve.

But the indirect results may make an improvement in the terms of trade, especially for a developed country, seem less desirable.

First, countries whose terms of trade have worsened may not be able to afford to buy the exports of the countries whose terms of trade have improved. For example, suppose that the price of wheat falls from £110 to £100 a tonne, but that '*A*' a major wheat exporting country, finds that demand increases only from 900,000 tonnes to 950,000 tonnes. Total expenditure on wheat falls, therefore, from £99 m to £95 m. But this expenditure equals approximately the income of her farmers who are exporting the bulk of their crop. As a result of the fall in income, their demand for the manufactured goods of '*B*', the wheat-importing country, would drop.

Second, the fall in income will also mean that less is spent on home-produced goods, thereby reducing profits. To the extent that firms of these countries are owned by British shareholders, lower dividend payments reduce the UK's invisible earnings.

Third, a fall in the incomes of less developed countries may mean that the loss must be made good by increased aid.

Fourth, the economies of countries which are dependent on foreign trade may be subjected to frequent adjustments if there are swings in the terms of trade. If, for instance, the price of gold fluctuates, incomes will be greater in South Africa when the price of gold is high, and smaller when the price of gold is low, because demand is inelastic. This has far-reaching effects on a policy aimed at stabilising income and employment.

37.4   FREE TRADE AND PROTECTION

Controlling international trade

Our earlier analysis suggests that trade should be as free as possible, for only then can maximum specialisation according to the law of comparative advantage take place. In practice, however, all countries follow policies which, to varying degrees, prevent goods from moving freely in response to differences in relative prices. Methods vary.

1.   Customs duties

Customs duties, e.g. the common external tariffs of the EU, are both revenue-raising and protective. They become protective when the imported good bears a higher rate of tax than the similar home-produced good.

2.   Subsidies

While countries which subscribe to the General Agreement on Tariffs and Trade (GATT) cannot follow a policy of 'dumping' exports by giving direct subsidies, the volume and pattern of international trade may be influenced indirectly by other means, e.g. government assistance to the shipbuilding industry. Less obviously, welfare benefits, e.g. child benefits and income supplements which keep down labour costs, may give one country a price advantage over another.

3.   Quotas

If demand is inelastic, the increase in price resulting from a customs duty will have little effect on the quantity imported. Thus, to restrict imports of a good to a definite quantity, quotas must be imposed. Compared with duties, quotas have two main disadvantages:

(a)   As a result of the artificial shortage of supply, the price may be increased by the foreign supplier or by the importer. Hence unless the government also introduces price control, they gain at the expense of consumers.

(b)   Quotas make for rigidity in the economy, for they are calculated on a formula, usually based on the volume of imports over a given period, which grows increasingly out of date with time. This penalises the efficient firm wishing to expand.

To avoid having formal quotas imposed, 'voluntary export restraints' may be agreed (e.g. on the import of Japanese cars to the UK).

4.   Currency control

A tighter check on the amount spent on imported goods can be achieved if quotas are fixed in terms of foreign currency. This necessitates some form of exchange control (see p. 503). All earnings of foreign currency or claims to foreign currency have to be handed over to the government and goods can be imported only under licence. Thus the government, not the free market, decides the priorities for imports.

5. Physical controls

A complete ban – an embargo – may be placed on the import or export of certain goods. Thus narcotics cannot be imported, while the export of certain high technology goods and works of art require a licence. Similarly, imposing strict technical standards for certain goods (e.g. milk) and regulating the importation of live animals (e.g. cattle, dogs and parrots) make trade more difficult.

6. Devices which divert trade

These include: 'Buy British' campaigns, Queen's Awards for Exporting, bilateral arrangements making import purchases dependent on the exporter buying goods of equal value from the importer, quarantine and health regulation and voluntary export restraints.

Reasons for government control of international trade

In general, trade is controlled because governments think and act nationally rather than internationally. Although people as a whole lose when trade is restricted, those of a particular country may gain.

Many reasons are put forward to justify control. Occasionally they have some logical justification; more usually they stem from a narrow interest seeking to gain advantages. We can examine the arguments, therefore, under three main headings: (1) those based on strategic, political, social, and moral grounds; (2) those having some economic basis; (3) those depending on shallow economic thinking.

1. Non-economic arguments

(a) *To encourage the production of a good of strategic importance.* Where a nation is dependent on another for a good of strategic importance, there is a danger of its supply being cut off in the event of war. Thus one argument for subsidising shipbuilding and aircraft production in the UK is to ensure the survival of plant and skilled labour.

(b) *To foster closer political ties.* As a member of the EU, Britain must impose a common external tariff as part of a movement towards political as well as economic unity.

(c) *To support political objectives.* Trade can be a weapon of foreign policy, e.g. the USA will not trade with Cuba because it disapproves of its communist policies.

(d) *To promote social policies.* Although in the past Britain has subsidised her agriculture mainly for strategic reasons, today the purposes are basically social – to avoid depression in rural districts.

2. Economic arguments having some justification

(a) *To raise revenue* (see p. 454).

(b) *To improve the terms of trade.* The incidence of a tax is shared between producer and consumer according to the relative elasticities of supply and demand (see p. 466). A government, therefore, can levy a tax on an imported good to improve the terms of trade if demand for the good is more elastic than the supply, for the increase in price is borne mainly by the producer, while the government has the proceeds of the tax. In practice this requires that: (i) the producing country has no alternative markets to which supplies can be easily diverted; (ii) her factors of production have few alternative uses; (iii) the demand for the exports of the country imposing the tariff must be unaffected by the loss of income suffered by countries who now find their sales abroad reduced.

(c) *To protect an 'infant industry'.* It may be possible to establish an industry in a country if, during its infancy, it is given protection from well-established competitors which are already producing on a large scale. Britain's car industry, for instance, benefited from such protection.

In practice, industries tend to rely on this protection, so that tariffs are never withdrawn; for example, American duties on manufactured goods imposed in the eighteenth century still persist today. Moreover, industries are often encouraged which without protection would have no chance of survival. This leads to maldistribution of a country's resources.

(d) *To enable an industry to decline gradually.* Fundamental changes in demand for a good may severely hit an industry. Such, for instance, was the fate of the British cotton industry in 1975. Restrictions on imports can cushion the shock, but in practice many industries do not make use of the breathing space to restructure.

(e) *To correct a temporary balance-of-payments disequilibrium.* A temporary drain on gold and foreign currency reserves may be halted by controlling imports. But if the depletion of the reserves is due to fundamental and lasting causes, other measures should be used (see Chapter 40).

(f) *To prevent 'dumping'.* Goods may be sold abroad at a lower price than on the home market. This may be possible because: (*a*) producers are given export subsidies; (*b*) discriminating monopoly is possible (see p. 189); or (*c*) it enables the producer to obtain the advantages of decreasing costs. People in the importing country benefit directly from the lower prices. If, however, the exporter is trying to obtain a monopoly position which he can exploit once home producers have been driven out, there is a case for protecting the home market.

3. Economic arguments having little validity

(a) *To retaliate against tariffs of another country*. The threat of a retaliatory tariff may be used to influence another country to change its restrictive policy. Thus in the 1992 GATT (subsequently the World Trade Organization) negotiations, the USA threatened to impose import duties on EU agricultural products unless EU subsidies were reduced. Such measures are usually ineffective, for countries often retaliate by imposing still higher duties, with everybody losing.

(b) *To maintain home employment in a period of depression*. Countries may place restrictions on imports to promote employment in the manufacture of home-produced goods. The difficulty is that other countries retaliate, thereby leading to an all-round contraction in world trade. GATT was set up to prevent this from happening (see p. 484).

(c) *To protect home industries from 'unfair' foreign competition*. The demand that British workers must be protected from competition by cheap, 'sweated' foreign labour usually comes from the industry facing competition. The argument, however, has little economic justification. First, it runs counter to the principle that a country should specialise where it has the greatest advantage. That advantage may be cheap labour. Second, low wages do not necessarily denote low labour costs. Wages may be low because labour is inefficient through low productivity. What is really significant is the wage-cost per unit of output. Thus the USA can export manufactured goods to the UK even though her labour is the-most highly paid in the world. The threatened industry can compete by improving productivity to reduce wage-cost per unit. Third, a tax on the goods of a poor country merely makes the country poorer and its labour cheaper. The way to raise wages (and the price of the good produced) is to increase demand in foreign markets. Indeed, if imports from poor countries are restricted, other help has to be given. They prefer 'trade to aid'. Fourth, protection, by reducing the income of the poorer countries, means that they have less to spend on Britain's exports. Fifth, the policy may lead to retaliation or aggressive competition elsewhere, thereby making it more difficult for the protecting country to sell abroad. One reason why Japan captured many of Britain's foreign markets for cotton goods was that her sales to Britain were restricted by protective barriers. Last, restrictions on competitive imports may allow home firms to raise their prices. If wage increases result, exports of goods generally could fall through higher prices.

Conclusions

While restriction of trade tends to lower living standards, there may be benefits – economic, political and social. Thus protection may be given to an industry because home workers cannot adjust quickly to other occupations or industries. Usually, however, such economic gains are doubtful. Others cannot be measured, and it has to be left to politicians to decide where the balance of advantage lies. It must, however, always be remembered that protection creates vested interests opposed to subsequent removal.

The General Agreement on Tariffs and Trade (GATT 1947–95) and the World Trade Organization (WTO 1995–)

The General Agreement on Tariffs and Trade, established in 1947, had three major objectives now embraced by the WTO: (i) to reduce existing trade barriers; (ii) to eliminate discrimination in international trade; and (iii) to prevent the establishment of further trade barriers by getting nations to agree to consult one another rather than take unilateral action. It operates as follows:

Member nations meet together periodically to try to agree on a round of tariff reductions. Here the 'most-favoured-nation' principle applies. This means that if one country grants a tariff concession to another it must apply automatically to all the other participating countries. Thus if the EU agrees to reduce tariffs on American automatic vending machines by 5 per cent in exchange for a 5 per cent reduction in the American tariff on EU man-made fibres, then both concessions must be extended to every other member of the WTO. This principle of non-discrimination also means that bilateral agreements and retaliatory tariffs against another country are out of harmony with the WTO.

Today (2006) there are over 149 member nations, accounting between them for over nine-tenths of world trade. Through the organisation, a progressive reduction in existing tariffs has been achieved, and the principle has been established that problems of international trade should be settled by cooperative discussion rather than by independent unilateral action. But difficulties have arisen:

(a) The principle of reciprocity means that low-tariff countries have to begin from an inferior bargaining position, and the concessions they can make are thus limited. Such countries may, therefore, prefer a low-tariff regional arrangement, such as the EU.

(b) In certain circumstances, the 'most-favoured-nation' principle may deter a country from making a tariff reduction to another country for the simple reason that it has to be applied to all.

(c) The Articles of the Agreement have had to be relaxed to allow for special circumstances – balance-of-payments difficulties, protection of agriculture, the establishment of 'infant' industries in less-developed countries, and the discriminatory character of the EU.

(d) While the WTO has been successful in dealing with tariffs and many physical barriers, it has been by-passed by the new forms of protection – voluntary export restraints, orderly marketing arrangements, subsidies for special groups of exports, and trading requirements as conditions for overseas investment.

The trade liberalisation procedure is through 'rounds' which bring together contracting parties. The Uruguay Round, the eighth, covered a period of hard bargaining between 1986 and 1994.

The WTO was established in 1995 to monitor the observance of the extensive agreements of the Uruguay Round. The importance of this round can be seen in the estimate of its value to world trade of £330 billion over ten years (including a 2 per cent increase in the UK's GDP.

The WTO aims to increase international trade by promoting lower trade barriers and providing a platform for the negotiation of trade. The WTO has a much broader scope than GATT. Whereas GATT regulated trade in merchandise goods, the WTO also covers trade in services, such as telecommunications and banking, and other issues such as intellectual property rights. China formally joined the WTO in December 2001 after a 15-year battle. Russia wants admission, but must first convince the EU and the US that it has reformed business practices.

The WTO follows these fundamental principles of trading:

1. A trading system should be free of discrimination in the sense that one country cannot privilege a particular trading partner above others within the system, nor can it discriminate against foreign products and services.
2. A trading system should tend toward more freedom, that is, toward fewer trade barriers (tariffs and non-tariff barriers).
3. A trading system should be predictable, with foreign companies and governments reassured that trade barriers will not be raised arbitrarily and that markets will remain open.
4. A trading system should tend toward greater competition.
5. A trading system should be more accommodating for less developed countries, giving them more time to adjust, greater flexibility and more privileges.

The stated aim of the WTO is to promote free trade and stimulate economic growth; but negotiations in recent years have been difficult, frequently failing to reach agreement. Many people argue that free trade does not make ordinary people's lives more prosperous but only results in the rich (both people and countries) becoming richer. WTO treaties have also been accused of a partial and unfair bias toward multinational corporations and wealthy nations.

CHAPTER SUMMARY

- International trade takes place because countries have different demands and different abilities to produce goods and services. Countries specialise where they have a comparative advantage in production and trade to obtain those goods where they do not.
- The terms of trade are the rate at which a country exchanges its exports for imports.
- An improvement in a country's terms of trade means that more imports can be obtained for a given quantity of exports.
- Despite the massive advantages of free trade, many countries in the world adopt protectionist measures to try to gain individually.
- The World Trade Organization exists to secure the advantages of free trade for its 149 member countries.

REVIEW QUESTIONS

- How can international trade improve living standards in a country?
- How are the terms of trade calculated?
- What would be the effect of a worsening of the terms of trade in the UK?
- What are the main advantages of international trade?
- Are there any valid arguments for protectionism?

 Visit the companion website for further questions

THE BALANCE OF PAYMENTS

LEARNING OBJECTIVES

After studying this chapter you should be able to:
- explain how exports pay for imports;
- analyse the UK balance of payments;
- describe the UK's trading position with the rest of the world.

38.1 PAYING FOR IMPORTS

Differences in currencies

Occasionally, international trade may take the form of a barter arrangement, one country agreeing to take so much of another country's produce in exchange for so much of its own. Normally, however, exchanges are arranged by private traders who, according to relative prices, decide whether it is profitable to export and import goods.

But different countries have different currencies – Japan (yen), EU countries (euros), the USA (dollars), the UK (£ sterling), and so on. This difference is important in international trade for two reasons: (a) sufficient foreign currency has to be obtained to pay for imports; (b) a rate has to be established at which one currency will exchange for another. The first will be considered forthwith, the second in the chapter which follows; but neither is independent of the other.

How are imports paid for?

We can best answer this question by first considering the purchases made by an individual, say Mrs Jones. Each week she buys a variety of goods. What is important for our purposes, however, is that there are at least seven sources from which she can obtain the money to pay for them.

The first and most usual source is the week's earnings, hers and her husband's, and Mrs Jones pays the shopkeeper on the spot with this money. It must be noted, however, that what in fact Mrs Jones is really doing is exchanging the goods which she and Mr Jones have specialised in producing for all the other goods needed. Thus, if Mr Jones is a tailor, the suits he makes are sold, and it is from the money thus obtained that Mrs Jones buys the goods the family needs. Furthermore, money is often earned, not by making goods, but by performing a service. Thus Mrs Jones herself may work a day each week for a shopkeeper, sending out accounts and answering correspondence. Last, interest on savings may provide some current income. Provided that all the weekly expenses are met out of this combined weekly income, we should say that the Jones family was 'paying its way'.

It might happen, however, that Mrs Jones's expenditure was not covered by the current weekly income. This might occur, for instance, because she bought a costly good, such as a dish-washer, which was not a regular item of weekly expenditure. In such circumstances Mrs Jones would have to raise the money from other sources. First, she could draw money from her National Savings account or from any another 'nest-egg'. Second, she could sell some household goods, such as the piano or the television set, for which she had a less urgent need. Third, she might be able to borrow the money from a friend or, what amounts to the same thing, ask the shopkeeper to forgo payment for the time being. Finally, if she were extremely fortunate, she might be able to obtain a gift of money, say from a doting father. Such methods of payment would be fairly satisfactory for a good which is in use over a long period, provided that her savings were gradually replenished, or the assets sold were replaced by assets of equal value, or that the loan was repaid during the lifetime of the good. Where, however, this does not happen, either because insufficient savings are put by out of weekly income or because the over-expenditure is a frequent occurrence, we would say that Mrs Jones is 'not paying her way'. In time her savings would run out, her home would be sold up, and she would be unable to obtain any more loans or credit from the shopkeeper.

Broadly speaking, a nation trading with other nations is in exactly the same position. The same alternatives are open to it in paying for goods it imports. The main source is money received from the sale of current exports. Figure 38.1 shows how an export earns foreign currency. In normal times importing and exporting are done by firms, and payments are arranged through banks, who exchange the currency of one country for the currency of another *provided that they have the necessary reserves of that currency*. Such reserves are earned by customers who export to foreign countries.

Let us assume that £1 sterling exchanges for $1.60 and that there are no currency restrictions. Suppose a British merchant X wishes to import cotton from A in the USA to the value of £100,000. The American exporter requires payment in dollars, for all payments, e.g. workers' wages, have to be made in dollars. Hence

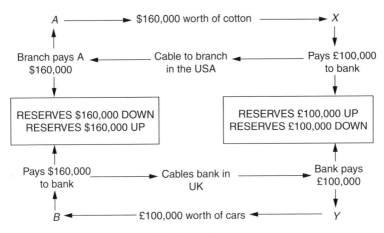

Figure 38.1 How exports pay for imports

the importer goes to a bank, pays in £100,000 and arranges a 'documentary credit'. The bank cables its branch in New York, authorising it to make the equivalent dollar payment to *A* on production of the necessary documents, e.g. the bill of lading. (Most banks have branches in foreign capitals; if not, they engage local banks to act for them.) But how is it that the branch has dollars available to honour the draft?

We can see this if we imagine that another British firm *Y* has sold £100,000 worth of cars to an importer *B* in the USA. This firm wants payment in £ sterling. Hence the American importer of the cars pays $160,000 into a bank in the USA, and the same procedure follows. It is obvious that the two transactions – buying cotton from the USA and selling cars from Britain – balance one another. The British bank's branch has had to pay out dollars, the American sterling. The British bank has received sterling, the American bank dollars. If the two get together, their requirements match. (In practice, it is more likely that they would meet their needs through the foreign-exchange market.) Thus the dollars needed for paying for the cotton are obtained by selling the cars and vice versa. In short, exports pay for imports.

'Exports' in the wider sense

In this connection the term 'exports' needs qualification. In the same way that Mrs Jones received payment for the service of sending out the shop-keeper's accounts, so a nation may receive payment, not only for the goods it exports, but also for services rendered to other countries. Goods exported are termed 'visible exports', because they can be seen and recorded as they cross the political boundaries between countries. Services performed for people of other countries, however, are called 'invisible exports', because they cannot be seen and recorded as they cross frontiers.

The main sources of invisible earnings and payments are:

1. *Government expenditure abroad,* e.g. overseas garrisons, diplomatic services.
2. *Shipping services,* e.g. an American travelling in the *Queen Elizabeth II* or shipping exports in a British merchantman.
3. *Civil aviation,* e.g. a German flying British Airways.
4. *Travel,* e.g. sterling required by an American tourist for spending on a visit to London.
5. *Financial services,* e.g. earnings of the City of London.
6. *Other services,* e.g. royalties earned on books and records, income from the transactions of overseas oil companies which ship direct from wells and refineries abroad to other countries.
7. *Interest, profits and dividends from overseas investments.*
8. *Government transfers,* e.g. net contribution to the EU.
9. *Private transfers,* e.g. remittances to relatives abroad.

Payments for any of the above transactions involve changing into another country's currency. Thus they represent 'imports' to the paying country and 'exports' to the receiving country.

38.2   THE BALANCE OF PAYMENTS

Most countries give an account each year of their monetary transactions with the rest of the world. The accounts presented are known as 'the balance of payments'. The balance of payments for the UK for the year ended 31 December 2005 is given in Table 38.1.

Table 38.1   The balance of payments of the UK, 2005 (£bn)

Trade deficit in goods	−65.6
Trade surplus in services	+18.7
Total trade	−46.9
Net investment income	+27.4
Net transfers	−12.4
Current balance	−31.9 (2.6 per cent of GDP)

Source: *Annual Abstract of Statistics.*

The current account

The current account shows, on the one hand, the foreign currency which has been *spent* on *imported goods* and *invisibles* in the course of the year, and, on the other, the foreign currency which has been *earned* by *exporting goods* and *invisibles*.

That part of the current account which shows the payments for just the goods exported and imported is known as the *visible balance* (formerly the *balance of trade*). Where the value of goods exported exceeds the value of goods imported, we say that there is a favourable visible balance. If the opposite occurs, the visible balance is 'unfavourable'. Too much, however, must not be read into the terms 'favourable' and 'unfavourable'. In the first place, we have to know the reasons for the unfavourable balance. It may be brought about, for instance, by an increased demand for raw materials and components as a country moves out of a recession. These will later be exported as manufactured goods. Or a less developed country may receive more aid, enabling her to import capital goods. Whereas the value of these is shown as 'imports', 'aid' will appear in the Financial Account. Secondly, a favourable or unfavourable visible balance can be reversed when the invisibles are taken into account.

When we add to the visible balance, payments and income on the invisible items, we have what is known as the *current balance*.

There is no special reason why earnings from goods and invisibles exported between 1 January and 31 December in any one year should equal expenditure on the goods and invisibles imported during that period. In fact, it would be an extraordinary coincidence if they did so. How often does what you earn during the week tally *exactly* with what you spend?

The current account is therefore likely to show a difference between earnings and expenditure. When the *value* of goods and invisibles exported exceeds the *value* of goods and invisibles imported, we say that there is a surplus current balance; when the reverse occurs, we say that there is a deficit current balance. The importance of the current balance is that it shows how far a country is paying its way.

However, the current account is only part of the statement covering a nation's overseas financial transactions. Capital flows must also be scrutinised. As we shall see, a current deficit need cause no alarm if it is covered by borrowing which will be put to a productive use. On the other hand, a current surplus may be insufficient to offset a heavy drain on the reserves through the outward movement of short- and long-term capital. The balance-of-payments statement must be examined as a whole.

The financial account

The *financial account* sets out the currency flow generated by current account balances and capital movements.

If the current-account transactions were a country's only dealings with the world, the balance-of-payments accounts would be quite simple. A surplus of

491

International trade

£100 million, for example, would add that amount to the reserves or allow the country to invest that amount overseas or to pay off short-term borrowings from the International Monetary Fund (IMF) or other foreign creditors. A deficit of £100 million would reduce the reserves by that amount or have to be financed by disinvestment or short-term borrowing abroad.

But *capital* flows also affect a country's ability to build up reserves or to pay off debts. Thus investment by private persons resident in the UK in factories or plant overseas (whether directly or by the purchase of shares), or a loan by the British government to a less-developed country, leads to an outflow of capital and the spending of foreign currency (negative sign in the accounts). Similarly, investment in the UK by persons overseas, or borrowing abroad by the British government, local authorities, or companies, leads to an inflow of foreign capital and the receipt of foreign currency (+ sign).

Whereas the current account covers *income* earning and spending in the course of the year, 'transactions in external assets and liabilities' show the movement of *capital* in and out of the country. This capital may be short- or long-term.

Short-term capital movements arise from the transfer of liquid funds to and from Britain. Because London is a world financial market centre, foreigners hold bank balances or short-term bills there. These short-term funds can move quickly from country to country to take advantage of higher interest rates or to guard against an exchange rate depreciation. They are thus often referred to as 'hot money'.

Long-term capital investment by British residents in factories or plant overseas (whether directly or by the purchase of shares), or a loan by the British government (e.g. to a less developed country or an international institution) leads to an outflow of capital. Similarly, investment in the UK by persons overseas or borrowing from abroad by the British government, local authorities, or companies leads to an inflow of foreign capital.

Any movement of capital out of Britain gives rise to a demand for foreign currency; a movement into Britain from abroad leads to the receipt of foreign currency.

No distinction is made between short- and long-term investment in presenting the overall balance of payments. In fact much of Britain's overseas investment is financed by short-term capital borrowed from foreigners, e.g. from the pool of Eurocurrency deposited in London. To the extent that this occurs, there is no net outflow of foreign currency. Britain's overseas investment which is undertaken in order to make a profit is, in fact, like private business ventures. And, just as the shopkeeper borrows from the bank to cover the holding of stocks before Christmas, so the UK borrows to finance investment overseas in factories, plantations, oil wells, nickel-mines, etc.

Thus the UK's balance-of-payments accounts concentrate on what is really significant to Britain – the extent to which currency flows as a whole influence the £ sterling exchange rate and her reserves of gold and foreign currencies.

The balancing item arises as follows. When all recorded capital transactions are added to the current balance, the total never adds up exactly to the amount of foreign currency the country has in fact gained or lost, which is known precisely to

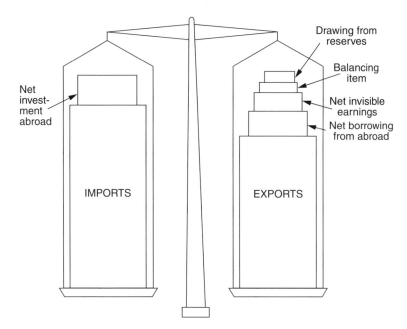

Figure 38.2   The balance of payments

the Bank of England. Government spending overseas, for instance, is easier to record exactly than the foreign spending of people taking holidays abroad. Exports, too, may go abroad in December, but payments for them come in the following February.

A 'balancing item' (see Figure 38.2) is therefore added to make up the difference between the total value of the transactions recorded and the precise accounts kept by the Bank of England. If the balancing item is '+', it means that more foreign currency has actually come in than the estimates of transactions have indicated. When there is a '−' balancing item, the opposite is the case.

The UK's balance of payments, 2005

The UK's current account deficit grew from £23.6 billion in 2004 to £31.9 billion in 2005. There were several contributory factors behind the increased deficit. The deficit on trade in goods increased by £5.2 billion to £65.6 billion as the UK became a net importer of oil for the first time since 1979. The surplus on trade in services declined by £2.7 billion to £18.7 billion, partly reflecting the payment of insurance claims associated with Hurricane Katrina. Net current transfer payments abroad increased by £1.5 billion to £12.4 billion as a result of a rise in payments to EU institutions reflecting the first full year of the enlarged EU. These effects were slightly offset by a small rise in the income surplus, which rose £1.0 billion to £27.4 billion.

The current account deficit in 2005 was equivalent to −2.6 per cent of GDP compared with −2.0 per cent in 2004 and is at its highest percentage since 1999. While the current account deficit is the highest on record in cash terms, as a percentage of GDP the deficits of the mid-1970s and late 1980s were far greater. Deficits at these times reached −4.0 per cent and −5.1 per cent of GDP respectively.

CHAPTER SUMMARY

....

- A nation pays for the goods and services it imports by exporting goods and services.
- If imports of goods and services exceed exports there is a trade deficit.
- If exports of goods and services exceed imports there is a trade surplus.
- Capital flows also affect the balance-of-payments accounts and they can be sufficient to turn a trade deficit into a balance-of-payments surplus; or a trade surplus into a balance-of-payments deficit.
- In 2005, the UK had a balance-of-payments deficit equivalent to 2.6 per cent of GDP.

REVIEW QUESTIONS

....

- How are a country's imports paid for?
- What are the different accounts of the UK balance of payments?
- What were the main features of the UK balance of payments in 2005?

 Visit the companion website for further questions

FOREIGN EXCHANGE RATES

39.1   HOW ARE EXCHANGE RATES DETERMINED?

Trade between countries involves, as we have seen, an exchange of their currencies. But how is the rate at which one currency exchanges for another determined? Why is it that we have to give a pound coin to obtain about 1.60 American dollars, 2.41 Swiss francs, 1.45 euros, and so on?

The simple answer is that the price of the pound sterling, like other prices, is determined by the forces of demand and supply. In this case the market is known as the 'foreign-exchange market'. It meets in no one place, but consists of all the institutions and persons – the banks of all kinds, dealers, and brokers – who are buying and selling foreign currencies. The foreign-exchange market is a world market, dealers throughout the world being in constant contact with one another by telecommunications.

Let us assume that we have 'freely fluctuating exchange rates'; that is, rates are not fixed by governments, but are free to move from day to day according to changes in the conditions of demand and supply. To discover how a change in the exchange rate can come about, we can glance once again at the mechanism of foreign payments.

When the British merchant wished to import cotton from the USA (see p. 489), he went to his bank to obtain the necessary dollars for payment. These dollars, we saw, were obtained from its branch in the USA, and this branch in its turn had received them from an American importer of cars who had deposited them in

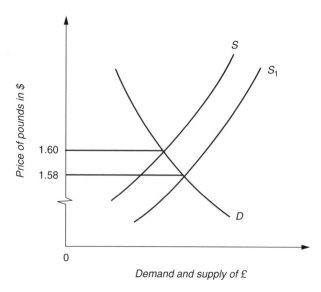

Figure 39.1   The determination of exchange rates

exchange for the pounds sterling he needed to pay the British motor firm. Let us assume that the existing exchange rate is $1.60 to the pound sterling and that trade is such that the same quantity of dollars is both demanded and supplied (Figure 39.1).

The situation, we will imagine, now changes. Imports of cotton from the USA increase in value, but exports of cars remain the same. The bank now finds that because more dollars are being demanded than are being deposited, its reserves of dollars are depleted. In short, the demand for dollars exceeds the supply. It is possible that the bank will be able to find on the foreign-exchange market another bank or dealer who is receiving more dollars than pounds sterling. But if its experience is typical of the rest of the market, that is, there has been a general increase in the demand for dollars relative to pounds, it will be able to replenish its reserves of dollars only by offering more pounds sterling in exchange, and the supply curve moves to S_1. The dollar thus appreciates in value to $1.58 to the pound. (As we shall see later, this will, to a large extent, bring a self-correcting mechanism into operation as regards the lack of balance between the value of imports and the value of exports.)

39.2   ARBITRAGE

We have concentrated our attention on the rate of exchange between the dollar and the pound. But there is also an exchange rate between the pound and the

Swiss franc, the euro, and so on; and all these rates are linked with one another. If, for instance, £1 = $2 and $1 = 2 Swiss francs, then £1 must equal 4 Swiss francs. Otherwise, what are known as arbitrage operations by foreign-exchange dealers would bring the rates into line. Thus suppose in London 5 Swiss francs can be obtained for the pound. A dealer would buy Swiss francs for pounds in London, sell them for dollars in New York, and exchange the dollars for pounds, making 25p profit on the deal. This would not last for long because the world market in foreign exchange is so perfect that the increased demand for Swiss francs in London would soon bring the price there into line with the world price.

39.3 WHAT ARE THE FACTORS UPON WHICH THE DEMAND FOR OR SUPPLY OF FOREIGN CURRENCY DEPEND?

It can be seen that an increased demand for dollars by people in Britain is one and the same thing as an increase in the supply of sterling being offered for dollars. An increased demand for dollars may be counteracted by an increased demand for sterling (that is, an increased supply of dollars) by Americans. For the sake of simplicity, we will concentrate our attention on the factors leading to a demand for sterling by Americans. These factors are:

1. To pay for the import of goods from Britain.
2. To pay for 'invisibles', e.g. a tour of Britain, government spending on diplomatic staff in Britain, etc.
3. To meet capital movements into Britain (p. 491).

39.4 WHAT ARE THE UNDERLYING ECONOMIC FORCES INFLUENCING HOW MUCH FOREIGN CURRENCY IS DEMANDED AND SUPPLIED?

So far we have merely indicated the items for which foreign currency will be demanded or supplied. Now we examine the economic forces which determine how large each of these items will be. They are:

1. Relative prices

The chief factor affecting trade, both visible and invisible, is the price of home-produced goods as compared with the price of similar goods abroad. If, for example, American prices are high, Americans will wish to import cheaper British goods, whereas the British will prefer home-produced goods to American.

The increased demand for sterling will, in a free exchange market, so raise the value of the pound sterling that eventually the prices of British goods are in line with those of the 'high-cost' American producer.

Some economists, notably Professor Gustav Cassel in 1922, carried this argument a stage further. They said quite categorically, in what became known as the *purchasing power parity theory*, that the value of a foreign currency in terms of another depends mainly on the relative purchasing power of the two currencies in their respective countries. In other words, the exchange rate settles at the level which makes the purchasing power of a given currency the same in whatever country it is spent.

For example, suppose that there is only one commodity, machines, and this machine sells for £200 in Britain and for $340 in the USA; then the rate of exchange would be 1.70 dollars to the pound. If now, through inflation, the price in Britain rises to £220, the rate of exchange will be 1.55 dollars to the pound. Thus a fall in the internal purchasing power of a currency through a rise in the general level of prices leads to a corresponding fall in its foreign-exchange value. Or mathematically, the purchasing power parity theory says that:

$$\text{Foreign exchange price of } £ \text{ (e.g. in dollars)} = \frac{\text{US price level}}{\text{British price level}}$$

When we are considering the long period, there is considerable truth in this theory. If, for instance, there is an inflation of prices in Britain relative to the USA, there will be less demand for British exports, but an increased demand for American imports. As a result, the price of the pound sterling falls in terms of the dollar. But, particularly in the short run, to say that overall purchasing power is the sole factor governing exchange rates is a gross oversimplification. The theory fails to allow for the following:

(a)   Not all goods enter into international trade. Quite a number, for instance Chinese herbal medicines, satisfy local and particular wants. Others, like houses, railway travel, gas and electricity, haircuts, and personal and professional services, cannot be transported easily from one country to another. The prices of such goods may rise considerably, whereas those of exports remain the same. Eventually, export industries will be forced by competition to pay higher wages, etc., but owing to immobility and imperfections of the market, this may take a very long time to come about. In the meantime, exchange rates will not be affected – in spite of the statistical rise in the general level of prices.

(b)   Such factors as indirect taxes, subsidies, and transport costs may change the prices of goods within a country but not affect exchange rates in the way the theory predicts. Suppose a 100 per cent tariff is placed on an important import, the demand for which is not absolutely inelastic. The price in the home market would rise, but since less *foreign* currency would be spent on it, the exchange rate would tend to improve!

(c)   A change in the exchange rate may originate in factors quite independent of the internal price level. When national income rises, for instance, imports are likely to increase in value relative to exports. As a result, the external value of the currency will depreciate. Similarly, a change in the terms of trade may affect the exchange rate. For instance, the 1986 fall in the price of oil led to a depreciation of the £ sterling on the foreign-exchange market.

(d)   The theory ignores the effect of movements of capital upon the exchange rates, an influence which is particularly important in the short period.

The purchasing power parity theory, therefore, is not a complete explanation of what determines exchange rates. In particular, it disregards the effect of capital movements both for investment and speculative purposes, and overlooks the fact that prices in the export industries may move differently from prices in other industries. But this does not mean that the theory has no value. Since imports and exports are the major items in a country's balance of payments, it draws attention to what, in the long run, is the dominant influence on exchange rates – how the internal price level moves relative to that of other countries. Indeed, there is a close link between this and the movement of capital for speculative purposes, for the latter is likely to reinforce changes in the exchange rates originating in the current account of the balance of payments.

2.   Relative money incomes

When a country's money income expands, its demand for imports increases. Potential exports also tend to be diverted to the home market.

3.   Long-term investment prospects

People can invest capital in foreign countries either by buying the bonds of foreign governments or the equities of companies there, or directly by building factories abroad as offshoots of parent companies in the UK. The chief factor influencing such investment decisions is how the prospective yield compares with that which could be obtained elsewhere.

Political risks, e.g. of default on loans, or possible changes in government policy, e.g. of a swingeing increase in corporation tax, have also to be assessed by those investing overseas.

4.   The rate of interest

Short-term capital moves from one country to another as changes take place in the rate of interest being offered by each. The government can therefore vary interest rates to attract or repel foreign capital as it sees fit.

5. Speculation on the future movements of the exchange rate

Inflation in a country will be interpreted by foreign holders of its currency as being likely to lead also to a fall in the external value of the currency. Selling of the currency follows, thereby helping to bring about the fulfilment of those expectations!

6. Government expenditure

Military expenditure and economic aid abroad now provide large sources of supply of certain currencies, e.g. the American dollar and the pound sterling, to foreigners.

It can be seen, therefore, that exchange rates are not dependent on any single factor. The only safe generalisation which can be made is that the value of a currency depends upon all the forces which give rise to the purchase or sale of that currency in the foreign-exchange market.

CHAPTER SUMMARY
....

- The value of the currency is determined by the demand for it and the supply of it on the foreign exchanges.
- Broadly speaking, demand for the currency is determined by the demand for the country's exports; and supply of the currency is determined by the demand for imports.
- Capital movements are also important and so the rate of interest influences the value of the currency.
- Other factors such as long-term investment prospects, the level of national income, speculation and government spending also have an influence on the exchange rate.

REVIEW QUESTIONS
....

- Illustrate how the value of a currency is determined in a free market or 'floating' situation.
- What are the main influences on the value of the UK currency?
- Why does the purchasing power parity theory not always hold?

 Visit the companion website for further questions

40

THE CORRECTION OF A BALANCE-OF-PAYMENTS DISEQUILIBRIUM

LEARNING OBJECTIVES

After studying this chapter you should be able to:

- explain why it is necessary for a country to correct a balance of payments disequilibrium;
- describe methods to correct an imbalance in the balance of payments;
- show the disadvantages of expenditure-reducing policies;
- assess the difficulties of expenditure-switching policies.

40.1 ALTERNATIVE APPROACHES

When do corrective measures become necessary?

Taken as a whole, the balance of payments must always balance. Foreign currency necessary for making payments abroad must have come from somewhere. If a current account deficit is not covered by private borrowing from overseas, there is an outward currency flow which has to come from the gold and foreign currency reserves or official borrowing.

In the short period, a balance-of-payments deficit may not be serious. It could easily happen that, just prior to 31 December, the date usually chosen for drawing up the accounts, imports of raw materials were running at a high rate. Later, when the goods manufactured from these raw materials are sold abroad, the reserves will be replenished. Reserves of gold and foreign currencies are held for this very purpose – to provide a 'cushion' when current earnings and private borrowing are temporarily insufficient to cover payments abroad. Even individuals usually carry spare cash to bridge the gap between income and spending.

Alternatively, a less developed country may run an adverse current balance for a number of years. The deficit is covered by borrowing, both private and official. Loans are used to buy capital equipment. Eventually, this equipment will allow her to export goods which will cover the interest due and then the repayment of the loan itself. Once again, the balance-of-payments deficit need not be frowned upon; it is just good business – like a firm obtaining a loan from the bank.

But the situation is different when year after year a country is running a current balance deficit and there is little likelihood of its being able to reverse the trend. This disequilibrium between credits and debits is then said to be of a 'fundamental nature'. If not corrected, foreign creditors will refuse to lend for they doubt whether the spendthrift will ever be in a position to repay and reserves will run out. Action has to be taken, therefore, to remedy the situation.

A broad analysis of the problem

A first-aid measure is for the authorities to raise the short-term rate of interest in order to reverse the outward flow of short-term capital. Furthermore, reserves could be strengthened by borrowing from other central banks and the IMF. This would help to restore confidence in the currency.

Eventually, however, exports must be increased in value and/or imports decreased in value.

There are two basic policies which can be followed: (1) reducing expenditure on imports; (2) switching expenditure, so that foreigners spend more on British exports and Britons spend less on imports in favour of home produced goods. Both policies can be followed simultaneously (though with a different emphasis on each), but it is easier to clarify the issues by considering them separately.

40.2   REDUCING EXPENDITURE ON IMPORTS: DEFLATION

The difficulty of increasing exports

A government may adopt policies to promote exports. Thus the British government guarantees payment through the Export Credits Guarantee Department and provides information on the possibility of developing markets abroad. Although under the terms of the WTO it is impossible to grant direct tax reliefs, incentives can be incorporated in indirect taxes; for example, zero-rating VAT on exports.

Increasing the value of exports by such means, however, takes time and is largely only marginal to the problem. The main immediate thrust has to be directed to reducing expenditure on-imports. This may be achieved by both physical controls and deflation of home income.

Physical controls

Physical controls may be exercised by import duties, quotas and exchange control.

1. Import duties and quotas

Tariffs may be levied to increase the price of imports. But if demand is inelastic, imports will not be greatly discouraged nor expenditure on them in terms of foreign currency greatly decreased. Sometimes, therefore, an import quota in terms of volume is imposed. As a result, however, the advantages of free trade are reduced, while the efficiency of home industry may be impaired by its protection from foreign competition. Moreover, other exporting countries may retaliate.

2. Exchange control

Exchange control may be introduced to:

(a) limit the amount of foreign currency spent on imports;
(b) discriminate against those countries whose currencies are 'hard' (that is, cannot easily be earned by exporting to them), and to favour those countries whose currencies are 'soft' (because they buy exports from the country concerned);
(c) distinguish between essential and non-essential imports;
(d) control the export of capital.

Exchange control is essential when a country's currency is overvalued – that is, its declared exchange rate is higher than it would be if it were determined by demand and supply on the foreign-exchange market. What this really means is that foreign currencies are valued below the market price – and so they have to be rationed.

Pegging the rate at a high level, however, may be advantageous to the country, particularly if her demand for imports and supply of exports are inelastic. In such circumstances, the balance of payments might not be improved by reducing the external value of the currency (see pp. 509–11).

Nevertheless, exchange control suffers from many of the disadvantages associated with rationing. Inefficient home firms are protected from foreign competition. Regulations are evaded and 'black markets' in the currencies occur. Many administrators are needed who could be more productively employed elsewhere. Moreover, it can lead to uncertainty in international trade. Countries may find their regular markets closed, while firms cannot plan ahead because of uncertainty as to whether they will be allowed to purchase their raw materials from a hard-currency area. Furthermore, the confidence of foreigners is impaired if any attempt is made to prohibit the movement of their funds out of a country. Finally, when people are prevented from buying in hard-currency countries, it often means that they are forced to purchase dearer or inferior goods elsewhere.

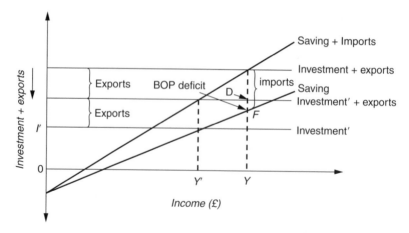

Figure 40.1 Achieving balance-of-payments equilibrium by deflation

Deflation of home income

Since imports increase as income expands, one way in which the value of imports can be brought into line with that of exports is by reducing income. Figure 40.1 explains the situation.

We assume an economy with no government spending or taxation, injections consisting of autonomous investment and exports, and leaks of saving and imports related to income. At the current level of income, Y, there is a current balance-of-payments deficit, DF. Assuming exports are maintained, this deficit can be eliminated by bringing down the level of investment to I' reducing income to Y'.

Such a deflationary policy would also tend to put a brake on any rise in home prices. More important, it allows adjustment to take place without altering currency-exchange rates (see below). This has the advantage that it facilitates trade by removing the uncertainty associated with fluctuating exchange rates (see p. 507). But there are serious disadvantages:

1. Unless home prices are flexible downwards, a deflationary policy can only succeed at the expense of creating unemployment. Thus in Figure 40.1 if Y were the full employment level of income, the fall to Y' would represent a rise in unemployment. In practice costs, particularly wage rates, prove to be rigid, so that home prices are sticky.
2. There is a low income-elasticity of demand for many imports, e.g. essential raw materials and components.
3. Any reduction of imports to Britain represents a loss of exports by other countries. Deflationary effects on their economies may result in a reduction in their demand for imports, thereby reducing British exports. In short, deflation is a 'beggar-my-neighbour' policy where the benefit is uncertain even to the deflating country.

The gold standard

The old gold standard was basically such a deflationary mechanism for correcting a balance-of-payments deficit. All major currencies had a declared value in terms of gold. If, for instance, Britain had a balance-of-payments deficit, foreign currency would be demanded. But the sterling exchange rate could not fall a great deal because it soon became cheaper to pay for imports with gold.

Purchases of gold were paid for by cheques drawn on the commercial banks, who drew gold from the Bank of England. This lowered their cash reserve and so the commercial banks had to reduce their lending. Furthermore, to protect its reserves, the Bank raised the bank rate. Other interest rates moved in sympathy.

Higher rates of interest attracted foreign capital, thereby halting the export of gold. But, by discouraging investment, they also set in motion a deflationary process. It was assumed that the contraction of income would result in a fall in costs, and thus lower home prices. In practice, as noted above, this proved difficult. As a result, restoration of balance-of-payments equilibrium was achieved, not so much by expanding exports but, as incomes fell, by a reduction in imports. Eventually unemployment did produce a fall in costs and, as exports became cheaper relative to foreign goods, the flow of trade was reversed.

In the meantime, however, the deflationary process caused severe suffering. Rather than continue with this, the UK and most other countries abandoned the gold standard in the 1930s.

It should be noted that a declared central exchange rate under the ERM (the Exchange Rate Mechanism of the European Union – the precursor of the euro) produced a similar sequence of events (see pp. 526–7).

40.3 EXPENDITURE-SWITCHING: DEPRECIATION OF THE EXCHANGE RATE

Expenditure-switching by exchange rate adjustment

The merits of a fixed exchange rate is that it facilitates trade and imposes a discipline on countries to maintain the internal value of the currency in order to hold the rate. Its big disadvantage is that a country cannot follow an independent internal monetary policy in order to promote full employment.

If it is decided to give employment priority, policy can take the form of expenditure-switching, with foreigners spending more on British exports and Britain spending less on imports. While some switching can be enforced by government control of import expenditure (p. 503), the most effective method is to alter the relative prices of imports and home-produced goods.

Prices of internationally traded goods are composed of: (1) the home producer's price, and (2) the exchange rate. Thus British exports can be made more competitive in world markets by lowering the rate at which the £ sterling exchanges for foreign currencies. Because fewer units of foreign currency have now to be given up to obtain a £ sterling, foreigners can buy British exports more cheaply. Similarly, imports to Britain now cost more in terms of sterling, encouraging Britons to switch to the relatively cheaper home-produced goods. Provided that, taken together, the demand for both exports and imports is sufficiently elastic, there will be a correction of Britain's balance-of-payments deficit (see pp. 509–11).

Such corrective exchange-rate adjustments occur automatically through the forces of demand and supply in a freely operating foreign-exchange market. Thus if the USA's exports to Britain are greater in value than her imports from Britain, the demand for dollars will increase, for British importers will be wanting them to pay for the USA goods. Consequently the exchange rate will move against sterling. This will raise the price in sterling of Britain's imports from the USA, and lower the price in dollars of British exports to the USA. Demand responses to these price changes tend to bring about equality in value of British imports and exports.

Advantages and disadvantages of exchange depreciation as a means of correcting a balance-of-payments disequilibrium

Exchange depreciation has the advantage that this correction is effected without the tribulations of deflation. Instead a country can follow its own internal monetary policy – even reflating if it thinks that this is desirable in the interests of reducing unemployment.

Moreover, with freely fluctuating exchange rates (when the value of the currency 'floats'), the correction is secured without the many controls which are often necessary when the exchange rate is 'pegged' (see p. 507) because reserves do not have to be protected.

Unfortunately, fluctuating exchange rates are themselves not without disadvantages.

First, the demand for exports and imports may be so inelastic that the balance-of-payments disequilibrium is made worse by depreciation rather than better (see p. 509). Supply, too, may be so inelastic that a country cannot take advantage of the expanded demand for its exports which follows a fall in the exchange value of its currency (see pp. 509–11). It should be emphasised, however, that such conditions are possible rather than likely.

Second, fluctuating exchange rates may deflect a government from pursuing policies to maintain the internal purchasing power of its currency. Instead export prices are made competitive by foreign exchange depreciation. Unfortunately, such depreciation tends to be continuous for, as the prices of imports also rise, home costs and prices are increased, giving a push to further inflation through wage demands, etc.

Third, freely fluctuating exchange rates encourage speculation, thereby making movements more frequent and pronounced. Speculative capital moves according to the holder's estimate of the future value of currencies. Similar speculation occurs with trade. Foreign importers of British goods who expect the price of sterling to depreciate delay paying for the goods as long as possible, a situation described as 'lags'. British importers of foreign goods make their payments in foreign currency as soon as possible, described as 'leads'. The importance of speculation is that it can bring about the very rise or fall in the exchange rate that was expected. On the other hand, dealers who quote fixed 'future' prices for foreign currencies on the 'forward' market serve, to some extent, to even out exchange rate fluctuations.

Fourth, fluctuating exchange rates add to the normal uncertainties associated with foreign trade for this usually involves granting credit and even entering into long-term contracts. By the time an exporter receives payment for his goods, the exchange rate may have moved so adversely that the expected profit has been turned into a loss. In such circumstances the exporter may prefer not to take the risk of an adverse movement in the exchange rate. Although this risk can usually be transferred to a foreign exchange dealer by a 'forward' exchange arrangement (that is, the foreign currency can be obtained at a given future date at an agreed price), trade may still not be worthwhile through the additional cost involved.

Finally, uncertainty of the future exchange rate can similarly discourage long-term international investment.

40.4 MANAGED FLEXIBILITY: 'PEGGED' EXCHANGE RATES BY INTERVENTION

The exchange equalisation account

When Britain left the gold standard in 1931, she followed a policy of flexible exchange rates. Nevertheless, to cancel out fluctuations in the exchange rate brought about by movements of short-term capital, the government set up the Exchange Equalisation Account.

The Account operates by the simple application of the laws of price. It has a stock of gold and foreign currencies (mostly borrowed against Treasury bills), and this stock is either replenished or offered on the market according to whether short-term capital is moving into or out of London. For instance, a movement of capital into London from the USA would increase the demand for the £ sterling and drive up its price; the Account can prevent this rise by offering pounds in exchange for dollars (see Figure 39.1). On the other hand, if there were a movement of capital out of London, the Account would offer dollars in exchange for pounds, thereby reducing its stock of dollars and increasing its holding of pounds.

The knowledge that such an Account exists to even out exchange fluctuations has done much to prevent speculation in the value of the pound. Provided it has adequate reserves of foreign currency, the Account can allow that value to appreciate or depreciate, and this it continues to do.

The International Monetary Fund (IMF)

The major defect of a system of freely fluctuating exchange rates is that it tends to discourage international trade. Countries, therefore, attempted to stabilise the exchange value of their currencies and an international code of behaviour to achieve this was drawn up at the Bretton Woods Conference in 1944. This established the International Monetary Fund (IMF) and the International Bank for Reconstruction and Development (IBRD, the 'World Bank'). Whereas the IMF makes short-term funds available to meet a temporary balance-of-payments deficit (see below), the World Bank provides long-term finance for reconstruction and development – the building of roads, irrigation schemes, power stations, etc. – especially in the less developed countries.

A system of 'managed flexibility' was operated through the IMF. Each member country agreed to maintain free convertibility of its currency at an agreed rate and contribute its quota of currency to a pool held by the IMF. From these reserves, the IMF could make foreign currency available to a country running a short-term balance of payments deficit. Should this balance-of-payments disequilibrium prove to be 'fundamental', devaluation of the country's currency was possible under agreed rules.

The Bretton Woods agreement worked tolerably well for twenty-five years. But it suffered from two main weaknesses:

1. The pressure of exchange adjustment fell almost entirely on debtor nations (who were forced to devalue) rather than on creditor nations (who could have eased part of the burden by revaluing).
2. Little provision was made for the expansion of international liquidity to service an increasing world trade.

We consider each in turn.

Exchange adjustment

While the UK and, later, the USA were frequent 'persistent debtor' nations, Germany and Japan were 'persistent creditor' countries. Both the latter countries, however, proved reluctant to revalue their currencies, fearing that the rise in the price of their exports which this would entail would make them uncompetitive in world markets.

The result was that, in order to maintain the existing exchange rate, the UK in particular had to deflate her economy (the 'stop' policy) whenever balance-of-payments difficulties arose. To some extent this could be regarded as the just penalty for her inability to prevent prices rising as her economy expanded.

The decisive step was taken in June 1972, when once again sterling came under pressure as the British economy expanded. The Heath government would not allow the maintenance of a fixed exchange rate to stand in the way of economic expansion. Thus the 'pegged' pound was abandoned: instead the pound was allowed to 'float', its value being arrived at on the foreign exchange market. Eventually all other major trading countries adopted floating exchange rates, but with intervention in the market through their own equivalent of the Exchange Equalisation Account.

Conditions necessary for successful exchange depreciation/devaluation

Where countries maintain an agreed rate of exchange between their currencies, depreciation takes the form of *devaluation* a once-for-all reduction in the value of a country's currency by definite government decision as opposed to a continuous fall on the foreign exchange market. But both depreciation and devaluation involve a reduction in the rate at which a country's currency exchanges for other currencies, so that, in examining the effects, the same broad principles apply.

Let us suppose that the UK trades only with the USA and that she has a persistent balance-of-payments deficit. The value of the pound falls from $1.65 to $1.50. Whether such depreciation is successful or not will depend upon the answers to the following questions.

1. What is the elasticity of demand for exports and imports?

The effect of the depreciation will be to make British exports cheaper in terms of dollars to the American buyer and imports from America dearer in terms of pounds to the British buyer.

A British good formerly selling in the USA for $1.65 need now cost only $1.50. This fall in price should lead to more British goods being demanded, and if elasticity of demand is greater than unity, more dollars will be earned.

Similarly, an American good worth $1.65 formerly cost the British buyer £1. After the depreciation, the price will rise to £1.10. But will this mean that we have to spend more *dollars* on our imports? The answer is 'no'. (Suppose that you are on a camping holiday in the USA and that the pound is devalued. Will your bread, camp site, etc. change in price?) The worst possible situation is when demand for imports is absolutely inelastic; then the same quantity of imports will be demanded and the same amount of dollars spent on them. Otherwise there will be some contraction of demand (because the price in terms of pounds has risen) and then expenditure in dollars will fall.

The two elasticities of demand for exports and imports must be considered together. Even if the demand for imports is absolutely inelastic (so that the same amount of foreign currency is spent on them), the balance of payments will not deteriorate provided that there is a gain of foreign currency from an increased demand for exports.

What is the probable situation in the real world for the UK as regards the elasticities of demand for imports and exports? Demand for imports is likely to be fairly inelastic, consisting, for instance, of raw-materials, essential components and tropical foodstuffs. Indeed, if her exports expand, demand for raw materials and components will increase. Offsetting this is a likely fall in British demand for luxuries and foreign travel on account of the greater cost, home-produced goods and holidays now being more competitive.

On the other hand, the demand for British exports as a whole is probably elastic. Not only could she undersell exporting competitors, e.g. in aero engines or electrical equipment, but the lower export price resulting from the depreciation would convert what were formerly 'potential exports' into real exports. Moreover, such items as tourism are likely to have a highly elastic demand. But it must be remembered that the price of exported goods will not fall by the entire amount of the depreciation. Their home price will rise when they are made from imported raw materials or components.

2. What is the elasticity of supply of exports?

It is on the supply side that the greatest obstacles to a successful depreciation are likely to be encountered. The fall in the price of exports will probably lead to an expansion of demand, but this will provide no lasting cost advantage if the supply of exports cannot be increased without the home price rising. Here the reaction of labour to the effects of depreciation is crucial. The increase in the cost of imports raises the cost of living. There is thus a strong temptation to demand wage increases. Moreover, labour is in a strong position, because demand for exports should increase following the devaluation. If the trade unions exploit their position, the resultant rise in wages could soon wipe out the cost advantage which Britain had gained and further depreciation would occur.

It should be noted, however, that where demand for British exports is inelastic, then inelasticity of supply may not be detrimental. The exporter can maintain his price *in terms of foreign currency* to foreign importers, and British earnings of foreign currency may not fall.

3. What is the elasticity of supply of imports?

If foreigners are dependent on the British market, and supply is inelastic, then they may be willing to reduce their prices. This may reduce Britain's expenditure of foreign currency, although in volume imports are almost as great.

4. What is the nature of British and American investments with each other?

Suppose British investments in the USA are mostly in the form of shares in companies there. Profits will be earned in dollars and so there will be no loss of foreign currency after depreciation.

On the other hand, if American investments in the UK are in stock with interest fixed in sterling, the USA will lose by depreciation of the pound for she gets fewer dollars than formerly in invisible earnings.

5. Will countries fear further depreciation?

Depreciation reduces the value of sterling securities held by foreigners, including the sterling balances held in London. In the first place, this may destroy confidence in sterling, undermining London's position as a banking centre. Business is transferred elsewhere, and invisible earnings are lost. Second, unless positive measures are taken to correct the underlying inflation, foreigners will fear further depreciation and so hasten to remove their capital from London, bringing about what they fear.

The above arguments suggest that, for a country like Britain, depreciation provides no escape from dealing with inflation. It may entail a serious deterioration in the terms of trade, a large amount of additional exports having to be given to achieve a small gain in the balance of payments. Indeed, where demand for both imports and exports is highly inelastic or where supply is inelastic, depreciation may cause the balance of payments to deteriorate still further. In this case, a country has to resort to physical controls to reduce imports.

The application of the above considerations to the UK's present balance of payments deficit is developed in Chapter 42.

40.5 INTERNATIONAL LIQUIDITY

Just as money in our pockets or at the bank is necessary to finance our everyday purchases, so people dealing in international markets require reserves of an acceptable form to finance international trade.

The one form that is always acceptable is gold. Unfortunately, the supply of gold does not increase fast enough to keep pace with the expansion of world trade and the corresponding need for larger reserves as surpluses and deficits increase in size. In the past, the difficulty was overcome by holding reserves in other currencies, e.g. dollars and sterling. These were convertible into gold, and were known as 'reserve currencies'. Holding reserve currencies instead of gold had the additional advantage that a rate of interest was earned, whereas there is no return on holding gold.

The willingness to hold a reserve currency, however, only lasts as long as there is little possibility of the reserve currency being devalued. Persistent balance-of-payments deficits undermine confidence, and there will then be a tendency to move out of the reserve currency. This is what happened in 1972 and 1973, first to the pound sterling, and then to the dollar.

To some extent the shortage of international liquidity has been made good by economising in the reserves through pooling arrangements, e.g. in the IMF and by the central banks of the Group of Ten. But what was needed was a new form of reserve to provide *additional* assets.

Special Drawing Rights (SDRs) – in contrast to the ordinary drawing rights of the IMF – are such an addition. Beginning in 1970, they have been issued by the IMF as a line of credit to members in proportion to their quotas. The value of SDRs is expressed in terms of a basket of sixteen major currencies weighted according to their international importance and calculated according to their daily value on the foreign exchange market.

Both the IMF and its members have agreed to honour SDRs. Thus a member country can use them to purchase foreign currency in order to support its exchange rate, and the countries with a strong balance of payments can be required to accept SDRs up to twice their own quota allocation.

By their creation, SDRs established an important principle – that internationally created credit could be used to finance world trade – and the creation of SDRs is likely to be the major source of extra international reserves in the future. Indeed, it has been suggested that SDRs could be created as a means of giving aid to the less developed countries.

The IMF today

The IMF's function of providing bridging finance has declined as most countries have allowed their currencies to float. At least for the major nations, bridging finance can be obtained through the private capital markets which, by being inter-national, can marry any excess or deficiency of funds. For the poorer nations, the IMF's approval of their schemes assists in their obtaining the necessary capital.

On the other hand, the increasing interdependence of the world economy has enhanced the importance of the fund's role of coordinating economic policies worldwide.

CHAPTER SUMMARY

- Persistent long-term balance-of-payments deficits require corrective action or other countries will lose confidence in the currency and economy of the country.
- Corrective action can be expenditure-reducing, which is deflationary and slows down the economy, or expenditure-switching, which attempts to increase the value of exports while reducing the value of imports.
- The success of expenditure-switching policies is largely dependent on the elasticity of demand for imports and exports.

REVIEW QUESTIONS

- If the balance of payments always balances, why are corrective measures necessary if there is an adverse current balance?
- What are the disadvantages of expenditure-reducing measures to correct a balance of payments problem?
- What are the difficulties of expenditure-switching measures to correct a balance of payments problem?
- How has international liquidity been maintained in an era of rapidly expanding international trade?

 Visit the companion website for further questions

THE EUROPEAN UNION

LEARNING OBJECTIVES

....

After studying this chapter you should be able to:

*   describe the development of the EU from 1949 to the present;
*   describe the institutions of the EU;
*   explain the economic objectives of the EU;
*   evaluate the Common Agricultural Policy of the EU;
*   assess the advantages and disadvantages of a single currency in the EU.

41.1   BACKGROUND TO THE EUROPEAN COMMUNITY

Supranational organisations

The two world wars convinced statesmen in Western European countries that some form of political unity was desirable, and in 1949 the Council of Europe was created – the basis, it was hoped, of a European parliament. But organisations with definite functions – the Organisation for European Economic Co-operation (founded in 1948), the North Atlantic Treaty Organisation (1949) and the Western European Union (1954) proved more fruitful than did the Council of Europe with its broad aims.

Although these organisations involved cooperation, they were merely voluntary associations, not federal bodies exercising supranational powers in the interests of members as a whole. While federation was the ultimate aim of European statesmen, they realised that it could only proceed piecemeal and on a functional basis. The first supranational organisation, the European Coal and Steel Community (ECSC) was formed in 1951 to control the whole of the iron, steel and coal resources of the six member countries – France, West Germany, Italy, Holland, Belgium and Luxembourg. The old divisions created by inward-looking national interests were thus broken down.

The success of the ECSC led to the setting up in 1957 of the Atomic Energy Community (EURATOM), a similar organisation for the peaceful use of atomic energy, and the European Economic Community (EEC), an organisation to develop a 'common market' between the six member countries. All three communities have now been brought within the European Union (EU).

Britain's attitude to the EU

When first offered membership of these organisations, Britain refused to join. Not only would joining the EEC have weakened Commonwealth ties, but she was also unwilling to forgo the right to follow independent policies in economics and defence. Instead, with six other nations, she joined the looser European Free Trade Area (EFTA).

Contrary to Britain's expectations, the EEC grew in strength, for difficulties were resolved as they arose. Moreover, Britain's trade with EEC countries increased at a faster rate than that with EFTA, since her goods were more complementary to their economies. Accordingly, after protracted negotiations, the UK joined the EEC in 1973. The other members are now: France, Germany, Italy, Belgium, the Netherlands, Luxembourg, Denmark, the Irish Republic, Greece, Spain, Portugal, Austria, Finland and Sweden; Cyprus, Czech Republic, Estonia, Hungary, Latvia, Lithuania, Malta, Poland, Slovakia and Slovenia joined in 2004; and Bulgaria and Romania are likely to join in 2007/8; Croatia, Macedonia and Turkey are in negotiations.

41.2 THE INSTITUTIONS OF THE EU

The essential point to grasp is that the 1957 Treaty of Rome set up a 'Community' with its own form of government and institutions.

There are four main institutions:

1. The Commission

This is the most important organ of the EU. Its 25 members serve for four years. Once chosen, however, the members of the Commission act as an independent body in the interests of the Community as a whole, and not as representatives of the individual governments that have nominated them. Each commissioner is responsible for a separate area of policy.

The Commission is responsible for formulating policy proposals and legislation, promoting the Community interest, trying to reconcile national viewpoints, executing Council decisions, and supervising the day-to-day running of community policies. As the guardian of the Treaty, it can also initiate action against member states which do not comply with EU rules.

2. The Council of Ministers

Each member country sends a cabinet minister (usually according to the subject under discussion) to the Council of Ministers. This is the supreme decision-making body, the Community's 'cabinet'. Its task is to harmonise the Commission's draft Community policies with the wishes of member governments. The Commission's representative in the Council is present by right, but only to discuss, not to vote. Proposals and compromise plans are exchanged between the Council and the Commission. If the Council becomes deadlocked, the Commission reconsiders the proposal in order to accommodate the views of the opposing countries. Over time, 'specialist' Councils have evolved dealing with particular areas of policy, e.g. agriculture, finance, industry, environment.

By the Single European Act of 1987 most single market measures are subject to majority voting with each member's vote weighted roughly according to its population. However, unanimity is still needed for the politically sensitive areas of taxation and the free movement of people. The UK has retained its right to exercise border controls on people entering.

Council meetings are chaired by the member state holding the *Presidency*, which rotates every six months. This carries with it the management of Community business, acting particularly as broker in promoting agreement.

The outgoing President also hosts the *European Council*, a summit of heads of government which meets twice a year and sets the agenda for the incoming Presidency. The major problems confronting them are reviewed in an informal and pragmatic way. The object is to suggest loosely-defined strategies so that each member can take into account the impact of its own policies on the others.

3. The European Parliament

This consists of representatives elected separately by each country, but they sit according to party affiliation, not nationality. The Assembly debates Community policies and examines the Community's budget. It can dismiss the Commission by a two-thirds majority.

Its powers were strengthened by the 'cooperation procedure' provided for by the Single Market Act 1987. On most single market proposals, Parliament gives a first opinion when the Commission make a proposal, and then gives a second opinion after the Council has reached a decision in principle.

Community legislation, therefore, results from a complex and often lengthy process of consultation and negotiation between the institutions.

4. The Court of Justice

This consists of judges appointed by member countries, for a six-year term. Its task is to rule on the interpretation of the Rome Treaty and to adjudicate on complaints, whether from member states, private enterprises or the institutions themselves. Its rulings are binding on member countries, community institutions, and individuals, and have primacy over national law.

5. Special institutions

Apart from the four main institutions above, there are also special institutions to deal with particular policies, e.g. the Economic and Social Committee, the European Investment Bank.

41.3 ECONOMIC OBJECTIVES OF THE EU

The overriding aim of the EU is to integrate the policies of its member countries. Its economic policy is based on two main principles: (1) a customs union, and (2) a common market.

1. A customs union

We have to distinguish between a free-trade area and a customs union. The former simply removes tariff barriers between member countries but allows individual members to impose their own rates of duty against outsiders. A customs union goes further. While it too has internal free trade, it also imposes common external tariffs.

The EU has a customs union, since this is essential for an integrated common market. Otherwise goods would enter the market through low-duty countries and be resold in those imposing higher rates.

2. A common market

The common market of the EU, however, goes further than a customs union for it envisages goods and factors of production moving freely within the Community through the operation of the price system; only in this way can the full benefits of the larger market be realised.

But it was recognised that this takes time to accomplish. Member countries had already developed their own individual taxes, welfare benefits, monopoly policies, methods of removing balance-of-payments imbalances, full employment policies and so on. Such differences could distort the working of the price system because they would give some members advantages over others. For example, suppose Britain taxed refrigerators but not binoculars. This would weight the possibilities of trade against Italy (which has a comparative advantage in producing refrigerators) and in favour of Germany (which has a comparative advantage in producing high-grade binoculars).

Alternatively, the comparative advantage of some countries may lie in the expertise of the professional services they can provide. Usually this means that such services have to be taken to where the customer is (e.g. know-how regarding property development). There must therefore be mobility of labour within the market, e.g. for property developers.

Policy was therefore directed towards the gradual introduction of 'harmonisation' measures prior to the Single Market coming into effect in 1993 (see p. 523). Examples of these are:

(a) *A Common External Tariff* (CET) by which members impose tariffs on imports from non-member countries at the same rates. However, some countries, particularly the developing countries, are given preferential concessions.

(b) *A common agricultural policy* (CAP) – see below.

(c) *Removal of barriers to trade and the movement of persons and capital between countries.*

(d) *Uniform rules on competition.* To prevent the distortion of competition in trade, uniform regulations have been introduced to cover price-fixing, sharing of markets and patent rights.

(e) *A common transport policy.* By regulating such items as freight rates, licences, taxation and working conditions, the EU can seek to ensure that transport undertakings compete on an equal footing. Any hidden advantages enjoyed by one country would distort the free movement of goods within the Community.

(f) *Harmonisation of tax systems.* As has already been shown, some standardisation of taxation is necessary in order to remove any 'hidden' barriers to trade. This applies particularly to indirect taxes. In the EC value added tax (VAT) is the basic form of indirect tax, and it is proposed that eventually all member countries will levy it at the same rates.

No proposals exist for harmonising income taxes, but most countries have adopted the 'imputation' system of corporation tax (see p. 453).

(g) *Exchange rate stability.* As we have seen, countries can adjust the prices of imports and exports by varying the exchange rate. If this were allowed within the EC, it could enable a member to obtain a competitive advantage over others by depreciating its currency. Thus through the Exchange Rate

Mechanism (ERM) countries agreed to maintain their currency at a fixed exchange rate within narrow limits. The UK joined the ERM in October 1990, but was forced to suspend membership two years later (see p. 526). Of course within the euro single currency area, no such exchange rate changes can happen.

(h) *A common regional policy.* Just as one nation cannot allow depressed areas to persist, so the EU is expected to help regions of high unemployment. Northern Ireland and southern Italy are two such regions, but the needs of special problem areas, e.g. south Wales and the north-east coast of the UK, have also to be recognised for depression partly stems from agreed EU policies, such as the contraction of steel-producing capacity and the reduction of the use of coal for environmental reasons.

(i) *A social policy.* This is concerned mainly with securing some uniformity of employment and working conditions embodied in the 'Social Chapter'. Assistance towards retraining is given from the Social Fund.

41.4 ADVANTAGES FOR THE UK OF BELONGING TO THE EU

Several advantages can accrue to countries by forming a common market.

First, it increases the possibility of specialisation. The EU provides a market of 460 million people, larger than that of the USA. This allows economies of scale to be achieved, especially as regards sophisticated products requiring high initial research expenditure, e.g. computers, drugs, nuclear reactors, supersonic aircraft and modern weapons. Such economies enable EU firms to compete more effectively in world markets.

Second, keener competition in the larger market can result in greater efficiency. Within the EU there are no trade barriers which in effect protect inefficient firms. Free trade means that goods and services can compete freely in all parts of the market and that factors of production can move to their most efficient uses, not merely within but also between countries. On the other hand, it must be recognised that protective duties may reduce competition from outside the market.

Third, a faster rate of growth should be achieved as a result of increased economies of scale and competition enjoyed by the EU countries. But it is also possible that the EU generates growth by increasing the *prospects* of growth.

Fourth, there could be significant political benefits. As already explained, the ultimate objective of the original advocates of European cooperation was some form of political union. A Western Europe which could speak with one voice would carry weight when dealing with other major powers, particularly the USA. Moreover, the integration of defence forces and strategy would give its members far greater security. Such benefits, it is held, more than compensate for any loss of political sovereignty.

Fifth, because she is a member of the EU and has a stable political background, the UK can attract investment from countries outside (particularly the USA and Japan) who are anxious to obtain the advantages of having a production base within the EU.

Sixth, the dynamic growth of the EU enables assistance to be given to its poorer regions and to the less developed countries of the world. Already the UK has been a major beneficiary from the Regional Development Fund, the Social Fund and the Agricultural Guidance and Guarantee Fund.

41.5 PROBLEMS FACING THE UK AS A MEMBER OF THE EU

While Britain's membership of the EU can secure important benefits and allow her to influence its future development, it does pose special problems.

1. The CET could lead to the diversion of trade towards less efficient EC suppliers

The duties imposed by the customs union may allow firms within the common market to compete in price with more efficient firms outside.

Suppose, for instance, that the same machine can be produced by both the USA and Germany but, because the American firm is more efficient, its machine is 10 per cent cheaper than the German. In these circumstances, Britain would, other things being equal, import from the USA. As a member of EU, however, Britain would have to discriminate against the American machine by the appropriate CET, say 20 per cent. This would make the German machine cheaper, and so trade would be diverted to the less efficient producer.

2. The CAP is a drain on the Community funds

Before joining the EU Britain imported food at the lowest world price that could be found. In so far as the UK farmer could not make an adequate living by selling at free market prices, British policy consisted of granting *deficiency payments* (financed out of taxation) sufficient to raise the price received by the farmer to a level set out in an Annual Review. The consumer paid a low price for food and the world had free access to the UK market. The taxpayer paid for farmer support.

But because the Community could not function satisfactorily if the cost of food to consumers differed appreciably in various parts of it, there has to be some equalisation of prices. Yet if this occurred through competition between producing countries it could destroy many small farmers, particularly in France and

520

Germany. Furthermore, because demand for agricultural products tends to be price-inelastic, even in the short run changes in the conditions of supply, e.g. through a good harvest, can have a far-reaching effect on farmers' incomes. Even in the long run farmers face relative falling prices for foodstuffs since demand is income-inelastic while supply conditions improve over time through technical innovation.

The CAP supports farmers' incomes by: (a) an intervention price; (b) granting direct production subsidies, e.g. on ewes held and land 'set-aside'; and (c) restricting imports by protective duties at the Community's external frontier.

Three prices are fixed for each product:

(i) a *target price*, which, it is estimated, will give farmers an adequate return in a normal year;

(ii) the *intervention price*, at which produce of a specified standard will be bought by the various agencies to prevent the price falling more than 8 per cent below the target price. Thus a farmer can choose between selling his corn on the market or 'putting it into intervention'.

(iii) a *threshold price*, which is the price set for calculating duties on imports when the world price is 10 per cent below the target price.

In practice, giving farmers a guaranteed price above the market clearing price for all they can produce simply encourages overproduction, and stocks accumulate which far exceed those necessary to draw on in the event of a poor harvest. Thus in Figure 41.1, the market-clearing price would be OP. However, if the guaranteed intervention price is OP_1, the demand curve becomes horizontal, D_1, at this price. At price P_1, consumers take OQ_1 but farmers supply OQ_2. There

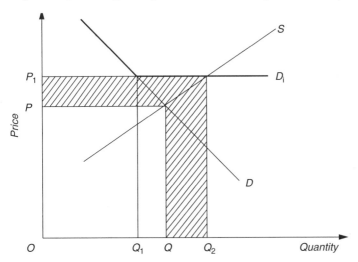

Figure 41.1   The effect on supply of a guaranteed 'intervention' price

is thus an excess supply of Q_1Q_2 which is bought for storage by the authorities of a cost of $P_1 \times Q_1Q_2$. The increase in farmer's incomes is shown by the shaded area.

To the extent that these stores are actually drawn on when harvests are poor, costs are recouped. In practice, however, improved techniques have so increased supply that it has regularly exceeded demand. Thus surpluses have accumulated, e.g. butter, beef and corn mountains and milk and wine lakes.

Not only does the system represent an inefficient use of resources, but it is inequitable in that it gives more support to the larger farmer. 50 billion euros are spent on the CAP (2006), almost half of the EU budget. The main beneficiaries are France, Spain, Germany, Italy and the UK, but 80 per cent of subsidies go to 20 per cent of farmers and the policy adds as much as £9 per week to household budgets in the UK.

3. 'Dumping' surplus produce on world markets injures the less-developed countries and antagonises the USA, Australia, etc.

Apart from the economic inefficiency resulting from subsidies and storage costs, the normal pattern of world trade in agricultural products is distorted. Not only have many world producers lost important markets in Europe, but EU surpluses are dumped on world markets. This depresses the price received by all exporting countries, including even the less-developed.

The USA, supported by Canada, Australia and New Zealand, linked EU agricultural protection with the Uruguay Round of GATT, making the reduction of tariffs on manufactured goods conditional on an EU reduction in price support for her agricultural produce. While this is in harmony with the British view (see below), it is difficult where the farming lobby is politically important.

A considerable reduction in milk output was achieved by the introduction of production quotas in 1984. As regards cereals, progressive reductions in the real prices received by farmers did not reduce overproduction. Hence in 1993 compulsory 'set aside' was introduced to take 15 per cent (since reduced) of the land under cereals out of production. In addition, intervention prices for cereals were cut by a third, with farmers given income compensation, reducing over three years. Subsidies on other agricultural activities are also being reduced.

4. There is insufficient control over the Community budget

A Community budget is necessary to meet the costs of administration and policies requiring expenditure, e.g. CAP and regional assistance. There are four main sources – agricultural levies on imported produce, import duties on non-Community goods, a VAT rate up to 1.4 per cent, and payments related to each member's GNP and which is relative to the economic wealth of each member state. The GNP resource therefore ensures that payments due to the Union reflect more closely the economic ability of each country to pay. This resource cannot exceed 1.27 per cent of the total EU GNP and, in fact, this ceiling has never been exceeded.

The GNP resource was introduced for another reason. The EU budget was consistently proving to be insufficient, particularly in the light of the massive EU spending on agriculture and more recently on regional funding. Over recent years, the GNP-based resource has steadily become the main source of EU revenue, representing – since 1999 – just under 50 per cent of the money that flows into the EU coffers.

In more simple terms, this financing system translates into the wealthier countries paying the lion's share of the Union's budget with the poorer members paying less. The leading paymasters are Germany, the Netherlands, Sweden and Austria all of which have increasingly showed their displeasure at what they see as an open chequebook for financing poorer EU countries. For instance, in 1997, Germany's share of the EU economy was 26 per cent but its contribution to the EU budget stood at 28.2 per cent, by far the largest and well ahead of the other large EU countries. However, calls for a fairer contribution met only with a token recognition in last year's budget debate, which decided on the EU's budget until the end of 2006.

On the other hand, the UK, another net contributor, succeeded, way back in 1984, to recoup a substantial share of its excess payment through a corrective measure known as a rebate. However, it must be said that even after the rebate, the UK remains a larger net contributor than other countries with more capacity to pay.

As to the contributions due to the EU by the new member states after the 2004 enlargement, this will be the subject of intense debate during the ongoing negotiations. The only thing that seems to be clear at this stage is that, judging by the level of economic development of the candidate countries, they are all likely to be net beneficiaries upon membership, which means that they will pay less to the EU budget than they will get.

41.6   THE SINGLE MARKET 1993

The Treaty of Rome 1957 which set up the European Economic Community envisaged a single unified market in which goods of member states could be freely exchanged, but which was protected from imports of other countries by common tariffs.

But even after tariffs between members had been scrapped, it was realised that there were other frictions to the free movement of goods and services. These included:

(a)   frontier delays, e.g. in checking documents, collecting excise duties;
(b)   transport control, e.g. licenses, national safety rules, lorry weights;

(c) differences in national product standards and in national trade mark and patent laws;
(d) restrictions on public purchasing;
(e) control over capital movements and restrictions on financial services offered across national frontiers by banks, insurance companies, etc;
(f) differences in recognised professional and technical qualifications;
(g) state subsidies to industry and agriculture;
(h) different rates of VAT, corporation tax, and of depreciation and other tax allowances; and
(i) the necessity of changing currencies.

It was recognised that the removal of such barriers would take time, but that in order to keep the momentum going there would have to be a set date. Thus the Single European Act provided for the single market to become operative on 1 January 1993. The Act: (a) required all countries to complete or be in the process of completing the necessary harmonisation measures, and (b) introduced qualified majority voting on most single market legislation so that progress would not be delayed by a few dissenting members.

Many of these non-tariff barriers were overcome by harmonisation of national requirements, e.g. as regards transport safety rules, product standards, acceptable professional standards. For example, a new trading form, the Single Administrative Document, replaced about 100 different documents for the export, import and transit of goods over EU frontiers. Alternatively, the Commission can persuade states to remove national restrictions, e.g. on public purchasing and capital movements.

As far as possible the Commission has sought to eliminate controls by deregulation generally rather than by dealing with each control individually. For instance, if one state imposed an excise duty on a good which was higher than that of another state the market would automatically transfer trade in that good from the dearer country to the cheaper, so that no regulation on duties would be necessary. Nevertheless it can make regulations specific to the practices of an individual state.

Conclusions

While the Single Market offers increased opportunities, the tougher competition presents challenges. Large-scale, low-cost producers will benefit at the expense of smaller higher-cost producers, some of whom could be taken over or go out of business. Even the larger British firms, with their greater reliance for expansion on equity finance through the capital market, are now more vulnerable to take-over or merger.

Certain regions, too, may find the readjustment painful, and the EU must provide extra finance through its Regional, Social and Agricultural Guidance Funds to promote their development.

For its part the Community has to decide whether it closes in on itself, secure from competition behind the common external tariff – 'fortress Europe' as this looking inwards has been termed. Or alternatively, whether it should maintain and develop a liberal policy of trading with the rest of the world allowing them to share in the benefits of growth.

The importance of the Single Market to the UK cannot be overemphasised. In value about 60 per cent of the UK's exports go to the EU and about 60 per cent of her imports come from there. Hence the government launched a 'Europe Open for Business' campaign to alert UK companies to the implications of the Single Market and to encourage them to act early to meet the opportunities and challenges it presents.

While the UK has been cooperative and even assiduous in removing barriers to the Single Market, she has fallen out of line in one major respect: hesitancy in joining a single currency.

41.7 A SINGLE CURRENCY

The advantages of a single currency

An exchange rate union which goes no further than irrevocably-locked exchange rates covers the basic requirements of the single market. But it has three weaknesses:

(a) a member could renege on the arrangement, realigning its exchange rate unilaterally;

(b) a risk premium against such a possible devaluation would mean a higher rate of interest would have to be set by the EU central bank; and

(c) costs would still be incurred in exchanging currencies.

A single currency eliminates all three weaknesses. It removes any uncertainty over exchange rate realignment, and in doing so should encourage trade and investment and eliminate the bias against small firms who experience more difficulty in absorbing the foreign exchange risk premium. More important, the single currency eliminates the costs of currency exchange for firms engaged in intra-EU trade and for individuals travelling within the EU, e.g. tourists.

Moreover, the single currency would have to be managed by a European Central Bank (ECB). Such an independent bank, committed to a low rate of inflation, would help to guarantee monetary stability since policy could not be slanted by a state-controlled central bank for electoral advantage. The resulting lower 'uncertainty premium' should produce a ECB rate of interest which would be lower than that required by an individual state to achieve the same level of inflation.

It is possible, too, that the new currency, the Euro, could be widely used as a reserve currency. If so it should reduce still further exchange risks with outside currencies, and even generate income for the ECB from its Euro holdings.

Finally, a single currency and a common ECB responsible for overall monetary policy would help to unify the single market, especially as cross-border transactions would no longer be distorted by currency uncertainties. Indeed, pricing all goods in Euros should, by making price differences transparent, promote competition within the single market.

In order to ensure that adoption of a single currency in the EU did not put an unacceptable strain on the economies of participating states, certain convergency criteria were made a condition of joining. The criteria were:

(a) *Exchange rate stability*, with exchange rates maintained within the narrow band for the previous two years. This would provide an indication of the once-for-all rate at which a country's currency would be valued in terms of the Euro.
(b) *Price stability*, with the index of consumer price inflation in the previous year to be no more than 1.5 per cent above that of the average of the best three performing member states.
(c) *Sustainability of government financial stability*, with government annual net borrowing to be below 3 per cent of GDP.
(d) *Convergence durability*, with the average nominal long-term government bond rate to be no more than 2 per cent above the average of the three best performing members.

Responsibility for the formulation and implementation of monetary policy would pass to the ECB, which would also decide on exchange rates with outside currencies, manage the reserves and intervene in the market. It would be the sole issuing authority of the single currency.

Possible difficulties arising from the single currency

The UK did not last long in the fixed exchange rate regime of the ERM. The £1–DM 2.95 exchange rate held until 16 September 1992, when the foreign exchange speculators, after forcing a devaluation of the Italian lira, turned on sterling. The magnitude of the selling took the government completely by surprise especially as, unlike Italy, the UK had foreign currency reserves of some £24 billion. The accepted counter measures – raising the minimum lending rate from 10 to 12 per cent and then to 15, spending £15 billion from the reserves, and support of between £5 billion and £10 billion from the Bundesbank and the Bank of France – proved quite ineffective. Consequently the UK suspended her membership of the ERM and allowed the £ to find its own parities on the foreign exchange market (around 2.45 DM, January 1992).

It must be recognised that the single currency could create difficulties for the EU as a whole.

First, there are the heavy initial costs of its introduction. Businesses would have to alter all their money machines (e.g. cash dispensers, tills, vending machines);

it is estimated that for the UK's retail sector alone the cost would be around £3.5 billion. In addition, computer programmes would have to be recalculated to allow for the change from the old currency to the euro.

Individuals, too, would have to adapt to the euro once the transitional period was over. Wages, salaries, state benefits, mortgages, monetary assets, etc., would all have to be expressed in euros. Since this would be less easy for older persons, there is here a 'psychological' cost.

Second, and more serious, is the inherent danger that without considerable assistance from the EC Structure, Social and Regional Funds, certain regions, especially those on the periphery, would be left facing long-term poverty. But this could mean that such distributions may run counter to the single market objective of securing the advantages of specialisation through the mobility of labour and capital. Through inflexible wage-rates and labour immobility, unemployment and poverty could persist in certain regions simply because subsidies reduce the need to accept lower wage rates or to move to the more prosperous regions.

In addition to the above, certain monetary conditions imposed by the ECB could adversely affect certain individual members in particular. It is these which are stressed by the UK, and which are considered in Chapter 42.

The single currency became a reality when in 1998 11 EU member states had met the convergence criteria and the eurozone came into existence with the official launch of the euro on 1 January 1999. Greece qualified in 2000 and was admitted on 1 January 2001, bringing total eurozone membership to its current level of 12 member states: Austria, Belgium, Finland, France (except Pacific territories using CFP franc), Germany, Greece, Ireland, Italy, Luxembourg, Netherlands, Portugal and Spain. Their combined population is over 307 million people.

The other 13 countries of the European Union that do not use the euro are: Denmark, Sweden, the United Kingdom, and the ten member states that joined the Union on 1 May 2004, namely Cyprus, the Czech Republic, Estonia, Hungary, Latvia, Lithuania, Malta, Poland, Slovakia and Slovenia.

CHAPTER SUMMARY

- The EU is a customs union and a common market for its member states.
- Because the market of the EU has a population of 460 million people, the advantages of specialisation and economies of scale are considerable.
- The absence of trade barriers within the EU should lead to increased competition and efficiency.
- Problems associated with the EU include trade diversion away from more efficient suppliers because of the common external tariff and the enormous cost of the Common Agricultural Policy.
- Twelve countries within the EU now use a single currency, the euro, but the UK has been hesitant about joining the eurozone since leaving the ERM in 1992.

REVIEW QUESTIONS

- What is meant by a 'customs union'?
- What are the advantages for the UK of membership of the EU?
- What is the effect on supply of a guaranteed price for agricultural produce?
- What are the advantages of a single currency within the EU?
- Why did the UK leave the ERM in 1992?

 Visit the companion website for further questions

PART
IX
LOOKING INTO THE FUTURE

42

CURRENT PROBLEMS AND POLICIES OF THE UK AND EUROPE

LEARNING OBJECTIVES

After studying this chapter you should be able to:

- describe the use of monetarism to try to control inflation in the UK;
- describe the balance-of payments difficulties of the UK;
- explain how industry in the UK has changed in the last 30 years;
- explain how population changes are important to the economy;
- assess the relationship between the UK and the EU.

The theoretical analysis set out in this book indicates that to some extent the main objectives of government stabilisation policy – full employment, a stable price level, a healthy balance of payments and a satisfactory rate of growth – are mutually incompatible, for success in one creates difficulties for others. Full employment, for instance, requires an adequate level of aggregate demand. But when aggregate demand is increased, so spending on imports rises and home-produced goods are diverted from exports to the home market. Thus the balance-of-payments position becomes less favourable. Full employment also means that eventually less efficient labour has to be employed, bottlenecks occur, and trade unions are in a stronger position to bargain for wage increases. On the cost side, therefore, there are forces which make for a rise in the price level as full employment is approached.

In essence, therefore, the government is somewhat like a juggler who is endeavouring to keep four balls in the air simultaneously. At any given moment, one is going up, a second has reached its peak, and a third is on the way down and the fourth is being passed from one hand to the other to be given a new upward thrust.

Nevertheless, other developed economies are in the same position, and until recently most of them, particularly Germany and Japan, have been more successful than Britain in achieving these objectives. Why is this? The simple answer is that the UK did not observe fundamental requirements: price stability to maintain exports, wage restraint to avoid rising wage-unit costs, restructuring industry to promote employment, and cost competition in exports. We now examine these weaknesses in the light of recent history.

42.1 INFLATION: A STUDY IN CHANGING POLICIES

Monetarism

Mrs Thatcher's Government of 1979 gave priority of economic macro objectives to that of bringing inflation under control. 'Fine-tuning' the economy by adjusting AD was replaced by naked monetarism (see p. 400).

This was embodied in the *medium-term financial strategy (MTFS)* which set targets for four years ahead to: (a) limit increases in the money supply; and (b) reduce the PSBR (now PSNCR) as a percentage of GDP. Each year projections were amended in the light of past experience.

But to control the money supply you need to have a measure of money. M3, the chosen aggregate, proved to be a misleading measure. Expansion of M3 was to be controlled by varying the rate of interest. In practice M3 did not prove to be interest-elastic. Indeed at times firms had to *increase* their borrowing when the rate of interest rose in order to tide them over the deflationary squeeze, while, because of the increasing habit of credit-card buying, higher interest rates often had a muted effect on borrowing. Moreover, the definition was too narrow; for instance it did not include building society deposits. Above all, the abolition of exchange control in 1979 and the development of the wholesale deposit markets enabled the banks to obtain funds for relending, and M3 raced ahead.

The reality is that, from the point of view of controlling AD, 'money' includes any asset which contains an element of immediate spending power or induces the owner to pare down money balances because it can be quickly turned into cash. Consequently there is no single aggregate which can be measured as representing the money supply. This was the rock on which Britain's experiment foundered, and in March 1987 the Chancellor of the Exchequer announced that he would stop setting targets for M3, but would retain M0, and also have regard to the wider aggregates when exercising his discretion as to the degree of monetary restraint required.

While M0, which is virtually coins and notes, appears to be more consistent, it is an 'indicator' not a 'target'. It simply *reflects* changes in GDP since cash is always made available by the Bank of England on demand. There is no *causal* connection between M0 and AD in the way that there is with M3. It is also affected by institutional changes, e.g. the increasing use of credit cards and automatic transfer arrangements.

Reducing the PSBR (now PSNCR)

Reducing the PSNCR was necessary because, if increased taxation or reduced expenditure are ruled out, a PSNCR can only be covered by creating money or by borrowing.

Initially, an excess of government spending over revenue is achieved by the government's paying its employees and contractors from its deposits at the Bank of England. Eventually this extra cash finds its way into the joint-stock banks, allowing them to expand their deposits, including advances.

But resorting to the 'printing press' in this way cannot be a permanent solution. The government has to cover its PSNCR by borrowing. Even so, if it does this by the cheapest method – the sale of Treasury bills – it runs into difficulties. The major holders of Treasury bills are the joint-stock banks, and they buy them as the increased offering forces up the yield. Such purchases, however, add directly to the banks' liquid assets, allowing them, as above, to increase their deposits. In other words, short-term borrowing involves an inflationary increase in the money supply.

As a result, the government has to rely on long-term borrowing, selling medium- and long-term bonds in the market to the *non-bank* sector, the institutions and private purchasers. Since such sources of funds rely mainly on current saving, this method is not inflationary. The difficulty, however, is that extra bonds can only be disposed of at a lower-price – that is, by a rise in the long-term rate of interest. This has the overall effect of discouraging investment, thereby increasing unemployment and retarding the rate of growth. Nor is this all. Interest payments on this borrowing add to the PSNCR. Furthermore, inasmuch as higher interest rates attract funds from abroad, the money supply is increased.

Unlike M3 which constantly overshot its target, the government was more successful in reducing the PSNCR, even achieving an annual surplus from 1987–9. Apart from strict control over its own spending, it was helped by increased tax receipts from an expanding economy and the proceeds of privatisation.

Other aspects of Thatcher monetarism

A policy for wages was implicitly embodied in the MTFS: instead of playing an active role in wage settlements, the government left employers to negotiate terms with the trade unions. It was hoped that holding to a MTFS would convince the unions that wage demands should be based on a *lower* expected rate of inflation. Nor would any inflationary wage increases be financed by an increase in the money supply. Instead firms' profits would fall, and unemployment follow. To limit the possibility of 'blood-letting' strikes and consequent damage to the economy, the government introduced legislation curtailing the powers of the unions.

The situation was somewhat different as regards labour in the public sector where output is not related to profits. Here, therefore, the government had virtually to impose a wages policy, and its strategy of limiting public sector spending helped to moderate union wage demands.

In addition to controlling the money supply, the Thatcher government took on board the politico-economic views of Friedman. He considers that the expansion of the public sector in most Western economies has undermined the willingness to accept risk-bearing and thus the ability to increase wealth. This view bore fruit in the privatisation policy, augmented by other measures to improve performance on the supply side (see pp. 404–7).

Inflation policy since leaving the ERM

While leaving the ERM represented a humiliating defeat for the government in the face of its repeated affirmation that it would take all necessary measures to maintain the agreed exchange rate, the U-turn on economic policy did permit a lowering of the rate of interest with the aim of stimulating the economy. By 13 November 1992 base rate was reduced to 7 per cent – lower than that of any other EC country.

This left the Chancellor with two basic problems: (1) the nature and extent of the measures required to 'kick-start' the economy; (2) how to control inflation now that sterling was no longer tied to the deutschemark.

His strategy was contained in the Autumn Statement 1992. Economic revival was to be promoted by additional public expenditure on infrastructure, e.g. the road programme, the 'Jubilee' line and housing, together with some reduction in taxation, e.g. an increased 40 per cent investment allowance for spending on machinery. To hold down public expenditure, public sector pay increases were to be limited to 1½ per cent.

The target for underlying inflation was to be within a 1 to 4 per cent range, with the long-term aim of 2 per cent or less. To achieve this: (a) the *target* annual growth range for M0 would be 0 to 4 per cent; (b) for M4 there would be a *monitored* range of 4 to 8 per cent. Additional indicators, e.g. house prices, exchange rate movements, would also be taken into account, but not targetted.

Furthermore, interest rate adjustments were to depend on prospective inflationary trends. The Chancellor of the Exchequer had monthly meetings with the Governor of the Bank of England where he listened to the Governor's views on the prospects of future inflation trends. But the final decision was his, and twice the Governor's recommendation to raise the base rate was overruled. However, as part of the policy of more openness on the reasoning behind decisions, each meeting was followed by a monthly report.

Control of inflation passes to an independent Bank of England

The above strategy succeeded in maintaining the rate of inflation at around 2.5 per cent. But where the decision to raise base rate rested with the Chancellor, there was always the danger that it could be unduly influenced by political considerations.

Thus the Labour government's determination to hold the rate of inflation to 2.5 per cent gained credibility when on 6 May 1997 Gordon Brown, the new Chancellor of the Exchequer, announced that henceforth the Bank of England would be completely independent of the government in deciding what changes in the base rate should be made to achieve the government's specified target, at present 2.5 per cent. In doing so he brought inflation control closely in line with the German method which has been so successful.

The Bank makes its base-rate decisions through a small Monetary Policy Committee specially chosen for the task. This meets on the Wednesday following the first Monday in each month, and again on the Thursday morning, after which its decision is announced. But controlling inflation is not an exact science. The Committee has to consider different factors, such as changes in the money supply, consumer spending, house and asset prices, the PSNCR, movements in the exchange rate and so forth, in order to form an opinion as to their bearing on what the rate of inflation is likely to be in two years' time. Minutes of its meetings are published within six weeks in furtherance of the 'openness' policy.

It should be noted that this new independence of the Bank of England puts the whole onus of controlling inflation on monetary policy and restricts government use of fiscal policy for demand management. Suppose, for instance, that the budget unexpectedly cut taxes in order to reduce unemployment. Other things being equal, the Bank of England could consider that this would lead to higher future inflation, and if so it would now have to respond by raising interest rates.

42.2 BALANCE-OF-PAYMENTS DIFFICULTIES

Post-war problems

Throughout the twentieth century Britain has been losing her share of international trade as other countries have industrialised and competed in world markets. But for a time net income from overseas investments which were accumulated during the prosperous nineteenth century covered the deficit on visible trade.

The two world wars aggravated Britain's difficulties. Overseas investments were sold and external debts incurred to pay for essential imports. Furthermore, when peace came, Britain's industry, which had been geared to the war effort, needed time to readjust and re-equip.

To make matters worse, although sterling was still used by foreigners as a reserve currency, Britain's gold and foreign currency reserves were too small to provide an adequate cushion when confidence in sterling faltered through a balance-of-payments weakness. At first, in order to protect the reserves and the value of the pound, deflationary measures – the 'stop-go' policy – had to be taken.

Eventually, in 1972, the pound was 'floated', leaving its value to be determined on the foreign exchange market, but subject to smoothing operations by the Exchange Equalisation Account.

The effect of North Sea oil

North Sea oil transformed the situation. Exploitation of oil and gas in the North Sea began in 1964. The earliest discoveries were of gas, but later exploration revealed large oil deposits. Between 1967 and 1974, 18 oilfields were developed and the first oil was piped onshore in 1975. By 1979 the UK was self-sufficient in oil, and then became a net exporter. Between 1986 and 1989 the UK's current account was in surplus, sales of North Sea oil covering the deficit on non-oil trade. Surpluses were used to accumulate overseas assets, which rose from £5 billion (net) in 1979 to £100 billion (net) by 1986.

Nevertheless, the emergence of the pound sterling as a petrocurrency was not without snags, for it meant that the sterling exchange rate became closely related to the price of oil, appreciating to $2.50 when in 1984 the price of oil rose above $30 a barrel. This made it still more difficult for British exports to compete, and manufacturing industries in particular were forced to cut capacity. In 1985 trade in manufactured goods moved from surplus to deficit. Similarly, when in 1986 the price of oil fell to $10 a barrel, the exchange value of the pound fell to $1.50.

Recession 1990–2

After 1985 the net value of oil exports fell, partly through a drop in the world price of oil to $18 a barrel, and partly through reduced UK production. Yet between 1985 and 1988 the rate of growth of the economy rose to a high of 4 per cent per annum. As it was consumer-spending led, this resulted in a 25 per cent increase in the value of imports over these four years. To make matters worse, from 1988 net invisible earnings from services fell (not recovering until 1993). Government measures to dampen down the overheating of the economy were not taken soon enough. By 1989 the current account deficit was £22 billion, equivalent to 4 per cent of GDP. DTI figures show that oil production peaked in 1999 and has since fallen 23 per cent below that level. Monument Securities says that, by 2010, production could be 50 per cent below peak levels. According to the Bank of England, output of North Sea oil in the first six months of 2005 was down nearly 10 per cent on 2004. Britain will become a net gas importer in 2006.

In order to support the rate of exchange of £1 = DM 2.95 within the ERM, the government raised the base rate. But current account deficits of £16 billion, £22 billion, £19 billion and £18 billion in the years 1988 to 1991, together with a worsening PSNCR, convinced speculators that sterling was overvalued. Even a base rate of 15 per cent and support from the reserves failed to stem the outflow of foreign funds. As a result, in September 1992 the UK suspended its membership of the ERM and the £ was floated on the foreign exchange market, eventually settling down at around DM 2.45.

As in the past, deflationary measures to maintain a fixed exchange rate had failed. Raising the rate of interest to protect the £ simply led to recession and unemployment.

Weaknesses of the depreciation/devaluation solution

Yet devaluation as an alternative policy also has weaknesses. First, speculation may lead to further downward pressure on the exchange rate as short-term capital moves out of sterling. Second, to halt the slide the rate of interest has to be raised. Third, depreciation/devaluation benefits all exporters alike, whether they are efficient or not. If firms can count on further depreciation/devaluation there is less incentive to strive for greater efficiency and reduced wage-costs per unit. Fourth, the benefits of increased exports through depreciation/devaluation can come up against inelasticity of supply (see p. 509). Even if slack in the economy should allow exports to be price-elastic, it is of little help if non-price considerations – e.g. design quality, firm delivery rates and after-sales service – are of paramount importance. Fifth, exchange rates are influenced by speculators moving short-term money.

What the policy can do is to provide a breathing space while the export base is enlarged.

Recovery from the 1990–2 recession

With no fixed exchange rate to be maintained, the rate of interest was reduced and growth gradually resumed (p. 534). In the past this had eventually paved the way for wage increases. This recovery, however, was different.

First, inflationary wage demands did not occur. This can be attributed to the level of unemployment which at the end of 1992 was just under 3 million. Job security was now uppermost in workers' objectives. Mrs Thatcher's curbing of trade union power was also a significant factor.

Second, although initially the recovery was consumer-led, within a year exports and investment had taken over. The volume of goods (excluding oil and erratics) exported from the UK in 1994 was almost 11 per cent higher than in the previous year, and for manufactured products the increase was even greater at over 13.5 per cent. Overall, net exports of goods and services accounted for 1 per cent of the 4.1 per cent growth in GDP in 1994.

This was largely brought about by the fall in export prices as a result of the £'s devaluation. On the supply side, however, there were factors which had made

British manufacturing industry more competitive: re-investment in modern machinery following the 1981–2 recession; the shedding of surplus labour; improved labour flexibility; spare capacity; better management and the adoption of modern methods and technology.

As a result the current account deficit fell sharply in 1994 to £2.5 billion and, although the economy grew by almost 4 per cent, the underlying inflation rate remained below 3 per cent.

Improving the UK's export performance

Over the last 30 years, recessions in the UK have been triggered by a serious deterioration in the balance of payments. To maintain steady and sustained growth it is essential to improve the UK's export performance. Three strands of policy can be identified: (1) ensuring that in the expansion of the economy export-growth keeps in step with consumer-spending growth; (2) improving the price-competitiveness of exports; and (3) expanding the export base of UK production.

1. Export-led growth

When the economy is expanding rapidly, for example as it comes out of recession, it is essential that an initial consumer-led recovery is not prolonged to the detriment of increasing exports. This is because as incomes expand part of the increased spending is on foreign goods and services, e.g. travel abroad. The UK's export position is at present so weak that a serious current account deficit can develop quite quickly. Thus the expansion of the economy in 1987–8 caused the current account to move from balance in 1986 to deficits of £16.5 billion in 1988 and £22 billion in 1989. This was the penalty of Chancellor Lawson's failure to take earlier action to squeeze credit.

2. Improving export competitiveness

UK exports must be kept price-competitive by firms reducing costs through stable money wage-rates and increased productivity; more specifically, by lower wage-costs per unit of output. How can this be achieved, and what are the prospects? While the government has an important part to play, in controlling consumer spending and inflation the major influence will be the response of both sides of industry, management and labour.

Until 1980 manufacturers were able to compensate for increased costs by raising prices. The Thatcher monetarist policy, by squeezing *AD*, prevented this. Instead employers, faced with a squeeze on profits, had to show greater resistance to wage demands, and, although the Thatcher government mismanaged the economy in 1988, its achievement in reducing the power of trade unions to intimidate management with the threat of disruptive action has to be acknowledged. Today, therefore, unemployment and a falling rate of inflation have moved labour away from excessive wage demands and confrontation towards job preservation and cooperation.

Furthermore, the recessions of 1980–2 and 1990–2 eliminated most surplus capacity and overmanning so that subsequently the UK's 4 per cent annual rate of increase of *productivity* in manufacturing exceeded that of other EC countries and the USA. However, this must be regarded as a special case since the improvement started from a low level.

Even so, new factors suggest that a steady increase in productivity could continue. The better employer-labour relationship means that management can now concentrate on a long-term strategy, and organise production accordingly, instead of having to devote time and energy to settling industrial disputes. Moreover, this improvement in worker attitude should stimulate investment in capital and training, especially if a lower rate of interest is possible as a result of greater certainty in the UK's ability to maintain a low level of inflation and to avoid deflationary policies resulting from balance-of-payments crises.

Nor must we ignore the benefits of direct investment by foreign firms e.g. Nissan, Toyota (Japan), Ford (USA), as they establish factories in the UK. Directly their production increases exports; indirectly, it could lead to a 'catch-up' process as domestic firms follow their improved management and production techniques e.g. single union agreements, greater attention to quality (often through a preferred supplier), control over the supply chain's 'just-in-time' component deliveries, and training of managers and operatives.

The government, too, has recognised the need for training. Education at school level is being improved, while young people and others returning to work are encouraged to develop their skills in the expanded universities and technical colleges.

3. Restructuring of British industry

While the above factors are helpful in reducing wage-costs per unit, it is doubtful whether this alone can effect the increase in exports on the scale required to turn round the precarious balance of payments situation. It is argued that this can only be achieved by a change in the export base of production by a restructuring of British industry towards manufacturing.

Until the 1960s the older basic industries – coal, steel, shipbuilding, textiles, engineering and vehicles, on which Britain's nineteenth-century prosperity had been based – were fully employed in making good the shortages created by the war. But there emerged newly industrialised countries of the Third World (e.g. Brazil, South Korea and Taiwan), while others grew rapidly (e.g. Japan). These adopted new techniques, and Britain lost its early comparative advantages in production.

In 1994 North Sea oil and gas contributed £1.3 billion net per annum to the UK's balance of payments, but this must be viewed as an asset which will eventually decline. Furthermore, net earnings from services may have already peaked. In any case, although in numbers employed and value of output, services are more than twice those of manufacturing, the value of its exports is little more than a third.

One bright spot is net overseas investment earnings – interest, profit and dividends. Largely as a result of increased private direct and portfolio investment since 1985, these have trebled in value to over 12 billion since 1994 as the rewards have come through.

It follows, therefore, that it is the balance of trade, where in value exports cover only four-fifths of imports, that has to be improved by expanding and developing those industries having a tradeable export content. In effect this involves dependence on manufacturing where all products are potentially tradeable (compared with services 20 per cent).

Employment in manufacturing industry in Britain fell from 37 per cent in 1971 to 20 per cent in 1992 and 11 per cent in 2005. While this relative decline is a long-term trend resulting from the switch to services as income increases, the fall was proportionately greater than that of other developed countries. To a large extent it was brought about by the decrease in manufacture exports as they became uncompetitive with those of other countries. This decline can be traced back to the early 1980s but it was exacerbated by the 4.5 per cent appreciation of the effective sterling exchange rate in 1987–8, the peak oil exporting years. While in 1979 the UK had a surplus of £6 billion in manufactures, by 1983 this had become a deficit, and by 2005 the deficit on UK trade in goods was a massive £65 billion. In the UK we have been importing on a remarkably large scale. The 'typical' family of four in Britain is, on average, a net importer of over £4,400 worth of goods each year (2005 figures). The prices of imported manufactured goods have also been dropping because of the liberalisation of the world economy and the emergence of low-cost countries such as Brazil, Russia, India and, most importantly, China. Lower prices have fuelled an appetite for imports, and in most product categories the UK could not produce substitutes at anything like the imported prices, if at all.

One cause of this rising adverse balance in manufactures is the penetration of the home market by foreign importers. This has applied not only to clothing, footwear, paper, printing and publishing products, and textiles, but, most disturbingly, to such high technology industries as office machinery, data processing equipment, electrical machinery, cars and cameras. Manufacturing industry must not only slow down the process of import penetration, but start to regain the home market from foreign firms.

But the trade deficit is so large that, if it is to be closed, tradeable output will have to rise as a share of GDP. This means that here again we must look to industrial production, and in particular, manufactured goods, for increased exports.

The need goes further than increasing sales abroad of current exports. A successful export base, as the Japanese have shown, depends on innovation – new ideas incorporated in new products having a high income elasticity of demand

and, on the supply side, new methods, first-class management and good labour relations with workers having a long-term loyalty to the firm. Given innovation, investment and jobs will follow.

Can the UK match the Japanese in these ways? In the past firms have been inhibited from innovating because of possible disruption through union Luddite resistance to new techniques and improved organisation. But that a more enlightened attitude now prevails is demonstrated by the fact that Japanese firms are choosing Britain for their production base within the EU. Indeed it is likely that British firms and production methods will be influenced through this closer contact with their Japanese counterparts. Above all, it is essential for Britain to identify and support innovative firms such as Vodafone (mobile phones), Glaxo (pharmaceuticals), Morgan Crucible (carbon fibre and ceramics), Pilkington (safety glass) and BOC (industrial gases) for these can not only reduce import penetration but, at the same time, increase exports.

42.3 THE PRESSURE ON FUTURE GOVERNMENT SPENDING OF THE UK'S AGEING POPULATION

The size of the future population

The UK population is projected to increase by 7.2 million over the period 2004 to 2031 (see Figure 42.1). This increase is equivalent to an average annual rate of growth of 0.42 per cent, or 12 per cent over the 27 years. The population is projected to grow until 2031. This is due to natural increase (more births than deaths) and because it is assumed there will be more immigrants than emigrants (a net inward flow of migrants).

The population is also projected to continue rising beyond 2031. However, long-term projections are very uncertain. With lower assumptions of future births, life expectancy or migration, the UK population could reach a peak in size by the middle of the century.

In common with most other countries, the UK has an ageing population (see Figure 42.2). The proportion of people aged over 65 is projected to increase from 16 per cent in 2004 to 23 per cent by 2031. This is an inevitable consequence of the age structure of the population alive today, in particular the ageing of the large numbers of people born after the Second World War and during the 1960s baby boom.

As a result, demographic support ratios will fall. In 2004, there were 3.33 people of working age for every person of state pensionable age. This ratio is projected to fall to 2.62 by 2031. The age structure of the UK population has become older in the last three decades, and is likely to become older still in the next three decades. The median age rose from 34.1 years in 1971 to 38.6 in 2004 and is projected to rise to 42.9 in 2031.

An ageing population is reflected in its pattern of consumption, and in a labour force which on balance is older and probably less mobile, and the loss of vitality associated with young persons. For the government today, however, it presents

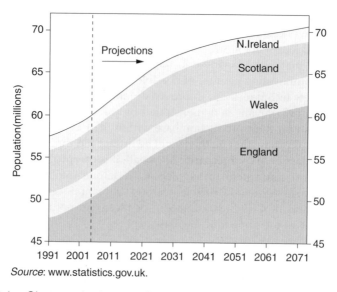

Source: www.statistics.gov.uk.

Figure 42.1   Changes in the population of the UK, 1991–2071

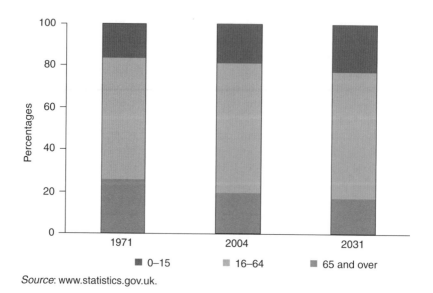

Source: www.statistics.gov.uk.

Figure 42.2   Population of the UK by age group, 1971–2031

the problem of looking ahead and providing to meet the mounting future cost of pensions and care homes for a growing number of older people.

The pension problem

Planned government spending on social security benefits for 2006–07 is £151 billion. Of the total, 38 per cent goes on meeting the cost of state retirement pensions and income support for those who have only the basic state pension to live on. The government has two problems.

First, the basic pension (£84.25 per week in 2006) is mean. It increases each year to allow for rises in the Retail Price Index. But it would be fairer to relate it to the higher rate of growth of average earnings, since this would allow all pensioners to share in the growth of the national income. Without an adequate pension, retired people have to fall back on income support.

Second, current retirement pensions are paid for out of current National Insurance contributions, that is, by taxation of those in work. The weakness of this present pay-as-you-go provision is that, because of the UK's ageing population, the number of contributors in the 16–64 group is falling relative to pension recipients in the 65+ group. Thus, whereas in 1991 there were four persons in the working group for every pensioner, in 2031 there will be only 2.5. We must also remember that because some of the working group may be unemployed, sick or already retired, the burden may be even heavier. Without a more generous basic pension and an overhaul of the pay-as-you-go scheme, retired persons with no company or private provision will be increasingly dependent on income support.

Both the Conservative party and the present Labour government realise that the solution lies in the introduction of a fully-funded scheme which would initially run in parallel to, but eventually replace, the existing pay-as-you-go method. This would be achieved by extra insurance deductions from persons as they start work so that they can build up a personal pension fund. The difficulty is that during the transition period finance would be required to pay pensions under the existing scheme. This might require additional contributions from new entrants, a reduction in the tax relief on private schemes, the squeezing of other social benefit expenditure, and a limited increase in the PSNCR. But the scheme should increase the UK's net saving ratio, and if additional savings are channelled into new investment it should raise the rate of growth. It is estimated that such a scheme would enable new participants to retire with a pension of £175 per week, while when fully in place (about 2060) there could be a saving of £40 billion a year in state spending.

It should be noted that this future pension deficit problem is so much more serious for Germany, France and Italy than for the UK because: (a) they have a higher future elderly dependency ratio; (b) their state pensions are more generous; (c) the UK has a higher proportion (60 per cent) of retired persons who have company or private pensions, and these are backed by funds amounting to more than £800 billion. This raises the problem of how EU monetary policy could avoid undermining her favourable situation should she join the single currency.

The need for care homes

Because more people are living into their 80s, there will be an increasing need for nursing and residential care homes. Of the over-85 group, about one-quarter will require residential care. Today the over-85 group numbers about 650,000 and by 2051 it is likely to be 2.8 million. Of these, about a quarter, some 700,000 old people, will be requiring care.

How will this be paid for? About 125,000 pay for their own private care, many out of past insurance. Those in long-stay hospital beds are cared for free, but once discharged into nursing homes they have to pay. The state helps with the fees provided no more than £16,000 worth of assets are held. It may mean selling a house if this is owned. Even so it is a mounting cost to the state.

42.4 THE UK'S RELATIONSHIP WITH THE EU

At present the relationship between the UK and the EU is strained. The UK cooperated fully in implementing the arrangements for establishing the single market and in doing so recognised, that some dimunition of sovereignty and majority voting had to be conceded as part and parcel of being a member of the EU.

But the proposal that the EU should adopt a single currency has been marked by the UK's distinct lack of enthusiasm. For the UK it opened up the question of whether it involved too much sovereignty being lost to EU bureaucrats on matters which ought to come within the competence of national governments.

Subsidiarity

One of the UK's apprehensions over the extension of bureacratic control is indicated by her emphasis on adhering to the principle of subsidiarity, which simply asserts that the functions of government should be devolved to the lowest competent level. The UK considers that this principle means that things should be done at the Community level only if they cannot be done at the national level. For instance with regard to the environment, dealing with greenhouse warming would be a Community function, but protecting national parks would be a national function.

At the other end of the spectrum, in contrast to the UK's view, the Commission would prefer a 'common interest' test of subsidiarity, the object being to widen the scope of its authority rather than limit it to the lowest common denominator. For the UK, this intepretation simply reflects her view that the Brussels bureaucrats wish to use their powers to abrogate to themselves rights and functions which can be performed efficiently by the nation state.

Until the meeting of the European Council in Edinburgh in November 1992, subsidiarity was little more than a slogan, with its practical application dependent on how it was interpreted by countries having different interests. The meeting moved towards the British view by laying down a three-stage test which new and existing legislation would have to pass. First, does the EC have the power to act? If it does, is it impossible to achieve the desired objectives at national level? If so, what is the minimum legislation necessary?

The UK's response to the introduction of a single currency

While recognising the advantages of a single currency (pp. 525–6), the UK has been lukewarm over the plan from the outset. Her main criticisms have focused on:

(a)   the possibility that a single rate of interest determined centrally by the ECB may differ in its impact on member countries;

(b)   the loss of exchange rate depreciation as a means of adjusting a country's economy to unexpected shocks; and

(c)   the extent and nature of the sovereignty which has to be conceded.

These are explained as follows:

The lack of symmetry between countries of ECB interest-rate changes

The impact of a change in the ECB's single rate of interest may differ from one member country to another. Two examples illustrate this.

A higher proportion of the UK's borrowing is at floating rates compared with Germany's fixed rate borrowing. Thus the UK would be more sensitive than Germany to a change in the ECB's rate. This means that the UK, together with other countries similarly placed, could bear a disproportionately large share of the burden of adjustment resulting from a tighter EU monetary policy.

Again, the UK makes more use of mortgage borrowing than Germany. This means that a single interest rate imposed on all EU countries may not be appropriate.

The loss of the weapon of exchange rate depreciation

It has to be conceded that, where national currencies exist, exchange rate depreciation by a country always remains a possibility, thereby affording it a competitive price advantage over other members' exports. But circumstances can be envisaged when depreciation rather than deflation may be the preferred policy.

Major disruptive economic events are always a possibility. But the immediate impact might be softened by depreciation, increased exports for instance absorbing some of the initial unemployment resulting from an economic shock. With a single currency, however, where no one country can depreciate, realignment would have to come about by the deflation of prices, including wages, and only after a prolonged period of unemployment. Such a policy has in the past proved unacceptable.

While the reverberations of economic shocks are usually felt by most countries, on occasions a shock may be more specific to a particular country. For the UK this might be the case if there were a considerable fall in the price of oil or if a major trading partner, such as the USA, ran into serious recession.

The 1992 experience of the UK trying to maintain a fixed ERM exchange rate against heavy speculation illustrates the point. Raising her rate of interest to support sterling merely added to her on-going recession and unemployment (see p. 534).

The retention of separate national currencies would, provided the chosen exchange rate was maintained, still leave considerable freedom of manoeuvre for national governments, for example as regards supervision of financial markets. With a single currency all such freedoms virtually vanish. Every element of money creation would be controlled as to timing, form and amount by the ECB. The central banks of members countries, such as the Bank of England, would retain only an advisory role through membership of the European System of Central Banks ESCB. Yet they would still be responsible for implementing the ECB's policy decisions. It also means that European banking systems and financial markets would have to be made more uniform.

Implications for sovereignty

Furthermore, in practice monetary control would extend to fiscal policy since, if the PSNCR is covered from the banking sector, there is an increase in the money supply. Indeed there may be binding rules on the size of a country's PSNCR, and 3 per cent of GDP has been provisionally agreed.

In short, what this means is that national governments would have to accept that macroeconomic control would have been largely surrendered to bureaucratic institutions which are largely outside the scrutiny of national parliaments.

Such control of monetary and fiscal policy by the ECB, together with the extension of majority voting, is a serious loss of political control for there is no real accountability to parliament. For the UK it has important constitutional implications because it goes directly to the heart of parliamentary sovereignty which rests on the ultimate control by the House of Commons of the public purse. It is for this reason that the loudest critics oppose the single currency and even see in the EMU a major step in the direction of a more federal Europe.

The UK government's policy on membership of the single currency (the euro) remains as set out by the Chancellor of the Exchequer in his statement to the House of Commons in October 1997, and again in the Chancellor's statement on the five tests assessment in June 2003.

The determining factor underpinning any UK decision on membership of the single currency is the national economic interest and whether the economic case for joining is clear and unambiguous. The Chancellor announced in the 2005 Budget that 'In this Budget the Treasury does not propose to initiate a further euro assessment'. The Treasury will again review the situation in the 2006 Budget.

The five economic tests

- *Convergence.* Are business cycles and economic structures compatible so that we and others could live comfortably with euro interest rates on a permanent basis?
- *Flexibility.* If problems emerge, is there sufficient flexibility to deal with them?
- *Investment.* Would joining the EMU create better conditions for firms making long-term decisions to invest in Britain?
- *Financial services.* What impact would entry into the EMU have on the competitive position of the UK's financial services industry, particularly the City's wholesale markets?
- *Growth, stability and employment.* In summary, will joining the EMU promote higher growth, stability and a lasting increase in jobs?

Current assessment

The five tests assessment of 9 June 2003 came to a clear position.

> Overall the Treasury assessment is that since 1997 the UK has made real progress towards meeting the five economic tests. But, on balance, though the potential benefits of increased investment, trade, a boost to financial services, growth and jobs are clear, we cannot at this point in time conclude that there is sustainable and durable convergence or sufficient flexibility to cope with any potential difficulties within the euro area.
>
> So, despite the risks and costs from delaying the benefits of joining, a clear and unambiguous case for UK membership of EMU has not at the present time been made and a decision to join now would not be in the national economic interest.

Concluding observations

At present there is no concensus view among politicians, economists, businesses or the public as to the advantages of joining or not joining the single currency for the UK. By staying outside from the beginning she loses the benefits of the single currency and also possibly any influence in the setting up of the ECB and other important structural issues – the same mistake as occured when the EEC came into being. Moreover, delaying entry could mean that future debate on economic policy might be dominated by speculation as to whether, how and when sterling should join.

On the other hand, it would appear that the UK's view that the programme is too rushed has been vindicated in that the cost of convergence for those seeking to join has been heavy. Four points relevant to arriving at a decision would seem to emerge from the foregoing discussion:

1. If the required convergence criteria were fundamental to the success of the single currency and have been achieved by some members only as a result of fudge, the UK should stand aside until it sees how the single currency arrangements work out.
2. The fact that the cost and disruption caused by replacing sterling with the Euro is so vast and so irreversible must be constantly borne in mind when a decision is taken.
3. The UK will still remain a member of the EU and its single market. While there is the risk that members joining might erect covert barriers which could put UK firms at a disadvantage, she can to some extent overcome this by retaining her relatively low wage costs.
4. Since not all EU members will be able to join at the outset, the door will still be open for the UK to enter at some future date.

The UK's present Labour government has committed itself to holding a referendum should it recommend joining, but whether people have the capacity to vote on such a complex issue is doubtful, especially as it is the voice of those against joining which in the past has been most frequently heard. Such propaganda, allied to the possible psychological reluctance of older people to accept the inconvenience of a completely new currency, could tilt the eventual decision against joining at the outset.

CHAPTER SUMMARY

....

-   Inflation has been the dominant economic problem of the UK for the last 30 years.
-   Continued weakness of the UK's balance of payments has also been a problem.
-   The structure of the British economy has changed significantly in the last 30 years, with growth in services and decline in manufacturing.
-   The UK has an ageing population structure and this poses economic problems for the twenty-first century.
-   The UK retains its own currency at present despite EU pressure to adopt the Euro.

REVIEW QUESTIONS

- Explain how monetary policy is used to control inflation in the UK
- Why does a balance-of-payments problem persist in the UK?
- What problems are likely to arise in the economy as a result of demographic changes in the early years of this century?
- Does the UK gain any advantages from retaining its own currency?

 Visit the companion website for further questions

INDEX